OPERATING SYSTEMS

COMPUTER SCIENCE SERIES

OPERATING SYSTEMS

A Pragmatic Approach

HARRY KATZAN, Jr.
Pratt Institute

 VAN NOSTRAND REINHOLD COMPANY
NEW YORK   CINCINNATI   TORONTO   LONDON   MELBOURNE

Library of Congress Catalog Card Number: 72-7413
ISBN: 0-442-24253-0
ISBN: 0-442-24838-5 pbk.

Manufactured in the United States of America

Published by Van Nostrand Reinhold Company
135 West 50th Street, New York, N.Y. 10020

Van Nostrand Reinhold Limited
1410 Birchmount Road
Scarborough, Ontario M1P 2E7, Canada

Van Nostrand Reinhold Australia Pty. Ltd.
17 Queen Street
Mitcham, Victoria 3132, Australia

Van Nostrand Reinhold Company Limited
Molly Millars Lane
Wokingham, Berkshire, England

15 14 13 12 11

Library of Congress Cataloging in Publication Data

Katzan, Harry.
  Operating systems.

  (Computer science series)
  Bibliography: p.
  1. Electronic digital computers—Programming.
I. Title.
QA76.6.K37   001.6'42   72-7413
ISBN 0-442-24253-0
ISBN 0-442-24838-5 pbk.

PREFACE

An *operating system* is an organized collection of programs and data that is specifically designed to manage the resources of a computer system and to facilitate the creation of computer programs and control their execution on that system.

This book presents an introduction to operating systems; it has two general features:

1. It includes a liberal amount of background and evolutionary material.
2. It presents the functional characteristics of two modern operating systems—an advanced multiprogramming system and a general-purpose time sharing system.

The latter feature includes a description of system structure, system utilization, and system operations for each system.

The book is composed of three parts: Fundamentals of Operating System Technology, Functional Characteristics of an Advanced Operating System, and Functional Characteristics of a General-Purpose Time Sharing System. As such, the book is designed for use as a college text or as a professional and reference book. Each part includes a list of questions designed to "encourage" the reader to think about the subject matter and to insure himself that he is familiar with the concepts presented. In a college environment, selected questions can be used as the basis for problem sets.

The book can also be used as background material for a course on operating systems principles; in this case, however, the book should be augmented with selected papers on operating systems from the computer science literature.

The basic premise of the book is that a significant amount of knowledge can be gained from studying complete systems—especially at the introductory level. The book emphasizes the "state of the art" in operating systems technology; however, the author recognizes the need to study theoretical and conceptual topics that will be of future value. For this reason, an extensive bibliography of operating system literature, in addition to the references, is included.

It is a pleasure to acknowledge the cooperation of the IBM Corporation in granting permission to include various figures and the useful comments and suggestions of Mr. Morton B. Lurie and Dr. Philip H. Enslow, Jr., Lieutenant Colonel, U.S. Army. The book is an outgrowth of C.S. 517: *Operating Systems*, a course taught by the author in the School of Engineering and Science at Pratt Institute. Special recognition is due to the students of that course, who studied from course notes and provided the motivation for "getting the material down on paper," to Pratt Institute for providing valuable administrative support, and to my wife Margaret for valuable assistance in the preparation of the manuscript.

HARRY KATZAN, JR.

CONTENTS

OPERATING SYSTEMS

PART ONE: FUNDAMENTALS OF OPERATING SYSTEM TECHNOLOGY

1 | INTRODUCTION

1.1 THE COMPUTER ENVIRONMENT

Prelude

This book concerns *operating systems.* More specifically, the material covers: (1) what an operating system is; (2) what an operating system does; and (3) how an operating system is designed. To some readers, the subject matter will be complicated. This is the case for two major reasons: (1) The reader is unaccustomed to dealing with large systems of programs; and (2) the reader may have limited experience in using an operating system. Chapter 1 is included to provide basic information on why an operating system is needed in most computer operating environments. The reader who is familiar with basic computing concepts can go directly to Chapter 2.

At this point, a general definition of the term "operating system" is needed.

An *operating system* is an organized collection of programs and data that is specifically designed to manage the resources of a computer system and to facilitate the creation of computer programs and control their execution on that system.

It follows that the effectiveness of an operating system is based on the extent to which it aids the program development effort and on how efficiently the resources of the computer system are managed.

3

Typical Computer Applications

The design of an operating system is greatly influenced by the applications for which the computer system is to be used. But once the operating system is designed and built, then that operating system along with the respective computer system determine the applications for which the combined systems would be most appropriate. In a sense, it is the "chicken and the egg" problem in another context. For this reason, a set of applications for which a general-purpose operating system would be appropriate is discussed. To a large extent, the diversity of applications underlies the complexity of most operating systems. The set of applications is not purported to be complete but exists simply as a representative sample of those applications that usually exist in any given operational environment.

The first category is those applications classed as *scientific computing* and is characterized by programs that input small amounts of data, perform a large amount of computation, and finally output a relatively small set of results. An engineering program that computes the design parameters for a bridge would probably fall into this category. The second category is those applications classed as *data processing* and is concerned with the processing of relatively large data files. Data processing applications handle large amounts of input and output; the amount of actual computation is characteristically low. A payroll program would fall into this category. The third category is those applications classed as *information retrieval*, in which large amounts of data are stored for access by a general-purpose retrieval system or by specially written programs. Frequently, information retrieval applications permit access to the system with telecommunications facilities. A file storage system for storing policy data by an insurance company would fall into this category. The fourth category of applications is given the name *real time systems*. In a real time system, the response time of the computer system is of prime importance. Message switching, industrial control, and data collection programs generally fall into this category. When a real time program is being processed, the system recognizes that it needs attention, upon demand, and assigns it a high operational priority. Although a variety of other applications, such as hybrid computation and data entry systems, exist, the above list is sufficiently complete so that it may be noted that: (1) Many programs possess one or more of the above characteristics; and (2) the operating system is usually designed to handle all of the applications and not a limited subset of them. In the chapters that follow, the alert reader will be able to detect a correspondence between a requirement (such as the capability of handling large data files efficiently) and a component of the operating system (in this case, data management). Therefore, even though design and analysis techniques for operating systems can be developed independently of a particular application, the impetus for "advanced" facilities in operating systems is frequently the result of "new" requirements in the applications area.

1.2 SYSTEM RESOURCES

Clearly, the function of an operating system is to control the execution of programs on a computer system and to facilitate the development of those programs. Thus, in one way or another, the operating system affects the major resources of a computer installation, that is, hardware resources, information resources, and human resources.

Hardware Resources

Hardware resources refer to the computer system itself and include the central processing unit (CPU), main storage, input/output (IO) devices, IO channel time, and space on direct-access storage devices. Each type of device has a cost/performance index that determines its economic effect on overall system efficiency. The implication, of course, is that the operating system will be more concerned with the utilization of a component with a high cost/performance index (such as the CPU) than a component with a low index (such as a card punch). This is indeed the case and most operating systems contain CPU scheduling and storage allocation routines that effectively control the execution of jobs in line with installation objectives.

Information Resources

Information resources include programs and data. An effective operating system facilitates the use of these information resources in two ways: (1) The information can be stored within the operating system for ready access by a user; and (2) the information can be shared, as required, among different users. Thus, the judicious use of information resources allows two or more users to work cooperatively while using the same programs and accessing the same data. Obviously, the capabilities in this regard differ between operating systems; in general, however, they range from a library of subroutines to the concurrent access to the same data file by several users.

Human Resources

Human resources are less clearly defined since they vary between installations. Most installations, however, have three classes of personnel that deal with the operating system: system programmers, applications programmers, and operations personnel. *System programmers* are concerned with the overall effectiveness of the computing system and are involved with the functional capability provided to the user and with the performance of the hardware-software system. An effective operating system allows the hardware and software systems to be configured to meet the precise needs of the installation and permits statistics to be recorded on the utilization of the various system components. Special conditions such as hardware errors that occur during processing, are also frequently recorded for subsequent analysis. *Applications programmers* are concerned with the development and use of programs to satisfy the computing requirements of an organization. Therefore, an operating system aids the programming effort by providing facilities that simplify the coding of sophisticated procedures, such as input and output routines, and by providing utility programs, such as a sort/ merge package, that eliminate the need to prepare a special program for a given task that must be performed. In many cases, an operating system reduces programming problems by allowing main storage to be managed on a dynamic basis; thus, the user can be less concerned with structuring his program to fit into a "fixed-size" area of storage. After a program is complete, an operating system alleviates operational problems involved with executing the program. Many operating systems also permit IO device types to be specified at run time instead of when the program is developed. Historically, operating systems have dealt with the operations side of running a computer. Even though modern operating systems also satisfy human and information needs, a great many features of an operating system continue to relate to the operational environment. In other words, an operating system reduces the problems associated with running a computer. Clearly, an operating system provides job-to-job transition so that operator intervention between jobs is not required. (This feature is discussed in considerable detail in later chapters.) However, an operating system aids *operations personnel* in other important ways. From a management viewpoint, most operating systems provide for priority job processing and collect computer usage accounting data for recording and billing purposes. For the computer operator, an effective operating system allows IO volumes to be mounted in advance and permits the system configuration to be modified dynamically when hardware components malfunction or when maintenance must be performed. Most operating systems also allow the operator to communicate with the system via a set of operator commands so that the console operator can control the execution of jobs in the system in much the same way that the programmer controls the execution of computer operations within a particular job.

1.3 SYSTEM PERFORMANCE

Performance

The measure of how efficiently a computer system operates is termed *performance*. Although performance is relative to the operational needs of a particular computer installation, it is usually considered to be a function of three factors: throughput, response time, and availability. (See Fig. 1.1.)

Throughput

Throughput refers to the total volume of work performed by a computer system in a given period of time. In general, throughput is a measure of both hardware

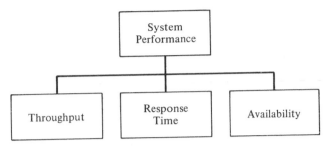

Fig. 1.1   Factors of system performance.

speed and software facilities and is especially important in a high-volume production environment.

Response Time

Response time refers to the time between when a user submits a job for processing and when he finally receives the results of that processing. Response time is used synonymously with "turnaround time" and can range from minutes to days; it usually includes nonsystem factors such as internal mail service and operational delays. (The term "response time" is also used in time sharing and in real time systems; in this context, it pertains to the time interval between when a request is made to the computer and when a reply is received over telecommunications facilities.)

Availability

Availability is a measure of a system's ability to handle requests for computation. If a system is frequently "down" for hardware repairs or software modification, then it has low availability. Availability is increased by including additional hardware resources and by designing error discovery procedures into the operation system.

The key point to be made here is that an effective operating system can increase system performance in each of the areas mentioned.

1.4 OPERATIONAL PHILOSOPHY

From an operational point of view, the need for an operating system is relatively straightforward and relates to the "setup" time between jobs. *Setup time* refers to the time spent by the computer system operator in loading the card reader, mounting tapes, setting switches, readying programs for execution, etc. Figure 1.2 depicts the relationship between operator time and computer time for relatively long running jobs (e.g., a data processing application). Although the

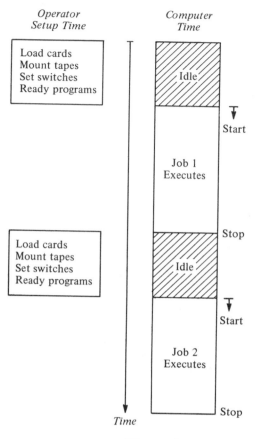

Idle: 1/3 of the time
Active: 2/3 of the time

Fig. 1.2 Relationship between idle and running time in a hypothetical data processing environment.

idle time of the computer is significant, it is not overwhelming as in Fig. 1.3, which depicts a series of small jobs. Moreover, increasing the speed of the computer only makes the idle time proportionately higher since jobs are processed in a shorter time but setup time remains the same.

Obviously, the average work load is probably a combination of long and short jobs that require varying degrees of operator setup time. However, the key point has been made. It is, simply, that human intervention between jobs is extremely "wasteful" of valuable computer time and that increasing the speed of the computer makes the operator setup time more significant. The ultimate objective is

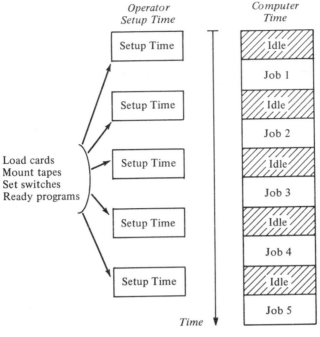

Idle: ½ of the time
Active: ½ of the time

Fig. 1.3   Relationship between idle and running time when processing small jobs.

the nonstop processing of jobs, and modern operating systems have approached that goal to a considerable degree.

1.5 OPERATING SYSTEM CONSIDERATIONS

The remainder of the book covers a variety of topics that are directly related to operating system technology or that reflects the manner in which an operating system is used. It is important to recognize that operating systems have evolved over the years and that some of the topics and/or components may not be pertinent to every operating system developed. In other cases, the need for a specific component may not be obvious due to the nature of the computer system hardware and the background of the reader. At this time, operating systems are not "computer-independent" as are many programming languages. (This fact is obvious from Chapter 3, "Computer Structures," which, to some extent, describes a broad class of machines.) Therefore, the remainder of this chapter presents a brief introduction to many of the software components that may be found in an operating system.

Data management is a generalization of the concept of an input/output control system (IOCS) that manages all IO for a multiplicity of jobs on a system-wide basis. A data management system provides flexibility in data organization and access and frequently allows device independence and a library reference system for data files.

Job control refers to the control information (i.e., job control language or control cards) used to direct the operation of the operating system and to the manner in which an operating system responds to requests for service.

All programs must be loaded into main storage for execution. *Linkage editing* pertains to the process of combining program modules prior to execution, and *loading* refers to the physical process of readying a job for execution.

Program management refers to the process of structuring a program so that it can operate in the storage space allotted to it. When program size is greater than the size of storage, the program must be segmented so that segments that are not currently used can be placed on secondary storage, such as a direct-access device. When a segment from secondary storage is needed, it is read in "on top of" a segment that is in main storage. The technique is referred to as *overlay* and is handled automatically by the operating system under control of user-supplied control information.

One of the major objectives of an operating system is to facilitate the programming process. *Catalogs and libraries*, maintained by the operating system, aid in this respect by allowing the name, location, and properties of a data file to be stored in a system catalog and by permitting programs and subroutines to be held in a program library—all for use by the programmer upon demand. Thus, programs and data may be shared among users without the necessity of the participants physically exchanging the information.

Checkpoint refers to the process of recording the status of a long-running job at specified intervals during its execution. Then if a system failure occurs before the job is complete, it can be *restarted* from its most recent checkpoint instead of from the beginning. In general, checkpoint/restart is a time-consuming and cumbersome process; the burden of taking a checkpoint and subsequently restarting is eased considerably by having operating system facilities for that purpose.

In many installations, users at a remote location are provided access to the computer via telecommunications equipment. The access usually takes one of two forms: (1) remote job entry (RJE) and remote job output (RJO); and (2) time sharing. With RJE, a user's job is simply entered into the input job stream, which is stored in a direct-access device, by the operating system, after it is received over telecommunications lines. For output (i.e., RJO), the information to be printed or punched is transmitted back over telecommunications lines, for printing and punching remotely, instead of being printed or punched at the central computer. The terminal device with an RJE/RJO system can be a specially designed I/O device or possibly a small computer. With *time sharing*, the user is permitted to enter into a conversation with the computer system during the process of problem solving or when retrieving or entering information. Although the user is given the operational advantage of having the machine to himself, the computer is actually switching control between users at a high rate on a periodic basis. The latter technique is referred to as "time slicing."

A *data base* is a named collection of physical data units organized as online and offline data files. The user normally has access to a data base on a system-wide basis. In a data base environment, the user provides descriptors for units of data with a data base descriptive language and those descriptors are stored in a data base directory. Information in a data base is accessed with a data base command language.

Most operating systems provide a set of *utility programs* that perform tasks that are frequently used but are unrelated to a particular user's job. Programs in this category usually include tape copy programs, disk storage initialization, and main storage printout (i.e., core dump).

System generation and maintenance refers to a process, normally performed by an installation's system programmer, whereby the required, alternative, and optional components of an operating system are combined to form a complete operating system oriented towards the needs of a particular installation. *System generation* is required when the supplier of an operating system provides components that are not necessarily needed by all computer installations that will use the operating system. *Maintenance* refers to the modification and updating of operating system components due to evolutionary design changes and system analysis and debugging.

The preceding topics are covered in detail in subsequent chapters.

2 | PROGRAM STRUCTURES

2.1 INTRODUCTION

A logically self-contained collection of computer instructions used to control the execution of a computer such that a specific result is obtained is termed a *program*. In the computer, information (which includes programs and data) is usually coded in an internal form, such as binary or binary coded decimal. Computer instructions are usually designed to execute primitive functions and are not convenient for the expression of algorithms. As a result, computer programs are prepared in a computer language that is more suitable for human use and data are frequently converted between an external form (such as BCD) and an internal form (such as binary) during the input or output process.

The remainder of the chapter is concerned with computer languages, how programs written in these languages are translated into computer instructions (i.e., machine language), and how programs are entered into the computer for execution. The chapter is also concerned with terminology relevant to these areas.

2.2 COMPUTER LANGUAGES

Languages that facilitate the programming of a digital computer are conveniently divided into three classes: assembler language, procedure-oriented languages, and problem-defining languages. Closely related to assembler language is the concept of an assembler language macro, which is also covered in this section.

Assembler Language

Assembler language closely resembles the internal language of the computer (i.e., machine language) except that the operations and operands, used to form instructions, are specified as mnemonic symbols and that locations are given symbolic names so that the corresponding machine address need not be used. The obvious benefits are that programs are easier to write (than in machine language) and that instructions do not reference specific machine addresses. Thus, instructions can be inserted or deleted without disrupting an entire program.

Location	Operation	Operand
	START	
	.	
	.	
	.	
LOOP	LOAD	8,L
	MULT	7,M
	ADD	8,N
	ST	8,K
	.	
	.	
	.	
	LOAD	5,I
	SUB	5,ONE
	ST	5,I
	COMP	5,ZERO
	BH	LOOP
	.	
	.	
	.	
ZERO	DC	$F'0'$
ONE	DC	$F'1'$
I	DS	F
K	DS	F
L	DS	F
M	DS	F
N	DS	F
	.	
	.	
	.	
	END	

Fig. 2.1 Simple example of assembler language. The first sequence of instructions computes K=L*M+N. The second sequence computes I=I−1 and compares the result with 0; if the result is greater than 0, a branch is made to the location named by LOOP. The last sequence defines constants and storage.

Figure 2.1 depicts a simple example of the use of assembler language. Because assembler language is closely related to machine language, it tends to differ among the various kinds of computers. However, one defining characteristic exists. It is that for each assembler language instruction written, one machine language instruction is generated by another program designed to translate programs from assembler language to machine language. It is termed an "assembler program" and is covered later in this chapter. Assembler instructions that can cause more than one machine language instruction to be generated are either special instructions or are macro instructions.

Macros

A *macro* is a well-defined sequence of assembler language statements that is given a name. When a user desires to use a macro in an assembler language program, he supplies the name of the macro along with arguments, if any. Figure 2.2 defines a simple macro that adds a sequence of numeric values and Fig. 2.3 shows how that macro might be used. Obviously, a macro must be defined before it can be used and is ordinarily supplied to the assembler program in one of two ways: by the system or by the user. User-defined macros are supplied by the user along with his program deck. System macros are stored by the operating system for subsequent retrieval and use.

Macros are useful for a variety of reasons. When the same sequence of instructions is used in many places in a program, a macro serves as a *convenience*. When sequences of instructions are sufficiently complicated to forestall their de-

Location	Operation	Operand
	MACRO	
	ADDUP	&V, &R
	LCLA	&I
&I	SETA	2
	AIF	(N'&V GT 0 AND N'&R LE 1).AOK
	MNOTE	OPERAND ERROR
	MEXIT	
.AOK	L	5,&V(1)
.NXT	AIF	(&I GT N'&V).STORE
	A	5,&V(&I)
&I	SETA	&I+1
	AGO	.NXT
.STORE	AIF	(N'&R EQ 0).DONE
	ST	5,&R
.DONE	MEND	

Fig. 2.2   A macro definition. &V and &R denote parameters (dummy variables) that represent arguments that can be supplied when the macro is used. (The macro is written in System/360 assembler language.)

Location	Operation	Operand
	ADDUP	(A,B),C
+	L	5,A
+	A	5,B
+	ST	5,C
	ADDUP	(X,Y,Z),T
+	L	5,X
+	A	5,Y
+	A	5,Z
+	ST	5,T
	ADDUP	F,G
+	L	5,F
+	ST	5,G
	ADDUP	(Q,R,S)
+	L	5,Q
+	A	5,R
+	A	5,S
	ADDUP	,W
+	OPERAND ERROR	

Fig. 2.3 Macro instructions. Examples of the use of the ADDUP macro defined in Fig. 2.2. The indicator (+) denotes an instruction generated by the macro processor, which is a part of the assembler program.

velopment by each user, a macro is used for *efficiency*. (IO macros fall into this category.) Macros are also used for *standardization.* When several programmers are working on the same project, appropriate macros are an aid in working cooperatively. In other cases, it is necessary that users of a computer system adhere to well-defined standards when passing program control between program modules or when using a system routine or accessing a system table. System macros, such as CALL and RETURN, fall into this latter category.

System macros are related, in one way or another, to the operating system and the computer system with which they are used. The topic was discussed briefly in an earlier paragraph. The key point to be made is that they represent a set of functions that are needed by many users and are also utilized by many routines of the operating system. Because of their frequent and widespread use, system macros are usually stored as a part of the operating system in the form of a data file (i.e., data set) termed a *macro library.* The macro library is searched by the assembler program during the assembly process and that search is facilitated by a *macro library index* that maintains a list of the names and locations of macros in the macro library.

Macros are an important part of operating system technology, especially from the user's point of view, and many of the features of an operating system are available to the user through macros. In cases when a higher-level language, such as PL/I, is used, the compiler for that language generates machine code that is equivalent to the macro expansion for a given function.

One remaining point on macros needs to be covered since it relates to the manner in which macros are used (and defined, as well). When a macro is defined, the first two constituents are *macro header* and *macro prototype* statements, written as follows:

MACRO
name   *param1,param2, . . .*
    .
    .
    .

That is, for example

MACRO
CALL   ENTRY,PARAM,VL
    .
    .
    .

In this example, the parameters are *positional* which means that arguments must be supplied in the operand field of the CALL macro instruction in the given order. The CALL macro under discussion might be used as follows:

CALL PLATO,(ABLE,BAKER),1

In other cases, it is desired to depart from the positional arrangement of parameters and denote an agrument by a *keyword*. The macro,

MACRO
LINK   EP=,PARAM=,VL=
    .
    .
    .

for example, might be used as follows:

LINK EP=PLATO,PARAM=(ABLE,BAKER),VL=1

which is equivalent to

LINK VL=1,EP=PLATO,PARAM=(ABLE,BAKER)

since arguments are denoted by keyword instead of by position.

Some forms of assembler language also permit positional and keyword parameters to be used together and allow default values to be specified for certain parameters.

Procedure-Oriented Languages

A *procedure-oriented language* is a form of computer language that permits the user to avoid the details of assembler language programming. When using a procedure-oriented language, the user specifies a series of statements to be executed in performing a particular task on the computer. In this respect, a procedure-oriented language is much like assembler language. The key difference is that a statement from a procedure-oriented language denotes an operational function that is equivalent to several machine language operations. A procedure-oriented language is oriented towards programming and is frequently referred to as a *programming language.* It is also convenient to design a procedure-oriented language around a particular class of applications so that familiar notation and technology can be employed. The following examples from FORTRAN (for scientific computing) and COBOL (for data processing), respectively, serve to illustrate the latter point:

$$SUM=SUM+A(I)*Y**Z \qquad \text{(FORTRAN)}$$
$$\text{MOVE NAME TO REPORT-FIELD.} \qquad \text{(COBOL)}$$

There is a multiplicity of procedure-oriented languages in widespread use; BASIC (an easy-to-learn language for the problem solver) and PL/I (a multipurpose programming language) are two other names that are frequently encountered. Collectively, programming languages have reduced the time and costs necessary for preparing programs and have enabled the nonprofessional programmer to utilize the computer effectively.

The different kinds of statements from programming languages can be conveniently grouped into five classes: data manipulation, program control, input and output, declarative, and subprogram. *Data manipulation* statements perform the calculations, data movement, list processing, or string editing required by a particular application. As a result of data manipulation, computation is performed and/or the value of data variables is replaced. Three simple examples are:

$$Y=A*B**Z+C \qquad \text{(FORTRAN)}$$
$$\text{MOVE RESULT TO ANSWER.} \qquad \text{(COBOL)}$$
$$\text{ADD PAY, GROSS GIVING TOTAL.} \qquad \text{(COBOL)}$$

Program control statements provide a facility for altering the sequential flow of execution in a program. Control statements are divided into four categories: (1) unconditional branches; (2) conditional branches and conditional statement execution; (3) looping; and (4) execution control. *Unconditional branches* alter sequential execution and denote the statement to be executed next; for example:

$$\text{GO TO 25} \qquad \text{(FORTRAN)}$$
$$\text{GO TO P1,P2 DEPENDING ON I.} \qquad \text{(COBOL)}$$

Conditional statements allow the user to change the sequence of execution or to execute a given statement on a conditional basis; for example:

IF(A+1)10,20,30	(FORTRAN)
IF(X.LT.0) X=0	(FORTRAN)
IF GROSS IS LESS THAN 600 MOVE 0 TO TAX.	(COBOL)
IF MALE NEXT SENTENCE OTHERWISE GOTO FEMALE-PAR.	(COBOL)

Looping statements allow a computer program to execute the same operations repetitively. During the execution of a loop, the statements comprising the body of the loop are executed using one or more of the following modes of control: (1) the loop is executed a specified number of times; (2) the loop is executed until a given condition is met; and (3) the loop is executed as a control variable assumes a given set of values. In FORTRAN, the body of a loop follows the looping statement as follows:

DO 100 I = 1,10

.

.

.

100 –

In COBOL, the looping statement specifies a paragraph or group of paragraphs that comprise the range of the loop; for example,

PERFORM B-BLOCK THRU E-BLOCK 7 TIMES.

The last type of program control statement concerns *execution control*, which denotes a class of statements to halt or terminate the execution of a program. A familiar example is the STOP statement. Statements in this category tend to vary between programming languages.

Input and output statements are used to transmit information between an external storage medium and the computer. Two forms of input and output (IO) are usually available: formatted IO and unformatted IO. During formatted IO, data are converted from an external form to an internal form during input under the control of format statements. The process is reversed during output. The following FORTRAN input statement illustrates formatted input (where 9000 is the statement number of a format statement):

READ(N,9000)K,(A(I),I=1,K)

During unformatted IO, information is transferred between an external medium and main storage without "software" conversion, even though hardware conversion may be required depending upon the physical IO device used. The following COBOL statements depict unformatted input and output statements, respectively:

READ A-FILE INTO B-RECORD, AT END GOTO DONE.
WRITE Z-FILE.

Declaration statements provide information on the manner in which data are to be stored and can be used to specify file types, establish storage requirements, and denote action to be taken when certain execution-time conditions arise. The following simple FORTRAN declaration specifies data attributes:

INTEGER B/7/,MATR(100,10)
REAL INCID(7,3,12)
COMMON MATR

Similarly, the following COBOL declaration found in the DATA DIVISION of a COBOL program, specifies a typical data record definition:

01 E-RECORD, CLASS IS ALPHANUMERIC, USAGE
IS DISPLAY.
02 NAME, SIZE IS 35 CHARACTERS.
02 BADGE, SIZE IS 4, CLASS IS NUMERIC.
02 SALARY, PICTURE IS S99999V99.

Subprogram statements allow a program to be structured into a main program and one or more subprograms. (Characteristics of subprograms are considered more fully in a later section of this chapter.) Subprogram statements are used, *in a subprogram*, to specify the name, attributes, and parameters of the subprogram and to cause the program to return to the calling program when the processing of the subprogram is complete. A statement of the former type is known as a *subprogram header*. The following FORTRAN statement initiates a function subprogram:

FUNCTION AVER(X,N)

while the subprogram header for a COBOL subroutine might look as follows:

E1: ENTER LINKAGE.
ENTRY 'ABLE' USING NAME, ADDR, CNT.
E2 ENTER COBOL.

Various forms of the RETURN statement are used to pass program control from the subprogram back to the calling program. In a *calling program*, a function is invoked by using the function name with appropriate arguments as a term in an expression, for example,

Y = AVER(BARRAY,NSIZE)+11.7   (FORTRAN)

and a subroutine is usually invoked with a CALL statement, that is, for example,

CALL ABLE(N1,ALOC,I)   (FORTRAN)

or the ENTER and CALL statements in COBOL:

CLA: ENTER LINKAGE.
     CALL 'ABLE' USES NAME, ADDRESS RETURNS COUNT.
CLB: ENTER COBOL.

Obviously, a variety of other statement types exist in programming languages. They cover facilities that range from dynamic storage allocation and the processing of interrupt conditions to block structure and macro facilities. The intent here has been to give the reader a flavor of the different kinds of statements; detailed information is available from one of the many good references on programming languages.

It is important to recognize that some statements use facilities in the operating system and others do not. Statements that relate to dynamic storage allocation do require operating system facilities and that fact is obvious. On the other hand, input and output statements also require operating system facilities, in a large percentage of systems, and this fact is not so obvious and is dependent upon how IO is handled in the computer being used. Therefore, a person knowledgeable in operating systems technology must also be reasonably familiar with programming languages and computer structures. (Computer structures are covered in Chapter 3.)

Problem Defining Languages

In assembler and procedure-oriented language, the user gives the steps necessary to execute a given procedure. In a *problem defining language*, the user specifies the characteristics of his problem and possibly input and output requirements but does not supply actual statements that should be executed. Problem defining languages are used for specialized applications and an appropriate program to solve the given problem is generated by a language translator called a *generator program*. A report program generator (RPG) falls into this category as do some sort/merge generators.

2.3 LANGUAGE PROCESSORS

Terminology

Programs that are designed to process other programs as input are generally referred to as *metaprograms*. (Operating systems, assemblers, and compilers, for example, generally fall into this category.) In operating system terminology, however, a program that processes a program written in a symbolic computer language is referred to as a *language processor*.

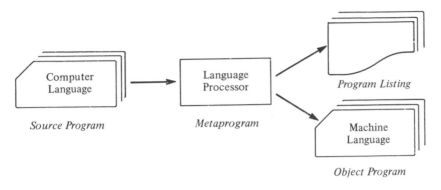

Fig. 2.4 Terminology relevant to language processing.

Input to a language processor is a program in symbolic form referred to as a *source program*. The output of a language processor is a program in machine language form called an *object program*. Figure 2.4 depicts terminology relevant to this area. Although source and object programs are depicted as card decks, this need not necessarily be the case. Source programs can reside on an external storage device or be entered at a computer terminal. Similarly, object programs can be deposited on an external storage device or be loaded into the computer for execution.

An object program is more than a sequence of machine language instructions. Control information is needed so that the instructions can be loaded into the computer and effectively combined with other object programs. For example, when the programmer uses statements such as

$$B = SQRT(X**2)$$

and

$$CALL\ BAKER(X,Y/3,25)$$

the subprograms SQRT and BAKER must be loaded into the computer and combined with the object program that contains these statements. An object program along with its control information is termed an *object module*. Later, programs will be introduced that operate on object modules and are capable of combining two or more object modules into a single object module.

Assembler Programs

An assembler program, or more simply an *assembler*, is a computer program that translates a program written in assembler language to an equivalent program in machine language. The translation procedure is frequently referred to as *assembly* or the *assembly process*.

Assembly is usually accomplished in two passes over the source program. In the first pass, addresses are assigned to symbols in the location field and macros are identified (i.e., located in the user's source input deck or retrieved from the macro library) and expanded. In the second pass over the source program, symbolic operation codes and operands are replaced by internal codes and addresses, respectively, and the object module and a program listing are produced. Error checking is performed and erroneous conditions are denoted, appropriately, in the program listing.

Assembly is essentially a straightforward replacement process, and the user has a great amount of flexibility in how he can use the assembler language. In general, the logical flow of a program written in assembler language is not analyzed so that the user can apply the features of the given computer to his particular problem.

It is important to recognize that the assembler program has access to the complete source program and that it must be completely translated to machine language before any attempt can be made at executing that program. Although the services of an assembler program are almost always supplied through an operating system, it is not an integral part of the operating system in the sense that it uses special features of the computer or of the operating system. To the operating system, the execution of the assembler program is simply another unit of work, much like a user's application program. The assembler program does use operating system facilities for input and output, storage, etc., but no more so than any other user program. (In operating system terminology, the assembler program is just another processing program to the operating system.)

Compiler Programs

The process of translating a program written in a procedure-oriented language to machine language is termed *compilation;* it is performed with a *compiler program*, which is another type of language processor. Functionally, the use of a procedure-oriented language subordinates the details of programming to the compiler program. For each statement in a procedure-oriented language, several machine language instructions are usually generated by the compiler. (This is in contrast to assembler language, characterized by the fact that one machine language instruction is usually generated for each assembler language statement by the assembler program.)

Compilers are necessarily dependent upon the language being processed; however, the following steps are usually involved:

1. The source program is read and analyzed on a statement-by-statement basis.
2. A *lexical analysis* routine scans each source statement and identifies reserved words, variables, operator symbols, constants, etc.
3. A *syntactical analysis* routine identifies the type of statements and verifies that the structure of that statement is admissible.

4. Tables and lists of symbols, expressions, and statements are maintained so that an inter-statement analysis can be made.
5. Analysis is made of logical flow of the source program and a global error analysis is made.
6. Machine language instructions, in an intermediate symbolic form internal to the compiler, are generated and optimization is performed, as required.
7. An object module is generated from the intermediate language and a program listing is produced.

Like an assembler program, the compiler is a processing program to the operating system. The compiler has nothing to do with the execution of a source program. It performs a translation of a source program to an object program and produces its result in the form of an object module. (As with an assembler, the compiler also produces a program listing with diagnostic information. When requested, most compilers have the capability of producing an assembler-type listing of the machine language code generated.)

Generators and Interpreters

Much like its counterparts, the assembler and the compiler, the *program generator* produces an object module that can be loaded into the computer and executed. It also operates as a processing program to the operating system and accepts a source program written in a problem-defining language as input.

The sequence of translating a source program into a machine language form, combining that program with required subprograms, loading it into the computer, and then causing execution to begin is a time-consuming process, and in many cases, the amount of work performed by the computer is not justified by the results obtained. This is particularly the case with very small "one-shot" jobs or in cases when "exploratory" work is being performed. A language processor that avoids the sequence of steps mentioned above is known as an interpreter. An *interpreter* is a language processor that interprets and executes a source program without producing an object program. It operates as follows:

1. The source program is processed on a statement-by-statement basis.
2. Each statement is scanned, analyzed, and interpreted to determine what operations should be performed.
3. The operations are executed by the interpreter and the intermediate results are saved.
4. The next statement to be executed is obtained and step 2 is repeated.

The technique of using an interpreter has several important characteristics:

1. The entire source program is *not* completely analyzed and is not translated to an object program before execution is initiated.
2. The next statement to be interpreted is dependent upon the results of the previous statement, such as with a GO TO statement.

3. Only intermediate results are saved and no object program is produced. (It should be noted that some interpreters convert a source program into an internal language to avoid reinterpreting a statement because of a loop or similar construct.)

Simple, easy-to-use languages are frequently implemented by using an interpretive technique.

Although most interpreters operate as normal processing programs, an interpreter is occasionally integrated into the operating system to provide a useful feature, such as a desk calculator language. When an interpreter is integrated in an operating system, it is usually shared among users of the facility provided.

2.4 PROGRAMS AND SUBPROGRAMS

Subprogram Structure

Programs are frequently structured into a main program and one or more subprograms for convenience, for efficiency, or simply to make use of subprogram libraries. A subprogram is characterized in three ways:

1. It is a function or subroutine.
2. It is open or closed.
3. It is external or internal.

As mentioned previously, a *function* returns an explicit result and can be used as a term in an expression. A *subroutine* does not return an explicit result and is usually invoked with a special statement of the language, such as the CALL statement.

Figure 2.5 depicts examples of open and closed subprograms. In any program, only one copy of a given *closed* subprogram exists. Each time that subprogram is used, linkage is established so that program control can be returned to the "point of call." However, in many cases, the overhead instructions necessary for using a closed subprogram are not justified by the size of the subprogram. In these cases, a copy of the subprogram is inserted by the compiler into the machine language program directly and no linkage is necessary. A subprogram of this type is termed an *open* subprogram since program control flows through it without executing additional linkage instructions.

Subprograms that are assembled or compiled independently of the calling program are referred to as *external* subprograms. An external subprogram has its own object module and is always incorporated into a program as a closed subprogram. Some programming languages allow a closed subprogram to be compiled as a part of the calling program such that only a single object module is produced. A subprogram of this type is referred to as an *internal* subprogram; its identity is known only to the object module in which it is included.

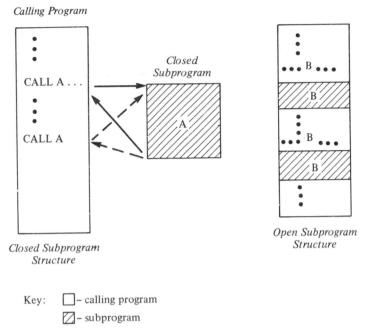

Fig. 2.5   Closed and open subprogram structure.

An operating system is not concerned (or even aware) of open and internal subprograms since their existence is known only to the compiler of the language used. An operating system is aware of the existence of a subprogram when it must be combined with a calling program during the "loading" process. The manner in which this is accomplished is covered in the following sections.

Linkage

The computer instructions necessary to call a subprogram and later return to the calling program are termed *linkage instructions*, and the process of actually executing those instructions is termed *linkage*. It is important to note that both the calling program and the subprogram participate in the linkage process. The calling program must supply arguments, establish a save area so that the subprogram can store the contents of machine registers, designate a return address, and branch to the subprogram. When it is activated, a subprogram saves machine registers in the designated save area and sets up parameters for execution. After the execution of a subprogram is complete, the return linkage instructions establish the explicit result (in the case of a function subprogram), restore machine registers, and branch to the return address supplied by the calling program. An

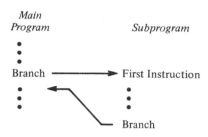

Fig. 2.6 Overview of subprogram linkage.

overview of subroutine linkage is depicted in Fig. 2.6. Subroutine linkage is necessarily machine dependent; however, the methods apply in general.

An example of subroutine linkage is given here to establish continuity between this section and the following section on program execution. The example provides a "skeleton" of subroutine linkage and uses basic assembler language (BAL); it is representative of the many linkage conventions that exist. In particular, the computer includes 16 general-purpose registers (numbered 0–15) that can be used for address manipulation and fixed-point arithmetic. (The computer also includes four floating-point registers [numbered 0,2,4,6] used in floating-point arithmetic operations.) The general-purpose registers are used in subprogram linkage as follows:

1. Register 15 is loaded with the subprogram entry address.
2. Register 14 is loaded with the return address (to the calling program).
3. Register 13 is loaded with the address of the first word in the register save area.
4. Register 1 is loaded with the address of an argument list.

The means used for returning the explicit result from a function subprogram obviously varies between systems and languages. With the procedure-oriented language FORTRAN, general register 0 has been used to return a fixed-point result and floating-point register 0 has been used to return a floating-point result. In cases where a return code is necessary, general register 15 has been used for that purpose.

The methods employed for passing arguments to a subprogram deserve special consideration. When the number of arguments to be passed is small and consists of numeric values, then these values can be placed in machine registers prior to passing program control to the subprogram. This technique possesses obvious limitations when the number of arguments is large or consists of nonnumeric values. A more general approach is to place the *addresses* of the arguments in a list of consecutive word locations. The address of the first entry in the argument list is placed in a general register providing the subprogram access to the complete list with a single register.   This method is used in the example which follows.

In the example (and it must be emphasized that the symbolic notation is hypothetical but based on existing computers), the assembler language statements represent a subroutine call of the form:

CALL PLATO(I,X+Y,25)

The argument list includes a symbolic name, a constant, and an expression that must be evaluated in floating point.   Each assembler language statement is divided logically into three fields—location, operation, and operand.   A sample of the machine code that would be generated for the above CALL statement is given in Fig. 2.7.   The functions performed by several of the statements are discussed.   Statement (1), the EXTRN statement, denotes that PLATO is an external subprogram that must be supplied at execution time.   Statements (2), (3), and (4) compute X+Y and store the result as a temporary variable.   (Obviously, the variables X,Y, and I are assigned values in another portion of the program.) Statements (5), (6), and (7) establish the following addresses respectively: register save area, argument list, and the address of the subroutine.   Statement (8) is a branch and link instruction that branches to the subroutine, whose address is in register 15, and places the address of the next statement to be executed in the calling program (the return address) in register 14.   Statement (9) defines an external address constant that will be filled by the linkage editor or the loader prior to program execution.   It will be loaded with the address in main storage of the subroutine PLATO.   Statements (13) through (18) define storage areas (DS) or define constants (DC).   In this case, F is an attribute that stands for fixed-point and E stands for a short floating-point word.

The subroutine PLATO would be programmed to use the arguments given in the argument list in performing its computation.   The last instruction to be executed in PLATO would be a branch to the main storage address contained in register 14.   This would cause program control to be returned to the statement following the BALR instruction in the program segment of Fig. 2.7.

2.5 PROGRAM EXECUTION

Object Modules

The output of a language processor is an object module that cannot be executed directly by the computer and must be prepared for execution by either of two service programs: a "linkage editor" or a "loader."   The reasons that a linkage editor or loader program is needed and the form of an object module are given followed by a description of the "linkage editing" process.

Assume that a particular program is composed of a main program and one or more external subprograms.   Prior to execution, the main program and the sub-

	Location	Operation	Operand	Comments
		.		
		.		
		.		
(1)		EXTRN	PLATO	SUBR ENTRY NAME.
		.		
		.		
		.		
(2)		LE	2,X	COMPUTE X+Y
(3)		AE	2,Y	... AND STORE IN
(4)		STE	2,TEMP	... TEMP LOC.
(5)		LA	13,SAVEAREA	LOAD ADDR OF SAVE AREA.
(6)		LA	1,ARGLIST	LOAD ADDR OF ARG LIST.
(7)		L	15,SUBADDR	LOAD ADDR OF 'PLATO'.
(8)		BALR	14,15	BR AND LINK TO 'PLATO'.
		.		
		.		
		.		
(9)	SUBADDR	DC	A(PLATO)	ADDR OF SUBR.
(10)	ARGLIST	DC	A(I)	ADDRESSES
(11)		DC	A(TEMP)	... OF
(12)		DC	A(F$25)	... ARGUMENTS.
(13)	SAVEAREA	DS	20F	REG SAVE AREA.
(14)	I	DS	F	DEFINE
(15)	TEMP	DS	E	... ST
(16)	X	DS	E	..... OR
(17)	Y	DS	E	.... AGE.
(18)	F$25	DC	F'25'	DEFINE CON-STANT.
		.		
		.		
		.		

Fig. 2.7 Sample expansion of the statement CALL PLATO (I,X+Y,25). (Included for illustrative purposes.)

programs exist as object modules. Before any program can be executed, the object modules of which the program is composed must be linked together so that program control can pass between modules without requiring the services of the operating system. (In the program segment of Fig. 2.7, for example, the address of subroutine PLATO would be stored as the address constant created for that purpose.) This process of combining object modules requires that the modules be relocatable. The characteristic of being *relocatable* simply means that the object program exists in a form where the address constants, contained therein, can be adjusted to compensate for a change of origin. (The implication here, obviously, is that when object modules are combined, they are relocated, requiring a change of origin.) The information necessary to relocate an object program, such as the location in the program of address constants, is generated by a language processor and exists along with other control information as a part of an object module. An object program that can be relocated is termed a *relocatable object program.* (Similarly, an object program that cannot be relocated and must be loaded into specific machine addresses is termed an *absolute object program.*) In general, most user programs exist as relocatable programs. This subject is discussed in Chapter 5.

Thus far, the form of an object module has been discussed in general terms. More detailed information is needed for the remainder of this chapter and for subsequent chapters. The logical structure of an object module consists of three entities: an external symbol dictionary, a relocation dictionary, and the text. The form of an object module is depicted in Fig. 2.8. The external symbol dictionary (ESD) contains an entry for each external symbol defined or referred to within the object program. An ESD entry includes the name of the external symbol (which is the symbol itself), the type of reference it is, and its location in the program. The relocation dictionary (RLD) contains an entry for each relocatable address constant that must be adjusted before a module is executed. An RLD entry specifies an address constant by indicating its location in the program. The text (TXT) contains the instructions and data of the object program.

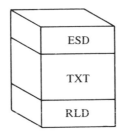

Fig. 2.8   Form of an object module.

Linkage Editing

The linking of object modules prior to execution is termed *linkage editing* and is performed by a service program termed the *linkage editor.* As depicted in Fig. 2.9, input to the linkage editor can take four forms:

1. object modules and linkage editor control information supplied by the user;
2. object modules from a user-supplied program library;
3. object modules from the system's "automatic call library"; and
4. load modules.

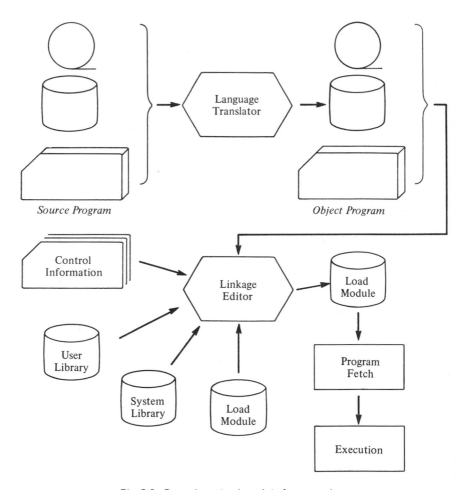

Fig. 2.9 Preparing a load module for execution.

Output from the linkage editor is a *load* module that can be loaded into main storage by a routine of the operating system for execution.

Each input module processed by the linkage editor possesses a program origin that was assigned during assembly, compilation, or a previous execution of the linkage editor. When producing an executable load module, the linkage editor assigns an origin to the text for the first module and adjusts address constants accordingly. The text for other modules, as well as address constants, is assigned addresses relative to that origin so that the combined text for all modules occupies consecutive addresses in the load module. External references between modules are resolved by matching the referenced symbols to defined symbols. Figure 2.10 depicts a load module produced by the linkage editor. The output load module is composed of all input object modules and input load modules processed by the linkage editor. The ESDs of the input modules are combined to form a composite external symbol dictionary (CESD). The output RLD includes relocation information for the complete text of the load module. The load module is in a relocatable format, as are the object modules, but the text represents executable machine code. It is placed in an executable program library for subsequent loading by *program fetch*, a routine of the operating system. When the user requests that his program be executed, program fetch retrieves it from the library and relocates it in main storage using the composite RLD. It is then ready for execution.

During its processing, the linkage editor attempts to resolve external references

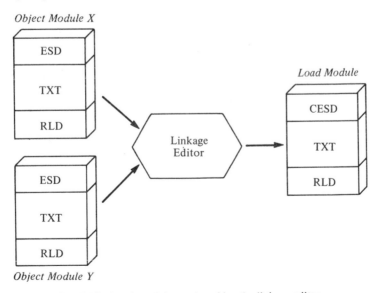

Fig. 2.10   Load module produced by the linkage editor.

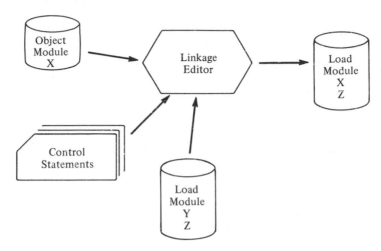

Fig. 2.11   An example of module editing using the linkage editor.

from the object modules supplied by the user. Symbols that are still undefined after all input modules have been processed cause the linkage editor to search a hierarchy of program libraries for the unresolved reference. User-defined libraries are searched first followed by a search of the system library. (A familiar example of this situation is the typical application program that uses the square root [SQRT] routine that is almost always retrieved from a library of subroutines maintained as part of the operating system.)

Another function performed by the linkage editor is the editing of load modules under the control of control statements provided by the user. Figure 2.11 depicts an example of linkage editor processing where one program module is deleted from a load module and another is added to the load module.

Loading

Some operating systems do not utilize the concept of a linkage editor and employ a *loader program* that effectively combines the linkage edit and program fetch phases. Other operating systems contain a linkage editor *and* a loader program.

A loader program is used when there is no need to produce distinct load modules for program libraries. The loader combines object modules produced by the language processors and loads them directly into main storage for execution. An example of the operation of a loader program is depicted in Fig. 2.12. Most loader programs are designed to search user-defined libraries and/or system libraries for resolving symbol references.

Actually, the primary difference between a loader and the "program fetch" routine of the operating system is one of degree rather than of function. The

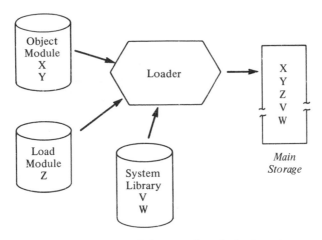

Fig. 2.12   An example of the operation of a loader program.

program fetch routine searches a program library for a requested load module and places it in main storage performing relocation of address constants, as required. (A load module is complete in the sense that additional subroutines are not needed for execution.) The loader does more. It combines object modules, in the same manner that the linkage editor does, and resolves external references by searching subroutine libraries. Unlike the linkage editor, however, the loader places the resultant "load module" into main storage for execution.

Job Execution

A *job* is the execution of a series of related processing programs that comprise a total processing application. The execution of a single processing program is termed a *job step*. (A simple sequence of job steps might be: (1) compilation, (2) assembly, (3) link editing, and (4) execution of the load module produced in the link editing step.)

When a user submits a unit of work to the operating system, he submits a job, which includes one or more job steps. More specifically, a job consists of control cards, programs, and data. Control cards must always be used since they direct the operating system to perform the desired functions. Programs or data may alternately be stored in libraries or data files, respectively, for retrieval by the operating system.

Information is placed on control cards using well-established conventions known as *job control language*. Most job control languages consist of a few major statements plus a variety of miscellaneous statements. Three major statements are discussed here:[†]

[†]These statement types are representative of those used in modern operating systems. Specific key words vary between systems.

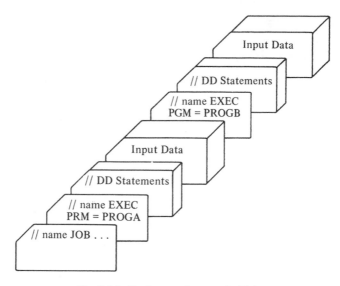

Fig. 2.13 Deck setup for a typical job.

1. The *job statement* (JOB) marks the beginning of a job, identifies the user, contains accounting information, and specifies general conditions that govern how the job is to be executed. (Only one JOB statement per job is needed.)
2. The *execute statement* (EXEC) marks the beginning of a job step and specifies the load module to be executed. The EXEC statement is also used to supply control information for the execution of that load module.
3. The *data definition statement* (DD) is used to describe a data file (frequently referred to as a data set) and to request the allocation of input/output resources. The DD statement is also used to specify the disposition of that data set after the job step is completed. One or more DD statements are used with each job step.

The input deck setup for a typical job is given in Fig. 2.13.

Usually, the job steps of a job are related in the sense that the results of one job step are used in a subsequent job step. Examples of typical job step sequences are given as follows:

Commercial Application	*Scientific Application*
1. Execute a load module of a user's processing program. (Load module fetched from the user's program library.)	1. Execute a FORTRAN compilation of a user's source module. (FORTRAN compiler loaded from system library.)

2. Execute a sort of a data file produced in step 1. (Sort program
loaded from the system library.)

2. Execute an assembler language assembly of a user's source module.
(Assembler program loaded from
system library.)

3. Execute a load module of a user's
processing program that generates

3. Execute the loader program to
link the object modules produced

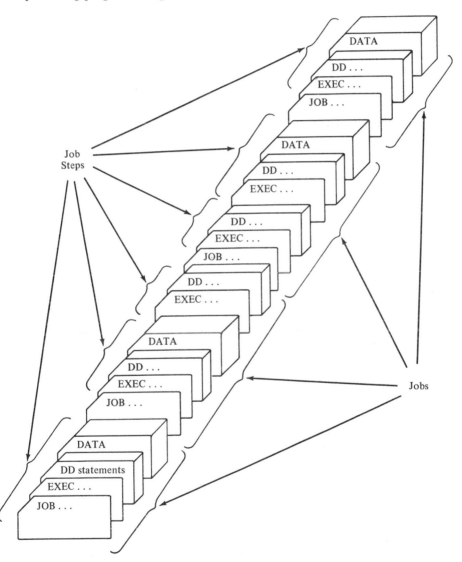

Fig. 2.14 The form of an input Job stream.

a report from the file sorted in step 2. (Load module loaded from the user's program library.)

in steps 1 and 2 and to initiate execution of the resultant load module. (Loader program is loaded for execution from the system library; user's program, after linking, is placed in storage for execution.)

Usually, a computer system is employed to service many users. Thus, input to the operating system takes the form of several jobs, arranged in a sequence called the *input job stream.* (See Fig. 2.14.) As input to the computer, the job stream, normally, can be read from punched cards, magnetic tape, or a direct-access device. In actual practice, however, the jobs may not be executed in the sequence in which they are found in the job stream. The nature of the operating system, the priorities of the respective jobs, and the availability of input and output devices generally determine how the resources of the computer system are utilized.

2.6 COMMENTS

It must be emphasized that this chapter has presented only an overview of program structures. Computer languages and language processors are fields of study in their own right and are not covered further in this book. Program structure, as it relates to reusable and reenterable code and to overlay structures, is covered in more detail later. The subject of program execution is covered in considerable detail. Program execution necessarily relates to the operating system and includes the "external appearance" of the operating system and its internal structure. The latter topics are the subject matter of this book.

3 | COMPUTER STRUCTURES

3.1 INTRODUCTION

There are several reasons for discussing computer structures in a book on operating systems. First, the reader is expected to have a background in computer technology and the extent of that knowledge should be stated. Secondly, several features of a computer are particularly relevant to the study of operating systems and these features should be covered to some degree. Lastly, terminology is important and this is an excellent place to resolve inconsistencies.[†]

Basic knowledge of a conventional stored program computer is assumed. That computer should include the following components:

1. central processing unit (CPU),
2. main storage,
3. input/output data channels,
4. input/output control units and devices, and
5. operator's console.

The other sections in this chapter cover particular aspects of these system components as they relate to operating systems technology.

Programs and data are held in directly addressable storage during execution so that computer instructions that reference storage include an address field. The

---

[†]The terminology has a "flavor" of the System/360/370 computers; however, it is illustrative of typical computer structures. The reader can easily extend the concepts to suit his particular needs.

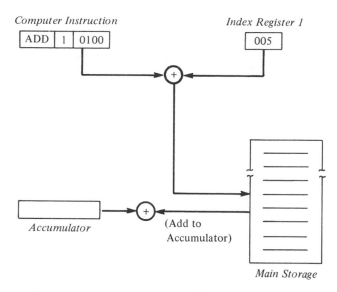

Fig. 3.1   Effective addressing using an index register.

address used to reference storage is termed an *effective address* and is usually generated in one of three ways:

1. as the address field in an instruction,
2. as the address field in an instruction incremented or decremented by the contents of an index register, or
3. as a displacement, contained in the instruction, incremented by the contents of base and index registers.

Two general forms of addressing are depicted in Figs. 3.1 and 3.2. This example is included to present a basic concept and serves to illustrate an important point. Although the knowledge of how an effective address is computed is not necessarily significant from an operating system point of view, the manner in which an effective address is utilized is important. Other topics in the area of computer structure should be treated similarly:

1. that BCD information is stored internal to the computer in a coded form—without necessarily knowing the exact code structure;
2. that IO operations are initiated by an IO instruction—without necessarily knowing precisely how that instruction operates; and
3. that IO data channels are controlled by channel commands, held in main storage, and that IO control units are controlled by orders sent by the channel—without necessarily knowing the exact form of the commands and orders and how they are used;

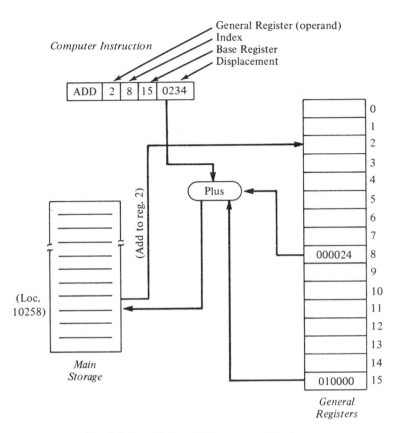

Fig. 3.2 Base, index, displacement addressing.

to name only a few. The reader also should recognize the characteristics of input/output devices—such as drum, disk, tape, and card units—as well as their respective storage medias.

Knowledge of other topics in computer technology is tacitly assumed:

1. word-oriented versus byte-oriented computers;
2. the manner in which a computer operates, including the initial program load (IPL) sequence and the synchronous and asynchronous modes of computer operation;
3. storage technology, including the use of buffer storage (cache) systems and interleaving;
4. the various types of computer instructions (i.e., data manipulation, branching and control, input and output, etc.); and
5. peripheral input/output devices such as graphic terminals, optical recognition devices, audio response units, and microfilm output units as well as

conventional devices such as card reader/punches, magnetic tape units, line printers, and disk and drum storage.

From a design standpoint, a reasonable knowledge of IO devices is necessary since most operating systems must provide the capability for supporting a wide range of devices.

There are many good books that provide a general introduction to computers and devices (see, e.g., Bohl [Boh71], Chapin [Cha71], or Davis [Dav69,71]).

3.2 SYSTEM ORGANIZATION

A computer system is an organized collection of components, which includes a CPU, main storage, IO data channels, and IO control units and devices. When a system contains more than one CPU (not necessarily connected in any way), it is termed a *multisystem*. Multisystems are used to overcome technological limitations and are employed for two major reasons:

1. to increase overall system performance, and
2. to increase system availability[†] (defined as the probability that the system adequately performs its specified function).

Multisystems are usually justified by a cost/performance index for a given workload. The following configurations are considered:

1. simplex systems,
2. duplex and n-plex systems, and
3. attached support processors.

System Configuration Technology

The manner in which the components of a computer system are connected determines how that system can be used. System components can be connected in one of two ways: (1) the centralized crossbar switch, and (2) the distributed crossbar switch. The two methods are depicted in Figs. 3.3 and 3.4, respectively. In general, the *crossbar switch* allows the connection of m CPUs to any one of n storage units. When $m \leqslant n$, the m connections can be made simultaneously.

When the *centralized crossbar switch* is used, each CPU and each storage unit has a single interconnection within a central switching network. The central switching network is essentially a major system component. When the *distributed crossbar switch* is used, each CPU (and IO data channel, as well) has a single connection, but storage units have multiple connections called *multiple tails*.

[†]More specifically, availability (A) is defined as:

$$A = \frac{t_u}{t_u + t_i}$$

where t_u is the mean time between user failures and t_i is the mean time to repair.

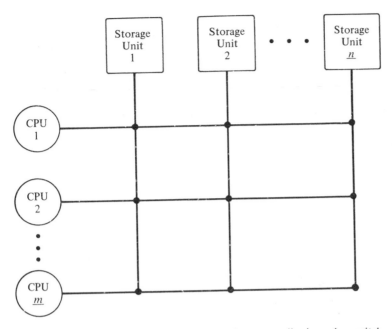

Fig. 3.3 Connection of system components using a centralized crossbar switch.

Obviously, systems differ in many respects; however, some general conclusions can still be drawn:

1. Systems employing a centralized crossbar switch operate faster since tie-breaking[†] circuitry is not needed.
2. The distributed crossbar switch has economic advantages since separate frames and cooling units are not required as each storage unit provides its own set of switches.
3. Systems employing the distributed crossbar switch provide availability and flexibility; the system may easily be reconfigured, storage units private to one CPU can be specified, and the failure of a single switching element does not cause the entire system to fail.

Although switching techniques (in the sense of the current discussion) are most frequently related to CPUs and storage units, they also apply to IO data channels, IO control units, and IO devices, as well.

The manner in which a system is configured determines, to a large extent,

---

[†]"Tie-breaking" refers to the situation where two components (CPUs, channel controllers, or a combination of either) attempt to reference a storage module at precisely the same instant. Obviously, one component must go first and circuitry is required to resolve the difference.

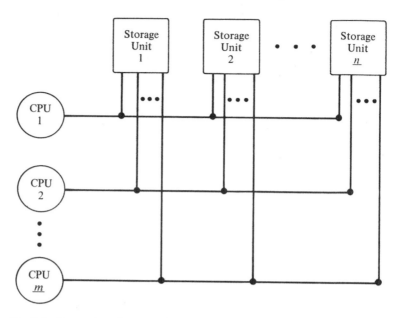

Fig. 3.4   Connection of system components using distributed network switches.

how it can be used by the software. The significance of this remark is inherent in the following sections.

Simplex Systems

A simplex system includes one central processor as depicted in Fig. 3.5. The vast majority of computers are simplex systems and are considered to be "CPU-oriented" in the sense that design objectives are usually to provide the CPU with information at the fastest possible rate. Towards this end, the system may include interleaved storage to decrease effective access time or a storage buffer (cache) to decrease the number of accesses to main storage.

Duplex and n-Plex Systems

Duplex (i.e., 2-plex) and *n*-plex systems are characterized by two or more CPUs, a configuration console,† several storage units, and channel controllers that permit an IO data channel to be connected to two or more CPUs. *N*-plex systems are usually "storage-oriented" in the sense that information in a single storage unit is accessible to two or more CPUs. A duplex system is depicted in Fig. 3.6.

---

†In general, a configuration console can be viewed as simply a means of configuring or reconfiguring the system. It contains manual switches for specifying the components that comprise the system and for denoting device addresses.

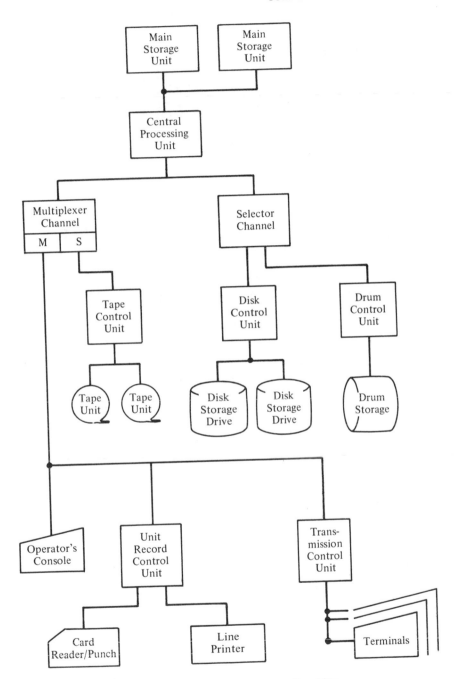

Fig. 3.5 Typical simplex system configuration.

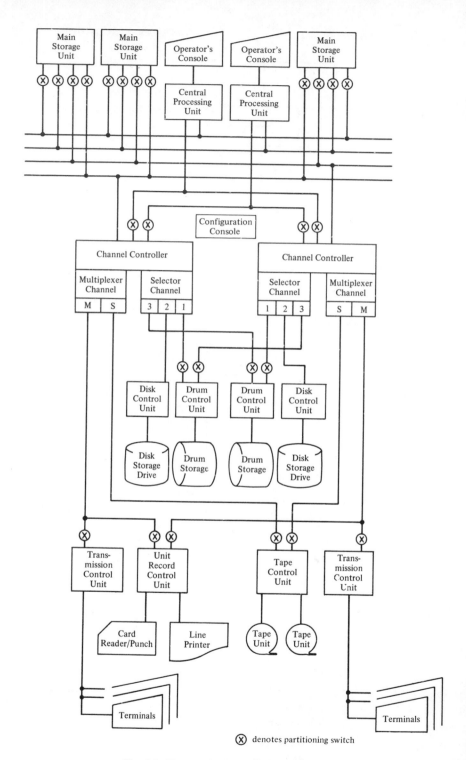

Fig. 3.6 Typical duplex system organization.

In an *n*-plex system, a failing component can be configured out of the system manually with the configuration console or dynamically under program control. This facility increases the "availability" of the system by allowing the system to continue operation in a "degraded" state.

Multiprocessing refers to the case where two or more CPUs share the same main storage and service the same work queue. When multiprocessing, the multiple CPUs operate concurrently such that a certain amount of "load leveling" is achieved. Also, the CPUs in a multiprocessing system frequently share the same routines, work areas, and tables resulting in more effective use of main storage (note the comment on "storage-oriented" given earlier).

Consider a duplex system (two CPUs) and the case where it is partitioned to form two complete computers—i.e., each with a CPU, one or more storage units, channels, etc. Each of the latter systems is termed a *half duplex system.* Two half duplex systems are more flexible than two stand-alone systems, since in a stand-alone system, all resources of a failing system are lost; whereas with half duplex systems, resources can be pooled and switched by means of the configuration console to meet the demands of a given situation.

Although multiprocessing obviously provides more computing power than a single system, a duplex system, for example, has less raw computing power than two equivalent stand-alone systems. Performance is usually degraded slightly because of hardware contention (e.g., when two CPUs attempt to access the same storage unit at the same time) and software contention (e.g., when two CPUs attempt to use the same routine or access the same data file and one of them is locked out). A high level of availability is usually the prime objective in multiprocessing systems design, although increased computing power is often of equal importance.

This discussion of multiprocessing and *n*-plex systems has presented the most general case—i.e., when the system can be configured on a dynamic basis. Multiprocessing systems also exist in which two or more CPUs operate concurrently on the same work queue without requiring additional equipment that permits reconfiguration. However, in most systems, even though they are "less complex," basic multiprocessing features (inter-CPU communication, shared resources, etc.) continue to exist. Specific details are a function of the particular equipment involved.

Attached Support Processors

In certain operating environments (e.g., in a large installation with many small jobs or with a high volume of unit record IO), the performance of a powerful CPU is degraded because of IO interference and an imbalance of other resource management facilities because of the excessive IO. In some cases, it is feasible to introduce a smaller CPU into the operating environment to handle low-speed IO devices and perform other housekeeping chores. Such a system is called an *at-*

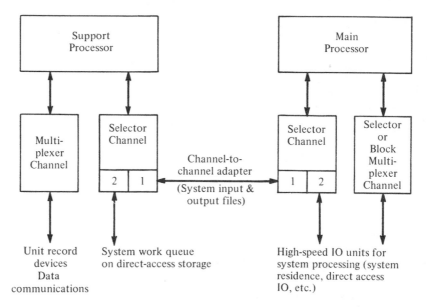

Fig. 3.7   Attached support processor (ASP) operating environment.

tached support processor (ASP), that is connected to the main computer via a channel-to-channel adapter or with a shared main storage (usually the former). The main computer's system IO devices are replaced by a channel-to-channel connection to the support processor that can supply normal system input and output data at electronic speeds. An ASP configuration is depicted in Fig. 3.7. A support processor is particularly useful for controlling data communications lines, performing data editing and translation, and executing some of the utility functions of the operating system.

3.3 CENTRAL PROCESSING UNIT

This section provides information on a generalized central processing unit (CPU) useful for the study of operating systems. Conceptually, the CPU controls the operation of the entire computer system. All storage references, data manipulation, and input/output operations are either performed by the CPU or initiated by it. These functions plus an understanding of sequence and control functions in the CPU and a knowledge of its control and execution units is assumed. Basic computer design philosophy is discussed here since it determines how an operating system is designed and how it operates. This information is not necessarily required by the user of the operating system although it may be required for the development of certain types of computer programs.

Status Word

Operating control of the computer is reflected in a computer word termed the *status word.*† The status word together with the machine registers reflect the current state of the CPU at any point in time. Changing the contents of the status word is tantamount to changing the status of the computer since the CPU uses it to determine how instructions and conditions that arise should be processed. The status word contains the following kinds of information:

1. the location in main storage of the instruction currently being executed;
2. the storage protection key (covered later);
3. codes that determine which interruptions (also covered later) can occur and specify conditions that currently exist; and
4. state indicators that govern the operational state of the CPU.

The status word is used in four ways: (1) to hold information that tells what *has* happened in the CPU; (2) to hold information that denotes what is currently happening in the CPU; (3) to hold information that governs what operations can or cannot be performed by the CPU; and (4) to hold information that denotes what can or cannot happen in the future. Thus, the status word is composed of mask fields, state bits, codes, lengths, and addresses.

The significance of the status word is amplified in subsequent paragraphs.

Program States

Modern computers are designed to accommodate several active users in main storage simultaneously—an operational technique known as *multiprogramming.* This technique requires that the operating system manage the resources of the computer system dynamically (including the CPU, storage, and IO facility) and that the users be protected from one another. It is not difficult to imagine the confusion and inefficiency that would result from several users attempting to perform their own IO, and utilize external storage as well, in a multiprogramming environment. For this reason, most modern computers limit the functions that can be performed by an applications program.

In general, two states of the CPU are defined: the supervisor state and the problem state. A program operating in the *supervisor state* has access to the facilities of the entire computer system. This is achieved through privileged and nonprivileged instructions. Privileged instructions are used to initiate IO, load the status word, manipulate storage keys, and perform other critical functions. (Several of these functions are discussed in other parts of this chapter.) Nonprivileged instructions are used to perform ordinary data processing functions—

---

†The status word is the same as the *program status word* (PSW) found in many modern computer systems.

those that cannot affect the program of another user. It follows that a program operating in the supervisor state can use both privileged and nonprivileged instructions.

The *problem state* is a state of the CPU that permits only nonprivileged instructions to be executed and is obviously intended for applications programs (often called processing programs).

Routines of the operating system that are involved with the overall management of the computer system normally operate in the supervisor state. When a program operating in the problem state requires the services of a routine that operates in the supervisor state, two functions must be performed:

1. Program control must be passed to the required routine.
2. The state of the CPU must be changed to the supervisor state.

The manner in which these two functions are implemented is discussed next under the subject title, "Interruptions."

The supervisor/problem state is perhaps the most obvious state that the CPU can be in since it determines the kinds of instructions that can be executed by an operating program. Other states that affect the operation of the CPU are: (1) the Stopped/Operating state, (2) the Wait/Running state, and (3) the Masked/Interruptable state.

When the CPU is in the stopped state, instructions cannot be executed and interruptions cannot be taken. (In other words, the computer is not operating.) If the CPU is in the operating state, then it is either waiting or running. If it is in the *running state*, then instructions are being processed and interruptions can be taken. In the *wait state*, instructions are not executed but interruptions can take place. Normally, the operating system will put the CPU into the wait state when it has no more work to do. The CPU is subsequently taken out of the wait state by an interruption that denotes an external event, a condition, or a request that must be attended to by the operating system.

When the CPU can be interrupted for a given event, that interruption is said to be *enabled* and a mask bit in the status word or an auxiliary control register is set. When the mask bit is not set, the interruption is said to be *masked off* or *disabled* and that particular interruption is not recognized. In general, a masked/interruptable state exists for each type of interruption; however, some interruptions are of prime importance and can never be masked off.

The CPU is put into a particular state by loading a status word with appropriate bits set. In general, a new status word is loaded with a "load status word" instruction that can be issued by a program executing in the supervisor state or as the result of an interruption that causes a new status word to be loaded.

Interruptions

The CPU is designed to execute instructions sequentially. The address of the current instruction (often called a location counter or the current address register) is maintained by the CPU.[†] Execution proceeds as follows:

1. The control unit of the CPU fetches the instruction located at the main storage address specified in the current address register.
2. The instruction is decoded by the control unit.
3. The current address register is incremented by the length attribute of the instruction fetched.
4. The specified computer operation is performed by the execution unit of the CPU.

The process continues with step 1, and in that way, instructions located in main storage are executed sequentially until one of two conditions arises:

1. An instruction is executed that alters the sequential order, or
2. an independent event interrupts normal computer processing.

An independent event that interrupts normal computer processing is called an *interruption* and can occur for one of many reasons:

1. The computer detects an erroneous or unusual condition in a program currently in execution.
2. A device external to the CPU needs attention.
3. The error detection circuitry of the computer detects a hardware malfunction.
4. A program executing in the problem state requires the services of a routine that executes in the supervisor state and issues an instruction that causes an interruption.

For each type of interruption recognized by the CPU[‡] there are two fixed locations in main storage—each of which can hold a replica of the status word. The first location is referred to as the *old status word* and the second is referred to as the *new status word*. When an interruption occurs, the *current status word* at the moment of interruption is stored in the old status word location and the status word located at the new status word location replaces the current status word for the CPU. The current address field of the new status word contains the main storage location of a routine developed to process that type of interruption, and the other bits of the status word are set appropriately. The switching of status words is performed automatically by the CPU when an interruption occurs for a condition that has been enabled. (See Fig. 3.8.) A disabled interruption may be ignored or left pending, depending upon the type of condition and the design of the CPU.

[†]It is assumed here that the current address register is maintained by the CPU as a part of the status word. In actual practice, the fields of the status word may exist in separate registers and may be assembled or disassembled when the status word is referenced.

[‡]The interruption scheme used in the 360/370 computer is described here.

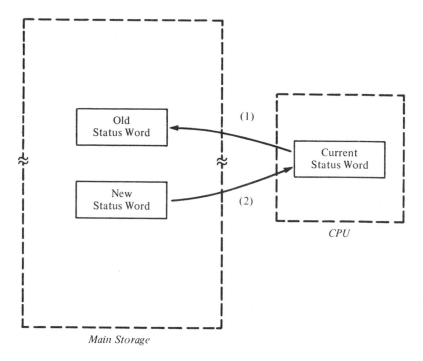

Fig. 3.8 Switching of the status word after an interruption.

Interruption systems are developed differently in different computers. Some computers permit interruptions to occur at different priority levels for a large number of independent events. Other computers permit only a small number of types of interruptions. Regardless of the design philosophy, additional information on the independent event causing the interruption is required; that information is stored as an interruption code in the old status word or elsewhere in main storage. The interruption code may specify the condition and/or the physical component associated with the interruption.

A basic set of interruptions are required for descriptive purposes. They are listed and described as follows:

1. *Input/output interruption*—signals to the CPU that an IO channel is free, that the activity of a specific channel or control unit has been completed, or that a special condition has arisen. The interruption code usually specifies the channel and control unit address of the associated IO device.

2. *Program interruption*—caused by an improper specification of computer hardware facilities or an illegal use of a computer instruction or of data. The condition causing the interruption is stored as the interruption code.

3. *Supervisor call interruption*—requests a change to the supervisor state from

the problem state.   Usually this type of interruption is issued to have a function performed that is permitted only by a program executing in the supervisor state.

4. *External interruption*—caused by a signal from a device external to the CPU or by an alarm from a timing device. System timers and inter-CPU communication features frequently use this facility.

5. *Machine check interruption*—results from a computer system malfunction. This type of interruption is dependent upon a particular model of computer.

(The experienced reader will recognize that the five basic types of interruptions are precisely the same as those available with the IBM 360/370 computers. However, this seems to be a basic set and it is not obvious how a system that utilizes the "interrupt philosophy" can operate with any less.) From an operating system point of view, the concept of an interruption is extremely important for three major reasons:

1. It allows system components that operate asychronously to communicate.
2. It allows computer programs to communicate.
3. It allows the computer system to monitor the execution of computer programs.

3.4 STORAGE

Although a general knowledge of main storage characteristics is generally assumed, two topics are of particular concern: large-capacity storage and storage protection.   Both facilities can be used by the operating system to control the allocation of hardware resources.

Large-Capacity Storage

Large-capacity storage, or LCS as it is usually called, is a directly addressable extension to main storage.   Access time to LCS is somewhat slower than to main storage, and when executing instructions or using data stored there, the performance of the CPU is degraded.   In many cases, however, the use of LCS as a bulk storage device is superior to using an auxiliary storage device (such as magnetic disk).   The combination of main storage and LCS constitutes a *storage hierarchy*.   For some applications, it is efficient to transfer instructions and data from LCS to main storage before processing.   In other cases, the overhead is not justified and the information is used directly from LCS.   (In the latter case, the CPU is said to be executing out of LCS.)

Some operating systems permit a user to specify whether he desires his programs and data to be loaded into main storage or into LCS.   Frequently, this facility is available on a "per object module" basis and can be used by the users and the installation to satisfy cost/performance objectives.

Storage Protection

One of the characteristics of most modern operating systems is that they permit one or more programs to reside concurrently in main storage. A hardware storage protection feature is available with many computer systems that prevents a program from making storage accesses to an area in storage occupied by another program.

Storage protection is implemented by dividing main storage into fixed-size blocks and by associating a storage key with each block. (The IBM 360/370 computers, for example, use a 2048-byte block for storage protection.) Each active program has a *protection key* that is usually maintained as a part of the status word. A store operation into an area of main storage is permitted only if the keys match or the protection key is zero. Keys are assigned by the operating system so that each block of storage assigned to the same program has the same storage key and so that the protection key assigned to that program matches the storage key. The zero protection key, taken generally to be the *master key*, is used by the operating system and is never assigned to a user's program.

Two levels of protection exist for main storage: store protection and fetch protection. *Store protection* guards against a store operation into a given block of main storage. *Fetch protection* guards against information being fetched from a given block of main storage.

Storage protection may also be provided through an advanced storage management technique known as *dynamic address translation*. Dynamic address translation is combined with a "paging" operation that effectively maps a user's "virtual" storage area into a combination of main storage and an auxiliary storage device. During dynamic address translation, each effective address is translated using page tables maintained by the operating system. When dynamic address translation and paging are being used, a private page (i.e., a fixed-size block of storage) of one user is protected against being accessed by another user for the simple reason that its main storage address or auxiliary storage location does not exist in the page tables of other users. Dynamic address translation and paging has other advantages in addition to storage protection. These advantages are presented in Part Three, where this subject is discussed in detail.

3.5   INPUT AND OUTPUT

In a complex computer system, input and output procedures are sophisticated for several reasons:

1. The input and output hardware components are inherently complicated.
2. Input and output operations are executed concurrently with CPU operations.
3. Input and output operations for multiple users can operate concurrently.
4. The CPU operates at electronic speeds and input and output devices oper-

ate at electromechanical speeds; hence, input and output data are frequently queued to compensate for differences in operating speeds.

Fortunately for most users,[†] modern operating systems provide input/output control systems (IOCS) or data management routines that relieve the user of the drudgery of programming his own IO. Data management facilities are presented in more detail later in the book. Input and output hardware components are considered here.

Input and Output Organization

In early computers, all data entering and leaving the computer passed through the CPU, forcing the CPU to operate at IO speeds in many cases. This obstacle to good performance was alleviated in the 1950s with the widespread use of the input and output data channel (referred to as an IO channel). An IO channel is essentially a small hard-wired or microprogrammed computer that controls the operation of an IO device or a group of IO devices. An IO channel has access to main storage independently of the CPU; in fact, the CPU and IO data channels are designed to operate concurrently. The structure of a sample IO subsystem is given in Fig. 3.9. The IO channel is the key link in an effective IO subsystem. An IO device is attached to an IO channel via an IO control unit. In general, peripheral devices external to the computer are referred to as IO devices regardless of whether they are used for input or output or for main storage.

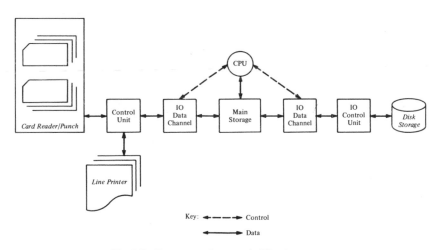

Fig. 3.9 Structure of a sample IO subsystem.

[†]This also includes experienced users since writing effective IO routines is a cumbersome process—even if one is knowledgeable in the subject.

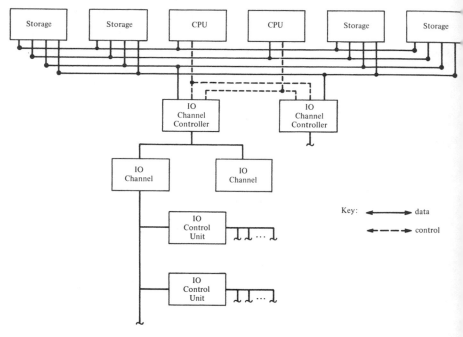

Fig. 3.10 Use of an IO channel controller to provide multiple CPUs with access to the same IO channels.

The manner in which an IO subsystem operates is directly related to its functional organization. The following hierarchy of operation is established:

1. The CPU controls the operation of the IO channels.
2. An IO channel controls the operation of IO control units attached to it.
3. An IO control unit controls the operation of IO devices attached to it.

Much like the CPU and main storage, an IO subsystem can be organized in different ways. First, an IO channel can be shared among two CPUs with an *IO channel controller*, as depicted in Fig. 3.10. An IO channel controller is designed to access main storage units while not interfering with the operation of the CPU and permits an IO channel to be controlled by either of the CPUs in the system. (An IO channel controller is used primarily in a multiprocessing system.) Next, an IO control unit can be shared between IO channels as depicted in Fig. 3.11. A shared IO control unit provides multiple paths to the same IO device; it is used when one IO channel controller or IO channel is unavailable for use with a particular IO operation or when it is necessary for two CPUs to share the same control unit. Lastly, IO devices can be shared among IO control units as depicted in Fig. 3.11. Clearly, the IO control units can be attached to IO channels for different CPUs or to IO channels of the same CPU. When the same CPU is involved,

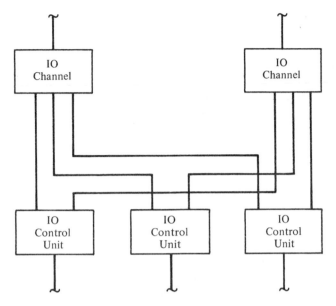

Fig. 3.11a Shared IO control units.

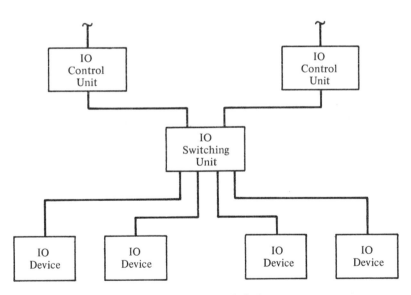

Fig. 3.11b Shared IO devices.

multiple paths to that device may be provided. When different CPUs are present, each system has access to a single shared device.

In each of the above cases, the components can be connected with a centralized crossbar switch or a distributed crossbar switch. In most cases, overall system availability is not directly related to the failure of IO devices, so IO devices are frequently connected to IO control units with the centralized switch.

In complex computing systems, the assignment of components to CPUs in particular, and the effective utilization of the hardware components in general, is the responsibility of the operating system. Regardless of the sophistication of the operating systems, the results can be very dramatic. In a relatively simple operating system, a typical benefit may be to select an alternate path to an IO device to bypass a failing IO control unit. In a relatively complex operating system that supports a multiprocessing system, a typical benefit may be to "reconfigure out" a failing storage unit without shutting down either of the CPUs. Obviously, this discussion is related to the configuration console mentioned previously. The key concept is that the computer system can be configured manually or under program control, or both, depending upon the characteristics of the hardware.

IO Data Channels

Clearly, an IO data channel (referred to hereafter simply as an "IO channel") directs and controls the flow of data between main storage and IO devices and allows the CPU to operate concurrently with IO operations. An IO channel must interface with two other components: main storage and an IO control unit, as depicted in Fig. 3.12. The amount of data that can pass between an IO channel and an IO control unit at one time is referred to as the *standard IO interface;* it is usually fixed for a given computer so that a variety of IO devices can be used. The IO channel operates as a hardware data buffer for the following reasons:

1. the large difference in data rates between main storage and IO devices;
2. the difference in access width between main storage and the IO channel and between the IO channel and the IO control unit; and

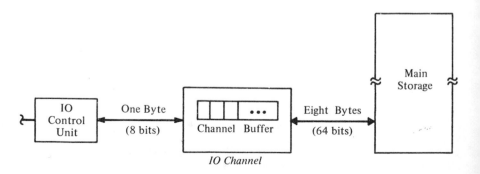

Fig. 3.12   Typical IO interface.

3. the fact that several IO channels and the CPU are competing for access to main storage, and once an IO channel gains that access, it is desirable to transmit enough data to make the effort worthwhile.

As a result, the IO channel requires storage facilities and logical circuitry to manage the control of IO facilities and the storage and transmission of data. Channel facilities required by a single IO operation are referred to as a *subchannel*. A subchannel requires, minimally, storage areas for the following kinds of information: a count, a main storage address used for data transmission, the main storage address of the IO command, control and status data, and a buffer storage area. Thus, a considerable amount of physical equipment is required to sustain a single IO operation. When the data rate of an IO device is high (e.g., 3 megabytes per second), then the use of a single IO channel for a single IO operation is certainly justified. However, when the data rate of an IO device is low (e.g., 10 bytes per second), then an IO channel must be shared to justify its existence. An IO channel is classified on the basis of the number of subchannels that it can sustain concurrently. In general, subchannels of a given IO channel share logical circuitry while storage facilities are not shared. Three types of IO channels are recognized: selector channel, byte-multiplexer channel, and block-multiplexer channel.

A *selector channel* is designed for use with high-speed IO devices, such as disk or drum storage. A selector channel includes a single subchannel and can sustain one IO operation at a time. Once a connection between a selector channel and an IO device is established, that connection is maintained until the IO operation is complete. In other words, the IO channel is "busy" for the duration of the IO operation. Several IO devices can use the same selector channel; however, only one device can be active at any one time.

A *byte-multiplexer channel* is designed for use with several low-speed IO devices and includes multiple subchannels. A byte-multiplexer channel can sustain an IO operation on each of its subchannels concurrently. A byte-multiplexer subchannel remains connected to an IO device for the duration of an IO operation; however, it utilizes channel facilities only for the transmission of a single unit of data, usually defined as a byte. (Hence, the name byte-multiplexer channel.) As a result, many low-speed devices share the channel, justifying its existence on a system-wide basis. Most byte-multiplexer channels also operate in a *burst* mode for short periods of time allowing medium-speed devices, such as magnetic tape, to be connected to the computer without requiring a selector channel.

The third type of IO channel is a *block-multiplexer channel* that combines the speed of a selector channel with the interleaved operation of a byte-multiplexer channel. The block-multiplexer channel is shared by multiple high-speed devices in the same way that the byte-multiplexer channel is shared by multiple low-speed devices. Instead of multiplexing bytes like the byte-multiplexer channel, the block-multiplexer channel multiplexes blocks, which correspond to physical data records. The design philosophy underlying the block-multiplexer channel is that it is freed during non-data transfer operations (such as disk seek) so that it can be used by another subchannel.

IO Control Units and Devices

An IO control unit controls the operation of one or more IO devices that fall in its domain. For example, there are disk control units for disk storage devices, magnetic tape control units for magnetic tape devices, and unit record control units for devices such as line printers and card reader/punches. A control unit manages the data flow to and from an IO device and performs other non-data transfer operations such as tape rewind or a disk seek. A single IO control unit frequently controls several IO devices.

An IO device is the component that physically interfaces with the IO medium. It is important to distinguish between an IO device and an IO volume. An IO volume is the physical medium on which data is recorded. (For example, a magnetic tape or a disk pack is an IO volume.) In any computer system, the number of IO devices is limited. There are n tape units, m disk units, etc. If an IO volume is removable, such as a magnetic tape or disk pack, then the amount of data that can be stored on that medium is theoretically unlimited. However, only a subset of the total amount of data is available to the computer at one time. Some devices, such as magnetic drum, have IO volumes that are not removable. Devices of this type are usually used for storing data on an intermediate basis or when frequent access to a large volume of data (such as in a stock quotation or airline system) is needed in a real time system.

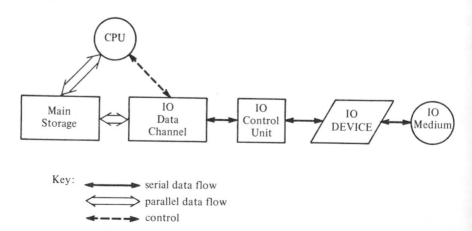

Fig. 3.13 Typical IO subsystem depicting the flow between main storage and an IO medium.

IO devices are used for input/output or for mass storage. Unit record devices, such as a card reader or line printer are usually used for input/output. Devices with removable volumes are used for either input/output or mass storage. Devices with nonremovable volumes are often used as intermediate storage—as mentioned above. Figure 3.13 depicts a typical IO subsystem.

IO Operations

An IO operation is initiated in the CPU by the execution of an instruction that specifies the IO channel and device addresses and indicates the main storage location of the beginning of a channel program. The channel program specifies the IO operations that should be executed and exists as a series of channel commands. (A channel command specifies a channel operation in the same way that a CPU instruction specifies a CPU instruction.) Some typical IO commands are: read, write, read backwards, control, and sense. A channel command usually requires a data address, a count, and the setting of some flags and control indicators. Depending upon the device involved and the requested operation, a channel program may exist as a single channel command or a series of channel commands that are executed successively by the IO channel. (It should be remembered here that while an IO channel is executing a channel program, the CPU can proceed concurrently.)

Although a detailed discussion of IO is dependent upon a given computer and inappropriate here, one particular procedure has significance from an operating systems point of view. The facility is termed *data chaining* and is used when it is desired to read parts of a data record into different locations. The process, also known as *scatter read* and *scatter write*, is depicted in Fig. 3.14. Data chaining

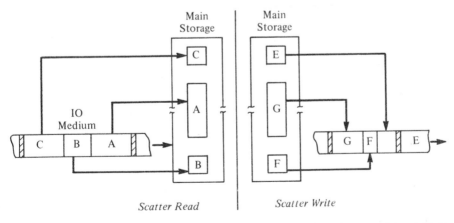

Scatter Read   *Scatter Write*

Fig. 3.14 Use of data chaining (in channel commands of a channel program) to perform a scatter read and a scatter write.

uses the control bit in a channel command that tells the IO channel to "continue the present operation with the address and count given in the *next* channel command." Assume here that RD means "read" and that CD specifies "data chaining." Then, the following commands specify the scatter read operation depicted in Fig. 3.14:

RD   A,350,CD
RD   B,100,CD
RD   C,200

(Where A, B, C denote storage locations and the numerals denote the "count" field in a channel command.) Scatter read is frequently used in an operating system to bring several routines (or distinct parts of a single routine) into main storage and place them at different locations with a single IO instruction.

An obvious question at this point might be, "If the CPU and an IO channel operate asynchronously, how does the CPU know when an IO operation is finished?" The answer is that the IO channel initiates an IO interruption that is accepted by the CPU and processed by an IO control routine. In general, an IO interruption can originate at an IO device, an IO control unit, or an IO channel. The nature of the event that caused the interruption is stored as part of an IO status word that is placed in main storage when the IO interruption is taken. The IO control routine uses the IO status word to determine the appropriate action to be taken. The processing of an IO interruption is generally considered to be a machine-dependent operation.

Direct-Access Storage

Much of modern operating systems technology involves the use of direct-access storage. Routines of the operating system are usually stored on a direct-access volume and most complicated IO procedures involve direct-access storage. (The device on which routines of the operating system are stored is frequently referred to as the *systems residence device*.) This section is limited to a discussion of disk storage. Other devices fall into the category of direct-access devices but disk is the most frequently used. The major objective of this section is to establish terminology since most readers are already familiar with the basic concepts. For those who are not, this section is pedagogical as well.

Disk storage is a recording medium similar in concept to that of a phonograph record except that the tracks are concentric instead of spiral. A disk volume has several recording disks, each coated on both sides with a magnetic material such as ferrous oxide, and mounted on a rotating shaft.

Data are recorded in tracks on the disk surfaces and are read or written as the disks rotate. A disk storage unit has three major components: the recording surfaces, the access arms and read-write heads, and the disk mechanism. (See Fig. 3.15.) Collectively, these components are referred to as a *disk module*.

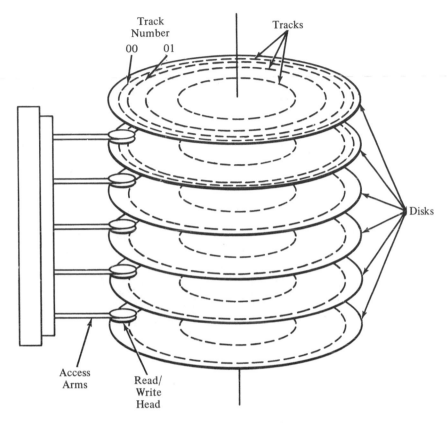

Fig. 3.15 Disk storage module.

Some disk drives (i.e., disk IO devices) include a single module and others include as many as nine modules. The disk mechanism causes the disks to rotate
and the access arms to move in and out as directed by the disk control unit. The
stack of disks is referred to as a *disk volume;* if the volume is removable, it is referred to as a *disk pack.*

Data are recorded on both surfaces of a disk (except possibly the top and bot-
tom surfaces of a volume) and a single access arm controls two read-write heads:
one for the upper surface and one for the lower surface. The access arms form a
comb-type assembly and usually move in and out together. (Notable exceptions
exist where the arms move independently in some disk mechanisms and are fixed
in other disk systems; however, the benefit of the comb-type approach is that it
is useful for introducing the cylinder concept.) Thus, a single read-write head is
used to access an entire surface.

Data are recorded serially by bit on a track, as implied in Fig. 3.16, so that a

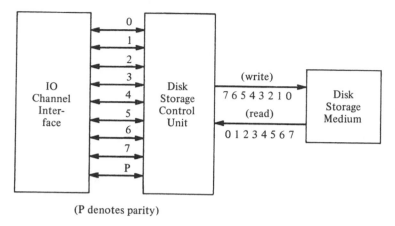

(P denotes parity)

Fig. 3.16   Data transfer between disk storage and the IO channel.

byte occupies 8 bit positions. The concentric tracks are designed so that each track holds the same amount of information. Since all read-write heads are always located in the same vertical position, several tracks (one corresponding to each recording surface) can be read or written without moving the access

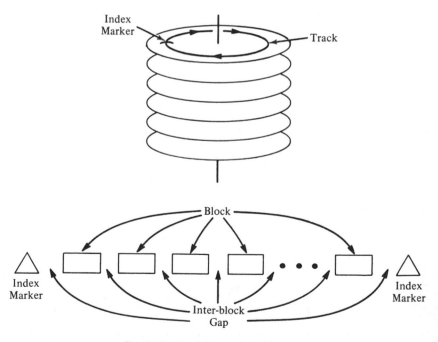

Fig. 3.17   Track format for disk storage.

mechanism. The positioning of the read-write heads at any track location provides access to a *cylinder* of information. There are as many cylinders per volume as there are tracks per surface. The cylinder concept is utilized by the data management facilities of an operating system to reduce the access time necessary to store or retrieve data.

Considering the above discussion, a specific track is located by read-write head number and by track number. (Another means of locating the same track would be by cylinder and head number, i.e., CCHH.) It seems reasonable to assume that most records written on a track would be either less than a track in length or greater than a track in length. Therefore, a track must be formatted using a combination of hardware and software facilities to enable it to be used effectively. Each track, as depicted in Fig. 3.17, is closed such that a single index marker denotes both the beginning and the end of the track. The index market is a property of the disk volume itself and not of a specific track. Data are recorded on a track as a series of consecutive bytes called a *block*. Blocks are separated by special gaps that are used for orientation and control. A single physical data record (see Chapter 4) is recorded as a series of three blocks, as depicted in Fig. 3.18. The *count block* denotes the beginning of a data record and contains flags, control information, the key length, the data length, and a record number. The *record number* is used to locate a specific record on a track. A typical count block is given as Fig. 3.19. The *key block*, which may be elided, contains a data field used to locate a particular record in a file. The *data block*, which never can be elided, contains the data portion of a data record.

As far as storing information on disk is concerned, several data records are stored on the same track provided that they each have a unique record number. When the data length of a record exceeds track length, it is stored as a spanned record (see Chapter 4) or on the next track of the same cylinder. The latter method can be used only if the disk storage mechanism has an automatic track overflow facility. Detailed programming operational procedures for disk storage are necessarily dependent upon a specific unit and are not considered here.

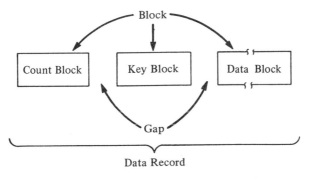

Fig. 3.18 Block format of a disk data record.

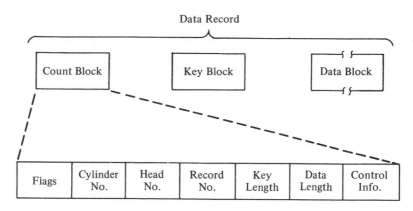

Fig. 3.19 Detailed information in the count block of a disk data record.

The objective of this chapter has been to discuss several aspects of computer systems technology that are most important from an operating systems point of view. For readers who would like to delve deeper: Flores [Flo69] and Foster [Fos70] give an introduction to computer architecture; Katzan [Kat71] discusses computer organization and the System/370; Davis [Dav71] provides a complete introduction to input and output devices; and Chapin [Cha71] gives a complete overview of the function and use of computers. These are only a few of the many references that exist in the area of computer structures. Reference manuals supplied by computer manufacturers are also an excellent source of information on computer systems and devices.

4 | DATA AND STORAGE STRUCTURES

4.1 INTRODUCTION

Algorithms from which computer programs are developed require a conceptualization of data called a *data structure*. Familiar examples are the table, list, or array; computer programs utilize data structures, such as these, to produce desired results. The concept holds true in general, and routines of the operating system use data structures in precisely the same manner as applications programs use data structures. The reader should recognize the difference between data structures and storage structures. *Storage structures* are the actual symbols (i.e., bits or bytes) that represent the data structures in the main storage unit and on the auxiliary storage units of the computer.

This chapter presents a brief summary of the data structures and the storage structures that are most frequently used in the study of operating systems. The presentation is primarily conceptual since storage structures for a specific computer are not considered.

It should be mentioned that data structures are frequently considered to be of two types: "program" data structures and "data" data structures. (The term *information structures*, which implies both program structures and data structures, is perhaps most appropriate here.) The present discussion is concerned with "data" data structures. "Program" data structures are more closely related to the study of programming languages and to the study of advanced concepts in operating systems technology.

4.2 BASIC DATA STRUCTURES

Scalar Data

The basic unit of data is known as a scalar. A *scalar* has one component, that is, its value, and exists in one of two familiar forms: problem data and program control data. *Problem data* can be of the types arithmetic or string, and include the following:

1. fixed-point numeric data items (e.g., 25.34);
2. floating-point numeric data items (e.g., .123×10^4);
3. character strings (e.g., 'TEA FOR TWO'); and
4. bit strings (e.g., '101101'B).

(Note here that no mention is made of how data are stored in the computer or even how they are used.) *Program control data* are concerned with the operability of a computer program and can be one of the following types: (1) label data, (2) pointer data (i.e., a computer address), (3) task data, (4) event data, etc. Although program control data can be structured in much the same manner as problem data, they tend to be machine-dependent and do not add appreciably to the presentation of data structures. (For example, an "event" data item may be represented as a single bit. If the event takes place, the bit is set to one; if the event does not take place, it is set to zero.)

Array Data

Most computer applications require that data be structured in some form or another. The most straightforward example is the complex number that includes real and imaginary parts. In a sense, the complex number is a special case since many programming languages, such as FORTRAN and PL/I, allow it as a special data type and have arithmetic operators defined over the domain of complex numbers. In general, a collection of data items, each with the same attributes, is termed an *array*. A one-dimensional array corresponds to the ordinary vector in mathematics. An element of a one-dimensional array is selected with an *index* (often called a subscript); thus, the term A(I) denotes the Ith element of array A. A two-dimensional array corresponds to the ordinary matrix in mathematics. An element of a two-dimensional array is selected with two indices: one for the row and the other for the column. Thus, the term B(J,K) denotes the element located at the junction of row J and column K of array B. In general, the concept is extended to as many dimensions as are required by a particular application.

Structure Data

A *structure* is a data aggregate in which individual data items are permitted to possess different attributes. The components of a structure may be either scalar values or arrays; in fact, arrays of structures are frequently used. Consider the following declaration of a structure in the PL/I langauge:

```
DECLARE  1  A,
            2  B   CHARACTER(5),
            2  C(3) FIXED BINARY,
            2  D,
               3 E CHARACTER(2),
               3 F PICTURE '999V99';
```

The declaration specifies a structure named A; B is a character data item; C is a one-dimensional array containing 3 elements in which each element is a binary fixed-point value; and D is a minor structure containing E, which is a character data item, and F, which is a numeric character data item. The level numbers 1, 2, and 3 specify the placement of a data item in the hierarchical structure. Level 1 is the highest level in a structure and level numbers with a greater magnitude specify a lower level. Data items with the same level number are structurally at the same level. Structurally, the structure A is depicted as:

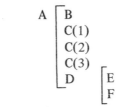

or

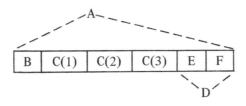

A structure frequently corresponds with the familiar data record used in data processing.

An *array of structures* defines a collection of structures, each with the same substructure. For example, the following PL/I declaration:

```
DECLARE  1  TABLE(10),
            2  KEY CHARACTER(8),
            2  VALUE FIXED DECIMAL;
```

specifies a collection (an array) of 10 structures each with the following form:

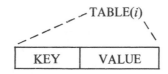

4.3 STORAGE STRUCTURES

Basic Concepts

Thus far, three types of basic data structures have been presented: scalars, arrays, and structures. No mention has been made of how these data structures are represented in storage or even what they represent. Consider, for example, an array of structures. It could represent a table, as illustrated in the preceding section, or it could represent a data file in which each element structure corresponds to a data record. The purpose of this section is to discuss how the basic data structures are represented in storage, or conversely, how storage is utilized in the representation of those data structures.

It is important to establish initially whether the concern is over main storage or auxiliary storage. A *unit of main storage* is usually taken to be a byte or a word. When a user utilizes or requests a certain amount of storage, he requests "so many" bytes or "so many" words. Sometimes, a fixed unit of storage such as a *page* is defined. (A typical page size is 4096 bytes.) Storage is then measured by the number of pages used. As far as auxiliary storage is concerned, the unit of storage depends on the medium involved. When a serial medium, such as magnetic tape, is used, the unit of storage is usually not given exactly; it is frequently measured by the number of feet used (of that medium) or the number of data records stored. When a direct-access medium, such as magnetic disk, is used, the unit of storage can be specified more precisely; it is usually measured by the number of tracks used or the number of cylinders used. Auxiliary storage can also utilize the page concept, and this is frequently the case when main storage is measured in page-size units. The correspondence between a physical page and the number of tracks or cylinders required to store that much information is usually determined by the data management properties of the operating system.

Storage Class

One of the attributes of a storage structure is its *storage class*, which determines when that storage is allocated. Storage can be allocated statically or dynamically. *Static storage* is allocated before the program that uses it begins execution. *Dynamic storage* is allocated during execution on an "as needed" basis.

Storage class is most frequently applied to main storage and applies to both programs and data. In modern operating systems, storage space for a program is allocated (by the operating system); the program to be executed is loaded into that space; and then execution is initiated. That program may utilize both static and dynamic data areas. A *static storage area* is established when the program is loaded. A *dynamic storage area* is requested by the program and allocated by the operating system on a dynamic basis.

The concept of static and dynamic storage also applies to space on an auxiliary storage media. Consider disk storage as an example. If the user knows that his job will require a given number of tracks or cylinders and he requests that space from the operating system (with control cards) before the execution of his program is initiated, then that storage is being allocated statically.[†] If auxiliary storage is allocated on an "as needed" basis, then it is allocated dynamically. The dynamic allocation of auxiliary storage during the execution of a program is a cumbersome process for the operating system, and except under special cases, tends to fragment the available space on auxiliary storage volume. One of the cases where the dynamic allocation of auxiliary storage is feasible is when auxiliary storage is organized and allocated in page-size increments.

Frequently, auxiliary storage is allocated both statically and dynamically during the execution of a single job. Before his job is executed, the user requests a *primary allocation* and a *secondary allocation*. The primary allocation is assigned to the job statically. If additional space is needed, it is assigned dynamically in storage units specified as the secondary allocation. Thus, the user is protected against "running out" of allocated storage space and thereby causing an abnormal termination of his job. By choosing primary and secondary allocations judiciously, he can use auxiliary storage efficiently without having to plan for the worst case. Also, some operating systems allow the user to "give back" storage that is allocated but unused.

A group of contiguous storage units (e.g., bytes) on an auxiliary storage medium is called an *extent*. Each time an operating system allocates auxiliary storage space to an operating program, it allocates contiguous bytes. However, different allocations do not necessarily occupy contiguous areas, so a data file written on auxiliary storage may occupy several noncontiguous extents.

Space on an auxiliary storage medium is allocated and maintained by the operating system in most modern large-scale operating systems. The user informs the operating system of his needs with control cards (i.e., job control information). In relatively small operating systems, the users must collectively manage auxiliary storage manually.

[†]Obviously, point of view is important here. Auxiliary storage that is allocated statically, as far as an individual job is concerned, is usually allocated dynamically as far as the operating system is concerned. However, one can easily imagine an operating system in which auxiliary storage is preallocated for various purposes.

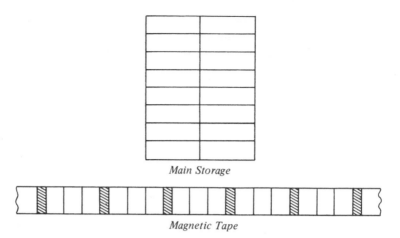

Fig. 4.1   Consecutive organization.

Storage Organization

Storage structures can be organized in four basic ways: consecutive, linked, keyed, and regional. *Consecutive organization* implies that a given allocation of storage occupies contiguous storage locations (see Fig. 4.1). Arrays held in main storage and data records placed on magnetic tape are familiar examples of storage structures that are organized consecutively. It should be noted that storage can also be organized consecutively on a direct-access medium by making the assignment in contiguous tracks or cylinders.

Linked organization does not require that units of storage (called *nodes*) occupy contiguous locations; nodes are connected by pointers (i.e., addresses) that point to succeeding and/or preceding nodes (see Fig. 4.2). Clearly, a node can be defined as any of the basic data structures. Linked organization applies to direct-access storage as well as main storage. Conceptually, the difference involves replacing address pointers with cylinder-head pointers.

Keyed organization implies a form of storage organization in which data are located by means of a data key that is part of a data record (or of a structure) or is maintained as a separate field, as in the key block in a direct-access data record (see Chapter 3). In keyed organization, data are retrieved by key—either by search or by using a table of keys that effectively points to the location of the corresponding data (see Fig. 4.3). Keyed organization is most frequently used with direct-access storage in which cylinder and track indices are used.[†] When direct-access storage is allocated in page-size increments, then relative page indices are used instead of cylinder and track indices. When a data file organized

[†]A form of data set organization known as "indexed sequential" uses a keyed organization permitting data records to be retrieved sequentially or directly.

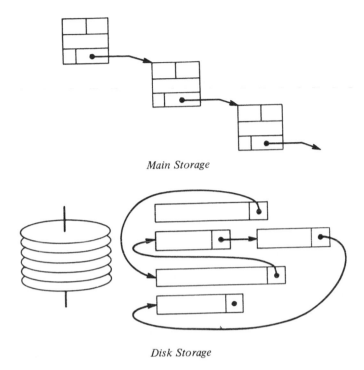

Main Storage

Disk Storage

Fig. 4.2   Linked organization.

by key is used, the index is first read into main storage from the storage medium. That index is subsequently used for accessing the desired information. A variation to keyed organization permits data to be located by applying a function to the key. The result of the function produces the location of the desired information.

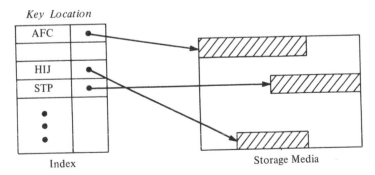

Key Location

Index

Storage Media

Fig. 4.3   Keyed organization.

Although keyed organization is most frequently used with direct-access storage devices (i.e., auxiliary storage), the techniques can be used very effectively for locating data in main storage or in directly addressable large-capacity storage by utilizing table lookup techniques.

Regional organization, like keyed organization, is most frequently used with data files but is also useful as an organization technique for main storage. A region of a storage area is located by name, index, or key. After a particular region is identified, data are located as though that region were organized consecutively (see Fig. 4.4). In many cases, regional organization simply defines partitions of a storage space allocated consecutively. A common example is a "library" of programs in object module format. The library is organized by proper name; once a program is located in the library, it is read sequentially. (A data file organized in this manner is referred to as a *partitioned data set*.)

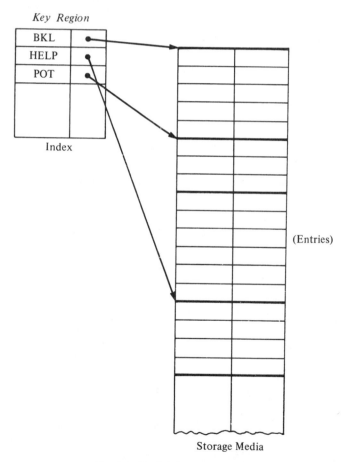

Fig. 4.4 Regional organization.

Obviously, "storage organization" is more complicated than has been implied here. The manner in which data are organized on a storage medium affects storage and retrieval processes, is related to data base management systems, and also has been studied theoretically. The objective here is to establish a conceptual framework, about the subject, that applies to both main storage and auxiliary storage structures. References on this subject are given at the end of the chapter.

Storage Access

Although the subject of storage access has been presented earlier, it is important to emphasize that the process should be viewed independently of storage organization or of how that storage is allocated (i.e., storage class).

Two methods of storage access are usually identified: sequential and direct. *Sequential access* denotes that the data elements (i.e., data records, nodes, entries, etc.) are referenced in a manner dependent upon the sequence in which the data elements are physically stored. Card decks, magnetic tape files, and simple lists organized in main storage are usually accessed sequentially; note however, that a linked list or a keyed file can also be accessed sequentially by following the pointers and by referencing the keys in order.

Direct access denotes that a data element is referenced without "passing over" or referencing preceding information. There are varying degrees of directness. When a data record or disk is referenced by passing directly to its cylinder-head number, the degree of directness is large. A similar situation arises in main storage when the physical address of a data item is known. Forms of direct access that are less direct exist in cases such as the following:

1. A key must be matched against a table that gives the physical location of the data (in fact, the table may be structured to require several "levels" of search[†]).
2. A functional transformation is performed on the key to give the relative position of a data item in a storage structure.
3. An element of an array is located by applying a mathematical formula that uses subscripts and the declared dimension of the array.[‡]

In summary, then, access applies to both main storage and auxiliary storage and includes sequential and direct modes of operation. These are basic methods of access. A given software program may define additional entry and search techniques over the basic methods. For example, sequential, interval, and binary search techniques are frequently used in data processing; each of these tech-

---

[†]On direct-access auxiliary storage, this technique is frequently referred to as *indexed sequential*, as mentioned in a previous footnote.
[‡]For example, the (I,J)th element of array A declared as DIMENSION A(M,N) in FORTRAN and stored in column order would be located with a formula of the form:

$$loc[A(I,J)] = loc[A(1,1] + M * (J\text{-}1) + (I\text{-}1)$$

niques uses either sequential or direct access defined on the methods employed for storage class and storage organization.

4.4   USER DATA STRUCTURES

As mentioned in Section 4.1, algorithms are developed in light of the way data are represented. This section presents some of the data structures that are most commonly used in creating algorithms, writing programs, and designing systems.

Fields and Numbers

A field is a unit of storage that would lose its meaning if "broken down" further. For example, a field of n characters might represent a person's name; a character in that field is simply a character in the alphabet. As a form of data structure, a *field* is used as a constituent of arrays, structures, data records, and files. By definition, a field is a scalar quantity.

A *number* is a field that has a meaning beyond that of the individual characters or bits that make up a field itself. A positional number system is practically always used and the numerical value of the field depends on the radix used. General attributes of a numeric field are: *mode* (real or complex), *base* (binary or decimal), *scale* (fixed-point or floating-point), *precision* (number of digits stored), and *scale factor* (implied location of the radix point in the field).

Array Characteristics

An array has several properties. The first is the *number of dimensions*. For example, a matrix has two dimensions: a row dimension and a column dimension. Each dimension is further characterized by a bounds and an extent. The *bounds* of a dimension are the beginning index and the ending index for that dimension and determine how elements are referenced. The *extent* is the number of elements in a dimension—regardless of the bounds. Consider the array A, defined as follows:

$$
\begin{array}{ccccc}
a_{1,-2} & a_{1,-1} & a_{1,0} & a_{1,1} & a_{1,2} \\
a_{2,-2} & a_{2,-1} & a_{2,0} & a_{2,1} & a_{2,2} \\
a_{3,-2} & a_{3,-1} & a_{3,0} & a_{3,1} & a_{3,2} \\
a_{4,-2} & a_{4,-1} & a_{4,0} & a_{4,1} & a_{4,2}
\end{array}
$$

A has two dimensions: 4 rows and 5 columns. The row bounds are (1:4) and the column bounds are (-2:2). The row extent is 4 while the column extent is 5.

Arrays are almost always stored in consecutive storage locations. An important consideration is whether the array is stored in row-major order or column-major order. *Row-major order*, also known as *index order* or *lexicographic order*, denotes that the elements of the array are stored in consecutive locations in a row-wise fashion. Row-major order is used with the COBOL and PL/I programming languages. *Column-major* order denotes that the elements of the array are stored in a column-wise fashion, and is used with FORTRAN. Examples of row-major order and column-major order for array A (given above) can be listed as follows:

Row-major Order	Index	Column-major Order
A(1,-2)	1	A(1,-2)
A(1,-1)	2	A(2,-2)
A(1,0)	3	A(3,-2)
A(1,1)	4	A(4,-2)
A(1,2)	5	A(1,-1)
A(2,-2)	6	A(2,-1)
A(2,-1)	7	A(3,-1)
A(2,0)	8	A(4,-1)
A(2,1)	9	A(1,0)
A(2,2)	10	A(2,0)
A(3,-2)	11	A(3,0)
A(3,-1)	12	A(4,0)
A(3,0)	13	A(1,1)
A(3,1)	14	A(2,1)
A(3,2)	15	A(3,1)
A(4,-2)	16	A(4,1)
A(4,-1)	17	A(1,2)
A(4,0)	18	A(2,2)
A(4,1)	19	A(3,2)
A(4,2)	20	A(4,2)

To bring the discussion into a familiar context, an array in FORTRAN declared as follows:

$$\text{DIMENSION } M(3,2)$$

has 3 rows, 2 columns, a row bounds of (1:3), a column bounds of (1:2), a row extent of 3, and a column extent of 2. It is stored as follows:

Array Element	Index
M(1,1)	1
M(2,1)	2
M(3,1)	3
M(1,2)	4
M(2,2)	5
M(3,2)	6

Sparse arrays (i.e., those with few nonzero elements) are occasionally stored as linked lists to conserve storage. Figure 4.5 depicts a sparse matrix stored in this form; the general format is due to Knuth [Knu68].

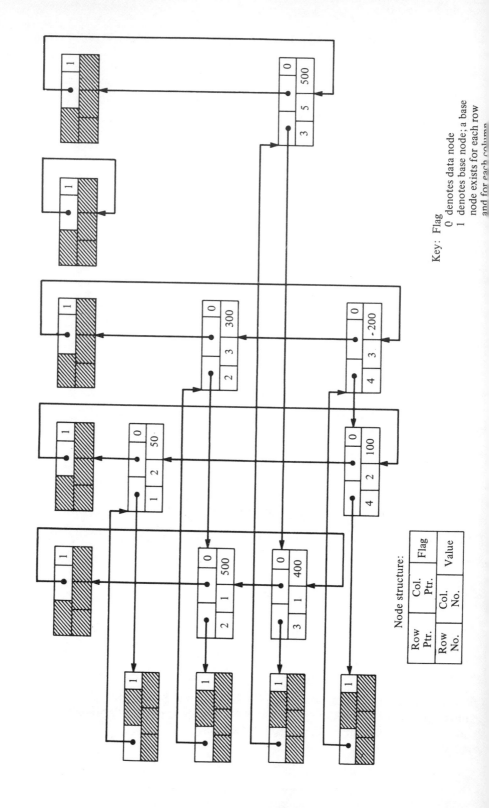

Key: Flag
0 denotes data node
1 denotes base node; a base
node exists for each row
and for each column

Node structure:

Row Ptr.		Flag
Row No.	Col. No.	
	Col. Ptr.	Value

Lists and Tables

A *list* is a one-dimensional structure of data items. Each data item in a list usually represents the same basic data structure, that is, they are all scalars or all structures. In main storage, a list is usually organized as an array or a linked list. On auxiliary storage, a list usually takes the form of a data file organized in one of the ways mentioned previously. Data processing operations are defined on lists in much the same manner as arithmetic and logical operations are defined on other data structures. Common list operations are: *sort, merge, collate*, and *search*. An important property of a list is whether it is ordered or not. In an *ordered* list, the relative sequence of entries is based upon the value of the data entry or a key field in the structure. Merge and collate operations are normally performed on ordered lists and the search operation is greatly facilitated when dealing with an ordered list.

A *table* is a list of symbol-value pairs of the form $<s,v>$; each entry takes the form of a structure. The symbol tables of Fig. 4.6 are common examples of the use of a table. Each entry in a table contains a key field used for posting, ordering, and retrieval. The value portion of a table entry may represent one or more data fields. Depending upon the program used to maintain the table, the entries may be sorted by the value of the key field or left unsorted. There are distinct advantages and disadvantages for maintaining a table in consecutive storage locations and as a linked list; similarly, there are advantages and disadvantages for

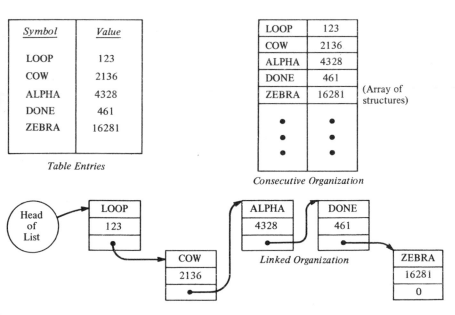

Fig. 4.6 A typical table organized as an array of structures and as a linked list.

maintaining the entries in a sorted and an unsorted form. The reader is referred to Knuth [Knu68] or Berztiss [Ber71] for a complete discussion of this topic.

A method frequently used in operating systems for maintaining a table is known as *hashing*. Several variations to hashing exist; a straightforward approach is given here. The method utilizes the fact that the key field in a table entry (usually a sequence of characters) is stored as consecutive bits—as a number is stored. A function is defined on the key field that partitions the universe of symbols into equivalence classes. Two symbols are in the same equivalence class if they hash to the same value. Table entries in each equivalence class are maintained as a linked list (or as an equivalent data structure) in either a sorted or an unsorted form. The objective is to decrease the average posting and search time over the type of symbols that can be used as key fields. Figure 4.7 depicts a typical hashing process.

A variety of algorithms are used as *hashing functions*. A sample method is to

Symbol	Value
BOND	1234
TIME	631
BAND	2381
ALPHA	15293
TURKEY	57

Table Entries

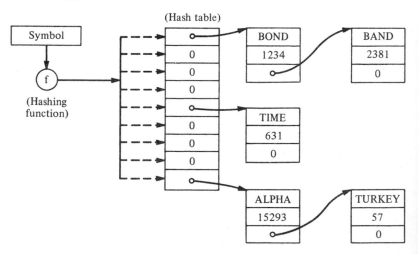

Fig. 4.7 Typical hashing process.

multiply the key field by itself and extract the middle n bits. This provides a displacement into a hash table, as shown in Fig. 4.7. Berztiss [Ber71] gives a summary of other frequently used hashing functions.

Stacks and Queues

Two user data structures in frequent use in systems programming are the stack and the queue. A *stack* is a list maintained on a last-in-first-out (LIFO) basis. A *queue* is a list maintained on a first-in-first-out (FIFO) basis. Either a stack or a queue can be stored in consecutive storage locations or as a linked list.

In systems programming, a stack is frequently used to convert an expression from infix notation to postfix notation or to save the return addresses in a procedure that is called recursively. A queue is frequently used to maintain a list of work to be done by the control program of an operating system or to maintain a list of storage blocks that can be allocated dynamically.

4.5 DATA MANAGEMENT STRUCTURES

Basic Concepts

Data management is concerned with how input and output are performed in an operating system and how data are organized for transmission between main storage and auxiliary storage. A definite distinction is made here between units of data and units of storage.

In main storage, a group of consecutive fields, which are related in some sense, is termed a *data record* (also, sometimes called a *logical record*). A familiar example of a data record is a single employee's record on a payroll file. A group of related data records is termed a *file*.

The unit of interchange between main storage and an IO medium is a *block*, which can be composed of one or more data records. The term block is often used interchangeably with the term *physical record*, commonly associated with magnetic tape, and corresponds directly with the disk block introduced in Chapter 3. On most IO media, consecutive blocks are separated by inter-block gaps and miscellaneous forms of control information. On a direct-access storage medium, a series of consecutive blocks is referred to as an extent. (This terminology is consistent with the definition for extent, given earlier.)

Record Formats

When performing input and output operations, the user deals with data records that form a file. The concepts of "data record" and "file" are units of data structure. However, the computer deals with storage structures. Blocks are comprised of data records and extents are comprised of blocks. The concepts of "block" and "extent" are units of storage structure. To an operating system, a named file is termed a *data set*, and is stored on an IO storage medium as one or

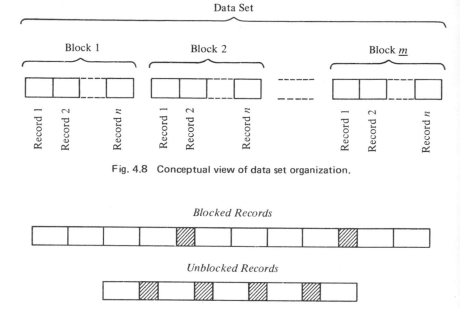

Fig. 4.8 Conceptual view of data set organization.

Fig. 4.9 Conceptual view of fixed-length records.

more extents. The location of the extents that comprise a data set plus the data set name and additional information are stored by the operating system in a *catalog;* thus, the user is able to access a data set by name without knowing its location on auxiliary storage and its attributes.

The manner in which logical records are grouped to form a block is referred to as *data record format* (Fig. 4.8). Logical records are grouped (frequently denoted as "blocked") according to one of four formats: fixed-length records, variable-length records, undefined-length records, and spanned records. The size of a *fixed-length record* is constant for all logical records in a block; moreover, the block size is also fixed, as depicted in Fig. 4.9. Fixed-length records may be blocked or unblocked. With *variable-length record* type, the size of logical records is variable in length and the length of the block is also variable. Obviously, a maximum block size must be stated so that IO buffer space can be allocated. Variable-length blocked records are depicted in Fig. 4.10; the block length (L) is included in the block and precedes the "block" data. The record size (l) is included with each logical record and precedes the "record" data. *Undefined-length records* (Fig. 4.11) are permitted in many operating systems to allow records to be processed that do not meet the requirements of the preceding two types. When undefined-length records are used, the user assumes responsibility for performing the housekeeping tasks associated with data manage-

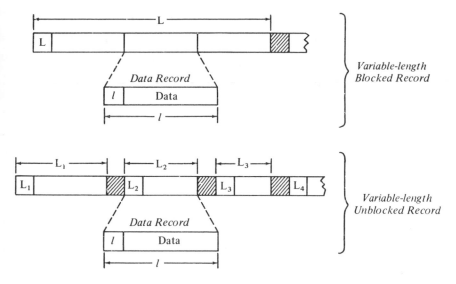

Fig. 4.10 Conceptual view of variable-length records.

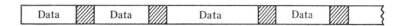

Fig. 4.11 Conceptual view of undefined-length records.

ment. A *spanned record* (Fig. 4.12) is a data record that spans two or more blocks. The spanned technique is used when the size of a block is fixed for some reason. The spanned record concept is usually defined by a processing program for its own needs or is provided by the data management facilities of the operating system. The various record formats are used for a variety of reasons; efficiency of IO operations, characteristics of a particular computer application, conservation of storage space, physical hardware limitations—to name only a few. A more comprehensive study of these topics is left as an exercise for the reader.

Data Management Operations

The processing of grouping logical records to form a block is referred to as *blocking;* the reverse process is termed *deblocking*. Normally, blocking and deblocking are performed by data management routines that are utilized with assembler language macros or statements in a programming language that perform the same functions.

Data management routines enable the user to perceive his file as a series of logical records. The blocking and deblocking processes are transparent to him.

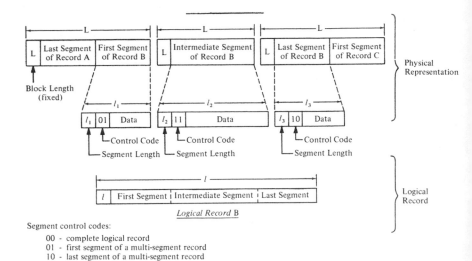

Segment control codes:
  00 - complete logical record
  01 - first segment of a multi-segment record
  10 - last segment of a multi-segment record
  11 - intermediate segment of a multi-segment record

Fig. 4.12 Conceptual view of spanned records.

Consider blocked input as an example. When the first logical record in a block is referenced by an operating program, the entire block is read from auxiliary storage and the first logical record of the block is passed to that program. When the following records in that block are referenced, data management does not have to perform a read operation and simply returns to the requesting program the next sequential logical record in that block. For output, a block is not written until it is filled with logical records.

The processing of reading and writing blocks is made more efficient by buffering. *Buffering* is the technique of establishing several storage areas for input and output. For input, blocks are read ahead of time so that when a data management routine needs a block, it is already in main storage. For output, the data management routines initiate the filling of a new block as soon as the preceding one has been filled and without waiting for the associated write operation to be completed. When using buffering, the CPU can effectively utilize the input/compute/output overlap capability provided by an IO channel.

Data access and data set organization are considered in more detail in later chapters.

4.6 COMMENTS

In addition to covering basic material on data and storage structures, the objective of this chapter has been to present most of the topics in a unified manner as they apply to either main storage or auxiliary storage. In this way, the similarities and differences between the various storage media are emphasized and the underlying concepts are reinforced. There are a variety of references on the subject matter of this chapter. The two references mentioned previously (i.e., Berztiss [Ber71] and Knuth [Knu68]) cover data structures. Chapin [Cha71], Flores [Flo70], and Dodd [Dod69] cover data management systems. Chapin [Cha68], Codd [Cod70,Cod71], and Mealy [Mea67] cover conceptual and theoretical topics in data organization. Aron [Aro69] surveys information systems in general.

5 | EVOLUTIONARY DEVELOPMENT OF OPERATING SYSTEM TECHNOLOGY

5.1 BASIC PROGRAMMING SUPPORT

The field of computer technology has progressed so rapidly in recent years that there are relatively few "old timers" around who once needed to program in machine language (i.e., binary, octal, or whatever the internal coding scheme of the computer was). In this day of advanced programming tools, the idea of doing such a thing sounds far-fetched; however, it is a fact that at one time, programmers used numerical operation codes, absolute storage locations, and storage maps to construct programs. "Object programs" were usually manually punched into cards (or punched tape) and loaded into storage with a "bootstrap" loader program—frequently consisting of one card. Once on the computer, the programmer would execute and debug his program using the lights and switches on the console. All of this was possible since computer time was allocated according to a schedule. The programmer signed up for a block of computer time and was usually constrained to operate in that time slot—regardless of the operational circumstances. Computer operators were not generally employed and the operational problems in using the computer were considered relatively great.

Primitive Assembly Systems

The first stage in the development of automatic programming components was the development of a primitive assembly system in which numeric operation codes are replaced with mnemonic symbols, as depicted in the following simple program:

```
ORG    100
LOAD   370
MULT   371
ADD    375
SUB    372
TMI    137
  .
  .
  .
ORG    370
DEC    0
DEC    2
DEC    16
  .
  .
  .
END
```

The source program, obviously, was prepared according to a fixed format; however, it was written to occupy fixed storage locations, and a "bootstrap" loader program was still used to load the object program into the fixed locations it would occupy. There were no program libraries, and a subroutine was used by inserting the symbolic cards of the subroutine into the symbolic deck of the program, prior to the assembly process.

The primitive assembly process is depicted in Fig. 5.1; the steps in the diagram are listed as follows:

1. The assembler program is loaded into the computer.
2. The assembler program reads the source program and performs the assembly process.
3. An object program is produced by the assembler program along with a program listing (not shown).
4. The object program is loaded into the computer.
5. The object program (during execution) reads data cards.
6. The object program produces results as determined by the particular application.

With the primitive assembly system, the operational procedures for using the computer remain essentially the same: The programmer signs up for a block of computer time and debugs and runs his own job using the dials and switches on the computer console.

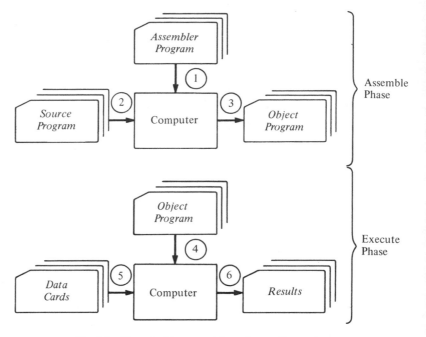

Fig. 5.1   The primitive assembly and execution process.

Translators, Program Structure, and Relocatable Loaders

The next stage in component development was the development of comprehensive assembly systems, compilers, and relocatable loaders. During this period of development, the program library also came into widespread use.

As assembly systems increased in complexity, the programmer was able to utilize symbolic locations and operands plus a variety of "assembler instructions" that effectively control the assembler program in much the same way that machine instructions control the computer.[†]   (Macro instructions came into widespread use at a later date.)   The need to facilitate programming gave rise to programming languages and their compilers, as discussed in Chapter 2. The importance of program structure became evident through the need to combine and use different program modules (i.e., main program and subroutines). Many features made available with a programming language were also implemented through the use of subroutines.

The need to share subroutines on a system-wide basis practically eliminates the possibility of using source program decks.   It was necessary that sharing be

---

[†]Typical "assembler instructions" are ORG (to set the location counter), DS (to define storage), EJECT (to provide listing control), and EQU (to equate a symbol to a specified value).

implemented at the object level (object modules). The desirability of incorporating the same subroutine in object form into diverse programs with different sizes and different organizational structures immediately ruled out programs written to occupy fixed main storage locations. The result was the capability to relocate object programs at load time—in essence, a relocatable format. In general, relocatable format provides information to the loader program as to which

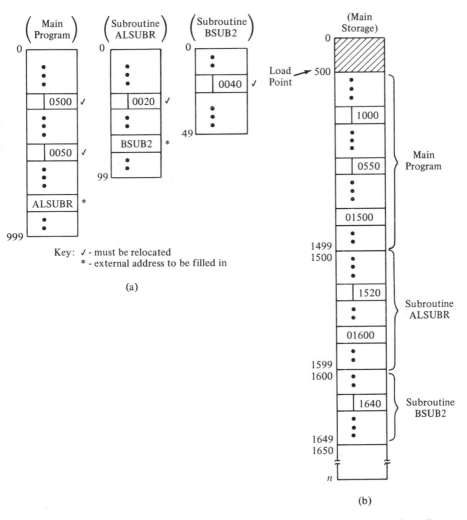

Fig. 5.2 The relocation of relocatable object modules during the process of loading. (a) Object modules prior to loading. (b) Load module after loading.

address fields (in computer instructions) are sensitive to absolute storage locations; these sensitive fields must be modified by the loader program at load time.

Figure 5.2 depicts several object modules prior to loading. Each module is assembled or compiled relative to a specified location (which is usually defaulted to zero); during the loading process, address fields and external addresses are modified to correspond to their relative position in main storage.

Clearly, the function of the loader program is expanded to the extent that it is a bona fide service program. Input to the loader program is a collection of object modules. As each object module is loaded into storage, a table is built of "subroutines" needed and "subroutines" present. After the last module is loaded, a library tape is searched for subroutines needed but not present. The process is depicted as Fig. 5.3. Clearly, as each object module is loaded, address fields and external addresses are modified accordingly. Heising and Larner [Hei61] and McCarthy, Corbato, and Daggett [Mcc63] give general characteristics of early loader programs.

In many early systems, the program library (usually on tape) was maintained on a system-wide basis. The most frequently used subroutines, for that installation, were placed on tape by a specially written utility program.

This stage in the development of effective automatic programming techniques also included the use of higher-speed IO devices, such as magnetic tape. Even though distinct job steps (assembly, compilation, loading, etc.) were initiated and controlled manually, the translators (e.g., assemblers, compilers) and service programs (e.g., loader) were frequently stored on tape for fast and easy loading. Moreover, translators and service programs frequently used magnetic tape for temporary storage.

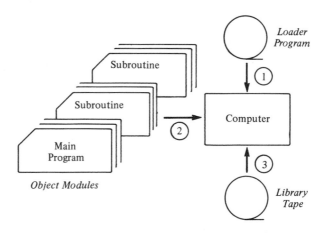

Fig. 5.3 Expanded function of the loader.

Sharing and IO Systems

The use of a program library is the first instance of sharing, except on a manual basis. In addition to subroutines, a typical program library might include at least one generalized program, such as a sort/merge package, that could be used with a variety of application structures. The program library was also a convenient place to store a frequently used application program, such as a payroll program or an inventory control system.

Input and output was as much a problem in earlier years of computing as it is now. Input/output packages (called IOPs) were frequently available for use by translators and service programs, generalized packages, and conventional application programs. Input and output routines were usually stored in the program library as subroutines. Although early IOPs were primitive in light of today's high level of achievement, they relieved the programmer of managing his own IO procedures. In several systems early IOPs even provided a limited capability for input/compute/output overlap.

Basic programming support is interesting, if only for academic value. Rosen [Rse64], Rosin [Rsi69], and Mealy [Mea62] give historical perspective on the subject.

5.2 EARLY BATCH PROCESSING SYSTEMS

The obvious inefficiencies in basic programming support led to the development of a simple control program that would provide job-to-job transition and would assist the system operator in running the computer. (By now, the advantages of employing a specialist to run the computer became obvious and most large-scale computer installations used at least one operator.) These control programs, called monitors or supervisor programs, are the forerunners of today's operating systems.

Monitor Systems

In its simplest form, a monitor system provides automatic transition between jobs. The respective jobs are placed in the card reader and the monitor system initiates the execution of the next job after the current job is finished, without operator intervention. Obviously, a certain amount of complexity is required: (1) The routines of the monitor system must be stored somewhere; and (2) the user must have a means of telling the monitor system what he wants done.

In the first case, the routines of the monitor system are stored on a *system tape* along with the language translators and the loader program (see Fig. 5.4). The routines of the monitor system are scatter-loaded (see Chapter 3), as required, from the system tape. The user informs the monitor system of processing requirements with control cards. Figure 5.5 lists simple control cards from a

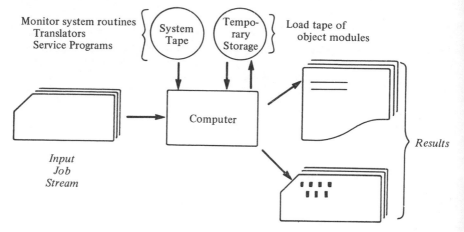

Fig. 5.4   Operational setup for an early monitor system.

Control Cards	Function
*JOB	Initiates a job.
*FORTRAN	Calls in the FORTRAN compiler.
*ASSEMBLE	Calls in the Assembler program.
*LOAD	Calls in the Loader program.
*DATA	Indicates that data cards follow.
*END	Signals end of data.

Fig. 5.5   Sample control cards from a typical monitor system.

typical monitor system. Operation of the system would progress somewhat as follows:

1. The JOB control card is read. The monitor system punches an accounting card to indicate the clock time when this job started. Another control card is read.

2. If the FORTRAN control card is read, the FORTRAN compiler is read into storage. It reads and compiles the source program that follows. The object program is placed on a "load" tape (see Fig. 5.4), and a program listing is printed.

3. If the ASSEMBLE control card is read, the assembler program is read in. It assembles the source program that follows from the card reader; as with the compiler, the object program is placed on the load tape and a program listing is produced. Control is returned to the monitor system to read another control card.

4. If the LOAD control card is read, the loader program is read into storage. It loads any object programs that are placed in the card reader between the LOAD card and the DATA card. Next, it loads object programs from the load tape and the program library. The loader initiates the execution of the program it just loaded. When the executable program has finished execution, it exits to the monitor system to read another JOB card and initiate the cycle again.

A sample input job stream is given as Fig. 5.6.

In an early monitor system, the user was allowed to specify to the compiler or assembler whether he wanted his object program punched, placed on the load tape, or both. Card punching was performed on-line as was card reading and printing.

Accounting procedures were also straightforward. The computer time charged

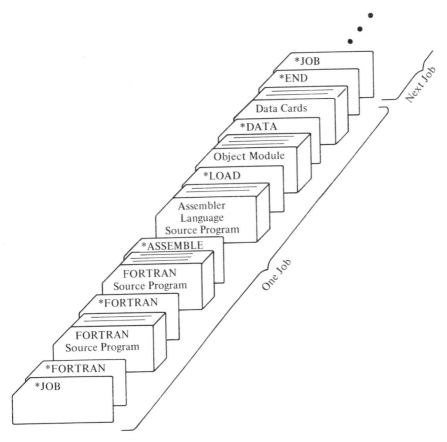

Fig. 5.6 Sample input job stream for a simple monitor system.

to a given job was computed as the time duration between the accounting card punched for its JOB card and the accounting card punched with the next JOB card since the user had control of *all* system resources during the intervening period.

The routines of the monitor system were fairly simple and included the following:

1. IO routines to read control cards and scatter load routines of the monitor system;
2. a routine to interpret control cards and call in language translators and service programs; and
3. routines to handle error conditions.

Obviously, language translators and service programs also existed; however, they rarely (if at all) occupied main storage when a user program was loaded. Early monitor systems occupied very little main storage; as an example, the beginning main storage address for programs to be loaded in one of the most widely used monitor systems was storage location 100 (i.e., for a word-oriented computer).

Peripheral Devices and Computers

The inefficiencies of reading cards, printing, and punching cards on-line led to the development of what is known as *batch processing*. Initially, a batch of jobs was collected on magnetic tape by a card-to-tape device. Either the magnetic tape was physically transported to the computer, or a switching device (see Chapter 3) was used to make the batch of jobs available to the monitor system. Similarly, printed output was written on a "print tape" and punched output was written on a "punch tape." Later, the two output tapes were printed and punched on tape-to-print and tape-to-punch devices, respectively. The result was to increase the performance of the main computer by exchanging low-speed IO devices with higher-speed devices. The process is depicted in Fig. 5.7.

Peripheral devices were subsequently replaced by a small *peripheral computer* (sometimes called a *satellite computer*) that could perform the three IO operations, as well as some processing of its own.

The use of special input and output tapes created the need to reserve specific tape units for specific functions. Some special units that were in widespread use are: (1) the *system tape* (for system routines); (2) the *program library tape;* (3) the *system input tape;* (4) the *system print tape;* (5) the *system punch tape;* (6) the *load tape* (for object modules produced by language translators); and (7) the *system utility tape(s).*

Storage Allocation in Early Batch Processing Systems

In an early batch processing system, a job runs serially until it is completed. During execution, a job has the complete resources of the system at its disposal—

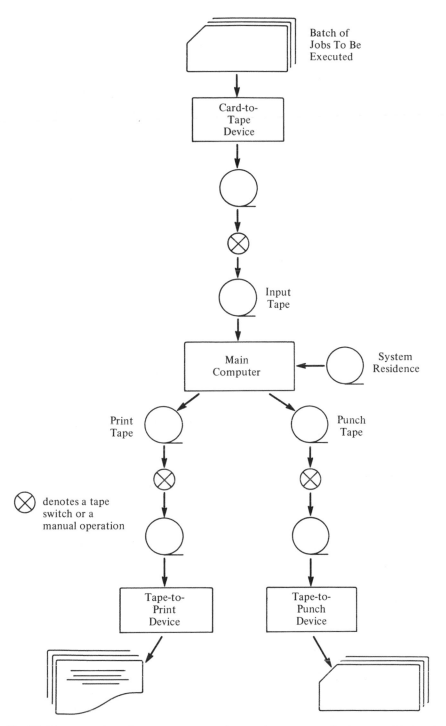

Fig. 5.7 The use of card-to-tape, tape-to-print, and tape-to-punch devices with batch processing.

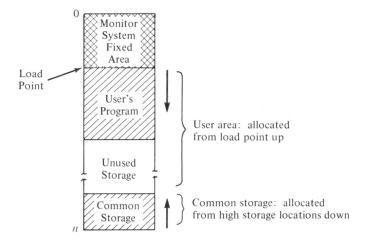

Fig. 5.8   Structural diagram of main storage in an early batch processing system.

including the CPU, main storage, and the IO equipment. (Some authors refer to this case as uniprogramming; however, this terminology is not used here.) Figure 5.8 depicts a structural diagram of main storage. Three areas are defined: (1) a fixed-size monitor system area; (2) a user area; and (3) a common storage area.

The *monitor system area* contains routines, buffers, and data areas of the monitor system. The extent of the monitor system area implicitly determines the load point for the user's program. The *user area* extends upward from the load point and until the common area is reached. The common area extends downward from high storage and extends to the user area. Thus, the storage boundary between the user area and the common area is maintained dynamically.

The *common area* is a repository for data that can be exchanged between object modules. Each object module addresses the common area directly and it is the user's responsibility to put the right data at the right place in the common area at the right time.† A frequent use of common storage of this type is as a place for large amounts of data that are shared among object modules. Although the size of the user area is a function of the size of the common area, it is constrained by the physical size of main storage. The need to run programs requiring more than the available main storage led to a technique known as chaining. In simple terms, *chaining* denotes the execution of successive program segments —each operating in the user area. After the ith program segment has finished

†Common storage of this type is known as *blank* COMMON.

execution, it calls the $(i + 1)$th program segment with a call statement of the form:

CALL CHAIN(name)

where *name* is the identifier of the $(i + 1)$th program segment. The $(i + 1)$th program segment is brought in from the "chain" tape and placed in the user area, completely "wiping out" the ith program segment. Clearly, each program segment resides on the load tape as a unique load module. Data are exchanged between program segments by placing them in the common area. (The process of successively executing program segments is known as a "ping pong" operation).

Chaining is implemented through the loader program. Figure 5.9 depicts a typical deck setup for chaining. The CHAIN control card causes flags to be set specifying that chaining is to take place and causes indicator data to be placed

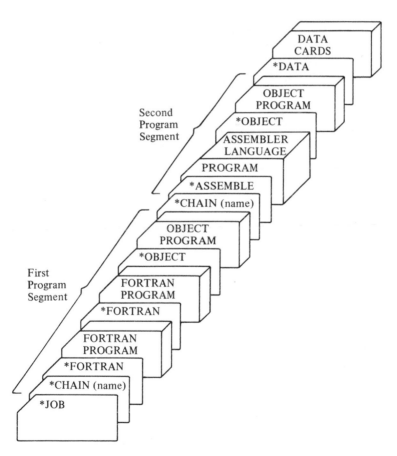

Fig. 5.9 Deck setup for chaining.

on the load tape. Object programs from the language translators and from the input job stream are placed on the load tape for subsequent linkage editing. After all object modules have been processed, object modules between chain indicators are linkage edited to form complete load modules; each load module is placed on a *chain tape* and identified. Thus, the loader links several load modules instead of the customary single load module. Instead of placing the load module in main storage for execution, it is placed on the chain tape as a binary record (or series of records).

Usually, a convention is established for determining which program segment (i.e., chain segment) should be executed first. The first chain segment constructed by the loader is frequently a good candidate. Later, execution of the

CALL CHAIN(*name*)

statement causes control to be transferred to a routine of the monitor system. Note that the monitor system must be used here since a new program segment completely overlays the previous one. The chain tape is searched for the requested segment, which is read into the user area, and execution is initiated. The common area is not changed and it is used to hold data that must be passed between segments.

5.3 DEVELOPMENT OF EXECUTIVE SYSTEMS

Thus far, an operating system has been described as a collection of routines to monitor the operation of a digital computer system. The word "executive" in the title of this section implies more than a simple monitor program, it implies a set of programs that manages the resources of a computer system to meet installation objectives.

The invention of the interruption and the development of the IO data channel provided the hardware capability necessary to extend the concept of an operating system beyond that of a simple monitor program. As mentioned previously, the IO data channel allows IO and computing to proceed concurrently and the interruption allows an external event (such as an IO condition) to interrupt the execution of the CPU.

This period in the development of operating systems is marked by diversity, with different systems emphasizing one or more of the following functions:

1. the execution of one or more IO operations concurrently with computing;
2. the execution of IO efficiently by providing a variety of buffering techniques;
3. the capability for supporting both scientific and commercial operating environments; and
4. the facility for structuring programs in a natural manner.

The significance of each of these functions is discussed in the following paragraphs.

System Components

The recognition that a collection of supervisory programs is a system in its own right (hence the name operating system) with organized components defined to perform specific functions was the first major step in the development of an operating system as we know it today. Mealy [Mea62] divided the components of an operating system into three categories: (1) input/output systems, (2) processors, and (3) supervisory systems. *Input/output systems* provide a software interface between programs and external IO devices and manage IO on a system-wide basis. *Processors* transform data and produce results. Language translators and problem programs fall into this category. *Supervisory systems* provide a logical interface between the hardware and the remainder of the software system. Scheduling, communications, and control routines fall into this category.

Resident and Nonresident Routines

The capability of computing and doing IO concurrently on a large-scale basis placed an additional responsibility on the operating system. The increased complexity required that a basic collection of routines (sometimes called the nucleus) be resident in main storage at all times. The *nucleus* provided common facilities for intercommunication and control among operating system routines and processing programs. Status information on hardware components (such as IO devices) as well as basic IO routines were considered to be a part of the nucleus. In many systems, error recovery routines were also a part of the nucleus. The nucleus has several properties of interest: (1) The nucleus is loaded during IPL (initial program load) and remains loaded throughout the operation of the computer system, and (2) only one active copy of the nucleus exists in the system. (Note here that no mention is made of the supervisor state or of storage protection. In this period, roughly 1961-1965, those hardware facilities had not come into widespread use.)

Although the size of main storage is an operating constraint in modern computing systems, it was more of a problem in previous generations of computers since main storage was considerably more limited in size at that time.† A well-designed "executive" system uses as little of main storage as possible; this design objective led to what is known as transient routines. A *transient routine* is a part of the executive system that is not resident in main storage at all times. It is scatter loaded when needed into a transient area of main storage on a temporary

---

†In modern systems, the amount of main storage that is allocated to the executive system is an economic consideration. A design tradeoff is made between the efficiency of CPU operations and the cost of the main storage used.

basis. When the operation of a transient routine is complete, the transient area of main storage is used for the execution of the next transient routine needed. A typical transient routine is one that processes a given type of control card.

Input/Output Control Systems

In general, an input/output control system (IOCS) is a collection of routines that improves the efficiency of IO operations and facilitates the programming of IO operations by the user. An IOCS is comprised of two components: (1) physical IOCS, and (2) logical IOCS. The *physical IOCS* (PIOCS) is the part of the nucleus that executes and manages IO operations on a system-wide basis. The use of a single IO supervisor eliminates the conflict that would ensue if each user were to do his own IO. *Logical IOCS* (LIOCS) routines are a part of the user's program and effectively link the program to physical IOCS routines. Logical IOCS routines perform blocking and deblocking of logical records and buffering, and allow symbolic device assignments to be used. Figure 5.10 depicts the use of an input/output control system. Bohl [Boh72] and Cenfetelli [Cen67] give brief introductions to the function and use of an input/output control system.

Spooling

The term *spooling* was derived from the acronym SPOOL (Simultaneous Peripheral Output On Line) which obviously refers to the process of computing and doing output concurrently. The term has been extended through usage to apply to both input and output.

The philosophy behind spooling is that unit record IO devices, operating at

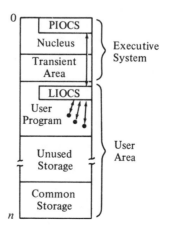

Key: PIOCS - Physical Input/Output Control System
      LIOCS - Logical Input/Output Control System

Fig. 5.10   The use of an input/output control system to manage IO operations.

electromechanical speeds, are sufficiently slow that the CPU could control their operation in addition to its normal load without a significant degradation of performance. The practice of spooling is briefly described as follows:

1. The spooling process operates at the highest priority. When it needs the services of the CPU, it gets the CPU on a demand basis. It signals the CPU with an interruption (previously called a *channel trap*).
2. The spooling program initiates a unit record IO operation; this process takes only a few machine cycles.
3. CPU control is turned over to a user program that can operate for a fairly large number of machine cycles.
4. A unit record IO operation interrupts the CPU and control is turned over to the spooling process.
5. The spooling program services the unit record IO request, taking a few machine cycles, and execution of the user's program is resumed from where it was interrupted. (The process continues with step 4.)

The spooling process is usually extended to include several unit record IO operations.

Figure 5.11 depicts the manner in which the spooling process operates. Spooling essentially replaces the card-to-tape and tape-to-print-or-punch operations

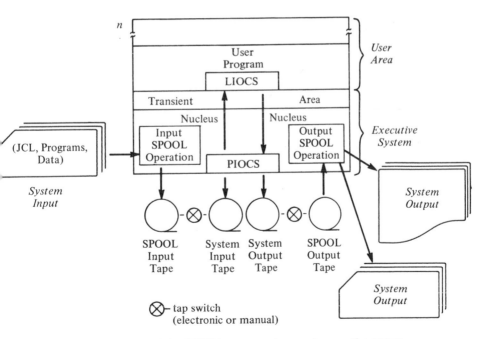

Fig. 5.11   The use of the SPOOLing process in an early executive system.

introduced previously; the process (of spooling) is transparent to the user's program and most routines of the executive system are not affected by the unit record IO that is being processed concurrently.

The alert reader will recognize that spooling was the first stage of multiprogramming as we know it today. In many executive systems, a direct-access device such as disk or drum was used instead of tape. Thus, the services of four or five magnetic tape devices were replaced by one direct-access device.

Direct-Coupled Systems

Another method used in this era to perform unit record IO operations was to couple two computer systems together via a core-to-core adapter. The second system, usually less powerful than the primary system, essentially acted as a slave to the primary system by maintaining input job streams and output files on magnetic tape or direct-access storage. Not only did the secondary computer system replace an IO channel of the primary system, it also relieved the nucleus of a portion of its processing functions and made additional main storage available for user programs. The secondary computer system in a direct-coupled system frequently performed IO editing for the primary computer system and was occasionally used to attach remote terminals to the primary computer.

The direct-coupled system is the predecessor to the attached support processor mentioned in Chapter 3.

Symbolic Device Assignments

A significant advance made during this period of executive systems was to allow symbolic device assignments. Previous to this in early batch systems, the user was required to "bind" his program to a particular IO device (such as tape unit number 10 on channel A) during assembly or compilation. Then, in the event of a malfunctioning IO device or a change in system configuration, the program had to be recompiled or reassembled.

During programming with the use of symbolic device assignments, the user uses a symbolic name, such as MFILE or unit 10, to specify an IO device. Prior to execution, the user assigns that symbolic name to a specific IO device with a control card of the general form:

*ASSIGN MFILE TO UNIT A13

The sample control card purposefully has been made hypothetical; however, it depicts the flexibility that is inherent in the use of control information made available to the operating system at run time.

On a small scale, the use of symbolic device assignment is an example of a facility that has extended the scope of operating system technology and made the operating system routines more complex. In later chapters, it will become evident that *device management* is one of the primary functions of an operating system.

Buffering

Recall that one of the characteristics of operating systems, as discussed thus far, is that only one user's program has been present in the "user area" of main storage. In some systems, however, the storage space left over was not wasted. (The case in which the user area was not big enough is covered next.) It was used for IO buffers. Obviously, the manner in which this space was used differs between systems. In some cases, the space was explicitly reserved for buffering by the user; in other cases, it was assigned automatically by the loader program for buffering. The result was the same. The logical IOCS routines could read data before they were to be used. Then when the program requested a read of those data, logical IOCS could simply move them from one place in storage to another or point to them in a buffer with an index register. On output, logical IOCS could reverse the process prior to a subsequent write operation by a physical IOCS routine. The process is depicted in Fig. 5.12.

Thus, the functions of the input/output control system (IOCS) have been extended to include input and output buffering as well as blocking and deblocking.

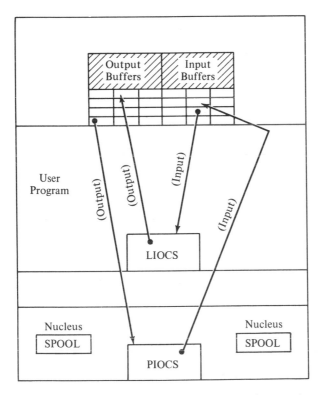

Fig. 5.12   The use of IOCS routines and buffering in an early executive system.

Input/output control systems were the forerunners of today's data management systems.

Overlay and Labeled Common

The case where the "user area" of main storage was not large enough for the user's program required a structuring of the object program similar to the method of chaining discussed previously. One of the disadvantages of chaining is that the user area is completely overlaid and the programmer must utilize common storage in an unnatural fashion. A more natural approach, obviously, is to structure the program like a tree such that only needed portions of storage are overlaid and common segments remain unchanged.

The more extensive overlay technique requires a certain amount of autonomy in the use of common storage unavailable with the previous method—referred to as "blank" common. Therefore, instead of reserving a large block of storage as common, smaller blocks, each given a name, are permitted. This feature allows two object modules to share the same common storage by using the same name. This facility is referred to as *labeled common*. Main storage space for a block of labeled common is assigned by the loader program.

An idea of how overlay and labeled common are used is demonstrated through an example. Consider the program tree of Fig. 5.13. The programs are depicted in Fig. 5.14. The programmer constructs his modules as though he had a very large main storage. The program is structured into overlay segments by the loader at load time; the user provides control cards that effectively tell the loader how to structure the program. A sample overlay structure developed by the loader is given as Fig. 5.15. The overlay structure developed by the loader is

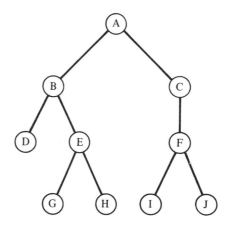

Fig. 5.13 Program tree for overlay and labeled common example. A is the root segment that calls routines B and C. Similarly, E calls G and H; F calls I and J.

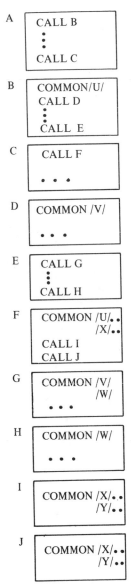

Fig. 5.14 Program modules to be used with overlay are developed as though the user had a very large main storage.

given as Fig. 5.16. The root segment (the segment of the program that is never overlaid) is placed in main storage and the other segments are placed on auxiliary storage as executable program segments. An overlay operation is initiated through the CALL statement. If the operand of the CALL statement is in another program segment (take CALL B in module A, for example), the loader

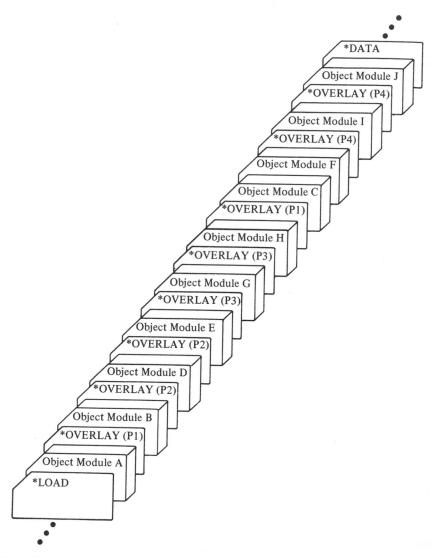

Fig. 5.15 Sample deck setup for the sample overlay structure given in Figs. 5.13, 5.14, and 5.16.

causes the execution of that CALL to activate the overlay monitor. The overlay monitor appropriately searches auxiliary storage for the correct overlay program segment and reads it into storage and resumes the CALL operation. This process is normally extended to as many levels as are necessary. Labeled common blocks are placed as high in the overlay structure as possible to permit the efficient utilization of main storage.

The user need not recompile or reassemble source modules to modify his over-

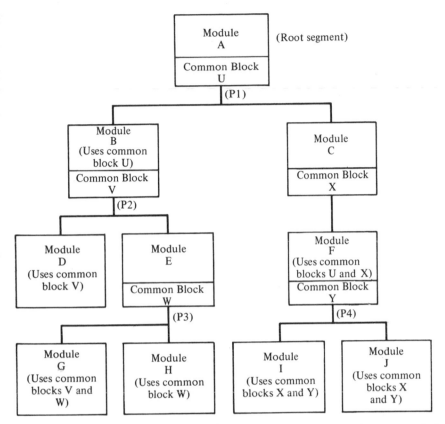

Fig. 5.16 Overlay structure for the program of Figs. 5.13 and 5.14. (See overlay deck setup in Fig. 5.15.) Note that labeled common blocks are placed at the highest possible level in the tree to permit efficient utilization of main storage.

lay structure. Since the overlay structure is governed by control cards, all the user need do is change his deck setup.

Lanzano [Lan69], Pankhurst [Pan68], and Sayre [Say69] discuss various aspects of loading and overlay techniques.

5.4 MULTIPROGRAMMING SYSTEMS

Multiprogramming is the current state of the art in operating systems technology; it is characterized by a refinement of old techniques and the addition of new operational facilities.

Operational Philosophy

Multiprogramming is an operational technique that allows several jobs to share the resources of the computer system. Usually, the various jobs co-reside in "main" storage and overflow to an auxiliary storage device, when necessary. Each job is given control of the CPU according to a scheduling algorithm. Functionally, a job executes in the CPU until one of two events occurs:

1. The program comes to a natural wait condition, such as for an input operation; or
2. the program has exceeded the burst of time allocated to it.

Control of the CPU is then given to another job and the process continues. In the latter case, termed *time slicing*, each user is given a short burst of time on a

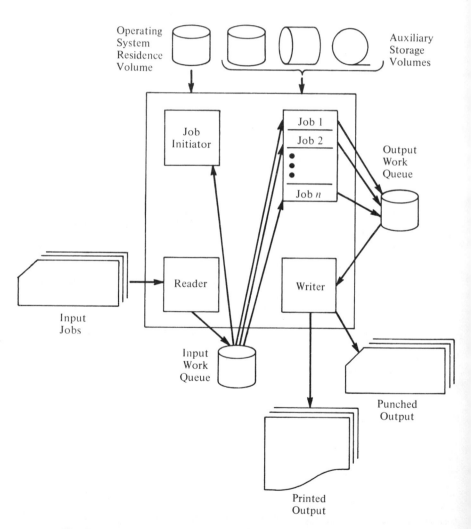

Fig. 5.17 Simplified description of a typical multiprogramming system.

periodic basis. A typical multiprogramming system is depicted in Fig. 5.17. Spooling is performed by an input *reader* and an output *writer*. Jobs are entered into the operating system from the input work queue by a *job initiator*. Not depicted in Fig. 5.17 are routines for managing the system, routines for managing a job, and routines for managing data. They are covered later in this section.

The major objectives of a multiprogramming system are twofold: (1) increased throughput, and (2) lowered response time. *Throughput* is increased by using the CPU "wait" time to run other programs. *Response time* is lowered by recognizing the priority of a job as it enters the system and by processing jobs on a priority basis. In this context, "response time" is used synonomously with "turnaround time." The spooling operation, mentioned earlier, is a normal function in a multiprogramming system. The *reader* and *writer* routines of the spooling package are simply assigned a high priority such that they are given CPU time, practically, on a demand basis. This operational philosophy allows unit record devices to be operated at close to maximum speed.

Structure of a Multiprogramming System

A multiprogramming system is, by definition, a more complex system of software routines than the simple monitor systems described previously; it is structured accordingly.

The structure of a multiprogramming operating system is depicted in Fig. 5.18. A multiprogramming operating system is composed of two types of programs:

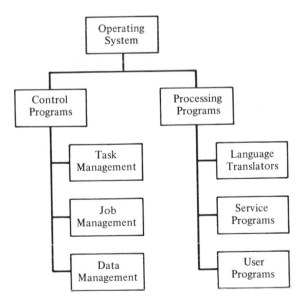

Fig. 5.18 Structure of a multiprogramming operating system.

control programs and processing programs. *Control programs* are concerned with the operation of the computer and the operation of a job. *Processing programs* operate under control of the control programs and exist as a unit of work to the system. Processing programs do not require privileged instructions or a special storage key and operate in the problem state. In general, the execution of one processing cannot affect the execution of another processing program or a control program. Processing programs are conveniently divided into three categories: *language translators* (such as a FORTRAN compiler), *service programs* (such as the linkage editor), and *user programs* (such as a payroll program).

The heart of an operating system is the control programs designed to manage the resources of the computer system. These routines are conveniently grouped into three classes: task management, job management, and data management. The function of each of these classes has been introduced previously. More precisely, *task management* provides a logical interface between the hardware and the remainder of the software system and is responsible for the allocation of the CPU and main storage. Task management routines, which operate in the supervisor state and are primarily core-resident, are frequently referred to as the *supervisor* of the operating system. The supervisor performs the following functions:

1. interruption handling and processing,
2. scheduling and execution supervision,
3. main storage allocation,
4. dynamic storage management, and
5. clocks and timer supervision.

Job management provides a logical interface between task management and a job or between task management and the system operator. Functions performed by job management are:

1. analyzing the input job stream,
2. preparing a job for execution,
3. obtaining system resources,
4. processing job terminations,
5. analyzing and processing operator commands, and
6. transmitting messages from an operating program to the system operator.

Job management routines are frequently regarded as ordinary "units of work" to the operating system and are multiprogrammed along with user jobs (later, units of work are referred to as *tasks*); however, most job management routines operate with a protection key of zero so that they have access to lists and tables on a system-wide basis.

Data management provides a software interface between processing programs and auxiliary storage. Functions performed by data management are:

1. assigning space on direct-access volumes,
2. maintaining a catalog of data sets,
3. performing support processing for IO operations (i.e., OPEN, CLOSE, etc.), and
4. processing IO operations (which includes IO supervision, access routines, data set sharing, etc.).

Most data management functions are service operations invoked by the SVC type interruption and processed by resident or nonresident routines (often called *transient routines*) of the supervisor. Thus, most data management routines execute in the supervisor state. The most notable exception to this convention is the access methods that reside in the work space of a job and provide blocking/deblocking and buffering facilities.

Job Control

The user prepares his job to be run in a multiprogramming system in precisely the same manner as when the operating system is not doing multiprogramming. Most systems permit a program to be segmented using an overlay technique such that it can be run in a portion of main storage—either a fixed-size partition or a bounded variable-size region. By constraining each user to operate in a portion of main storage, the level of multiprogramming is increased, as discussed later. (It should be mentioned here that main storage is usually larger when a multiprogramming system is being used. As a result, the level of multiprogramming is usually a function of the size of main storage.)

As input to an operating system, a job consists of the following kinds of information: (1) job control information, (2) input/output requirements, (3) programs (in source or object form), and (4) data. Only job control information is absolutely required since programs can be stored in a job library and data can be retrieved with the operating system's data management facilities. Input/output requirements may be included in the job control information or be included as cataloged procedure. (A cataloged procedure is a predefined set of control cards that are stored as a part of the operating system.)

As implied in the preceding paragraph, input data can be included in the input job stream or be prestored as a data file (called a *data set*). Frequently, the input job stream is "spooled" to disk; however, most operating systems allow a great amount of flexibility in this regard and permit the input job stream to be the card reader, magnetic tape, or any other system device. In fact, the input job stream can usually be changed dynamically by the computer operator. Similarly, system output is usually placed on disk and is later "spooled" to a printer or a card punch. It is necessary, therefore, that a processing program use symbolic device names for system input and system output, such that the operating system can assign any device it chooses to those functions. A symbolic name frequently used for the system input device is SYSIN; similarly, a symbolic name frequently used for the system output device is SYSOUT.

Operation of a Multiprogramming System

A multiprogramming system, as any other system, is characterized by the functions it performs. Some of these functions are essentially unrelated to the structure of the system; that is, the structure of the system would not be affected if the operation of those functions were changed. Two examples are the spooling operation and the use of utility programs. Other functions make the system what it is; these functions are of prime concern and are mentioned here.

A job becomes a unit of work to the operating system when its JOB control card is read from SYSIN by an operating system routine designed for that purpose. An initial program structure is created for the job and a *control block* is built to hold control information (i.e., registers, location counter, pointers to other control blocks, etc.) that is maintained dynamically for that job. (The control block of OS/360, for example, is referred to as the TCB, which stands for "task control block"; similarly, the control block for TSS/360 is the TSI, which stands for "task status index.") After a job is initiated as a unit of work, IO devices are assigned, and the load module for the first job step of that job is loaded. The job is then ready for execution and is subsequently given control of the CPU by a scheduler routine of the operating system. At any given time during system operation, there are usually several jobs in various stages of execution—some beginning, some part-way through execution, and others finishing. However, only one program can be actively executing in the CPU. Thus, there is one active job, zero or more jobs that are ready for execution, and zero or more jobs that are waiting for some event, such as IO completion. If no job is active or ready, the computer is usually put into the wait state until more work enters the system or one of the waiting jobs is put into the ready state. (The manner in which the system is given work to do is covered later.)

As a job enters the system for execution, it is assigned an internal priority computed as a function of external priority and arrival sequence. When the supervisor routine of the operating system has no more "supervisory" work to do, CPU control is given to a scheduler routine to dispatch the CPU to a processing program. The scheduler selects for execution the job with the highest internal priority that is in the "ready" state. That job operates until an interruption occurs, which means that the supervisor program of the operating system has more work to do. That interruption may be caused by IO completion for another job, a machine check interruption, or a program, supervisor call, or timer interruption for the active job. Each type of interruption is processed appropriately by a supervisor routine designed to process that type of interruption. Usually, the supervisor "queues up" the various interruptions and has them processed by priority (some types of interruptions are defined to be more important than others) and by arrival sequence, much like the processing of user jobs.[†] When the supervisor has processed all interruptions and has done all of its housekeeping, it can then dispatch the CPU to a processing program. CPU control is passed to the scheduler routine and the above process is repeated.

Interruptions can take place anytime—i.e., when a processing program is executing or when a supervisor routine is executing. If a processing program is executing when an interruption occurs, the registers, location counter, and other control information for that job is stored in its control block. When that program is activated again, execution is resumed from where it left off. However, the "state" of that program may change. If the interruption is independent of the executing program, then the state does not change from "ready." If that program caused the interruption (for an IO request, or because the timer has run down, etc.), then the state of the program is frequently changed from "ready" to another one of the permissible internal states. Note here that priority and scheduling takes care of itself. A high-priority job that loses control of the CPU because of an event independent to it eventually gains control of the CPU again, when the supervisor is finished with its work. If a higher-priority job becomes ready for execution, then it gains control of the CPU the next time around.

If an interruption occurs when the CPU is executing in the supervisor state, then that interruption is "queued up" and the supervisor routine resumes execution from its point of interruption. Thus, the supervisor can complete its work in an orderly manner.

An operating system that operates in a manner similar to that described above is said to be *interrupt driven* in the sense that a program continues to execute until it is interrupted. Interruptions take place automatically when a need arises; in a sense, the computing system monitors itself. Only one type of interruption is initiated by an operating program; that is the *supervisor call interruption* (SVC), which is issued to initiate a service request.

The manner in which interruptions are handled by the CPU (i.e., the switching of PSWs) is described in Chapter 3.

Obviously, there is a lot more to the operation of a multiprogramming system. Thus far, an overview of task management has been given. Job and data management perform important functions in the overall operation of the system; however, job and data management are more conveniently introduced with regard to a particular mode of operation—i.e., batched processing with multiprogramming or general-purpose time sharing. General-purpose time sharing is introduced in the next section on terminal-oriented systems.

[†]The process of "queuing up" an interruption involves the dynamic construction of a control block to represent the event that caused the interruption as well as to store status and control information. Usually, a control block is added to an appropriate list for that class of interruption.

5.5   TERMINAL-ORIENTED SYSTEMS

Terminal-oriented systems are used for two basic reasons: (1) to make the computational and data processing facilities of a computer system more appropriate to the needs of the user; and (2) to provide an operational capability that is usually not available with traditional batch processing systems. Remote batch processing, conversational remote job entry, and time sharing fall into the first category. They are the subject matter of this section. Applications such as data acquisition, message switching, and data base/data communications (DB/DC) fall into the second category. They are usually implemented as a high-priority job (i.e., task) that uses telecommunications facilities while running in a multiprogramming environment. This general class of applications is not discussed further.

Remote Batch Processing

By design, batch processing systems are more system-oriented than user-oriented. Turnaround time can range from two hours to several days. Batch processing provides for efficient utilization of the equipment since work is queued up for each resource in the system. (For example, there usually exist, in most systems, an input job queue, a queue of tasks ready for execution, and an output queue.) Moreover, processing time is only a small part of turnaround time. Other times include delivery time to the computer, setup time, and delivery time to the user. In addition, several passes through the batch loop are usually required to eliminate program errors. Thus, the elapsed time for problem solution is lengthy and frustrating. Many jobs that need to be done are not done because results are needed before they can be compared.

Remote batch processing (frequently called remote job entry [RJE] or remote job output [RJO]) permits a user with a terminal-oriented work station to enter his job into the input work queue and receive his output directly from the output queue. Turnaround time is reduced by eliminating delivery and wait times. However, the user cannot interact with his job once it is in the work queue, and the normal operational delays, inherent in batch processing, still exist.

The effectiveness of a remote batch processing system is dependent upon the needs of a particular installation. This facility is provided by most operating systems as an adjunct to normal batch processing with multiprogramming.

Conversational Remote Job Entry

An alternate approach to the submission of jobs in a batch processing mode is conversational remote job entry (CRJE). The user, at a low-speed keyboard-type or a CRT-type† terminal, creates a data set that can be entered into the input work queue as a job—including control cards, programs, and data. The data set is

†CRT is an acronym for "cathode ray tube."

saved on-line for subsequent editing and reprocessing. CRJE is not time sharing but frequently approaches that mode of operation by providing diagnostic and control information to the user.

Output from a system providing CRJE support is usually returned to the user via the normal batch delivery service; however, low-speed printed output is sometimes available at the remote location with the same terminal device.

Time Sharing

Through years of development, batch processing systems have evolved to a high level of sophistication. The knowledgeable user is provided with a tremendous computational capability. On the other hand, a considerable amount of knowledge is required to run a simple job; this fact has contributed to the characteristic delays of batch processing mentioned previously.

Time sharing is a user-oriented means of utilizing a computer system. When *time sharing*, multiple users concurrently engage in a series of interactions with the system via remote terminal devices. The user is able to respond immediately to system responses, and similarly, the system can respond immediately to requests for service by the user. Actually, the time sharing control program is designed to service many users on a "round-robin" basis; each user is given a "time slice" of CPU time. Users' think and reaction times are used to perform other work in the CPU. Thus, a user has the operational advantage of having a machine to himself as in the days of console debugging. In reality, the system is time sharing. When a program error is detected by the system, the user is informed immediately. At that point the user can correct his error and continue. Response time is measured in seconds and turnaround time is rarely even considered. Obviously, CPU time is used to provide this sort of time sharing service. A tradeoff is made between efficient CPU utilization and effective user service. Not all jobs lend themselves to time sharing. A long-running file processing job, for example, is perhaps more effectively run in a batch processing mode of operation. A short one-shot FORTRAN program is perhaps best developed in a time sharing mode of operation.

Time sharing systems differ in capability and in complexity; they are conveniently divided into two categories: closed and open. In a *closed* system, the user is limited to a single programming language, such as BASIC or APL. Closed time sharing systems are frequently designed to operate as a single high-priority job in a multiprogramming environment. When implemented in this fashion, the time sharing system usually performs its own scheduling and storage allocation for the users in its domain. Another method of implementing a closed system is to dedicate a complete computer system to that service (called a *dedicated system*). The advantage of the first method of implementation is that the computer can be used to run background batch jobs when the time sharing workload is light.

In an *open* time sharing system, the user is provided with access to all of the capability of the system—assembler language, programming languages, data management, utilities, etc. The primary difference between open time sharing and batch processing is that the user can access to the system with a terminal device and that the system permits an interactive mode of operation. Most open time sharing systems permit two modes of operation: the conversational mode and the batch mode. The facilities of the system are essentially the same in both modes except for the ability to interact with the system to enter programs and data, to perform debugging, and to enter modifications. Moreover, the ability to initiate a batch job from a terminal and to start a job in the conversational mode and complete it in the batch mode is usually provided. Precise terminology differs between systems; the conversational mode is sometimes called the *foreground* and the batch mode is called the *background.*

Several open time sharing systems have become well-known and provide excellent background material on the subject. Four of the better known systems are: CTSS [Cor63] and MULTICS [Cor65, Dal68, Vys65] at M.I.T. and Kinlow's system [Kin64] and TSS/360 [Com65, Gib66, Let68] at IBM. Most computer manufacturers and a great many universities have produced open time sharing systems with varying degrees of success. Some of the lesser known systems are the most successful. The University of Michigan's Michigan Terminal System (MTS) [Ale72] and Carnegie-Mellon's C-MU system [Lau67, Fik68] are notable examples of productive systems in an academic environment.

The subject of time sharing operations is presented in Part Three of this book.

QUESTIONS FOR PART ONE

Chapter 1

1. Quickly review the history of digital computer applications. What "new" areas of application resulted in changes in the operating environment?
2. Consider a nontrivial computer application with which you are familiar. What "additional" operating system capabilities would facilitate the processing of that job? If you currently use a sophisticated operating system, what capabilities *do* facilitate the processing of that job?
3. Extend the set of computer applications given in the chapter and classify them accordingly. Do the additional applications require "new" operating system facilities? (This is a good question for discussion.)
4. The need for an operating system has been stated. In what areas of application would an operating system be undesirable? Give examples.
5. What are some disadvantages of using an operating system? Can these disadvantages be classified?

Chapter 2

6. Distinguish between positional and keyword parameters.
7. What are the key differences between a compiler, a generator, and an interpreter?
8. In what sense is a language processor regarded as a "problem program" to the operating system?
9. What is the difference between a macro and a subroutine?
10. Why are open and internal subprograms actually of very little interest in operating systems technology?
11. Give instances when the use of an *absolute object program* would be desirable.
12. Distinguish between linkage editing and loading.
13. In what kind of applications is the process of linkage editing and the use of load modules superior to the customary loading process?

Chapter 3

14. Discuss advantages and disadvantages (if any) of a byte-oriented computer vs. a word-oriented computer, as far as operating systems technology is concerned.
15. What is the essential difference between a simplex system and a half duplex system?
16. Discuss the advantages and disadvantages of allocating specific devices to a problem program and not control units and devices.
17. Outline a method by which the storage protection feature of a computer could be used to allow several users to share a common routine.
18. In what way does base/index/displacement addressing offer advantages over address/index register addressing as far as operating systems are concerned? (Consider loading and relocation.)

19. What is the significance of the status word from an operating system control point of view?
20. What is the relationship between an operating system and the supervisor state?
21. Describe how an IO channel and the interruption scheme operate together to provide effective IO processing.
22. Discuss the influence of direct-access storage on the development of operating systems technology.

Chapter 4

23. Distinguish between *storage class, storage organization,* and *storage access.*
24. In what way are "blocking" and "buffering" used to achieve the same objectives?
25. Give examples of a data structure. Storage structure.
26. Describe how keyed organization can be used for both sequential and direct access.
27. A triangular matrix is symmetric around the main diagonal such that $a_{ij} = a_{ji}$. Thus, a triangular matrix A with three rows and three columns can be stored as follows:

$$A(1,1)$$
$$A(2,1)$$
$$A(2,2)$$
$$A(3,1)$$
$$A(3,2)$$
$$A(3,3)$$

where duplicate elements are elided. Develop a formula for locating $A(I,J)$ where $I < J, I = J$, and $I > J$.
28. Consider an array of structures declared as follows:

DECLARE 1 TABLE(5),
        2 A CHARACTER(3),
        2 B(2) FIXED BINARY(16),
        2 C FLOAT BINARY;

The declaration specifies a table (TABLE) of 5 entries. Each entry is composed of a character item (A) with a size of 3 bytes, a 2-element array (B), and a floating-point binary element (C). Each element of B occupies 16 bits or 2 bytes. Assume that C occupies 4 bytes. Develop a formula for computing the location of TABLE(I).A, TABLE(I).B(J), and TABLE(I).C.
29. List the obvious problems that have to be accounted for in the design of an operating system when main storage is allocated dynamically to problem programs.

Chapter 5

30. Compare an attached support processor with the use of SPOOLing. Consider: economics, performance, capability, etc.

31. Imagine a CPU without an interruption scheme. How would an operating system be designed in this environment?
32. What other kinds of interruptions (than those given) would be desirable?
33. Why and in what way should an operating system control the use of LCS?
34. Most disk drives use a comb-type assembler for read/write heads such that all heads move in and out together. How would read/write heads that move in and out independently be useful to an operating system?
35. Describe how relocatable object modules, the subroutine library, and the loader work together.
36. Discuss the attached support processor as a natural extension to the use of peripheral computers. Does the concept have a "deeper" significance?
37. Compare the use of "chaining" and "overlay."
38. Why does the SPOOLing program require a high operational priority? Explain.
39. What are the advantages (and disadvantages) of symbolic device assignments?
40. Distinguish between blank common and labeled common.
41. Describe how you think time slicing is implemented in a multiprogramming system. Why would time slicing be used in a multiprogramming system?
42. What is the significance of the use of transient routines?
43. Distinguish between remote batch and time sharing.

PART TWO: FUNCTIONAL CHARACTERISTICS OF AN ADVANCED OPERATING SYSTEM

6 | SYSTEM STRUCTURE

6.1 INTRODUCTION

The purpose of this part of the book is to present the functional characteristics of an advanced operating system. The vehicle used for this purpose is OS/MVT, which is an acronym for *Operating System/Multiprogramming with a Variable Number of Tasks*. The motivation for presenting a real-life system is that it includes all of the components necessary for an effective working system. It is most important that the reader be exposed to the overall structure of a system, since in most systems, the interface between components is at least as important as the manner in which the discrete components function. (A component is an element of a system; in an operating system, a component may be a routine, a table, a queue, or a control block.)

OS/MVT was developed by the IBM Corporation for the 360 series of computers. OS/MVT (hereafter called simply OS) is appropriate for study since it includes most of the facilities available in a given multiprogrammed operating system. In fact OS has been criticized in some circles, perhaps unfairly, as being "everything to everybody."

The study of OS requires a general familiarity with the 360/370 type computers. All of the required topics have been covered in Chapters 1-5. In particular, the following orientation of computer characteristics is assumed:

1. supervisor/problem states;
2. storage protection;

3. privileged/nonprivileged instructions;
4. IO channels;
5. comprehensive interruption system including machine check, IO, program, external, and supervisor call (SVC) interruptions; and
6. byte-organized storage.

In fact, a general introduction to OS is presented as Section 5.4, "Multiprogramming Systems." The material covered there is amplified here through a presentation of the facilities available to the user and the manner in which the operating system operates in response to the user's requests for service.

6.2 FUNCTIONAL CAPABILITY

Job Structure

The basic unit of work that is input to the system is a job. A *job* is a series of job steps, as depicted in Fig. 6.1. Each *job step* specifies the execution of a single processing program. Within a job, job steps are executed sequentially. However, the input job stream usually contains several jobs that may be in

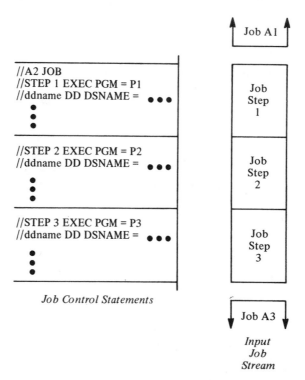

Fig. 6.1 Input job stream depicting a job and job steps.

various stages of execution as a result of the multiprogramming mode of operation.

The job steps that comprise a job are frequently related. For example, a series of job steps might be a compile, an assemble, a link edit, and an execution of the load module produced from the link edit. Similarly, the results of one job step might produce a data file that is used in the next job step (e.g., a sort followed by the execution of a report program).

The execution of a job step may also be conditional upon the successful completion of a previous job step. If a given condition is not met, then the job step is bypassed. A typical example of conditional job step execution might be the bypass of a link edit after an unsuccessful compile.

When a job is accepted for execution by the operating system, the user is given an area of main storage in which to operate. That area of main storage is called a *region;* except under special conditions, the user is constrained to operate in that region. The processing programs that comprise the job steps of a job occupy the region successively. That is, the first processing program is loaded into the region and executed. When the second processing program is to be executed, it is loaded into the same area of storage as occupied by the first processing program and then executed.

From the user's point of view, most of the facilities of the operating system are available through the job control language (i.e., control cards) available for using the system and through macro instructions. Job control language (almost always referred to as JCL) and macros are introduced in the next section; later JCL is covered in more detail.

Job Control

In any given installation, a program can be in any one of several stages of development or can be in a "production status." Data can be stored on auxiliary storage volume or can exist as a card deck. Also, programs and data can be carried over from previous job steps (i.e., in that job). The job control language is designed with sufficient flexibility to allow all of the cases mentioned previously, while allowing device independence and permitting late binding (i.e., at execution time) of access methods to data files.

OS job control language (JCL) adheres to a simple structure and includes six types of statements. Three statement types are introduced here (JOB, EXEC, and DD) and the remainder are covered in a later chapter. The structure of a JCL statement includes *name, operation, operand,* and *comments* fields as follows:

//name operation operand(s) comments

For example, a simple JOB statement might be written as

//RUN3 JOB 916,JONES,REGION=64K,TIME=(2,30) SAMPLE RUN

Fields are separated by blanks, and operands, which may be of positional or keyword variety, are separated by a comma.

The JOB statement marks the beginning of a job and specifies operational parameters such as an accounting number, time limit, region size, and priority class. The JOB statement may also specify conditions under which the job is to be terminated. A sample JOB statement was given in the preceding paragraph.

The EXEC statement marks the beginning of a job step and identifies the processing program to be executed or the cataloged procedure to be used. (A *cataloged procedure* is a series of JCL statements that is given a name and stored as part of a data set. When the procedure name is used, the statements are retrieved and interpreted as though they had been placed in the input job stream.) The EXEC statement also permits the user to set a time limit on the job step, to pass parameters to the job step, to specify region size in the event that it is not given with the JOB statement, and to provide for conditional execution of the job step. Other facilities are available which are covered later. A sample EXEC statement is given as follows:

//BLD EXEC PGM=IEWL,REGION=96K,TIME=(1,30)

The DD statement is used to specify the characteristics of a data set that is to be used with a processing program. Each data set used by a processing program requires a DD card that is placed after the EXEC card for that program. The form of the DD statement is:

//MFILE DD DSNAME=SHOP.MASTER(0),
              DISP=OLD,UNIT=2314,VOL=SER=123456

In summary, each job requires one JOB statement; each job step requires one EXEC statement and zero or more DD statements. The DD statements for each job step follow the EXEC statement marking the beginning of the job step.

Although JCL is an effective means of utilizing the facilities of the operating system, the preparation of JCL statements must be preplanned. Thus, the use of JCL is not appropriate when it is desired to use the system on a dynamic basis— i.e., when requests for service are data-dependent. As an example, the EXEC statement in JCL is a means of having a load module loaded into the user's region and executed. To perform the same function dynamically requires an additional capability of the operating system and an understanding of how the operating system operates. First, the EXEC card prepared by the user is read by a Job Management routine and it causes the load module to be loaded. For the most part, Job Management routines operate in the problem state, and the routine to do the loading is part of the Supervisor and operates in the supervisor state. ("Why" and "how" are explained later.) In short, the Job Management routine issues an appropriate SVC interruption that activates the Supervisor routine that does the loading. (The routine is known as "program fetch.")

Could a user's processing program issue the same SVC interruption? The answer is yes; moreover, an assembler language macro is available to make it easier to use. For example, if a user desired to have a load module with entry point APROG loaded and executed dynamically from a processing program, he would include the following macro instruction at the appropriate point in his program:

LINK EP=APROG

(This is a simplified use of the LINK macro.) The assembler program would expand the LINK macro to include the appropriate instructions for having the load module that contains the entry point APROG loaded and for passing program control to it.

A great many of the facilities of the operating system are available through macro instructions, such as this.

Tasks and Multitasking

To the user and to computer operations personnel, a unit of work is the job. To the Supervisor, a unit of work is a task. More specifically, a *task* is an independent unit of work that can compete for the resources of the computing system. Associated with each task in the system is a *task control block* (TCB), which is an area of storage containing control information for that task. Task representation is suggested by Fig. 6.2. Each task has a priority (assigned by the user, the system, or both) and a state (active, ready, or waiting). The TCBs are arranged by priority on a *task queue;* the task queue is implemented as a linked list. When the Supervisor allocates the CPU to a task, it chooses the first TCB on the task queue that is in the ready state.

Ordinarily, at least one task exists for each job and corresponds to the active job step; thus, if there are n jobs in some stage of execution, there are at least n tasks in the system. However, tasks may exist for two other reasons: (1) Control program routines that execute in the problem state operate as tasks to the Supervisor routines; and (2) a user task can initiate a *subtask* that executes concurrently with the parent task. A control program routine that operates as a task is called a *system task* to distinguish it from a *user task* that is created for a processing program. Most system tasks perform job management functions.

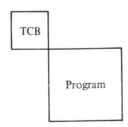

Fig. 6.2 Symbolic representation of a task.

In the operating system, a task is created with the execution of an ATTACH macro instruction; ATTACH, which requires several operands, expands to an SVC instruction that initiates an interruption when executed. The routine that processes the ATTACH SVC interruption causes a task to be established (i.e., put on the task queue, etc.) with a given priority. One of the operands to ATTACH is the entry point name of the task to be attached.

A task is created as a result of one of the following actions:

1. The operator performs the IPL sequence and a "master scheduler" task is created; this is a Job Management routine discussed later in this chapter.
2. The EXEC job control language statement is read; a Job Management routine (system task) subsequently issues an ATTACH for the load module to be executed.
3. An ATTACH macro instruction is executed in a system task (e.g., the "master scheduler" attaches another Job Management routine).
4. An ATTACH macro instruction is executed in a user task, thereby creating a subtask.

Task synchronization is also important. Later, an *event control block* (ECB) is defined. When a subtask terminates, the control program routine posts a "completion" status in the ECB; the parent task can query the ECB, achieving the desired synchronization.

Multitasking is a complex process. As this part of the book unfolds, the functions introduced above will be expounded and related to the components of the operating system.

Program Structure

The reader is assumed to be familiar with the concept of a load module, introduced previously. Clearly, the notion of a load module embodies those of main program and subprogram; moreover, a load module is a static entity. That is, its structure does not change between different invocations. Even though a load module is produced by the operating system, only processing programs are involved in load module creation, and the control programs are not involved per se, with the load module being produced.[†] However, the dynamic behavior of that load module (during execution) is significant since it may require participation of the control programs.

The dynamic behavior of a program can be placed into one of four structural categories: (1) simple structure, (2) planned overlay, (3) dynamic serial structure, and (4) dynamic parallel structure.

A program with *simple structure* is loaded into main storage as a single entity

---

[†]In other words, load modules are produced by the linkage editor, which runs as a processing program.

and executed. The program segment placed in main storage contains the entire program. (The particular instructions that are executed in that load module are not significant to the operating system—even though the program may require operating system services.)

A program with *planned overlay structure* is produced by the linkage editor as a single load module; however, program segments that need not be in main storage at the same time are identified. Thus, the same area in main storage can be reused on a hierarchical basis. The technique, known as *overlay*, requires a minimum amount of control program assistance to bring an overlay segment into main storage.

Programs with a simple structure or a planned overlay structure utilize a single load module.

As the execution-time behavior of programs becomes more complex, the efficiency and flexibility of planned overlay structures tends to decrease. The remaining types of program structure allow more than one load module to be executed during the course of program execution. In a program with *dynamic serial structure*, more than one load module is used. Four macro instructions are provided for the management of load modules and for linkage between load modules; they are LINK, XCTL, LOAD, and DELETE. The LINK macro instruction, as depicted in Fig. 6.3, causes a load module to be placed in main storage and executed. Control is returned to the calling program with the RETURN macro, which releases the occupied space but does not reassign it. Later, if the same load module is requested again (and the load module has the correct at-

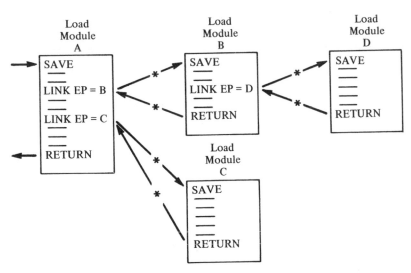

Fig. 6.3 The LINK macro instruction used in a program with dynamic serial structure.

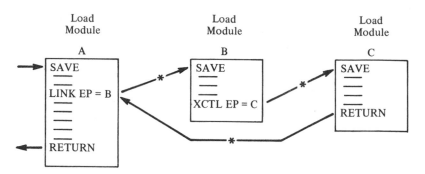

Fig. 6.4 The XCTL macro instruction used in a program with dynamic serial structure.

tributes) and the copy in main storage is still intact, it is reused without requiring a "fetch" operation. The LINK macro instruction and this form of the RETURN macro instruction require the assistance of the control program (i.e., LINK and RETURN expand into appropriate SVC instructions).

The XCTL macro instruction causes a load module to be "fetched" and executed, as does the LINK macro instruction. However, XCTL is used when the program is executed in phases, and the execution of the load module containing the XCTL macro is complete and will not be executed again. Figure 6.4 depicts the use of the XCTL macro instruction; in that figure, the space occupied by load module B is released for further use. Execution of the XCTL macro involves control program assistance.

The LOAD macro instruction causes a load module to be loaded but not executed. It is subsequently used with an ordinary BRANCH instruction. A load module loaded with the LOAD macro instruction can be removed from main storage with the DELETE macro instruction. As depicted in Fig. 6.5, a load module loaded with the LOAD macro instruction can be executed successively provided that it possesses the correct attributes. Execution of both LOAD and DELETE macro instructions involves control program assistance.

A program with *dynamic parallel structure* uses the ATTACH macro instruction to create a subtask that is executed concurrently with the parent task. Whereas with simple structure, planned overlay structure, and dynamic serial structure, a single task and a single TCB exist, with dynamic parallel structure, an additional task is created for each ATTACH that is executed. The use of the ATTACH macro for two typical cases of subtasking is suggested in Fig. 6.6. (The figure includes two task synchronization macros—i.e., WAIT and POST— that are covered later.)

Each load module, stored in a program library, is one of three types: not reusable, serially reusable, and reenterable. A *not reusable* load module is fetched

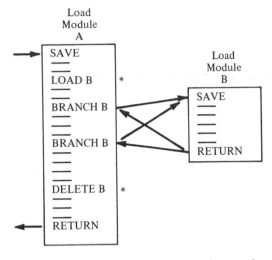

*Denotes that control program assistance is required.

Fig. 6.5 LOAD and DELETE macro instructions used in a program with dynamic serial structure.

from the library each time it is referenced. A module of this type modifies itself during execution requiring a fresh copy each time it is used.

A *serially reusable load module* is self-initializing so that any modifications from a previous execution are restored before it is reexecuted. A load module of this type normally carries the same storage key as that of the job step to which it is attached. More than one subtask of the job step may use a serially reusable load module provided that is is used by only one task at one time. Normally, when two subtasks of the same job step wish to use the same serially reusable load module concurrently, another copy is fetched from the library. The second copy can be avoided with the use of enqueuing and dequeuing facilities of the operating system that permit tasks to become "queued up" waiting for the previous execution of a serially usable load module to be completed.

A *reenterable load module* does not modify itself during execution. System tasks are frequently designed to be reenterable and have a storage key of zero. A reenterable load module can be used by any active task in the system; data and control information are kept in machine registers and in "private control sections" that are a part of the user's program and not of the reenterable load module. In a multiprogramming system, the use of reenterable load modules is a desirable feature since main storage space requirements are minimized. Reenterable load modules have an interesting and useful property. Since the storage oc-

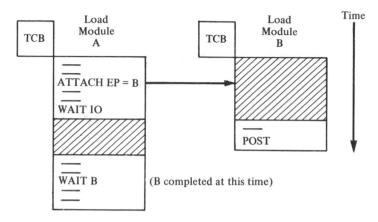

Case (1): A has higher priority than B; delay expected in A.

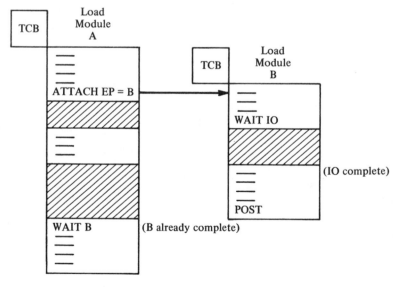

Case (2): B has higher priority than A; delay expected in B.

 Key: denotes wait

Fig. 6.6 Use of the ATTACH macro to create a subtask. Case (1): A has higher priority than B; delay expected in A. Case (2): B has higher priority than A; delay expected in B.

cupied by these load modules need be read only by the active task, the protection key in the program status word (PSW) need not match the storage key of the load modules. This explains how any task in the system can use reenterable system routines such as OPEN, CLOSE, and the access methods.

Main Storage Allocation

In OS/MVT, main storage is allocated dynamically except for the resident routines of the control program; the size of the resident area is established during "system generation" and loaded at IPL time. The structure of main storage is discussed later in this chapter in the section entitled "Control Program Structure."

The user area of main storage is maintained dynamically, depending upon the needs of the jobs that enter the system. This function is performed by a Task Management routine in response to requests by other control program routines, system tasks, and user tasks. As each job is readied for execution, its main storage requirements are determined from the REGION parameter of the JOB card; if that parameter is omitted, the space requirement for each job step is determined from the REGION parameter, if present, of the EXEC card for that job step or it is assigned by default as a function of the priority and job class of that job. The main storage that comprises a region is assigned in 2048 (2K) byte increments and is given a storage key that matches the PSW protection key assigned to the job. This fact is significant. System/360, for example, has 16 possible storage protection keys numbered 0-15. The storage protection key numbered zero is assigned to the Supervisor; thus, the number of active jobs in the system is limited to 15. However, a subtask assumes the same storage protection key as its parent task; similarly, system tasks run with a storage protection key of zero. Therefore, although the number of jobs is limited to 15, the number of tasks can be fairly large.

Except for cases where "roll out/roll in" is used, a job is constrained to operate in the region assigned to it. ("Roll out/roll in" refers to the technique of moving a program or a part of a program to an auxiliary device to provide main storage space for the execution of another program. Subsequently, the first program is read back into main storage to resume execution. This topic is covered later.) Storage in a region is assigned either implicitly or explicitly by a Supervisor routine. An *implicit* storage assignment is generated internally to the control program as a result of a request to load a program. In this case, a Supervisor routine finds a load module in a library, allocates space to it, and then reads it into the space allocated to it and readies it for execution. An *explicit* storage assignment results from a request for working storage from an operating task. Two macros are defined for this purpose: GETMAIN and GETPOOL. GETMAIN is usually used to obtain storage for a single task. GETPOOL is frequently used to obtain main storage that is to be shared among independent subtasks within the same job step. Storage allocated explicitly can be a fixed or variable size and be requested on a conditional or unconditional basis, as determined by the following definitions of the terms:

1. *Fixed-size area.* A precise amount of main storage is requested and that amount is explicitly allocated to the requesting task.
2. *Variable-size area.* A minimum amount and a preferred amount of main storage are requested. If the preferred amount is not available, the largest amount greater than the minimum is assigned.
3. *Conditional allocation.* Main storage is requested but the task can proceed without it.
4. *Unconditional allocation.* The requesting task cannot proceed without the amount of main storage requested.

The above criteria are well-defined in the sense that the Supervisor is provided with a certain amount of flexibility in choosing the manner in which main storage, one of the system's primary resources, is assigned.

In a multiprogrammed operating system, main storage is usually allocated to as many jobs as the size of main storage will support. Obviously, this number varies on a dynamic basis. If a high-priority job (i.e., higher than any active job) enters the system and insufficient main storage is currently available to satisfy its requirements for region size, then that job must wait until a sufficient amount of main storage becomes available through job or task terminations. Main storage allocation is also related to "roll out/roll in," which is presented later in this chapter.

6.3 DATA SETS, VOLUMES, LIBRARIES, CATALOGS, AND INPUT/OUTPUT

This section serves as an introduction to the structural properties of OS data management facilities. To be sure, these facilities satisfy the input and output requirements of an operating system. However, OS data management provides considerably more than IO capability. Other facilities include:

1. device independence,
2. allocation of space on direct-access devices,
3. late binding of programs to data files—thus, specifications such as buffer size, blocking factors, device identification, and device type need not be specified until execution time for a particular job step,
4. automatic location of data files by name, and
5. protection of data files on the same device, against unauthorized access, and against concurrent update and access.

This capability is provided through a system of data sets, volumes, libraries, and catalogs. These topics are the subject matter of this section, which provides a foundation for the data management portion of Chapter 7.

Data Sets

The concept of a data file is generalized to what is known as a data set. Whereas a data file usually refers to a group of data records related in some form to a data processing function, a data set refers to one of several categories of information, such as a source program, an object program, a numerical table, a payroll file, or a collection of subroutines. Thus, a *data set* is a collection of related data items, such as one of the above examples, together with a "data set label," stored along with the data set. The *data set label* includes the name of the data set, its physical attributes, and its boundaries on a storage medium. Common examples of a data set are an ordinary data file, a library of object programs, and a source program stored as a set of source data records. A data set name can be stored in a catalog. A data set is stored on a volume and possesses a data set organization —a term that denotes its physical characteristics. It is accessed by an IO routine termed an access method.

The data set label mentioned above should be distinguished from a tape label or a file label used for identification purposes in data processing. With direct-access devices, the data set label is termed a *data set control block* (DSCB); it is stored on the direct-access volume containing the data set. With magnetic tape, the data set label is a part of the data set header label and includes a data set sequence number. The reason for a data set sequence number on magnetic tape, obviously, is for checking and positioning when more than one data set is stored on the same magnetic tape reel.

Volumes

A standard unit of auxiliary storage is termed a *volume*, such as a magnetic tape reel, a disk pack, or a drum. Several data sets can reside on a single volume, which is usually the case, or a single data set may span two or more volumes. Each volume has a volume label that identifies the volume and can be used during "automatic volume recognition." *Automatic volume recognition* is a Job Management function that allows the operator to premount requested volumes. Job Management routines manage a table of "volume identifications" for volumes mounted on input and output units of the computer system. If the identification of a requested volume is found in the table, then the system need not issue a mount request to the operator.

Magnetic tape volumes can be labeled or unlabeled. A labeled volume includes the following:

1. volume label (one per volume),
2. data set header label (including data set sequence number) for each data set,
3. data set trailer label for each data set, and
4. user labels, as required.

The identity of unlabeled tapes is not verified by the operating system; however, in some cases, it is necessary for the operating system to create a volume label for an unlabeled tape. (This is a detailed question for which manufacturers' reference manuals should be consulted.)

Each direct-access storage device (DASD) volume is labeled in a standard location (usually the first track—corresponding to read/write head 0—of cylinder 0). Each DASD volume label includes the following:

1. volume label identifier,
2. volume label number,
3. volume serial number,

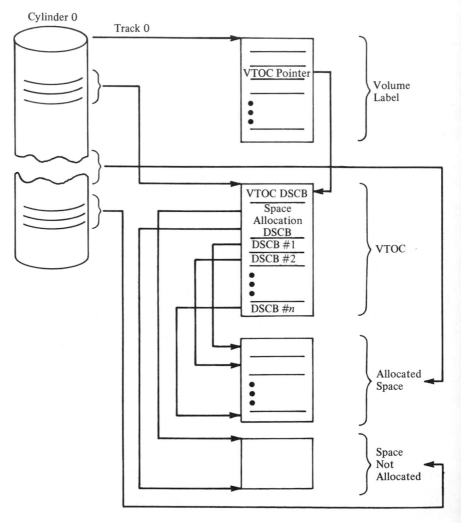

Fig. 6.7   DASD organization (simplified).

4. volume security byte,
5. VTOC pointer,
6. manufacturer's information,
7. owner's information, and
8. blank space.

The volume table of contents (VTOC) is important since it includes the DSCBs of all the data sets stored on the volume. More specifically, the VTOC contains:

1. a DSCB for the VTOC itself,
2. a DSCB for each data set on the volume, and
3. a DSCB for all tracks on the volume that are available for allocation.

The volume label and a skeletal VTOC are placed on a DASD volume when it is initialized by a utility program. When a data set is to be stored on a DASD volume, the attributes and space requirements of that data set must be supplied to the operating system. These specifications are used by DASD space allocation routines in maintaining the VTOC for a given volume. DASD organization is suggested in Fig. 6.7.

Catalogs

In utilizing the concepts that have been presented thus far, the operating system needs the following information to retrieve a data set: data set name, the device type, a volume identification, and possibly a data set sequence number. Specification of this information can be cumbersome to the user, especially when several users are working cooperatively. A *catalog* allows data sets to be referenced by name alone.

A *data set name* is a simple name (1–8 alphameric characters the first of which must be alphabetic) or a series of simple names separated by periods, such as DIV15.YORK.ABC. The *catalog* is a tree-organized set of indices held in direct-access storage. The master index is a basic structural entity in the catalog; the level of subsequent indices is determined by the users of the system. Figure 6.8 depicts the catalog structure and search procedure. When the user specifies an "already existing" data set by name alone, the system can determine its attributes by performing a catalog search and retrieving the file characteristics from the DSCB of the data set.

Not all data sets need be cataloged, depending upon the needs of a particular user and upon the operating practices of an installation. Every OS system has a catalog that resides on the system residence volume (SYSRES). When it is desired to conserve space on SYSRES or when a data set is used infrequently, its name is not cataloged. A data set name is usually cataloged upon request only.

Libraries

A *partitioned data set* (see the regionally organized file discussed earlier) is a data file that is divided into sequentially organized members. Each member is

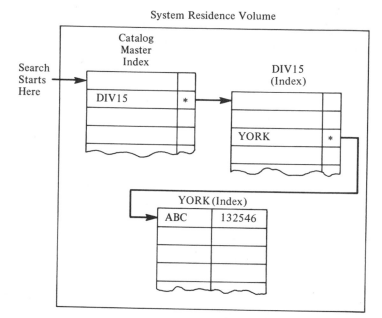

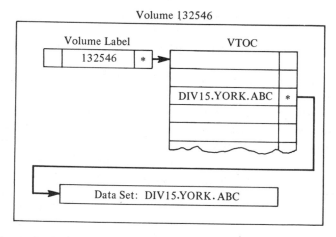

Fig. 6.8 Catalog and search procedure. (The catalog is searched for a data set named DIV15.YORK.ABC.)

composed of records. In a logical sense, a partitioned data set (PDS) is a file of files. Each PDS includes a directory that points to the beginning of each member.

Data sets of this type are most frequently used to store object programs—each member corresponds to a single object program. The PDS as a whole is referred

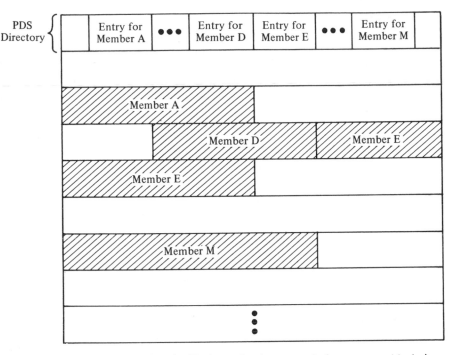

Fig. 6.9 Partitioned data set (PDS). (Each member is composed of one or more blocks.)

to as a *library*. Operating system libraries and user libraries are stored in this fashion. Figure 6.9 depicts a typical partitioned data set.

Member entries in the PDS directory vary in length depending upon the nature of the respective members. Using a NOTE macro instruction, the user can develop pointers to blocks within a PDS and have the pointer information stored in the directory along with the member name. (Pointers of this type are used to update a record in place.) Macro instructions are available for adding or deleting directory entries; similarly, other macro instructions are available for adding or deleting members to the PDS itself. (All operations on PDS directory or PDS members are regarded as IO operations since all information is stored on a DASD volume; therefore, they are utilized as typical IO operations are used.) A secondary entry point to an object module in a PDS is stored in the PDS directory with an "alias" flag set. Thus, a member can be accessed by a "primary" name or by one of several "secondary" names.

An ordinary data set is referred to by name. For example, data sets MFILE and RIVER.JOHNS would be specified in JCL statements as:

DSNAME=MFILE

or

DSNAME=RIVER.JOHNS

where DSNAME is the keyword for the parameter. When a member of a partitioned data set (PDS) is specified, the member name is enclosed in parentheses following the PDS name. For example, member APROG of partitioned data set BIGLIB is specified as:

$$DSNAME=BIGLIB(APROG)$$

Control Volumes

A volume that contains all or a part of the system catalog or contains libraries that include operating system control programs is termed a *control volume*. Usually, the operating system control programs and the master index of the catalog are stored on a single control volume termed the *system residence volume* (SYSRES). Frequently, the indices of the catalog spill over to other control volumes. SYSRES libraries are presented in Section 6.4.

Input and Output

The manner in which IO operations are performed is determined by the needs of the user and the physical attributes of the data set. Several factors are involved:

1. mode of operation (basic or queued);
2. data set organization (sequential, direct, indexed sequential, or partitioned); and
3. blocking and buffering facilities.

A value for each of these factors collectively determines a method of doing input or output; a routine for doing the input or output is termed an *access method*—i.e., a means of referencing a particular data set. From the point of view of this book, the facilities for doing IO are not as significant as how it is performed within the operating system.

All input and output is performed by pre-assembled routines (object code as compared to interpreted code) that are connected to a user's program when a data set is opened. "Open" results from the execution of an OPEN macro instruction (or an appropriate SVC instruction). At this time, the entries of a data control block (DCB), which is included in a user's program, are completed. (The DCB is a control block that describes the characteristics of a data set and associated IO operations; it is used by an access method during IO processing. Thus, the access method can be shared among users since information peculiar to a given program and to a given data set is stored in the program itself. In fact, a program frequently uses the same access method routine for different data sets. Each data set has a DCB, and when an IO operation is being executed on that data set, its own DCB is used.) The entries in the DCB are formed from the information in the user's DD statement for the data set, the DSCB for the data set, and the parameters of the OPEN macro; these entries control the execution of an IO operation and point to an OS-supplied IO processing program (i.e., the access method mentioned above). Actual input and output is controlled by an input/ output supervisor (IOS) located in the nucleus (resident portion) of the Supervisor, which communicates with the appropriate access method to provide the desired IO processing. An IO processing function is logically disconnected from a processing program when a CLOSE macro instruction is executed.

Input/output structures and the control blocks used (such as the DCB) are presented in detail later. However, the above presentation is included as an aid in understanding control program structure—covered next.

6.4 CONTROL PROGRAM STRUCTURE

The structure of operating system routines is related to several factors:

1. the functions performed by the various control programs,
2. the libraries used to store operating system programs,
3. the organization of main storage, and
4. the manner in which the system operates.

The first three topics are presented here. Chapter 8 is devoted entirely to the operation of the system.

Functions of the Control Program

Control program routines are divided into three categories: (1) task management routines, (2) job management routines, and (3) data management routines. *Task Management* (referred to as the Supervisor) performs the following functions on a system-wide basis:

1. interruption handling,
2. task supervision (including multitask operations),
3. main storage supervision,
4. contents supervision (of main storage),
5. overlay supervision,
6. timer management (timers, clocks, etc.)
7. input/output supervision, and
8. processing of exceptional and error conditions.

Supervisor routines execute in the supervisor state; the most frequently used of these routines are core resident. The others are loaded on a demand basis.

Job Management routines provide communication facilities between the user and the operating system. This function involves two types of input:

1. operator commands, and
2. the input job stream.

Operator commands control the execution of the system by causing system tasks to be attached. These system tasks, such as the "reader/interpreter," control job processing. The input job stream, obviously, determines the jobs that are processed. Job Management routines respond to the input job stream in much the same manner that the computer responds to the execution of instructions. The primary function of Job Management are:

1. reading, interpreting, and analysis of the job stream;
2. allocation of IO devices;
3. job initiation; and
4. overall system scheduling (i.e., the "master scheduler").

Job Management routines normally operate as system tasks.

Data Management routines control all input and output operations; these functions include:

1. catalog management,
2. auxiliary storage management,
3. channel and IO operations,
4. IO initialization and termination, and
5. IO error processing.

Processing programs and control programs both use Data Management facilities. Processing programs use Data Management mainly for input and output. Control programs use Data Management for locating data sets and reserving space, in addition to input and output. Most Data Management routines, except for access methods, operate in the supervisor state.

The routines that perform the above functions are presented later in this section.

System Libraries

Routines of the operating system are stored in three program libraries: SYS1.LINKLIB, SYS1.SVCLIB, and SYS1.NUCLEUS. SYS1.SVCLIB and SYS1.NUCLEUS reside on the system residence device (SYSRES). SYS1.-LINKLIB may reside upon SYSRES depending on how the system is generated.

All system libraries are partitioned data sets. Resident routines of the Supervisor, that operate with a PSW protection key of zero, reside on SYS1.NUCLEUS as a single load module (i.e., the various routines are link edited together). Nonresident Supervisor routines reside on SYS1.SVCLIB and operate from transient areas in the "nucleus" or from an area called the "link pack area." Nonresident Supervisor routines also operate with PSW protection keys of zero. (The "nucleus," the "link pack area," and the "system queue area" relate to main storage organization; they are discussed in the next section.)

Job Management routines access fixed storage areas ("nucleus" and the "system queue area") and must operate with a PSW protection key of zero. They reside on SYS1.LINKLIB and operate out of the user area and the "link pack area."

Data Management routines reside on SYS1.SVCLIB and operate out of one of the following areas:

1. SVC transient area,
2. link pack area, or
3. region of the requesting task.

Access routines operate with the same PSW protection key as the task that calls them; other Data Management routines operate with a PSW protection key of zero.

Several areas of main storage have been mentioned; it is virtually impossible to present main storage organization without system libraries and vice versa. (It is much like the chicken and the egg problem.) The areas of main storage presented here are defined next.

Organization of Main Storage

The organization of main storage uses the storage protection feature. (Protection key zero is used for the Supervisor; protection keys 1-15 are used for job steps.) During the IPL sequence, four areas are established:

1. *Fixed area.* Contains the resident portion of the Supervisor (called the *nucleus*). The storage protection key of this storage area is zero. Two transient areas are embedded in the nucleus: the SVC transient area and the IO Supervisor transient area. These transient areas are used by nonresident SVC routines and nonresident IO error handling routines, respectively. The nucleus is loaded from SYS1.NUCLEUS when the system is IPLed; routines that operate from either of the transient areas reside on SYS1.SVCLIB.
2. *System queue area.* The system queue area is a fixed-size area of storage adjacent to the fixed area. The system queue area supplies storage for queues and tables that are built and used by the Supervisor during operation of the system. The system queue area is initialized by a nucleus initialization program (NIP) during IPL and operates with the storage protection key of zero so that it cannot be accessed by processing programs.
3. *Link pack area.* The link pack area is located in upper storage and is loaded during IPL. It contains reenterable routines from SYS1.LINKLIB and SYS1.SVCLIB. These routines are used by any task that requires them. The link pack area also contains the track addresses of other routines that reside on SYS1.LINKLIB and SYS1.SVCLIB so that these routines can be retrieved quickly and loaded into the user's region. The routines that comprise the link pack area are specified when a particular installation's version of OS is "generated." Frequently used control program routines are placed in the link pack area so that they can be shared and thereby eliminate excessive loading.
4. *Dynamic area.* The dynamic area extends from the system queue area to the link pack area. As job steps and system tasks are initiated as units of

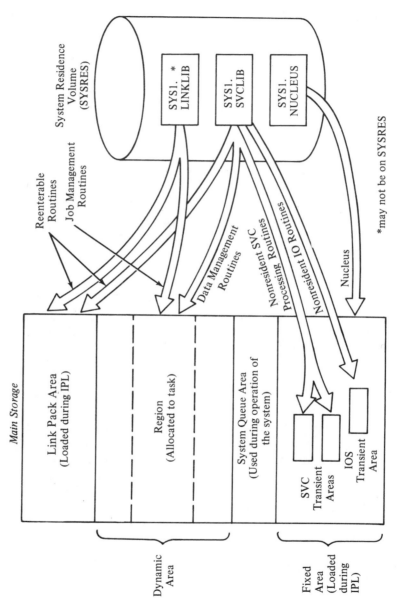

Fig. 6.10 Organization of main storage.

work to the system, main storage space is allocated to them in blocks of 2048 bytes from the dynamic area. The storage assigned to a unique job step is termed a *region*. The dynamic area can be extended by using large-capacity storage. One of the input parameters to the linkage editor and the loader indicates whether the load module should be loaded in high-speed main storage or low-speed main storage.

Main storage organization is depicted in Fig. 6.10.

The size of the various areas of main storage usually varies depending upon the needs of a particular installation. The number of transient areas, the size of the system queue area, the routines that comprise the link pack area, as well as other parameters, are entered into a *system generation process* that generates a version of the operating system for a given installation. Thus the supplier of the operating system, IBM in this case, provides a basic (starter) operating system with a variety of options; the user performs a system generation procedure that adapts the system to his needs.

Supervisor Structure

It is virtually impossible to separate the structure of the Supervisor from its method of operation; moreover, several routines are involved compared to Job and Data Management, which utilize relatively few.

As mentioned previously, the system is interrupt driven. This means that all Supervisor processing begins with an interruption. (Recall here the five types of interruption: supervisor call—SVC, external, input/output, program, and machine check.) The overall flow of the Supervisor is as follows:

1. A task is executing.
2. An interruption occurs.
3. A new PSW is loaded and a Supervisor routine is given control of the CPU.
4. The interruption is analyzed.
5. The requested service or required action is performed.
6. The CPU is dispatched to a task.

The flow is depicted in Fig. 6.11.

The Supervisor is organized according to the functions that it performs. When an interruption is accepted by the CPU, it is initially processed by a First Level Interruption Handler (FLIH). The FLIH determines if the routine for processing that interruption is in storage; if so, CPU control is passed directly to that routine. This method of operation is suggested by Fig. 6.12, which gives the modular control flow of the Supervisor. If the routine for processing the interruption is not core-resident, then control is passed to a Second Level Interruption Handler (SLIH) to bring the needed routine into one of the transient areas. If the Supervisor must wait for the needed routine to be brought into main storage, then CPU is frequently passed to the Dispatcher to give the CPU to a ready task

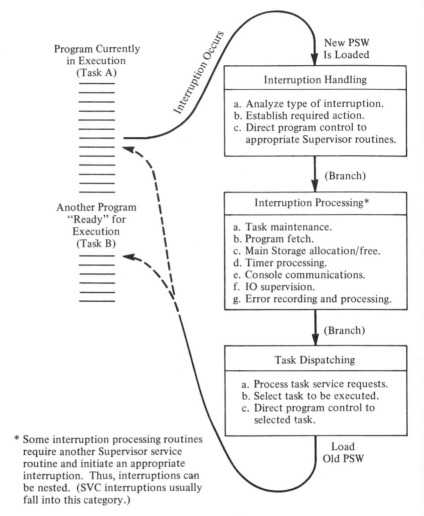

Program Currently
in Execution
(Task A)

Interruption Occurs

New PSW
Is Loaded

Interruption Handling

a. Analyze type of interruption.
b. Establish required action.
c. Direct program control to
appropriate Supervisor routines.

(Branch)

Another Program
"Ready" for
Execution
(Task B)

Interruption Processing*

a. Task maintenance.
b. Program fetch.
c. Main Storage allocation/free.
d. Timer processing.
e. Console communications.
f. IO supervision.
g. Error recording and processing.

(Branch)

Task Dispatching

a. Process task service requests.
b. Select task to be executed.
c. Direct program control to
selected task.

Load
Old PSW

* Some interruption processing routines
require another Supervisor service
routine and initiate an appropriate
interruption. Thus, interruptions can
be nested. (SVC interruptions usually
fall into this category.)

Fig. 6.11   Flow of interruption processing.

until the needed routine can be read in. The structure of the Supervisor is suggested by Fig. 6.12.   Specific details on how the system operates are presented in Chapter 8, "System Operation."   For now, the overall flow and structure of the system are most important.

Job Management Structure

The two major functions provided by Job Management routines are command
processing and job processing.   These functions are performed by a master

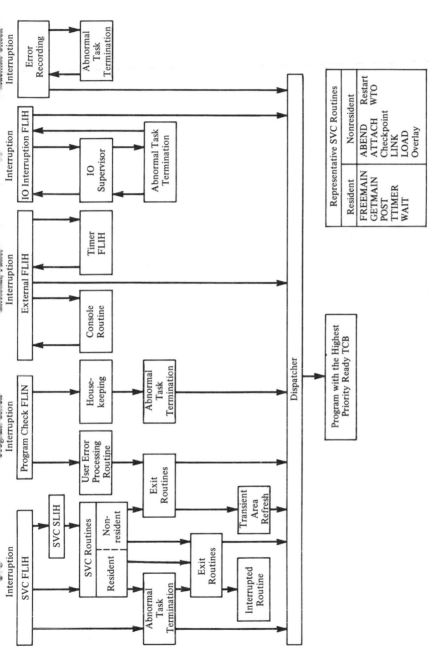

Fig. 6.12 Overall structure of the Supervisor. (Adapted from [OSm], p. 348.)

scheduler and a job scheduler, two groups of routines that operate as system tasks with PSW protection keys of zero. Each system task is assigned a region of main storage; if a routine used by one of these system tasks is not in the link pack area, it is loaded into the region for execution. Figure 6.13 depicts the overall structure of Job Management and the flow of work through the system.

The operation of the system is controlled by the master scheduler. The *master scheduler* is a system task that is established during IPL; in fact, it is the only task that exists when the system is initialized. The master scheduler handles operator commands and messages to the operator. Operator commands are of prime importance since they are used to create job scheduler routines as system tasks. Operator commands are entered into the system from the console or are included in the input job stream. (If a command is entered via the input job stream, it is passed by the reader/interpreter to the master scheduler.) A command is processed in three steps:

1. It is read.
2. It is scheduled.
3. It is executed.

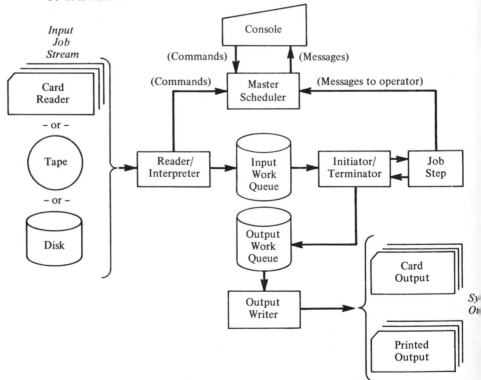

Fig. 6.13 Job management structure and information flow.

Each of the above steps may require a separate system task or are a part of a single task, depending upon the command.

Job processing involves three kinds of tasks: (1) reading tasks, (2) initiating tasks, and (3) writing tasks. These tasks are created in response to a START command entered by the operator. In general, a reading task or a writing task exists for each input or output device.

The *reading task* (frequently referred to as the *reader/interpreter*) reads input job stream records until an end-of-data condition arises; JCL statements are stored in an internal queue and input data are placed on a direct-access volume as an input data set. The reader/interpreter operates in one of three modes:

1. The reading and interpreting are done directly, as mentioned above. The JCL is interpreted and placed in an input work queue. Input data sets are created.
2. The reading and interpreting are performed as separate tasks. The reading task (called *automatic SYSIN* batching) reads the input records and creates a batch work queue. The interpreter is attached as a separate task to interpret the batch work queue.
3. The input records are entered into an intermediate input queue by *remote job entry* (RJE) routines. The interpreter reads the intermediate input queue as input.

The manner in which the reader/interpreter operates is presented in Chapter 8.

The input work queue constructed by the interpreter is a collection of control blocks and tables chained together as records and referred to as the work queue data set (SYS1.SYSJOBQE). Each input job comprises an entry in the work queue; it is referred to as a *work queue entry*. Elements of the work queue entry are presented later. In OS/MVT, there can be 15 job classes—specified by the CLASS parameter of the JOB statement. Thus, there can be 15 input work queues.

Like the reading tasks, the *initiating task* (referred to as the *initiator/ terminator*) is also established with the operator START command. An initiator is assigned to one or more job classes; the first entry on an input work queue is selected and the following processing is performed in response to that unit of work:

1. A region of main storage is acquired.
2. Input data sets are located.
3. Required IO devices are assigned.
4. Auxiliary storage for "new" data sets is reserved.
5. A task for that job step is attached.

When a job step is complete, the *Terminator* routine disposes of data sets used or created, releases IO devices, and removes the job step's TCB from the system.

Upon job termination (i.e., after the last job step in the job), the terminator deletes the job's work queue entry from the SYS1.SYSJOBQE data set and creates entries in output work queues for that job's system output data sets.

System output data sets are written on a direct-access storage device for processing by an output writer task. Each class of system output (there are 36 in all) has an associated output work queue. An entry in the output work queue is made by the terminator, for each output data set created by a job step. As with other job processing tasks, an *output writer task* is attached with the operator's START command and assigned to an output class. An output writer task dequeues output work queue entries and performs the required output function. When output work queue entries are exhausted, the output writer enters the "wait state" until a job terminates and the terminator places an output queue entry in the output work queue.

Data Management Structure

Data Management functions presented earlier are performed by four types of routines:

1. *Direct-access device space management SVC routines.* These routines are used primarily by Job Management during job step initiation and control the allocation of space on a direct access volume through the volume table of contents (VTOC) of that volume.
2. *Catalog management routines.* These SVC processing routines are used by Job Management during job step initiation and termination to catalog or uncatalog data sets used during the job step.
3. *IO support processing routines.* These SVC processing routines perform open processing, close processing, and end-of-volume processing. As part of their normal function, IO support processing routines insure proper volume mounting, construct tables and control blocks, and cause access method routines to be loaded.
4. *IO processing routines.* IO processing operations are performed in two parts: (1) Problem state routines (i.e., access methods) that prepare control information required by the IO supervisor to start an IO operation; and (2) Supervisor state routines (i.e., the IO supervisor) that initiate and control IO operations.

The structure of an IO processing operation is suggested by Fig. 6.14.

All Data Management routines are loaded from SYS1.SVCLIB. SVC processing routines operate in the supervisor state from either the link pack area or the SVC transient area. Access methods operate in the problem state from the link pack area or the region of a task. The IO supervisor is part of the nucleus and operates as a Supervisor routine.

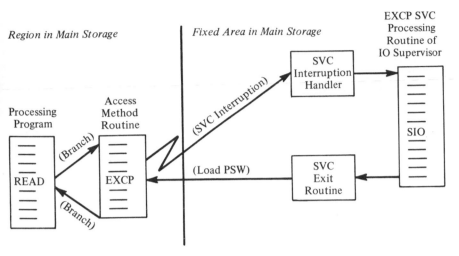

Fig. 6.14 Structure of an IO processing operation. (READ and EXCP are macro instructions.)

Remarks on Control Program Structure

It is cumbersome to describe the structure of control programs without referring to the tables, lists, and control blocks that are built and used. Stated briefly, control program routines can be viewed as "mini" processors that operate on tables and lists, modifying them, and creating new ones. Tables, lists, and control blocks are presented in Chapter 8, which gives an overview of how the system operates.

No attempt has been made here to describe all control program routines. For example, volume management and recovery management have not been mentioned. The viewpoint is pedagogical, and toward that end, topics of most significance are covered.

6.5 OPTIONS AND FACILITIES

This section presents a collection of topics that provide background material for Chapters 7 and 8 and for operating systems in general. Several of the topics provide "food for thought" since the manner in which they are used depends upon a particular operational environment; others are included simply to give evidence as to the "state of the art" in operating systems technology.

Checkpoint/Restart

One of the problems with long-running jobs is the possibility of a failure late in the run, due to program or system failure, such that a significant amount of processing time is lost. A means of minimizing risk of this type is to take a checkpoint. Actually, the term *checkpoint* has two meanings:

1. It is the point in the execution of a job step at which execution can be restarted.
2. It is the process of recording the status of a job step (storage contents, registers, data set positioning, etc.) so that it can be restarted upon demand.

When a checkpoint is taken, a checkpoint data set is written. That data set is used in a subsequent restart procedure. A checkpoint is specified with the assembler language macro instruction CHKPT; obviously, some points during program execution are more appropriate for a checkpoint than others. In general, this is the user's responsibility. With the CHKPT macro, the user can specify an automatic restart or a deferred restart.

Restart can be one of four types:

1. automatic step restart,
2. automatic checkpoint restart (restart at a checkpoint),
3. deferred step restart, and
4. deferred checkpoint restart (restart at a checkpoint).

A restart definition (RD) parameter exists for the JOB and EXEC job control statements. The RD parameter operates in conjunction with the CHKPT macro and controls automatic restart.

If the RD parameter specifies *restart:*

1. The job step is automatically restarted from the beginning if failure occurs (no CHKPT need be taken).
2. However, if CHKPT is executed, a restart is performed from the point of checkpoint (unless deferred). A CHKPT overrides automatic step restart.

If the RD parameter specifies *no automatic restart:*

1. The job step is not automatically restarted from the beginning.
2. The automatic restart specified with the CHKPT is not performed. However, that checkpoint can be used for a deferred restart.

If the RD parameter specifies *no checkpoint:*

1. No automatic step restart is performed.
2. The action of the CHKPT macro is suppressed. (Thus, a program that includes the CHKPT macro can be executed when the checkpoint is not desired.)

If the RD parameter specifies *restart and no checkpoint:*

1. Automatic step restart from the beginning is performed if failure occurs.
2. However, the execution the CHKPT macro is completely suppressed.

```
//JOB1 JOB MSGLEVEL=1,RD=R
//STEPA EXEC . . .
       —
       —
       —
//STEPB EXEC . . .
       —
       —
       —
```

Fig. 6.15 Specification of an automatic step restart for any job step that fails.


```
//JOB1 JOB MSGLEVEL=1
//STEPA EXEC . . .
       —
       —
       —
//STEPB EXEC PGM=PROGB,RD=R
       —
       —
       —
```

Fig. 6.16 Specification of an automatic step restart for job step STEPB, if it fails during execution.

Finally, if the RD parameter is not used on a JOB card or the EXEC card of the job step in which a failure occurs, checkpoint/restart is governed by the execution of the CHKPT macro (if it has been executed). If no RD parameter is given and no CHKPT macro is executed, then a checkpoint is not taken and an automatic restart is not performed. Figures 6.15 and 6.16 give two simple examples of automatic step restart.

A *deferred restart* is initiated with the RESTART parameter on the JOB card for a job step that was terminated abnormally. A *deferred step restart* is the restart of a job at the beginning of a specified job step. A deferred step restart is actually a resubmission of a job; the user must provide the correct operating environment (i.e., data sets, etc.) for the execution of that step. Figure 6.17 depicts original and resubmitted decks for a deferred step restart.

A *deferred checkpoint restart* allows a job step to be restarted at the point at which a specific checkpoint was taken. The data set on which the checkpoint was taken must be specified with the resubmitted deck along with the identifier of the checkpoint. When the RESTART parameter is used with a deferred checkpoint restart, both the step and the checkpoint identifier must be specified. Figure 6.18 gives an example of a deferred checkpoint restart.

```
//JOB1 JOB MSGLEVEL=1
//STEPA EXEC PGM=PROGA ...
    —
    —
    —
//STEPB EXEC PGM=PROGB ...    (Step that is terminated abnormally)
    —
    —
    —
```

Original Deck


```
//JOB1 JOB MSGLEVEL=1,RESTART=STEPB
//STEPA EXEC PGM=PROGA ...
    —
    —
    —
//STEPB EXEC PGM=PROGB ...    (Step to be restarted)
    —
    —
    —
```

Resubmitted Deck

Fig. 6.17 Deferred step restart (STEPB) for a job step that was terminated abnormally (no checkpoint taken).

Roll Out/Roll In

Normally, a processing program is assigned main storage from its region, and if insufficient main storage is available, the job step is abnormally terminated. The ROLL parameter used on a JOB or EXEC card permits additional main storage to be obtained.

If the ROLL parameter is used and a job step requires more main storage than was requested in the REGION parameter, the roll out/roll in routines attempt to assign additional main storage from the dynamic area. If insufficient main storage is available in the dynamic area, then another job step with a lower priority may have to be temporarily transferred to secondary storage; the process is referred to as *roll out*. The job step requesting the additional space is assigned space from the main storage area occupied by the job step that was rolled out. Later, when the additional space is no longer needed, the job step that was rolled out is read back into main storage to continue execution.

The ROLL parameter is used on a JOB or EXEC card (in the operand field) and takes the following form:

$$ROLL=(x,y)$$

```
//JOB1 JOB MSGLEVEL=1,RD=NR      (No restart can occur)
//STEPA EXEC PGM=PROGA
    —
    —
    —
//STEPB EXEC PGM=PROGB      (Includes CHKPT macro)
//DD1 DD DSNAME=CHKDS       (Checkpoint data set)
    —
    —
```

Original Deck

```
//JOB1 JOB MSGLEVEL=1,RESTART=(STEPB,CHKO1)      (Restart at point
                                                  CHKO1 in
                                                  step B)
//SYSCHK DD DSNAME=CHKDS      (Checkpoint data set containing CHKO1)
//STEPA EXEC PGM=PROGA . . .
    —
    —
    —
//STEPB EXEC PGM=PROGB . . .      (Step to be restarted)
//DD1 DD DSNAME=CHKDS      (Included for additional checkpoints)
    —
    —
    —
```

Resubmitted Deck

Fig. 6.18 Deferred checkpoint restart (STEPB at CHKO1) for a job step that was terminated abnormally (checkpoint taken on data set CHKDS).

The value x pertains to the job containing the ROLL parameter; if x is YES, then steps of that job can be rolled out. If x is NO, then the steps of that job cannot be rolled out. The value y determines whether additional main storage (i.e., of the region) can be requested. If y is YES, additional storage may be obtained from the dynamic area; if main storage is not available in the dynamic area, then a lower-priority job step can be rolled out. In short, if y is YES, then the job can cause roll out. If y is NO, then the job cannot cause roll out and main storage space over the allocated region cannot be assigned. For example, the JOB statement:

```
//JOB1 JOB ROLL=(NO,YES),REGION=80K
```

specifies that the job cannot be rolled out but can cause roll out of another job step if more than 80K of main storage is required.

Main Storage Hierarchy

Main storage hierarchy refers to the utilization of main storage and large-capacity storage (LCS) in a single computer system. LCS is a logical extension to main storage and is directly addressable by an executing program. Access time to LCS is slower than main storage so that the CPU is essentially operating in a degraded state when executing a program "out of LCS." In many cases, however, executing a routine "out of LCS" is preferred to bringing it into main storage since the overhead involved is not justified. In a sense, the effective utilization of LCS is an alternate to overlay in some cases.

In order to use LCS, the user must do two things:

1. reserve the required amount of LCS; and
2. specify how LCS should be used.

LCS is reserved with the REGION parameter on the JOB or EXEC card; it takes the form:

$$REGION=(v_1K,v_2K)$$

where v_1 specifies the number of contiguous 1024-byte areas in main storage; v_2 specifies the number of contiguous 1024-byte areas in LCS. Thus if a user entered the following job card:[†]

$$//JOB1\ JOB\ REGION=(100K,200K)$$

he would be requesting 100K bytes of main storage and 200K bytes of LCS. (OS takes care of the case when the user requests LCS, but it is not included in the system configuration; he is assigned additional main storage that may be discontiguous to that requested with the v_1 parameter.)

LCS is normally used in two ways: (1) by placing sections of load modules there for execution; and (2) for the dynamic allocation of storage in response to GETMAIN and GETPOOL macro instructions.

If a user desires that a section of a load module be executed out of LCS, he specifies to the linkage editor that LCS be used with a linkage editor control statement. When that program is subsequently loaded, the appropriate sections are scatter loaded to main storage and to LCS. Similarly, when storage is requested dynamically, one of the parameters to the GETMAIN or GETPOOL macro instruction specifies the hierarchy of storage that is desired.

Block and Scatter Loading

Block loading refers to the practice of placing a load module into a contiguous area of main storage. Ordinarily, block loading is used when sufficient contiguous storage exists within the user's region. If sufficient contiguous storage does

---

[†]"K" refers to 1024 bytes of main storage; thus, 4K is equivalent to 4096 bytes.

not exist in a user's region to block load a load module, then the sections of that load module are scatter loaded by the Supervisor. *Scatter loading* refers to the practice of placing the sections of a load module in discontiguous areas of main storage.

When a load module is produced by the linkage editor, it is normally in block format, which means that it cannot be scatter loaded. The user can specify a scatter format with a parameter that is passed to the linkage editor by Job Management, as follows:

//LKED EXEC PGM=IEWL,PARM='SCTR,...'

where IEWL is the program name of the linkage editor and SCTR specifies scatter format. If a load module is produced in scatter format, then it can be block or scatter loaded depending upon the status of a user's region.

If main storage hierarchy is specified for a load module, then the load module must be produced in scatter format so that it can be effectively scatter loaded by the Supervisor to main storage and large-capacity storage.

Private and Public Storage

One of the basic concepts in operating systems technology is whether on-line auxiliary storage is for public use or for private use. The problem becomes significant when it is remembered that a direct-access volume can be used concurrently by more than one job. The extensive use of public storage and the system catalog frees the user of concern over the management of storage volumes. The use of private storage permits the user to control his storage volumes directly. Auxiliary storage is managed on a volume basis.

Each volume is assigned a "mount" attribute and a "use" attribute. The *mount attribute* controls when and how the volume is demounted. The *use attribute* determines the manner in which data sets are assigned to volumes. The mount attributes are:

1. *Permanently resident*—volumes that cannot be demounted. This category includes system control volumes and volumes that cannot be physically demounted (such as a drum).
2. *Reserved*—volumes that remain mounted until an UNLOAD operator command is issued. A volume is reserved with the MOUNT operator command to avoid excessive mounting and demounting between tasks and job steps.
3. *Removable*—volumes that are removed when the job step using them is completed or the associated device is needed for another purpose.

Before the use attribute is presented, an important concept is necessary. When a user refers to an auxiliary storage volume, he can denote a specific volume or any volume (referred to as a nonspecific volume). For example, the user may not specifically care where a temporary data set is placed. On the other hand, a particular data file may reside on a given volume and he may wish to use that file. In the first case, a user might use a nonspecific volume, and in the second case, he would request a specific volume. An example of a DD card requesting a specific volume is given as follows:

```
//ABC   DD   DSNAME=JONES,UNIT=2311,DISP=OLD,
             VOLUME=(PRIVATE,,,SER=683201)
```

The *use attributes* are:

1. *Public*—a volume that the system can allocate to a nonspecific request for a temporary data set. A public volume can be used for a permanent or a cataloged data set only when a specific volume request is made.
2. *Private*—a volume that is designed to a specific user. A private volume is not used for the allocation of temporary data sets. A specific volume request must be made to use an existing private volume. When a user requests a nonspecific private volume (for a new data set), the operator is requested to mount a new volume.
3. *Storage*—a volume used for nonspecific volume requests when PRIVATE is not used. Storage volumes are considered as an extension to main storage and are used for temporary and nontemporary data sets.
4. *Scratch*—a magnetic tape volume used for temporary data sets. If the PRIVATE attribute is used or the data set is nontemporary, the volume becomes private.

When a user defines a data set with a DD card, he specifies (explicitly or implicitly) a mount attribute and a use attribute. It is up to the installation to determine how many public volumes are permanently mounted for temporary data sets and how many storage volumes are permanently mounted for temporary and nontemporary data sets. The catalog is also of concern and can overflow the SYSRES control volume and must be moved to a separate public volume that is permanently mounted.

In general, a public volume is usually permanently mounted and is shared among several users. It is frequently referred to as *public storage*. A private volume is usually removable and its use is restricted to a single user or group of users working cooperatively. It is frequently referred to as *private storage*.

Event Control

In a multiprogramming environment, the need to synchronize events rises out of multitasking and overlapped IO. Events are synchronized through the use of an "event control block." An *event control block* (ECB) is a word in main storage established by the user. (The precise format of the ECB is not necessary for this presentation.) An event is established in one of two ways:

1. A macro instruction such as ATTACH, READ, or WRITE is executed that implies event synchronization.

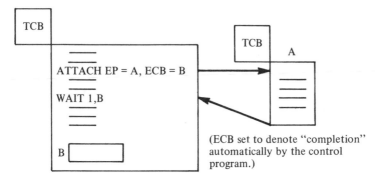

Fig. 6.19   An example of event synchronization.

2. Event synchronization is specified explicitly with the WAIT macro instruction.

After the event has occurred, the ECB for that event is set to denote "completion" by a POST macro instruction. After the ECB is set to denote "completion," the requesting task can proceed past the WAIT point. An event control block can be POSTed by a control program routine or by a user program. Two obvious examples of automatic POSTing by a control program routine involve subtasking and input/output. A subtask created with an ATTACH macro with the ECB parameter causes that ECB to be set to "completion" automatically by the control program when the subtask terminates. (See Fig. 6.19.) Similarly, the completion of an IO operation automatically causes an ECB for that IO operation to be set to denote "completion."

Time Slicing

Another feature that is frequently available with advanced multiprogrammed operating systems is a time slicing option. Normally, a task loses control of the CPU through one of the following: task completion, a higher-priority task becoming ready, or a wait condition. Thus, certain types of tasks can monopolize CPU time if none of the above conditions arises. Time slicing permits each task in a time slice group (i.e., a collection of tasks with the same priority) to have control of the CPU for a short burst of time, called a *time slice*. A time slice group loses control of the CPU when a higher-priority task not in the time slice group becomes ready for execution. Time slicing pertains to the execution of processing programs.

Other Topics

A variety of other options exists in OS/MVT that are beyond the scope of this book. However, several of these topics are of academic and practical interest and make good assignments (see the problems for Part Two).

Multiprocessing refers to two interconnected CPUs sharing the same main storage and most IO devices. The two CPUs execute distinct processing programs concurrently; they share the same control program routines. This feature increases the reliability, availability, and throughput of the system. When two CPUs attempt to use the same control program routine simultaneously, one of them is locked out until the other has completed the use of the routine (called software lockout). Witt [Wit68] discusses OS/360 multiprocessing and Madnick [Mad68] discusses software lockout.

System generation refers to the process of modifying a "starter" operating system to operate on a specific computer system configuration to meet the operational requirements of a given installation. *Accounting facilities* record operational statistics for each job so that users can be billed appropriately. *Graphics support* refers to the use of graphic input and output devices as an adjunct to normal system functions. *Time sharing option* (TSO) refers to an "open" time sharing facility that augments conventional system functions such as batch processing, telecommunications, and graphics. TSO creates a time sharing environment in a batch processing oriented system. A variety of other facilities require operating system support: use of the interval timer, shared direct-access storage devices among different CPUs, and teleprocessing—to name only a few. The reader is directed to the bibliography and references for information on these important topics.

7 | SYSTEM UTILIZATION

7.1 INTRODUCTION

Although this book is not intended as a user's guide to a particular operating system, the basic concepts of system utilization are required since the system operates in response to users' requests for service. This chapter covers two topics: data management and job control language.

Data Management is concerned with record formats, interface with the operating system, data set description, access methods, buffering, and indexed sequential input/output processing.

Job control language is concerned with the input job stream, job control, data definition, parameters, and cataloged procedures.

7.2 DATA MANAGEMENT

The data set naming capability together with the system catalog and the property of device independence allow the user to store and classify data according to his installation's needs. In general, these facilities use the DSCB and VTOC features† mentioned previously and frequently require the system catalog and the Data Management routines for using the catalog.

Data sets are organized according to the manner in which they are used. Under OS, four methods of data set organization are identified: (1) sequential, (2) in-

---

†DSCB and VTOC are acronyms for Data Set Control Block and Volume Table of Contents, respectively.

dexed sequential, (3) direct, and (4) partitioned. Each method of organization has been introduced previously. In general, *sequential organization* is used with magnetic tape and direct-access devices, and a considerable amount of device independence is permitted. *Indexed sequential, direct,* and *partitioned organization* are available for use on direct-access devices only. This section is primarily concerned with how data records are formatted and how they are accessed. Data record format is essentially independent of the method of organization; method of access is not.

Basic knowledge of the concepts of volumes, catalogs, libraries, data sets, and input and output is generally assumed.

Data Record Formats

The concept of a data record format is introduced in chapter 4. This section presents a concrete example of data record formats in an advanced multiprogrammed operating system.

A data set is a collection of data records stored on a storage volume as a series of blocks separated by inter-record gaps. Each block consists of one or more data records (also referred to as logical records). The process of grouping data records to form a block (also referred to as a physical record) is called *blocking*; the reverse process is called *deblocking*.

In many cases, record formats are an operational consideration. When using the FORTRAN language, for example, record formatting is done with control cards and the user has very little concern over the machine language operations that take place. A specific record format is selected for efficiency or to conserve storage. When programming in assembler language, however, the user must be concerned with record formats since he is required to program many of the housekeeping chores necessary for a particular set of IO functions.

The size of fixed-length data records is constant for every record in a data set; the size of each block is also constant except for a short block that may exist at the end of a data set. Fixed-length records are depicted in Fig. 7.1. The size of a data record is called *logical record size*; the size of a block is called *block size*. When each block contains a single logical record, the data set is regarded as unblocked. The first character of a data record is often interpreted as a control character by a particular IO operation. (The control character is frequently used for carriage control with print files.)

Many applications require variable-length data records. (The decision to use variable-length records is actually one of systems design and involves a trade-off between the cost of carrying unused data bytes in a fixed-length record versus the overhead required with variable-length records.) A variable-length block consists of a *block descriptor word* (BDW) followed by one or more data records or segments of data records. The BDW occupies 4 bytes and gives the length of the block. (For basic access the user must supply the BDW; for queued access,

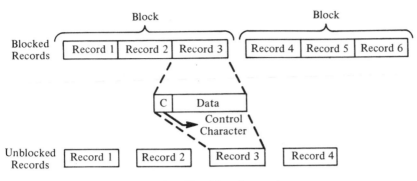

Fig. 7.1 Fixed-length records.

the access method provides the BDW for the user. Basic and queued access are covered later.) Each data record is composed of a 4-byte *record descriptor word* (RDW) followed by the data. Variable-length records are depicted in Fig. 7.2. When generating variable-length records, the user is required to provide the maximum block size and the maximum record size.

Undefined-length records are defined for data sets that do not conform to fixed-length or variable-length specifications. Fig. 7.3 depicts undefined-length records. Blocking and deblocking must be performed by the user when undefined-length records are used.

Spanned records exist in two principal forms. They can be defined *in* a processing program to adhere to a convention established by the user or they can be defined to the data management system. (OS recognizes only one type of spanned record; it is used with variable-length records of "basic direct" data sets.

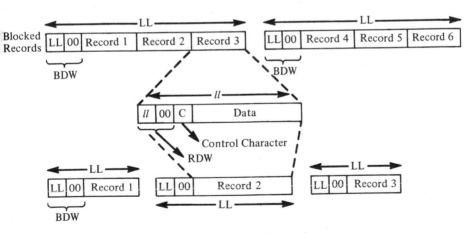

Fig. 7.2 Variable-length records.

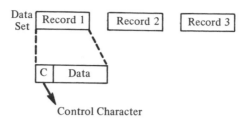

Fig. 7.3 Undefined-length records.

The reader is directed to reference [OSc] for additional information on spanned records.)

Data Control Block

The primary method of communication between a processing program and the Data Management routines of the operating system is a storage block in the processing program called a *data control block* (DCB). A DCB is required for each data set used by a program. In assembler language, a data control block is created with the DCB macro. When using a programming language, the DCB is generated by the compiler.

The purpose of the DCB is to describe the characteristics of the data set. Information for the DCB is supplied in three ways:

1. It is preassembled into the DCB;
2. from the DD statement for that data set; and
3. from the data set label for that data set (the data set control block—DSCB— in the case of direct-access storage).

Since the DCB is a storage area in a program, the various fields in it can be modified dynamically during program execution. (In fact, the execution of the OPEN macro causes the DCB to be completed dynamically.)

One of the most significant advantages of using the DCB concept is that it allows data set independence. This is the case since data set description information can be supplied to the DCB at run time with the DD statement.

Data Set Description

Each data set used in a program requires a DCB, and in addition, a DD statement. Information for the DCB can be supplied from either source or the data set label, if the data set existed previous to the job step. The correspondence between a DD statement and a DCB is made by using the DDNAME of the DD statement in the DCB macro instruction. For example, a DCB macro of the form:

location	*operation*	*operand*
SAMPDCB	DCB	DDNAME=MTAPE,DSORG=PS,...

is logically associated with a DD statement of the form:

//MTAPE DD DSNAME=MFILE,...

A data set is described by the following 28 parameters that are contained in the DCB:

Buffer alignment (BFALN)
Buffering technique (BFTEK)
Block size (BLKSIZE)
Buffer pool control block (BUFCB)
Buffer length (BUFLN)
Buffer number (BUFNO)
Cylinder overflow tracks (CYLO)
Data definition name (DDNAME)
Device type (DEVD)
Data set organization (DSORG)
End of data exit address (EODAD)
Error options for uncorrectable IO errors (EROPT)
Problem program exit list (EXLST)
Buffer pool storage hierarchy (HIARCHY)
Data set key length (KEYLEN)
Direct-access search limit in tracks (LIMCT)
Logical record length (LRECL)
Macro instruction and facilities (MACRF)
Master index location for indexed sequential (MSHI)
Work area location (MSWA)
Number of READ or WRITE macro executions before CHECK (NCP)
Number of tracks in master index/cylinder (NTM)
Optional control program services (OPTCD)
Record format (RECFM)
Relative key position (RKP)
Size of main storage for highest-level index of data set (SMSI)
Size of main storage work area (SMSW)—see MSWA
Error exit address (SYNAD)

Each parameter is not described, although several are referenced later in the chapter. Collectively, the parameters are indicative of the information necessary to describe and process a data set.

Open and Close

The operations necessary for preparing a data set for processing are independent of the functions involved with preparing a load module for execution. In many programs, several data sets are defined but only a few are used in any given computer run. Therefore, the convention of readying data sets for processing only when they are going to be used reduces the amount of system overhead and lessens the work load of the system operator.

A data set is readied for processing when it is opened. *Open* is a data management function, performed in the supervisor state by an SVC routine, that performs the following functions:

1. completes the data control block;
2. loads the required access routines (if necessary) into the user's region;
3. requests volume mounting;
4. initiates data set processing by checking old labels or writing new labels and control information; and
5. constructs the system control blocks and buffers necessary for IO processing and performs data set positioning.

Open is initiated by the execution of the OPEN macro instruction, which takes the form:

location	*operation*	*operand*
[symbol]	OPEN	(DCB-address, ...)

The key point is that the address of a data control block (DCB) is given which describes a data set to be opened. (The OPEN macro expands to an SVC instruction that invokes an SVC processing routine.) This is where the DDNAME comes in. The OPEN routine searches a chain of job file control blocks (JFCBs) built by Job Management when it processes a DD card.[†] OPEN then performs the DCB merge suggested by Fig. 7.4 to complete the DCB. The DCB merge is shown in more detail in Fig. 7.5. After the DCB merge is complete, the JFCB is updated (to reflect the updated DCB). The JFCB is used to create a "new" data set label and also during CLOSE processing. After the DCB merge and JFCB merge, the appropriate access routine is determined and loaded (if necessary). Input/output buffers are created and channel command words (CCWs)[‡] are created for the particular IO operations to be used. The addresses of the access routine, the buffers, and the CCW list are placed in the DCB for use during IO processing, and in the case of queued access, an input buffer is also primed. Input/output program flow is suggested by Fig. 7.6.

When IO processing is complete, a data set must be closed. The close operation (initiated with the CLOSE macro) empties IO buffers, completes the data set label, and handles the disposition of the data set. CLOSE also restores the DCB to its original state so that it can be used again.

[†]The JFCB is covered in Chapter 8. Unfortunately, operating systems are sufficiently complex that it is not feasible to define all terms prior to their use.

[‡]A channel command word (CCW) is an IO command that is passed to the data channel for execution. Typical channel commands are read, write, seek, and sense.

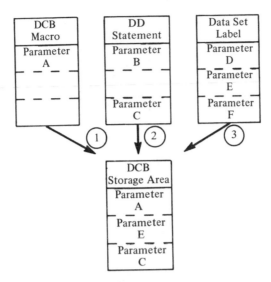

Fig. 7.4 Conceptual view of the DCB merge. (The DCB takes priority over the DD statement that takes priority over the data set label.)

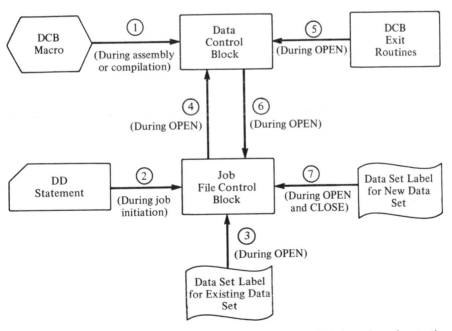

Fig. 7.5 Source of information for the DCB merge. (The circled numbers denote the order in which functions are performed.)

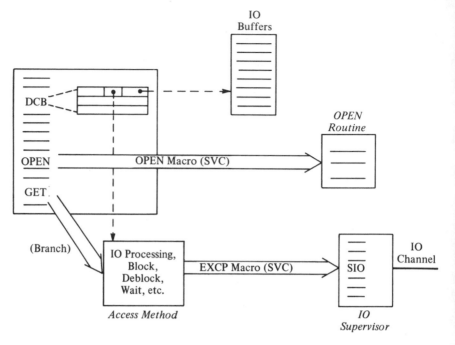

Fig. 7.6   Conceptual view of program flow during IO operations.

Access Methods

The characteristics of a data set as described in the DCB determine the access method that is assigned during OPEN. An access method is the combination of data set organization and a technique used to access the data.

Two data access techniques are defined: queued and basic. The *queued access* technique provides automatic blocking and deblocking on data transfers between main storage and IO devices. Queued access also provides look-ahead buffering and automatic synchronization of IO operation and CPU processing. The access method routine controls the use of buffers such that sufficient input blocks are in main storage at one time to prevent the delay of CPU processing. The GET macro instruction is used for input and the PUT macro instruction is used for output. When using queued access, the user need not test for IO completion, errors, or exceptional conditions. After the execution of a GET or PUT macro instruction, control is not returned to the processing program until the operation is logically complete. Buffering techniques are discussed in the next section.

The *basic access* technique does not provide automatic blocking and deblocking; neither does it provide anticipatory buffering or automatic event synchronization. Basic access is used when the sequence in which records are processed

TABLE 7.1   ACCESS METHODS

| Data Set | Data Access Techniques | |
Organization	Basic	Queued
Sequential	BSAM	QSAM
Partitioned	BPAM	
Indexed sequential	BISAM	QISAM
Direct	BDAM	

cannot be predicted in advance. With the basic access technique, the user must perform his own blocking and deblocking. The READ macro instruction is used for input and the WRITE macro instruction is used for output. READ and WRITE macros only initiate IO processing; both operations must be checked for completion with the CHECK macro. In other words, automatic event synchronization is not provided.

The access techniques are combined with data set organization to determine access methods. The basic access technique is used with all forms of data set organization; queued access is used only with sequential and indexed sequential organization. Six access methods are given in the following list and summarized in Table 7.1:

Basic Sequential Access Method (BSAM)
Basic Partitioned Access Method (BPAM)
Basic Index Sequential Access Method (BISAM)
Basic Direct Access Method (BDAM)
Queued Sequential Access Method (QSAM)
Queued Indexed Sequential Access Method (QISAM)

The processing of each of the above access methods is performed by an access method routine. Each routine uses the data set description in the DCB to control IO processing.

Additional function exists. First, additional capabilities exist through access methods which have not been described. Next, telecommunications and graphics are supported by appropriate access methods. Last, the above access methods are designed for "normal" processing on "standard" devices. An execute channel program (EXCP) assembler language macro instruction is available for the user who desires to create his own channel program. EXCP uses conventional system functions for IO scheduling, interruption procedures, error handling, and special conditions.

Buffering

A *buffer* is a storage area used to compensate for a difference in operating speeds of two physical devices. In the case of data management in an operating system environment, an *input buffer* is an area of main storage used to hold input blocks prior to processing. Similarly, an *output buffer* is an area of main storage used to hold blocks prior to the output operation.

A collection of contiguous buffers is termed a *buffer pool*, which can be assigned to a single data set or to a group of data sets. A buffer pool is contructed in one of three ways:

1. by creating the necessary storage area in the processing program and by executing a macro instruction (the BUILD macro) that effectively connects the buffer pool to the appropriate data set(s);
2. by executing a GETPOOL macro instruction that requests that the operating system create the buffer pool (the buffer pool is subsequently released with the FREEPOOL macro instruction); and
3. by letting the operating system create the buffer pool automatically when the data set is opened.

When *basic access* is used, buffers are controlled in two ways:

1. A buffer is obtained *directly* from a buffer pool with the GETBUF macro and returned with the FREEBUF macro. That buffer is subsequently used with a READ or WRITE operation.
2. A buffer is obtained *dynamically* by requesting a buffer with the READ or WRITE macro instruction.

When *queued access* is used, buffering achieves its greatest utility. Three transmittal modes are defined:

1. *Move mode*—the record is moved to the program's work area or from the work area to an output buffer.
2. *Locate mode*—the record is not moved but the address of the buffer holding the input record is placed in a general-purpose register (for input) or the address of the next output buffer is placed in a general-purpose register (for output).
3. *Substitute mode*—the record is not moved; the address of the next input or output buffer is interchanged with the address of the current work area.

The transmittal modes are used to form two fundamental buffering techniques: simple buffering and exchange buffering.

With *simple buffering*, the buffers in a buffer pool are associated with a single data set. A channel command (word) is associated with each buffer so that each record must be moved from an input buffer to an output buffer. Processing can be performed in either buffer or in a work area. Four cases of simple buffering are identified: GET(move)/PUT(move), GET(locate)/PUT(locate), GET(locate)/PUT(move), GET(move)/PUT(locate).

GET(move)/PUT(move) is depicted in Fig. 7.7. The GET macro instruction

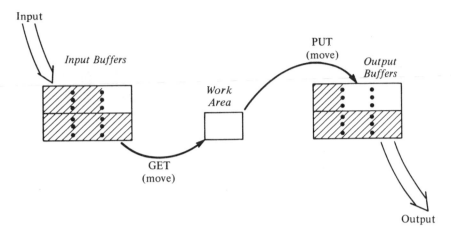

Fig. 7.7 Simple buffering—GET (move)/PUT (move).

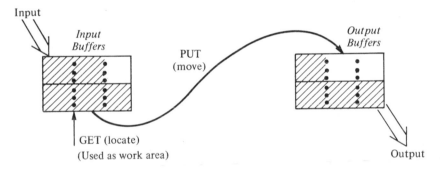

Fig. 7.8 Simple buffering—GET (locate)/PUT (move).

specifies the address of a work area into which the access method moves the next record from the input buffer. The PUT macro specifies the address of a work area from which the access method moves the output record into the next output buffer. *GET(locate)/PUT(move)* is depicted in Fig. 7.8. The GET macro locates the next input record in an input buffer. (The address is passed in a general-purpose register.) The PUT macro specifies the address of the output record (usually in an input buffer) from which the access method moves the output record into the next output buffer. *GET(move)/PUT(locate)* is depicted in Fig. 7.9. The preceding PUT macro locates the address of the next available output buffer segment. (The address is passed in a general-purpose register.) The GET macro specifies the address of the next output buffer into which the access method moves the next record from the input buffer. *GET(locate)/*

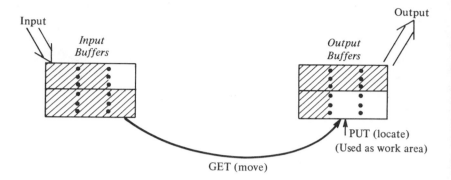

Fig. 7.9   Simple buffering—GET (move)/PUT (locate).

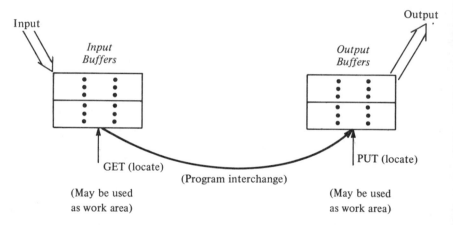

Fig. 7.10   Simple buffering—GET (locate)/PUT (locate).

PUT(locate) is depicted in Fig. 7.10. The preceding PUT macro locates the address of the next available output buffer segment. The GET macro locates the next input record in an input buffer. The processing program moves the data from the input buffer to the output buffer. Processing can be performed in either buffer.

With *exchange buffering*, the segments of a buffer are not necessarily contiguous in main storage and are not always assigned to the same data set. The substitute transmittal mode is used for input or output or both. Exchange buffering eliminates the need to move the record. Fig. 7.11 depicts exchange buffering of the form *GET(substitute)/PUT(substitute)*. In step 1, the GET macro specifies the address of a work area which is essentially an unused buffer. The address of the work area is exchanged by the access method for the address of the

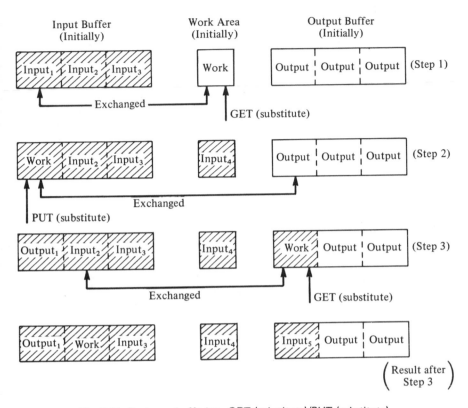

Fig. 7.11 Exchange buffering—GET (substitute)/PUT (substitute).

next input record, which can be processed in the input buffer. In step 2, the PUT macro specifies the address of the output record and receives the address of an empty buffer in return. Step 3 is a repetition of step 1 with different buffer areas. As exchange buffering operates, the roles of the buffer areas are constantly changing.

The management of buffers using the substitute mode is essentially a problem of managing queues of buffers implemented as linked lists. Five queues are involved: input queue, processing input queue, work queue (usually one buffer), processing output queue, and output queue. (Implementation of this technique or a variation to it is a useful exercise.) The substitute mode is frequently combined with the move and locate modes to provide a considerable amount of processing flexibility.

Several fields in the DCB concern buffering. MACRF determines the buffer processing mode; and BFALN, BFTEK, BUFCB, BUFLN, and BUFNO describe the characteristics of the buffers. This is the means by which the user tells the access method how he wants his IO processed. Here is where the DD card comes into use. The DCB merge that is performed at OPEN time enables the user to specify his buffering needs with the DD statement at the time the job step is run.

Indexed Sequential

The indexed sequential method of data set organization is of special concern since it allows the data set to be processed directly or sequentially. Records can be inserted or deleted, and basic or queued access can be used. The defining characteristic of an indexed sequential data set is that the records are arranged, by collating sequence, according to a *key field* contained in each record. Indexes of keys are maintained to provide direct or sequential access.

An indexed sequential data set must reside on a direct-access storage volume. As any other data set, it possesses a data set control block (DSCB) stored in the volume table of contents (VTOC) for that volume. Each indexed sequential data can use three different storage areas:

1. The *prime area*—contains data records and track indexes. The prime area is always used.
2. The *overflow area*—contains overflow from the prime area when new records are added to the data set. Use of the overflow area is optional.
3. The *index area*—contains master and cylinder indexes for the data set and is used when the data set occupies more than one cylinder (see Chapter 3).

The access to records is managed through indexes. When records are written in the prime area, the system keeps record of the highest key (i.e., the last record) for each track and forms a track index—one entry per track. There is a track index for each cylinder of the data set. If the data set occupies more than one cylinder, then a *cylinder index* exists for each cylinder; each entry in the cylinder index reflects the key of the last record in the cylinder. A *master index* is developed for groups of cylinders to increase the speed of searching the cylinder index. An indexed sequential data set is depicted conceptually in Fig. 7.12.

The *track index* contains one entry for each track of a cylinder. Each track index entry includes a normal entry and an overflow entry. Initially, the normal and overflow entries are the same. When an overflow is associated with a track (due to an insert operation), the overflow entry contains the key of the highest overflow record and the address of the lowest overflow record associated with that track. A track index is generated automatically for each cylinder.

As each track index is generated, the system creates a cylinder index entry. If more than one cylinder index entry is created, then a *cylinder index* is formed. The *master index* is optional; the user can specify the number of tracks of the cylinder index that correspond to a master index entry.

As far as access is concerned, both queued and basic are defined. The queued index sequential access method (QISAM) is used to create an indexed sequential data set and add records to the end. The basic indexed sequential access method

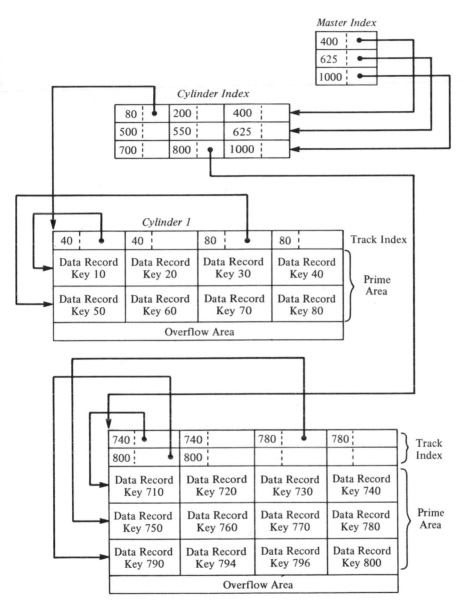

Fig. 7.12 Conceptual view of indexed sequential data set organization.

(BISAM) is used to insert new records, update old records, and access records directly. Both QISAM and BISAM can be used to access the data set sequentially. QISAM is more efficient when large amounts of data are being read sequentially. Blocked records are permitted and the system automatically precedes each block with the key of the last record (i.e., with the highest key) in the block.

Comments on Data Management

The reader should be cautioned against unconsciously thinking that OS data management facilities are limited to those presented in the preceding discussion. Direct and partitioned access methods have not been described and a multitude of control and housekeeping functions have not even been mentioned. Additional IO macro instructions also exist.

Data management is a complicated area. Most computer manufacturers' reference manuals give this area excellent coverage because of its complexity. Reference [OSc] entitled *Data Management Services* is exceptionally useful because of its clarity and completeness. Books on the subject are scarce; however, Flores [Flo70] and Thomas [Tho71] both cover the structure and programming of OS data management.

7.3 JOB CONTROL LANGUAGE

Job control language (JCL) is the user's primary method of interfacing with the operating system. This subject has been introduced previously (Chapter 6), and the intent here is to give some idea of the functional capability available with JCL.

OS job control is practically a field of study in its own right. In fact, at least three authors (Brown [Bro70], Cadow [Cad70], and Flores [Flo71]) have written books on the subject.

The JOB Statement

The JOB statement initiates a job and provides the system with the following information:

1. name of job (jobname field),
2. accounting information (positional parameter in operand field),
3. user's name (positional parameter in operand field), and
4. parameters (keyword parameters in operand field).

The general format of the JOB statement is:

//jobname JOB operands commends

For example,

//COW JOB 123,JONES,CLASS=A,REGION=100K

The parameters are of prime concern; they govern the manner in which jobs are processed. The parameters are: job class, conditional execution, message class, message level, notify (for time sharing), job priority, restart definition, region size, restart execution, roll (for roll out/roll in) time, and run type. These parameters are summarized in Table 7.2.

TABLE 7.2 JOB STATEMENT PARAMETERS

Parameter	Positional or Keyword	Function
Accounting information	1	Provides accounting information to system.
User's name	2	Identifies user.
Job class	CLASS =	Assigns a job class.
Conditional execution	COND =	Specifies conditions that terminate job execution.
Message class	MSGCLASS =	Specifies output routine for system messages.
Message level	MSGLEVEL =	Specifies JCL information that should be printed.
Notify	NOTIFY =	Requests message sent to time sharing terminal.
Job priority	PRTY =	Specifies job priority.
Restart definition	RD =	Controls automatic step restart and checkpoint processing.
Region size	REGION =	Specifies main storage and large-capacity storage requirements.
Restart control	RESTART =	Requests a restart of a job step.
Roll out/roll in	ROLL =	Permits and causes roll out (and subsequently roll in).
Time limit	TIME =	Specifies execution time limit for job.
Hold job execution	TYPRUN =	Postpones job execution until operator command.

The EXEC Statement

The EXEC statement is the first statement of a job step; it specifies a program to be executed or gives the name of a cataloged procedure. The EXEC statement takes the form:

//stepname EXEC operands comments

For example,

//A34T EXEC PGM=AMODT,TIME=6,REGION=120K

The "stepname" identifies the job step and allows it to be referenced in other JCL statements. Either one of two positional parameters is required: program name (PGM) or cataloged procedure name (PROC). Keyword parameters allow the following kinds of information to be provided to Job Management routines: accounting information, conditional execution, dispatching priority, parameters, restart definition, region size, roll out/roll in, and a time limit. These functions are summarized in Table 7.3.

The DD Statement

The data definition (DD) statement describes a data set to be used with a job step and may specify IO facilities required for using that data set. A DD statement must be present for each data set used in a job step. The DD cards for a job step follow the EXEC card. The format of the DD statement is:

//ddname DD operands comments

For example,

//ABL DD DSNAME=MFILE,UNIT-2314,
        DISP=(NEW,KEEP),SPACE=(CYL,(10,2))

The "ddname" logically connects the DD statement with the DCB of a data set. Parameters are coded in the "operand" field and serve to complete the DCB, specify device requirements, and supply control information. One of four positional parameters and a variety of keyword parameters can be used. DD statement parameters are summarized in Table 7.4. There is a considerable amount of function inherent in JCL and especially in the DD statement. OS was designed to provide a great deal of flexibility and functional capability. In a less complex operating system, many of the DD parameters would be assigned default values. A useful exercise for the reader is to attempt to determine (perhaps only hypothetically) a relationship between the percentage of functional capability and a given set of parameters.

DCB Subparameters

From an operational point of view, the most significant parameter of the DD statement is the DCB parameter. The DCB parameter is used to complete the

TABLE 7.3 EXEC STATEMENT PARAMETERS

Parameter	Positional or Keyword		Function
Program or procedure name[a]	PGM= or PROC= or Procedure name	} Positional	Specifies name of program or cataloged procedure.
Accounting information	ACCT=		Provides job step accounting information.
Conditional execution	COND=		Specifies conditions for bypassing job step.
Dispatching priority	DPRTY=		Assigns dispatching priority to job step.
Parameter	PARM=		Provides parameters to job step.
Restart definition	RD=		Controls automatic step restart and checkpoint processing.
Region size	REGION=		Specifies main and large-capacity storage to be allocated to the job step.
Roll out/roll in	ROLL=		Permits and causes roll out (and subsequently roll in).
Time limit	TIME=		Specifies execution time limit for job step.

[a]See "libraries" in this section.

TABLE 7.4 DD STATEMENT PARAMETERS

Parameter	Positional or Keyword	Function
Input data	* or DATA	Specifies that data following this statement are to be entered in the input stream.
Special input data	} Positional	Specifies that the input data following this statement may have // in columns 1 and 2.
Dummy data set	DUMMY or DYNAM	Creates a dummy data set (EOD returned when accessed). Specifies the dynamic allocation of data sets (used with time sharing option).
Affinity (to another address)	AFF=	Causes channel separation relative to other data sets.
Data control block	DCB=	Completes the DCB.
Reference to other ddname	DDNAME=	Postpones data definition.
Data set disposition	DISP=	Gives disposition of data set after job step is complete.
Data set name	DSNAME= or DSN	Specifies the data set name.

Forms control buffer	FCB=	Specifies an image for the forms control buffer (3211 printer).
Data set label	LABEL=	Describes the data set label.
System output limit	OUTLIM=	Specifies a limit for the number of records on the system output data set.
Teleprocessing data	QNAME=	Defines data to be accessed by telecommunications methods.
Separation	SEP=	Specifies channel separation.
DASD space allocation	SPACE=	Requests space allocation on DASD.
DASD space allocation	SPLIT=	Allocates DASD space among several cylinders.
DASD space allocation	SUBALLOC=	Specifies that DASD space should be allocated from another data set.
System output data set	SYSOUT=	Assigns a data set to a system output writer.
Terminal IO	TERM=	Specifies a time sharing terminal as an input or output device.
Universal character set	UCS=	Specifies a set of print characters.
IO unit	UNIT=	Specifies or indicates device type or unit address.
Volume specifications	VOLUME= or VOL=	Identifies an IO volume and supplies its attributes.

DCB and exists as an alternate means of specifying IO characteristics. Parameters that do not vary between "runs" of a program are placed in the DCB during assembly. Parameters that vary between "runs" and are established at run time are supplied via the DCB parameter. The DCB subparameters are listed in Section 7.1; any of the DCB fields can be assigned values with the DD statement. The general form of the DCB parameter is:

$$DCB=(\text{list of attributes})$$

or

$$DCB = (\left\{ \begin{array}{l} \text{dsname} \\ \text{*.ddname} \\ \text{*.stepname.ddname} \\ \text{*.stepname.procstepname.ddname} \end{array} \right\} \quad [,\text{list of attributes}])$$

where:

[ ]   denotes optional material;

{ }   denotes selection;

dsname specifies that DCB information should be copied from the data set label of the cataloged data set name "dsname";

*.ddname specifies that DCB information should be copied from an earlier DD statement in the job step;

*.stepname.ddname specifies that DCB information should be copied from an earlier DD statement in the named job step; and

*.stepname.procstepname.ddname specifies that DCB information should be copied from a job step in a cataloged procedure.

The most important concept to be gained here is that one DD statement can reference another DD statement—using one of the above forms (as in the third DD statement given below). Sample DD statements depicting the DCB parameter are listed as follows:

```
//ONE  DD  DSNAME=JOE,DISP=(NEW,CATLG),
           DCB=(RECFM=FB,LRECL=140,BLKSIZE=840),
           UNIT=2400

//TWO  DD  DSNAME=MIKE,DISP=OLD,DCB=(RECFM=FB,LRECL=80,
           BLKSIZE=400)

//THREE  DD  DSNAME=PETE,DISP=(NEW,KEEP),UNIT=2400,
             LABEL=(,SL),DCB=*.TWO
```

In the last case, the parentheses for the DCB parameter can be elided if one subparameter is used.

Values used with DD statement parameters are coded values. For example, RECFM=FB above denotes a record format that is "fixed blocked." Coded values are not considered here since they represent nominal conventions established during system development.

Control Statements

A variety of JCL statement types are defined to serve control and informational functions.

The *operator command* statement is written as

// command operand comments

For example,

// START READER

In OS/MVT, the following commands are defined: CANCEL, DISPLAY, HOLD, LOG, MODIFY, MOUNT, RELEASE, REPLY, RESET, SET, START, STOP, UNLOAD, VARY, and WRITELOG. Reference [OSi] should be consulted for a description of the functions performed by these commands.

The *comments* statement is coded as:

//* comment

and permits a comments card to be placed in the input job stream.

The *delimiter* statement is coded as

/* comments

and denotes end-of-data; for example:

```
//J1  JOB SMITH,A34T,MSGLEVEL=1
//S1  EXEC PGM=ABC
//D1  DD  *
           .
           .
           .
        data
           .
           .
           .
/*    END OF INPUT DATA
```

The *null* statement is coded as a blank card with slash characters (i.e., soldius) in columns one and two. The null statement denotes the end of a job.

Two additional statements exist: PROC and PEND. They are used with cataloged and in-stream procedures.

Standard ddnames

Several "ddnames" have special meaning to the operating system and specify that the user desires to use a special facility. For example, the DD statement:

//JOBLIB DD DSNAME=MATH.LIB,DISP=(OLD,PASS)

denotes a user library of programs that should be searched for requested load modules.

The special ddnames are given in the following list:

JOBLIB—defines a private library for use in the job.

STEPLIB—defines a private library for use in the job step.

SYSABEND—defines a data set on which a dump can be written if the job step terminates abnormally. The dump gives the nucleus, the program region, and a trace table.

SYSUDUMP—defines a data set on which a dump can be written if the job step terminates abnormally. The dump gives only the program region.

SYSCHK—defines a checkpoint data set.

The five ddnames denote important functions to the user and to the operating system; these are basic features that should, in general, be included in the design of an operating system. Of greater significance, however, is the technique of utilizing special ddnames. A variety of other functions could be added to the operating system in a similar manner.

Libraries

When a request is made to load a load module, the Supervisor checks to see if it is already in main storage (in the user's region, in the link pack area, or in the module list held in the link pack area). If the load module is not found, the link library (SYS1.LINKLIB) is searched for that module. (The link library is referred to as the *system library*.) The user can also establish temporary libraries and private libraries.

A *private library* is a partitioned data set used to store a collection of load modules. When the user specifies a job library by using the JOBLIB ddname in a DD statement, he tells the system to search the JOBLIB before searching the LINKLIB. An example of a DD statement with a ddname of JOBLIB was given previously. When a JOBLIB is used, the DD statement is placed directly following the JOB statement—implying obviously that the library is defined for the entire job. If a step library is specified with a DD statement named STEP-LIB, then the step library overrides the job library (if it exists) for that job step.

A temporary library is defined for a series of job steps and is used to hold a load module prior to an execute step. For example, if it is desired to compile, link edit, and then execute a program in a single job, a temporary library would probably be used. A *temporary library* is a partitioned data set created in one job step to hold a load module to be used in a following job step. When the load module is required, the PGM parameter of the EXEC statement can be used to refer back to the DD statement of the library. The extended form of the PGM parameter is:

$$PGM = \begin{cases} \text{program name} \\ *.\text{stepname.ddname} \\ *.\text{stepname.procstepname.ddname} \end{cases}$$

where the constituents of the parameter are defined under the topic *DCB parameters* presented previously in this section. The following JCL statements depict the use of a temporary library:

```
//LINK   EXEC PGM=IEWL
//SYSLMOD DD DSNAME=&&MYLIB(APROG),UNIT=2314,
                DISP=PASS,SPACE=(1024,(100,10,1) )
//DOIT   EXEC PGM=*.LINK.SYSLMOD
```

where IEWL is the name of the linkage editor, the double ampersands (&&) denote a temporary data set defined only for the job, and APROG is the name of the load module. The concept of a temporary library is a generalization of a "load tape" or a standard library file found in earlier and less complex systems.

Concatenated Data Sets

Frequently, the input file to a program consists of one or more data sets that should be logically connected—i.e., concatenated. This is accomplished under Job Management facilities by omitting the ddnames from all DD statements except the first, as depicted in the following example:

```
//IN DD DSNAME=BIG.PARTA,DISP=OLD
//   DD DSNAME=BIG.PARTB,UNIT=2400,VOLUME=SER=3841,DISP=OLD
//   DD DSNAME=BIG.PARTC,UNIT=2311,VOLUME=222134,
           DISP=(OLD,DELETE)
```

Concatenated data sets are commonly used to chain together a series of private libraries, as depicted in the following example:

```
//J1 JOB MSGLEVEL=1,REGION=240K
//JOBLIB DD DSNAME=MYLIB.MATH,DISP=(OLD,PASS)
//       DD DSNAME=MISCLIB,DISP=(OLD,PASS),UNIT=2311,
               VOLUME=SER=123456
//       DD DSNAME=MYLIB.PHYS,DISP=(OLD,PASS)
```

The private libraries are searched in the order in which the DD statements appear; thus, a hierarchy of libraries can be established.

Cataloged and In-Stream Procedures

A procedure in the sense of job control language is a series of JCL statements that have been assigned a name. If the procedure is placed in a partitioned data set known as the procedure library, it is called a *cataloged procedure*. If the procedure precedes its reference in the input job stream, it is referred to as an *in-stream procedure*. Cataloged procedures facilitate the use of the operating system and are ordinarily employed to avoid errors and assure standardization in the use of the JCL. In-stream procedures are used to avoid repeating the same statements in a single job.

A cataloged procedure is placed in a procedure library named SYS1.PROCLIB with a utility program. At that time, the procedure is assigned a name. If the cataloged procedure is to use symbolic parameters, then a PROC statement must be used. A PROC statement takes the form:

//name PROC operands comments

For example, the following statements define a procedure named ABC and utilize symbolic parameters (denoted by a single ampersand, as in assembler language):

```
//SIMPLE PROC OPT,ID
//DOIT    EXEC PGM=UPDATE,PARM='&OPT'
//INDS1   DSNAME=&ID.MATH,DISP=OLD
//INDS2   DSNAME=&ID.PHYS,UNIT=2311,VOL=SER=123456,
         DISP=OLD
```

Assume the procedure is invoked by an EXEC statement of the form:

// EXEC SIMPLE,OPT=AB,ID=HART

The procedure would be retrieved from the library, the parameters would be replaced, and the following statements would be entered into the input job stream:

```
//DOIT  EXEC PGM=UPDATE,PARM='AB'
//INDS1 DD   DSNAME=HART.MATH,DISP=OLD
//INDS2 DD   DSNAME=HART.PHYS,UNIT=2311,VOL=SER=123456,
           DISP=OLD
```

A variety of facilities are defined for: assigning values to parameters; overriding, adding, and nullifying parameters; and adding DD statements to a procedure.

As *in-stream procedure* takes the general form:

//name PROC operands comments

.

.

.

JCL statements

.

.

.

//   PEND

and is used in a similar manner. The primary differences between cataloged and in-stream procedures are that the latter exist solely for the duration of a job and are not stored in a cataloged procedure library.

The reader is directed to any of the following references for additional information on procedures: Brown [Bro70], Cadow [Cad70], Flores [Flo71], and the JCL reference manual [OSi].

Comments on Job Control Language

Although job control language is oriented towards the operational conventions for using an operating system, it reflects the complexity of the operating system, and to some degree, the computer system. A good rule of thumb is that as the functional capability of the system increases, so does the complexity of the job control language. This is an empirical fact and is not necessarily causal in nature. As a result, ordinary features such as default conventions and procedures become increasingly important. Conceptually, the process is one of adding an additional level of software support.

8 | SYSTEM OPERATION

8.1 INTRODUCTION

OS/MVT is an advanced operating system, and there is great benefit in considering how the system operates. This subject was introduced to some extent in Chapter 6 because it is difficult to completely separate structure from operation. The objective of this chapter is to give the reader a reasonably good idea of system operation without going into excessive detail. The balance between useful information and excessive detail is indeed a "fine line." However, the reader can always gain additional material by consulting the references. A collection of topics deemed to be of greatest interest and pedagogical value are presented.

Overall System Flow

The overall flow of control and information in OS/MVT is given in Fig. 8.1. The system is designed for a multitask batch environment. The overall design of the system is not response-oriented but functions so as to optimize the use of system resources—especially the CPU. The design philosophy is almost directly opposed to interactive computing systems in which the objective of the operating system is to provide a level of computing service to the users.

As a result of the system's design objective, there is an emphasis on job input and output (as suggested in Fig. 8.1). Much of the material included in this chapter relates to the manner in which the operating system operates in response to requests for service.

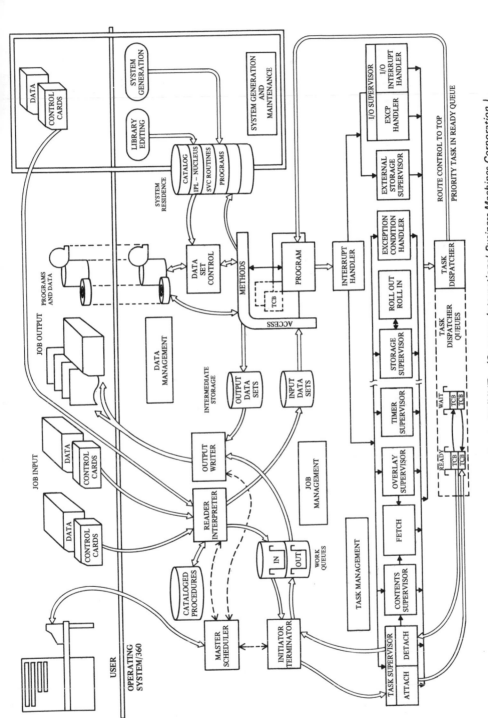

Fig. 8.1 Flow of control and information in OS/MVT. (Courtesy International Business Machines Corporation.)

Initial Program Load

The operation of the system begins with initial program load (IPL). During IPL, the IPL program bootstraps itself into main storage and performs housekeeping functions (such as determining the size of main storage and setting the storage protection keys to zero). The IPL program then relocates itself into upper storage and reads the nucleus into lower storage. The IPL program then passes control to the nucleus initialization program (NIP). NIP, which is actually a section of the nucleus, performs a variety of system-oriented functions. Some of the "better known" functions performed by the nucleus initialization program are:

1. initializes tables;
2. determines the locations and sizes of routines;
3. establishes the timer system;
4. determines and initializes the system console;
5. defines the system queue area;
6. loads the link pack area; and
7. creates the master scheduler task.

NIP passes control to the master scheduler. After IPL, the task structure of the system is suggested by Fig. 8.2.

Master Scheduler

The routines of the master scheduler prepare the system for job processing by initializing input and output work queues, by executing automatic operator commands, and by opening and initializing data recording data sets, such as the system log and the accounting data set. If the master scheduler has not created additional tasks by way of the automatic operator commands,† the system is put into the wait state.

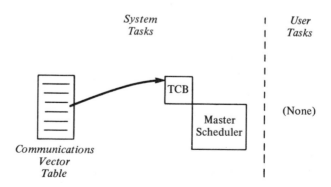

Fig. 8.2 Task structure of the system immediately after IPL.

†An automatic operator command is a procedure that is automatically executed when the system is initialized; it corresponds in function to a bona fide operator command.

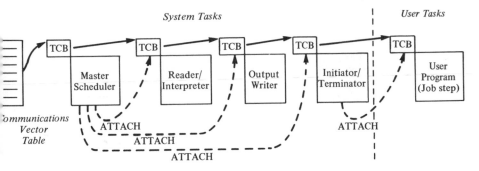

Fig. 8.3 Conceptual view of task structure after the operator has started a reader, a writer, and an initiator.

The master scheduler operates in response to operator commands, such as

START RDR.id,input device,,,job classes
START INIT.id,,,job classes
START WTR.id,device,,,output classes

to attach additional system tasks such as the reader/interpreter, initiator/terminator, or the output writer. The initiator, as part of its normal function, ATTACHes user tasks. The process is suggested by Fig. 8.3.

Command Processing

Actually, the processing of an operator command is more complicated since the routines to do the processing may not be resident in main storage and the CPU can be allocated to another task while a routine is being brought in. It should also be recognized that commands are entered by the operator while the system is running. He starts and stops readers, initiators, and writers as the work load varies. Therefore, command processing is divided into three phases:

1. reading the command,
2. scheduling the command for execution, and
3. executing the command.

The three phases may operate as three system tasks or a single system task—depending upon the command. (For example, a command may originate at the console or from the input job stream; thus the reading task may vary depending upon the source.) Command processing gives some insight into how the system operates and is described further.

One of the functions performed by the master scheduler is to link to a console initialization routine. A console communications task is established that manages console communications. Upon initialization, this task issues a WAIT macro to place the task in the wait state until an attention from the console is received. Figure 8.4 depicts command processing. The operator pushes "attention" to

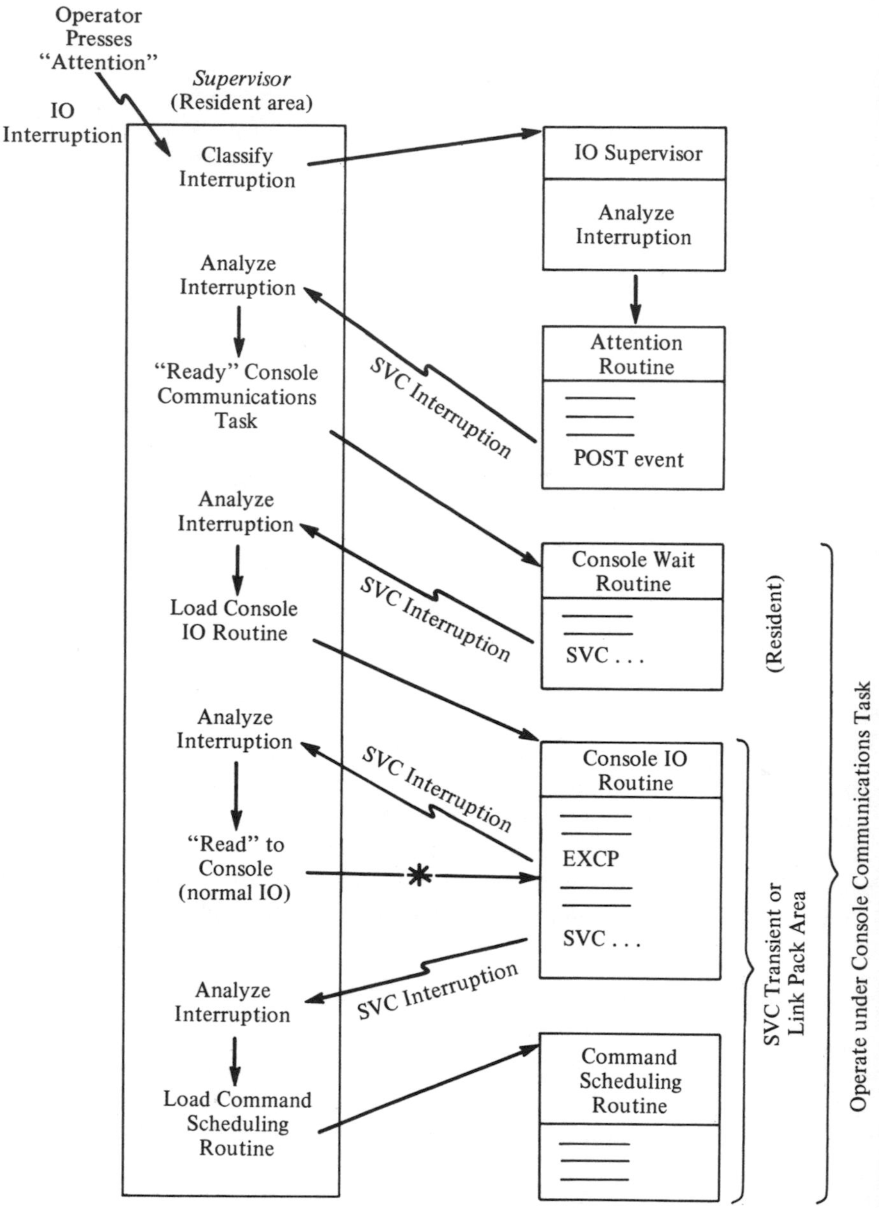

*Normal multitasking takes place here

Fig. 8.4 Flow of system control when a command is entered from the operator's console. (Reference: *MVT Guide* [OSk] ; this is an adaption of a similar figure given on p. 109.)

obtain use of the console. The attention is processed by the Supervisor and then the IO Supervisor. The IO Supervisor analyzes the attention and issues a POST macro, which effectively activates the console communications task. The console IO routine is loaded and issues a "read" to the console, and the user enters a command. The command is analyzed and a command scheduling routine is loaded to schedule the command for execution. (Commands must be scheduled for execution in an orderly manner since it is impossible to synchronize operator input with the operation of the system in a multitasking environment.) The operation of command processing is typical of how the system operates. Most functions are performed asynchronously; interruptions are used for communications and for passing control from one routine to the next. Synchronization is achieved through event control blocks.

8.2 JOB PROCESSING

Job processing begins when a reader/interpreter and an initiator/terminator are started in response to operator commands. A detailed version of Fig. 6.13 is

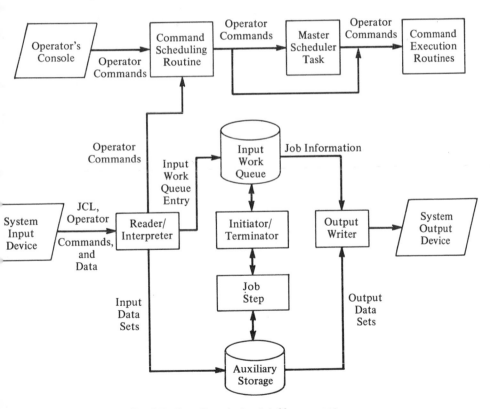

Fig. 8.5 Data flow during Job Management.

given as Fig. 8.5. It depicts data flow during job management. Other than the master scheduler, Job Management functions are executed by three routines: (1) the reader/interpreter, (2) the initiator/terminator, (3) the output writer. The three routines are described briefly, followed by a "walkthrough" of job processing.

Reader/Interpreter

The reader/interpreter performs seven basic functions:

1. reads the input job stream;
2. scans and interprets JCL statements and builds appropriate tables;
3. places system messages, intended for the user, in an output queue entry;
4. creates output queue entries for output data sets;
5. copies input data in the input job stream to auxiliary storage and places pointers to that data set in the job's work queue entry;
6. sends operator commands to the command scheduler; and
7. creates an input work queue entry for the job.

The reader and the interpreter can operate as a single task or as two separate tasks—depending upon the needs of a given installation. A combined reader/ interpreter is described here.

The reader/interpreter reads the input job stream. Control blocks and table

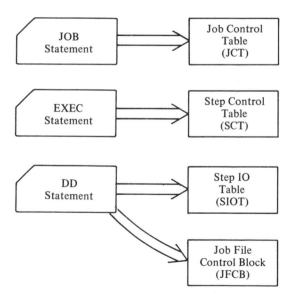

Fig. 8.6 Control blocks and tables that are built from JCL statements by the "interpreter."

entries are built from the JCL statements. Commands are dispatched to the "command scheduling routine" (see Fig. 8.5). A temporary "system input" data set is created for data that are encountered in the input job stream. The relationship between control blocks and tables and JCL statements is given in Fig. 8.6. The *job control table* (JCT) is built from the JOB statement and contains job information and job step information that apply to all job steps in that job. The *step control table* (SCT) is built for each EXEC statement and contains job step information. The *step input/output table* (SIOT) is built for each DD statement and contains IO device requirements for that data set. The *job file control block* (JFCB) is also built for each DD statement and contains the data set attributes specified on that DD card. (When the data set is opened, the JFCB is completed.) Collectively, the four blocks and tables (except those pertaining to output data sets) constitute an *input work queue entry*. A "queue manager" routine is invoked to place the input work queue entry on the input work queue. A typical input work queue entry is depicted in Fig. 8.7. The tables and

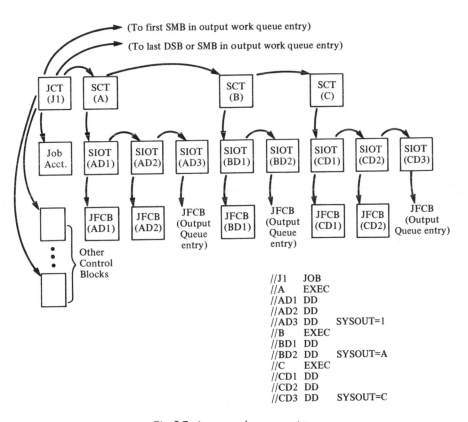

Fig. 8.7 Input work queue entry.

blocks are implemented as records chained together in a system data set named SYS1.SYSJOBQE. (The methodology is covered in Chapter 4.)

The JFCBs for output data sets are combined with system message blocks (SMB) to form an output work queue entry. Each output work queue entry describes the system output, in a given output class, for a single job. A data set block (DSB) exists for each output data set; the DSB points to the JFCB for the data set. Entires on the output work queue are processed by an output writer when the job is completed. Figure 8.8 depicts a typical output work queue entry. The output work queues also reside on SYS1.SYSJOBQE as data records chained together.

The operation of the reader/interpreter is terminated when an end-of-data condition is received from the input device or the operator issues a STOP command for that reader/interpreter task.

Initiator/Terminator

The initiator/terminator prepares job steps for processing and does termination processing when job steps are complete.

The initiator/terminator is a system task that is assigned to one or more job classes with a START INITIATOR command. The order in which the classes are listed in the operand field of the operator's command determine the order in which input work queue entries are selected from input work queues for processing. The initiator selects an input work queue entry from an input work queue, and the initiation, execution, and termination of that task are performed sequentially under the control of the initiator. The initiator processes only one job at a time without multiprogramming. Multiprogramming is achieved when another job initiator is started by the operator. (Note, however, that multitasking, which is a Task Management function, is not ruled out and may take place even though only a single job is being processed.) The initiator performs the following functions:

1. acquires a region of main storage;
2. locates data sets;
3. allocates IO devices to data sets;
4. allocates auxiliary storage space for "new" data sets; and
5. attaches job steps for execution.

In performing most of the above functions, the initiator calls upon SVC routines. Main storage requirements for a job step are obtained from the step control table (SCT); if the space requirements for the job step or the initiator cannot be satisfied or there is insufficient space in the system queue area for queues and tables, the initiator is put into the wait state until sufficient storage is available. Input data sets are located via a catalog management SVC routine, and input/

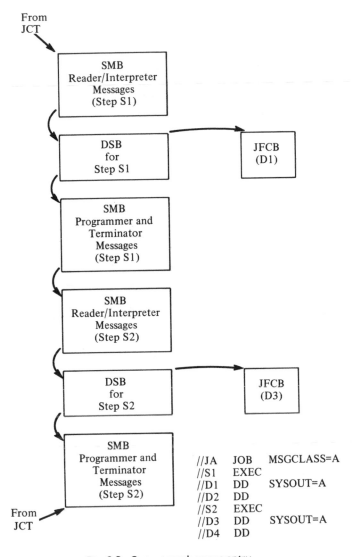

Fig. 8.8 Output work queue entry.

output devices are assigned from a task input/output table (TIOT) built from the job control table (JCT), step control table (SCT), and step input/output table (SIOT). The data set control blocks (DSCBs) for new data sets are created from their respective job file control blocks (JFCBs). The process of building the TIOT and the DSCBs for new data sets is suggested by Fig. 8.9. Auxiliary stor-

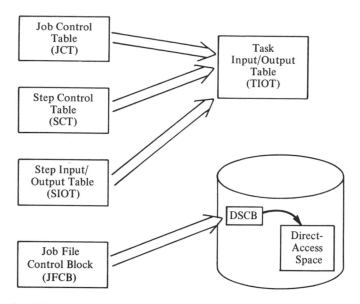

Fig. 8.9   Building of the TIOT and the DSCB during job step initiation.

age space is reserved by the Direct Access Device Space Management routine of Data Management. A DSCB for "new" data sets is partially built during job step initiation; the DSCB, as well as the JFCB, is completed when the data set is opened.

A job step is put into execution when the initiator issues an ATTACH macro for the load module comprising the job step. The "ATTACH" SVC routine creates a task control block (TCB) for the task and places it on the task queue for subsequent execution. The initiator is placed in the wait state until the job step is complete.

When the initiator finds no work to be performed in any of its input work queues, it writes a message to the operator informing him of the situation and invokes the initiator wait routine, which executes a WAIT macro. When a queue manager places an input work queue entry on an input work queue, the initiator wait routine's event control block (ECB) is posted and the initiator wait routine is "readied" for subsequent execution.

A job step is terminated for one of three reasons:

1. The job step is complete.
2. The specified time for the job step has been exceeded.
3. An error prevents further processing of that job step.

The terminator removes the job step's TCB from the system with a DETACH macro, deletes the input work queue entry from SYS1.SYSJOBQE, and completes the output work queue entry on SYS1.SYSJOBQE. The output work queue manager posts an event control block for an output writer; this process makes the output work queue entry available for processing by an output writer.

Output Writer

An output writer operates in an analogous manner to a reader/interpreter. It is assigned to an output class or group of output classes and processes messages and output data sets assigned to that class on a job basis.

An output writer task is created by the master scheduler (or one of its routines) in response to a START WRITER command. (Multiple output writers may be started, depending upon the needs of an installation.) The output writer obtains an output work queue entry from the queue manager and writes the messages and data sets. When all output work queue entries for classes to which a particular output writer is assigned have been processed, the output writer task is put into the wait state with a WAIT macro specifying an event control block. The output writer is placed in the ready state when an output work queue entry is placed on the output queues associated with the output writer task.

Job Processing Walkthrough

Figure 8.10 shows the flow of operating system control as it processes a single job. The description is simplified and applies to the execution of that job; no multiporgramming or multitasking is depicted. The objective is to give an indication of the functions performed by the various system components and the order in which those functions are performed.

Comments on Job Processing

Ordinarily, the job processing aspects of an operating system are relatively straightforward; however, the Job Management facilities of OS/MVT are complex for several important reasons:

1. to allow multiprogramming and multitasking;
2. to allow the operating system to be used on computer systems with medium-sized main storage;
3. to allow a variety of device types; and
4. to operate effectively for a variety of workloads.

To meet these needs, the design of OS/MVT Job Management includes a variety of queues and tables and a complex collection of system tasks and subtasks that operate on the queues and tables.

The reader is directed to Witt [Wit66], the *MVT Job Management Program Logic Manual* [OSl], and the *MVT Guide* [OSk] for additional information on Job Management.

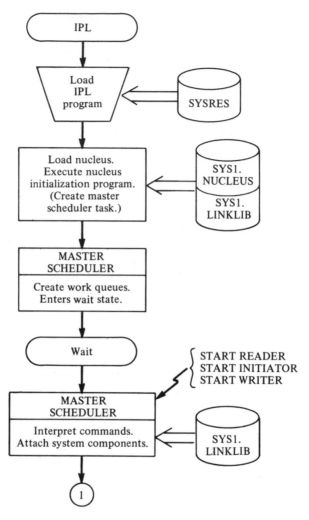

Fig. 8.10 Part I

8.3 THE SUPERVISOR AND RESOURCE MANAGEMENT

Task management routines have been introduced previously. The concepts are extended here through a discussion of the following topics:

1. task control,
2. interruption processing,
3. task supervision,

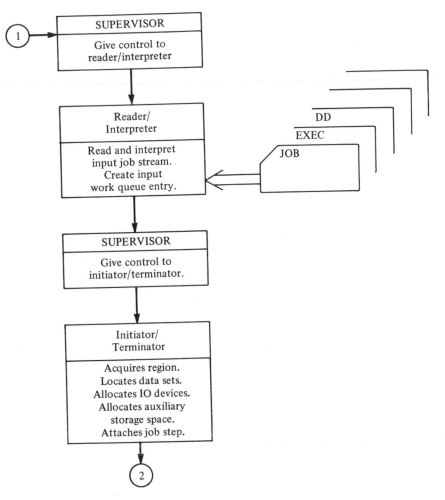

Fig. 8.10 Part II

4. main storage supervision, and
5. contents supervision.

In controlling the operation of the computing system, Task Management routines manage system resources: the CPU, main storage, and the services of Task Management routines. Each resource is managed by a *resource manager*—a group of Task Management routines. *All work is performed under task control.* Some resources are designed to be allocated immediately; others can be delayed. When a resource is being used by another task, a request for that resource must be queued up and the requesting task must wait.

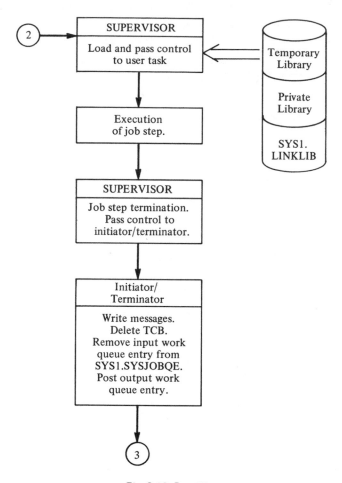

Fig. 8.10 Part III

The IO supervisor, which is part of the nucleus, is discussed in the next section, "IO Communications and the IO Supervisor."

Task Control

Task control is managed with the *task queue* and with control blocks. A control block in the Supervisor called the *communication vector table* (CVT) points to the task queue. A task control block (TCB) exists for each system task and for each user task. The TCBs in the task queue are ordered by priority. (The task queue is implemented as a linked list.) The system resources and programs associated with each task are represented by control blocks that are chained to

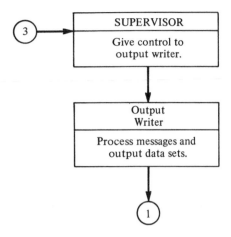

Fig. 8.10 Part IV

Fig. 8.10 Simplified "walkthrough" of job processing (multiprogramming, multitasking, data management, task management, etc. are not depicted).

that task's TCB. (Remember that a task can be a reader, an initiator, a user program, etc.) Figure 8.11 depicts some of the control blocks used for task control.

A *request block* (RB) exists for each program (load module) or control program routine that is executed for a task. The RBs are linked in reverse order to the sequence in which the programs are activated. Thus, if a task is interrupted, the TCB points to the last one in execution. As new load modules (e.g., with a LINK macro) or SVC routines are activated, RBs are created and chained to the TCB. As a routine or load module completes execution, its request block is removed from the chain. The process is depicted in Fig. 8.12.

Four types of request blocks are defined:

1. *Program request blocks* (PRBs)—represent nonsupervisor programs activated with ATTACH, LINK, and XCTL.
2. *Supervisor request blocks* (SVRBs)—represent supervisor SVC routines activated by SVC handling routines.
3. *System interruption request block* (SIRB)—represents a routine activated because of a system error.
4. *Interruption request blocks* (IRBs)—represent asynchronous interruption control routines.

The need for program request blocks is evident from the previous discussion of dynamic serial program structure. Supervisor request blocks represent SVC routines that *can* issue SVC interruptions. (The SVRB is used to store control information when an SVC is handled.) An example of an SVC routine that re-

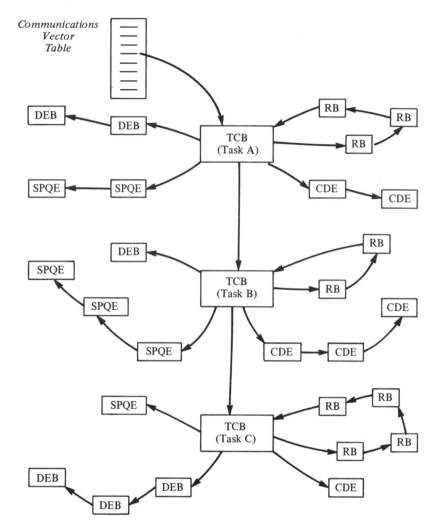

Key: RB – control block for task management
SPQE – control block for main storage management
DEB – control block for data management
CDE – control block for contents management

Fig. 8.11 Control blocks used for task control.

quires an SVRB is the routine that processes the SVC interruption associated with the execution of the ATTACH macro. The attach routine creates a task and uses other system macros (such as GETMAIN) that generate additional SVC interruptions. System interruption request blocks and interruption request blocks are not discussed further.

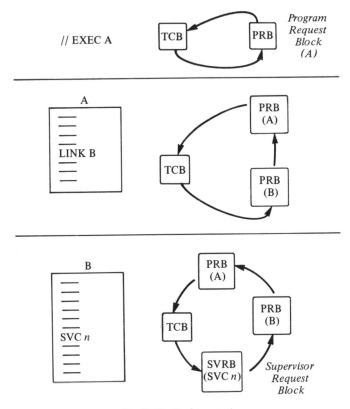

Fig. 8.12   Task control.

Other control blocks are chained to the TCB. Control blocks that represent the main storage allocated to a task are chained to the TCB as are control blocks that represent data management structures. This subject is pursued further under "Main Storage Supervision" and "IO Communications and IO Supervision," respectively. Control blocks for the use of the system timer are also chained to the TCB; the study of timer supervision is planned as an exercise for the reader.

Interruption Processing

Interruptions are classified on the basis of the manner in which they operate. The structure of interruption processing is depicted as Fig. 6.12; SVC interruptions are further classified here by whether the execution of additional SVC instructions is required during processing. Interruptions are "fielded" by interruption handlers; except for machine check processing, the interruption handler routine runs disabled (i.e., interruptions masked off) so that it is not interrupted again before critical information can be saved.

SVC processing routines that cannot issue SVC instructions pass control to

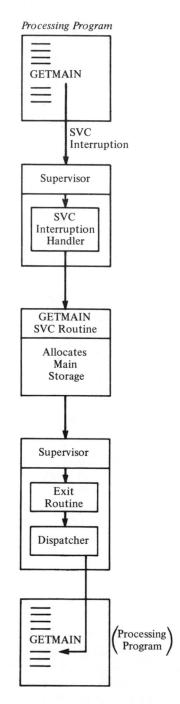

Fig. 8.13 Simplified walkthrough of the processing of a typical SVC interruption.

other service routines with the branch instruction. These routines are resident in main storage and represent the following type of macro instructions: CHAP (change priority), EXIT, EXTRACT (extract control information from protected storage), FREEMAIN, GETMAIN, POST, TIME, TTIMER, and WAIT. Figure 8.13 depicts a simplified walkthrough of the processing of a typical SVC interruption.

Supervisor request blocks (SVRBs) are created for nonresident SVC processing routines and SVC processing routines that can issue SVC instructions or can be interrupted. After the SVRB is created and linked, control can pass directly to the routine or a request is made to have the routine brought in from a library to a transient area. The SVC interruption handler determines the attributes of SVC processing routines through an SVC table.

Program interruptions are handled directly as governed by control information in a task's TCB. Similarly, external and machine check interruptions are processed directly as determined by the characteristics of a given computing system (uniprocessor or multiprocessor) and the level of "system generation." IO interruptions are handled directly by the IO supervisor.

Task Supervision

Task supervision involves task creation, task control, task dispatching, and task synchronization. Task control has been covered previously.

A task is created with the ATTACH macro instruction. The SVC processing routine that corresponds to the ATTACH macro instruction performs the following functions:

1. creates a TCB by obtaining storage from the system queue area for the TCB and places control information for the task (or a subtask) in that TCB;
2. requests that main storage be allocated to the task;
3. places the address of the TCB on the system's task queue and on the subtask queue of the parent task; and
4. calls upon "contents supervision" to fetch the first load module of the task.

After the Supervisor has completed its interruption processing, it allocates the CPU to a task. As a result of certain types of interruptions, program control is passed directly back to the program that was interrupted. When it is possible that another task of a higher priority is placed in the ready state by the processing of the interruption, then control is passed to the task dispatcher. The task dispatcher selects the highest-priority ready task and passes control to the first program in its queue of request blocks. Thus, the states of a task are: (1) an input work queue entry; (2) ready; (3) waiting; (4) active; and (5) complete.

Time slicing refers to the practice of giving tasks in a time slice group control of the CPU for a specified time interval on a periodic basis. Time slicing operates as follows:

1. A task in a time slice group is given control of the CPU.

2. The task executes until one of the following occurs: the time interval expires, a higher priority task becomes ready, it must wait for the completion of an event, or the task is complete. If a task with a priority higher than the priority of the time slice group becomes ready, the CPU is given to it. Otherwise, the CPU is dispatched to the next task in the time slice group.
3. If a task in a time slice group loses the CPU because of a wait or because a higher-priority task becomes available, it loses the remainder of its time slice. When the time slice group again gains control, the next task in the time slice group is given the CPU.
4. The dispatching of the CPU to tasks in a time slice group continues until all the tasks are waiting or are complete or a higher-priority task becomes ready.

Task synchronization is achieved through the WAIT/POST event facilities or through the enqueue/dequeue facilities. The latter are described here. As mentioned previously, resources of the system are managed by resource managers. (A resource can be access to a table, the use of a Supervisor service routine, and so on.) When one of these resources is needed, the program requesting the facility issues an enqueue (ENQ) macro instruction which places a queue element (QEL) on a queue associated with that resource. If the resource is currently free, the ENQ routine allows the issuing task access to the facility. If the resource is not free, the ENQ routine issues a wait condition for the issuing task. When a task completes its use of a resource, it issues a DEQ macro to eliminate its queue element. This reduces the wait count for the resource and allows the next user of that resource to be placed in the ready state; the now ready task is given access to the resource the next time it is dispatched for execution.

Main Storage Supervision

Main storage is allocated in response to the execution of a GETMAIN macro instruction; the GETMAIN routine operates as a resident SVC processing routine. In general, main storage supervisor routines control and allocate storage in three areas:

1. in the dynamic area as regions for job steps and system tasks;
2. in the system queue area as control blocks; and
3. in a user's region in response to requests by the parent tasks and subtasks.

After the system is initialized and the master scheduler task is created, the organization of main storage is as depicted in Fig. 8.14. The dynamic area is allocated as regions in blocks of 2K increments. The first three words of each free block of storage in the dynamic area are occupied by a control block called the *free block queue element* (FBQE). The FBQE contains the number of bytes in

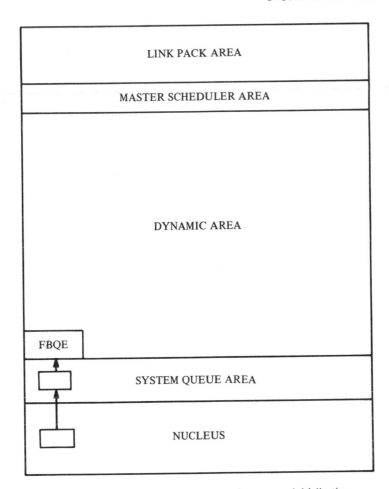

Fig. 8.14   Organization of main storage after system initialization.

this free block of storage (in 2K increments) and includes forward and backward pointers to other elements on a FBQE chain.

When a task is created, contiguous storage is assigned to it in blocks of 2K bytes. If insufficient storage for that region is free in the dynamic area, the initiating task is put into the wait state until the required storage becomes free. After the system has been in operation for a period of time, the structure of main storage looks somewhat as depicted in Fig. 8.15. (Note that the FBQE control block which is first in the chain is pointed to from a control block located in the System Queue Area; that control block is in turn pointed to from a table located in the Nucleus.

The system control blocks, located in the system queue area, are of interest

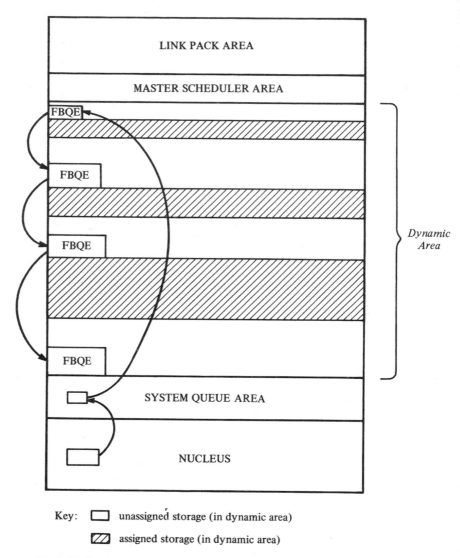

Key: □ unassigned storage (in dynamic area)

▨ assigned storage (in dynamic area)

Fig. 8.15 Typical organization of main storage after a period of system operation.

since they exist for both allocated storage and free storage. A field in a table† in the nucleus points to (i.e., contains the address of) a *dummy partition queue element* (DPQE); the major purpose of the DPQE is to point to partition queue

†More specifically, the address of the dummy partition queue element is contained in field PQEPTR located at an offset of 8 from the GOVRFLB table in the nucleus. However, the knowledge that the DPQE is located via a table in the nucleus is sufficient for a conceptual understanding of the Supervisor.

elements (PQEs) that describe a chain of FBQEs. The PQE contains pointers to the first and last FBQEs associated with the storage described by the PQE. If large-capacity storage is used, then an additional PQE exists for that hierarchy of storage.

When a region of main storage is assigned in response to the execution of the GETMAIN macro instruction, the GETMAIN routine searches the FBQE chain to find the first block of free storage that is large enough to satisfy the request. The beginning address (a_R) of the region to be assigned is computed as follows:

$$a_R = s_{FB} - s_R + a_{FB}$$

where:

s_{FB} is the size of the free block of storage;
s_R is the size of the region requested;
a_{FB} is the address of the free block.

The size of the free block is then reduced as follows:

$$s_{FB} = s_{FB} - s_R$$

Next the GETMAIN routine builds FBQE, DPQE, and PQE control blocks for the region. The size of the region is placed in the FBQE. The size of the region and the region address are placed in the PQE (i.e., the PQE points to the FBQE). The DPQE is made to point to the PQE and the address of the DPQE is placed in the TCB for the task. If a storage hierarchy is used, then a PQE is constructed for the assigned segment of storage. (Note here that the control blocks serve other purposes than those stated. Only the major functions served by a control block are given because of the complexity of the system.) The relationship between allocated and unallocated storage is depicted in Fig. 8.16.

A region is deallocated with a FREEMAIN macro instruction. The FBQE for the space freed is inserted at the appropriate place in the chain of FBQEs for free storage. In the event the newly freed space is adjacent to an area of free storage, then only a single FBQE is used for the contiguous areas of storage.

The System Queue Area (or *space* as it is sometimes called) is used to build system control blocks. The size of the system queue area is specified at the time the system is generated. When a GETMAIN request for the system queue area cannot be satisfied, the routine tries to free unused control blocks with a purging routine. If this attempt fails to release the needed space, then the system queue space is expanded by assigning to it adjacent blocks of free storage in 2K increments from the dynamic area. If adjacent storage is not available, then the requesting task is placed in a wait state until space becomes available. As with the dynamic area, control blocks are used to manage storage allocation in the system queue area.

Main storage within a region is managed in a similar manner to the way that storage in the dynamic area is managed—with a chain of free block queue ele-

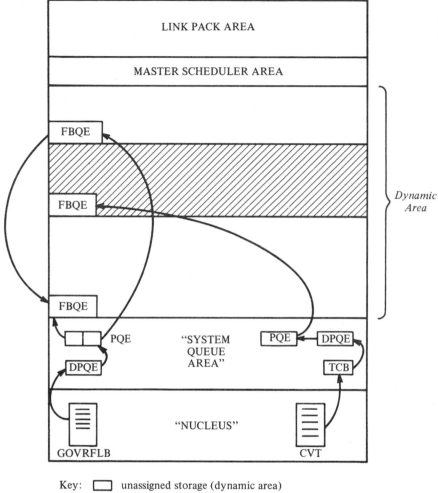

Fig. 8.16 Structure of region allocation.

ments (FBQEs). Recall here that a task can attach subtasks such that more than one task can be using the same region. When storage is requested in a region, it is assigned in 2K increments to a subpool. A subpool queue element (SPQE) exists for each subpool of a region. The subpools used by a task are reflected in a chain of SPQEs that is chained to the TCB for that task (see Fig. 8.11). Each SPQE, in turn, points to a queue of descriptor queue elements (DQEs) that represent the storage assigned to that subpool from the region. A subpool can be shared among one or more subtasks.

Each subpool represents storage established for a class of routines or for a certain function. Typical subpools usually exist for:

1. register save areas and parameter information (operate with the storage key of the region),
2. reentrant modules from SYS1.SVCLIB or SYS1.LINKLIB (operate with a storage key of zero), and
3. nonreentrant or JOBLIB modules (operate with the storage key of the region).

A related area of study concerns the operation of roll out/roll in routines and the manner in which they utilize the queues built for main storage allocation. The reader is directed to reference [OSm] for additional information on this subject.

Contents Supervision

Contents supervision involves bringing nonresident load modules into main storage and keeping track of the contents of the link pack area and the dynamic area. Load modules are brought into main storage by the execution of a LINK, ATTACH, XCTL, or LOAD macro instruction.

Contents supervision is managed with the aid of a "contents directory." The *contents directory* is a set of queues denoting the load modules that exist in the above two areas and also in a user's region. The Supervisor maintains two "system-oriented" contents directory queues: one for the link pack area and the other for subpools (of user's regions) that contain reenterable modules from SYS1.LINKLIB and SYS1.SVCLIB.† A contents directory queue is a list of control blocks—each termed a *contents directory entry* (CDE). A CDE describes a module by giving its name, aliases, entry point, the address of the request block that requested the module, plus a variety of module attributes. The contents directory queue for the link pack area is pointed to from the communications vector table. The contents directory queue for a region is pointed to from the first TCB for that region. Figure 8.17 suggests the use of the contents directory queue.

Contents supervision routines perform the following functions:

1. search for the module name in a contents directory queue;
2. create CDEs to describe requested modules;
3. determine if a module is ready for use;
4. fetch and load modules;
5. manage deferred requests for modules; and
6. do a variety of housekeeping and control services.

Contents supervision routines also fetch nonresident SVC and IO error handling routines and supervise the loading of segments in an overlay structure. The

†More specifically, these subpools are referred to as the *job pack area.*

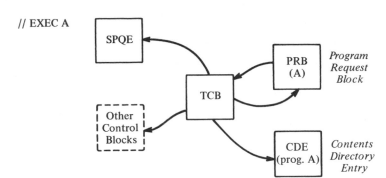

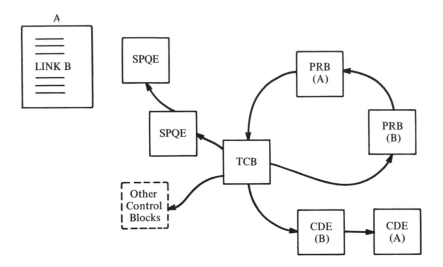

Fig. 8.17   Conceptualization of the contents directory queue.

process of fetching and loading modules is discussed here. The loading of system routines and overlay management are natural extensions to the fetching and loading operations.

The *program fetch* routine is called by the Contents or Overlay Supervisors to locate and load a requested module. Program fetch performs the following functions:

1. *Initialization*—obtains a work area for the fetch and load process and builds IO control blocks, channel programs, event control blocks, IO buffers, and a buffer table to be used during the IO transfer operation of a load module into storage.

2. *Loading*—transfers text (TXT) and the relocation list dictionary (RLD) to main storage.
3. *Relocation*—relocates relative address constants found in the program.
4. *Termination*—performs housekeeping functions, sets the return code, and returns to the calling program (i.e., the contents or overlay supervisor).

The overall flow of the processing of loading a module (or an overlay segment) is depicted in Fig. 8.18. A specific example of how a module is read in and relocated is given as follows:

1. The text (TXT) record is read into its appropriate block of main storage.
2. The relocation list dictionary (RLD) is read into an RLD buffer. (The RLD denotes which address constants should be adjusted.)
3. A relocation subroutine adjusts each address constant specified in the RLD by adding or subtracting, as specified, a relocation factor. For a block loaded module, the relocation factor is the difference between the address assigned by the linkage editor (usually zero) and the address of the first byte of storage into which the module is loaded. (For scatter loading modules, each RLD entry contains a position pointer that is used to locate the specific address constant.)

Conceptually, the process of loading a module is straightforward. In actual practice, the process is "messy" because of the "loose ends" that must be handled and the special conditions that arise.

Contents supervision routines rely heavily on the IO facilities of the operating system; they are covered in the next section.

Comments on the Supervisor and Resource Management

The objective of this section has been to give the overall flow and operational characteristics of the Supervisor while eliminating as much of the detail as possible. Many of the problems that would ordinarily be encountered in implementing a system with the capability of OS/MVT have not even been implied. Moreover, several important topics such as management of the system timer, abnormal terminations, error recovery, system environment recording, and the operation of checkpoint/restart have not been mentioned. The reader can consult one of the references for additional information on these topics. However, the topics covered (i.e., task control, interruption processing, task supervision, main storage supervision, and contents supervision) do have counterparts in other operating systems, and a significant amount of the knowledge contained here can be transferred directly.

8.4 IO COMMUNICATIONS AND THE IO SUPERVISOR

Data management is introduced in Chapter 6. Direct-access device space management routines and catalog management routines are utilized by Job Management

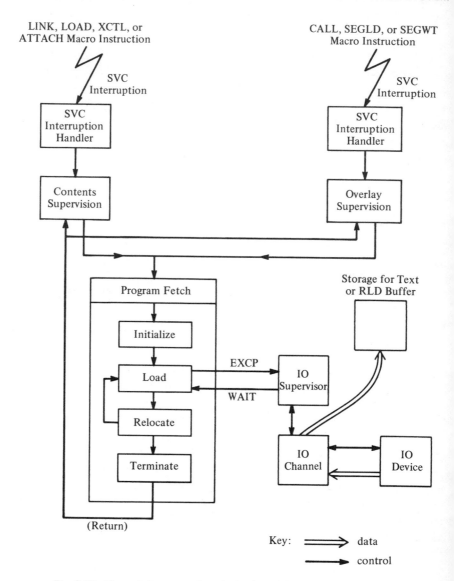

Fig. 8.18 Flow of the processing of a load module or an overlay segment.

even though they are logically data management functions. All topics cannot be covered in an introductory book and direct-access device space and catalog management routines are least related to how IO is actually performed in an operating system. They are not discussed further. IO support processing routines (in particular, open and close processing) are discussed briefly with regard to the construction of control blocks used for IO processing. The primary emphasis of this section is on the operation of the operating system during IO processing.

Overview of IO Processing

IO processing can be done with an access method or without an access method. When an access method is used, the user must supply a data control block (DCB), and he initiates input or output with a macro instruction such as READ and WRITE or GET and PUT. Execution of one of these macro instructions passes control to an access method routine that resides in the user's region or in the link pack area. The access method then handles the IO processing for the processing program. A processing program is logically connected to an access method when a data set is opened. (The reader should recall that the open routine provides for correct volume mounting, as required.) In addition to completing the data control block (DCB), job file control block (JFCB), and data set control block (DSCB), the open routine also constructs a data extent block (DEB) for each DCB opened. (A DCB exists for each data set used.) The DEB is a logical extension to the DCB; it contains information on the volume location, data set boundaries, and access method, and additionally, points to the unit control block (UCB) for the associated IO device. (The UCB is introduced a little later.) The DEB is constructed in the system queue area and is chained to the TCB for the task (see Fig. 8.11). Figure 8.19 depicts the sources of information for the DEB. The access method provides the IO supervisor an input/output "control" block (IOB—which is also introduced briefly), buffers, and a channel program, and initiates IO requests with the EXCP macro instruction.

When an access method is not used by the user, he must create his own buffers, input/output "control" block, and channel program; however, he may issue an EXCP macro just as an access method does.

The execute channel program (EXCP) macro instruction is assembled as an SVC instruction that specifies the address of the IOB for a particular IO request. The resultant SVC interruption is handled by the SVC interruption handler that passes control to the IO supervisor.

When the IO supervisor receives control, it first verifies the correctness of the control blocks it has to use. The IO supervisor then constructs a "request element" that includes the addresses of the IOB, DEB, and the UCB, as well as control information about the channel program. The "request element" facilitates the access to the control blocks since some effort is involved in determining their actual addresses. (More specifically, the IO supervisor locates the DCB from the IOB, locates the DEB from the DCB, and locates the UCB from the DEB.) If the channel or device (specified in the IOB) is busy, the request element is placed in a request element table and an exit is made to the processing program. If the channel and device are free, the IO supervisor initiates the requested IO operation and control is returned to the processing program.

IO interruptions are discussed after the IO supervisor is introduced.

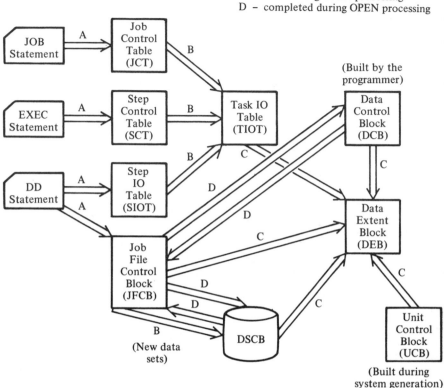

Key: A – built by the job interpreter
     B – built by the job step initiator
     C – built during OPEN processing
     D – completed during OPEN processing

Fig. 8.19 Source of information for control blocks used during IO processing.

Control Blocks and Tables

Because CPU processing and IO processing operate asynchronously and because several IO operations can be in progress concurrently, control information is stored in control blocks and tables. The control blocks and tables are used to initiate an IO operation, to associate an interruption with a particular IO operation, and to handle IO error conditions.

Five control blocks are used during IO processing: (1) input/output block (IOB), (2) data control block (DCB), (3) data extent block (DEB), (4) event control block (ECB), and (5) unit control block (UCB). The logical relationship between these control blocks is given as Fig. 8.20. The *input/output block* (IOB) is used for communication between the routine that issues the EXCP macro and the IO supervisor. (The address of the IOB is passed with the SVC instruction.)

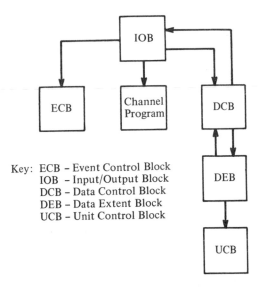

Key: ECB – Event Control Block
     IOB – Input/Output Block
     DCB – Data Control Block
     DEB – Data Extent Block
     UCB – Unit Control Block

Fig. 8.20   Logical relationships between IO control blocks.

The IOB contains the address of the channel program, a storage area for a channel status word (provided by the IO supervisor upon IO completion), the initial seek address for a direct-access storage device, the addresses of the DCB and ECB, and other control information.   The *data control block* (DCB) contains data management information (see Chapter 7), the address of the DEB, and information on error procedures.   One DCB exists per data set.   The *data extent block* (DEB) supplements the DCB and contains information on the volume, data set, boundaries, and access method. The DEB points to the UCB. One DEB exists for each DCB.   The *event control block* (ECB) is used by the IO supervisor to POST the completion of an IO operation. The ECB is pointed to by the IOB.   The *unit control block* (UCB) describes an IO channel and device. It contains the channel and device addresses, the device type, flag bits, and an area for sense information, table references, and a work area for error recovery. The UCB points to the request element for an IO operation. One UCB exists per IO device; it is built during system generation.

   Seven tables are identified: (1) UCB lookup table, (2) channel table, (3) device table, (4) statistics table, (5) attention table, (6) request element table, and (7) logical channel word table. The *UCB lookup table* contains the addresses of the UCBs in the system. When an IO interruption occurs or when an IO operation is to be started, the supervisor determines the UCB that represents the IO device from this table. The *channel table* is used to locate a channel search module for a given channel. A channel search module exists for each type of channel and is used to locate channel queues of request elements. The channel table is used to start IO operations that are "queued up." The *device table* is used to locate device-dependent routines which initiate IO operations on a specific device. The *statistics table* is used to record IO error statistics. The statistics table contains an entry for each device attached to the system. The *attention table* is used to locate routines that process "attention" conditions for IO devices. This table is built when the operating system is generated (i.e., system generation). The *request element table* contains request elements that represent IO operations. Each request element contains: UCB, DEB, IOB, and TCB addresses and the priority of the request. The *logical channel word table* contains an entry for each logical channel queue in the system. (The set of all physical channel paths to a single device is called a *logical channel.* Through IO switching, an IO device can be connected to one of several physical channels.) Each logical channel word points to the first and last request element for each logical channel queue. Each logical channel possesses a *logical channel queue* that is used to represent IO operations that are awaiting execution. A logical channel queue is composed of request elements.

In general, the IO supervisor calls upon routines to do its processing. Whenever a routine is needed for a special purpose, its address is determined from one of the above tables, depending upon the existing conditions. The control blocks and tables are also used to associate an IO interruption with a particular IO operation and to initiate IO operations.

Operation of the IO Supervisor

The IO supervisor resides in the Nucleus and supervises IO operations on a system-wide basis. The IO supervisor executes in the supervisor state and issues privileged IO instructions. The IO supervisor performs two major functions:

1. It handles IO requests.
2. It handles IO interruptions.

To perform these functions, the IO supervisor is divided into an "EXCP supervisor" and an "IO interruption supervisor." During its operation, the IO supervisor uses the IO supervisor transient area and the SVC transient area for non-resident routines.

The five major sections of the IO supervisor are:

1. *Test channel* section—determines if a channel is available for the IO device that is to be used with an IO operation.
2. *Enqueue and dequeue* section—queues IO requests that cannot be started. After an IO operation is started, the request is removed from the queue.
3. *Start input/output* section—initiates an IO operation on a given channel and device.
4. *Channel search* section—searches channel queues for the next IO request.

Channel search is activated when one IO operation is completed and another can be initiated.

5. *Trapcode* section—provides information on an IO operation and an IO device after an IO interruption associated with that device has been received.

The "test channel," "enqueue and dequeue," and "start input/output" sections are logically a part of the EXCP supervisor; the "channel search" and "trapcode" sections are logically a part of the IO interruption supervisor. However, all five sections are assembled together as the IO supervisor. The five major sections of the IO supervisor are reflected in Fig. 8.21, which gives the functional flow of the IO supervisor.

Operation of the EXCP Supervisor

The EXCP supervisor starts the channel program necessary to perform an IO operation. It receives control from the SVC interruption handler (see Fig. 6.12). The EXCP supervisor operates as follows:

1. A validity check routine checks the control blocks and performs initialization of the IOB.
2. A request element is constructed for the IO operation.
3. The UCBs for the device are inspected to see if the device is available.
4. A test channel routine is entered to obtain a physical channel to the device. (The test channel routine is located via the logical channel word table.)
5. A start input/output module is selected for execution by means of the device table and control is passed to it.
6. Control is passed by means of the SVC exit routine to the dispatcher.
7. If the IO operation cannot be started, then the request element is queued on the logical channel queue and control is passed to the dispatcher.

In reality, the EXCP supervisor is considerably more complicated. However, the overall flow of IO operations is most important, and extensive detail, which certainly exists in the case of input and output, tends to obscure the concepts involved.

Operation of the IO Interruption Supervisor

The IO interruption supervisor receives control from the IO interruption handler (see Fig. 6.12). The objective of the IO interruption supervisor is to analyze IO interruptions, post IO completions, initiate queued IO requests, and process error conditions. The IO interruption supervisor operates as follows:

1. The address of the UCB for the channel or device from which the interruption was received is determined by means of the UCB lookup table.
2. The status bits stored with the IO interruption are analyzed to determine the processing required.

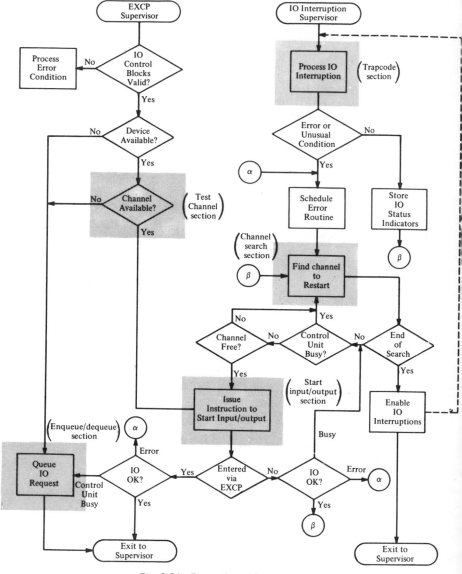

Fig. 8.21 Flow of the IO supervisor.

3. If the interruption is to record IO completion, then the ECB for that IO request is posted.
4. The channel queues are searched for an IO operation that can be started on the channel that is made available by the interruption.

5. If a request element is found for that channel, that IO operation is started and an exit is made to the dispatcher, as described below.
6. If no request element for that channel is available, then the IO interruption supervisor exits to the dispatcher, as described below.

The IO supervisor executes with all interruptions (except for machine check) disabled. After an IO interruption has been processed and before the IO interruption supervisor exits to the dispatcher, two checks are made:

1. A channel search is made to see if a channel can be started for a stacked IO operation. If so, a channel restart procedure is executed.
2. IO interruptions are enabled to test for IO interruptions that may have been stacked during the IO processing.

If no interruptions are pending, then IO interruptions are again disabled and the IO supervisor returns to the dispatcher. Figure 8.22 depicts a simplified walk-through of IO processing.

Other conditions arise as IO interruptions. When an attention condition is received for a particular device, the attention table is used to locate an attention routine for that device. After an appropriate attention routine has completed execution, it returns to the IO supervisor. The statistics table is used in a similar manner. This table contains an entry for each IO device attached to the system. Each entry can contain a variety of counters to record occurrences such as read errors, write errors, and equipment checks. The statistics table is used by system error routines to maintain error records for later recall and analysis.

Like the EXCP supervisor, the IO interruption supervisor is fairly detailed. In fact, the amount of detail involved forestalls any attempt to describe its flow in a reasonably sized flow diagram. Much of the processing of IO interruptions is machine dependent, and as such, is not appropriate for general study. The overall concepts and the manner in which control blocks, tables, and queues are used are important. The reader who is interested in the details of IO communications and the IO supervisor is directed to Clark [Cla66] and the *Input/Output Supervisor Program Logic Manual* [OSd].

8.5 COMMENTS ON SYSTEM OPERATION

As any large system, OS/MVT has specific characteristics. The criterion that "all work is done under task control" is carried through to include IO processing. Most "supervisor state" routines execute with interruptions disabled; thus, the work that has to be done gets done as fast as possible. This design philosophy is particularly appropriate for batch-oriented multiprogramming systems in that the level of system throughput is kept very high and that high-priority jobs are completed as quickly as possible within the limits of normal multiprogramming.

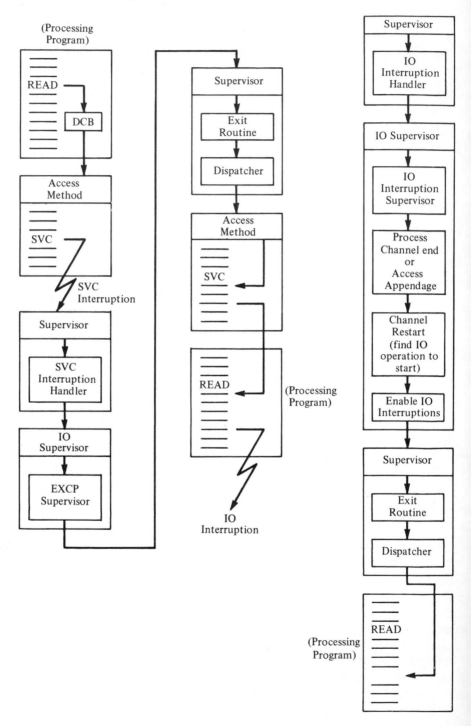

Fig. 8.22   Simplified walkthrough of IO processing.

The reader who is interested in an overview of OS/360 is directed to Mealy [Mea66].

Part Three of this book describes a time shared operating system that is response-oriented. The reader will recognize that the design philosophy, at least as far as the supervisor is concerned, is considerably different.

QUESTIONS FOR PART TWO

Chapter 6

1. Compare the concept of a job and a job step with the "sample input job stream" given as Fig. 5.6. In what way are the concepts both similar and different? (Consider the influence of the commercial data processing environment.)
2. Discuss the feasibility of developing a user program that reads control cards and executes appropriate macros in lieu of using Job Management facilities. (Consider: storage allocation, device assignment, error processing, and so forth.)
3. When and why would a user utilize multitasking facilities?
4. The concept of a *system task* raises a conceptual question. Are there any advantages in including the program that comprises the system task as a part of the control program? (Consider the size of the machine with which the operating system is to be used.)
5. Distinguish between a job step and a task.
6. The use of LOAD, LINK, ATTACH, XCTL, and DELETE macros is referred to as *dynamic linkage*. Evaluate the concept of dynamic linkage in terms of *hardware, information,* and *human resources.*
7. Compare the *variable-size region* concept of main storage allocation with the concept of a *fixed-size partition* in which jobs are assigned to a partition on the basis of attributes of the job. Under what circumstances would each of these technqiues be appropriate?
8. When, for example, would a user request that a block of main storage be allocated to his program on a conditional basis? Variable-size area? Both?
9. What is the relationship between a data set name, the catalog, and the volume table of contents?
10. Distinguish between an IO device and a volume.
11. Why is the catalog structured as a tree rather than a simple list?
12. Why do Job and Data Management routines execute with a zero PSW protection key?
13. Summarize how a job is processed by the operating system.
14. Explain why an operator might want to place an operator command in the input job stream.
15. Describe how the system generation process might be useful to an installation.
16. As described, checkpoint/restart is a "rather general" facility that can be used almost anywhere in a program. What information would have to be stored to enable a job step to be restarted?
17. By restricting when a checkpoint could be taken, how could the process be made more efficient?
18. In what way would an installation want to restrict the use of roll out/roll in?
19. Assume that it is desired to control the use of large-capacity storage (LCS) by the operating system to maximize the utilization of system resources. What "heuristic methods" could be applied?
20. In a multiprogramming system, such as OS/MVT, there must be a point

where the use of public storage can be justified economically. What factors should be considered? Is it possible to develop an economic model describing the situation?

Chapter 7

21. Describe the relationship between a DCB and an access method.
22. Give examples of the following (a) when it would be desirable to use the same DCB with different data sets; and (b) when it would be necessary to open and close a file more than once in a single computer run.
23. Distinguish between the READ macro instruction and a READ statement in a language such as FORTRAN or COBOL. Also, between the PUT macro instruction and the WRITE statement.
24. When would the move mode be used? Locate mode? Substitute mode? Is it possible to establish a decision criterion?
25. In what ways could indexed sequential be an inefficient way of doing business?
26. When could the DSNAME in a DD statement be omitted?
27. Why is a "data set disposition" an important parameter?
28. There seems to be an analogy between assembler language and macros and between JCL and cataloged/in-stream procedures. Can this analogy be carried any further? Is it feasible to do so?
29. Is it feasible to develop a standard JCL, similar to the standard FORTRAN or COBOL?
30. In what way could cataloged procedures augment the DCB merge?

Chapter 8

31. Why is the IPL sequence necessary?
32. Describe why the Master Scheduler is so named.
33. Describe how the posting of an event control block (ECB) can "ready" a task for execution.
34. Discuss, in your own words, why the use of *requests blocks* is necessary.
35. Develop a flow diagram of interruption processing.
36. What function does the FBQE serve?
37. Why does the Supervisor need both request blocks and contents directory entries (CDEs)? Consider abnormal task termination and dynamic linkage.
38. Distinguish between "program fetch" and "loading."
39. Describe how the IO supervisor can associate a task with a given IO interruption.
40. Why does the IO interruption supervisor execute with interruptions disabled?
41. The address of a channel program is passed to the EXCP supervisor. What type of minimal checking must be performed on this channel program?
42. After the reader/interpreter has completed its work, the operating system essentially operates on queues, lists, and tables. Comment on the feasibility of implementing the operating system control programs as part of the computer—perhaps using microprogram logic.

PART THREE: FUNCTIONAL CHARACTERISTICS OF A GENERAL-PURPOSE TIME SHARING SYSTEM

9 | SYSTEM CHARACTERISTICS

9.1 BASIC CONCEPTS

Introduction

Time sharing is described as the concurrent use of the resources of a computer system by a large number of users via terminal devices. Time sharing is conversational in the sense that the user can engage in a series of interactions with the system to enter data or a program, to process a program, to retrieve information, and so on. One of the characteristics of time sharing is that each user appears to have the entire computer to himself; actually the system is switching rapidly between users—called multiplexing. In a sense, the time sharing system is using the users' think time, reaction time, and IO time to run other programs in the computer.

With time sharing, the objective is to provide service to the user, and rapid response time is important. The CPU is shared on a scheduled basis. When doing multiprogramming on a batch-oriented operating system, as a comparison, the prime objective is to keep the computer busy and response time is not a major concern. In this case, the CPU is shared on a demand basis.

Time sharing is a popular concept, and a variety of design philosophies exist. The major emphasis in this part of the book is to discuss an "open" time sharing system in which the user has access to all of the traditional facilities of an operating system—namely, assembler language and macro instructions, language processors, data management, and job control facilities—by using a remote terminal device. A user can use an open time sharing system to:

1. solve a problem,
2. create a program,
3. enter or retrieve information from the system,
4. run a nonconversational program,
5. manipulate data files, or
6. any combination of the above.

This part of the book presents a model of a general-purpose time sharing system for study, for analysis, and for a thorough understanding of the basic concepts. The vehicle used is the TSS/360 operating system developed by IBM for the System/360 model 67 computer. At the time of this writing, few general-purpose time sharing systems are in widespread use. TSS/360 is selected because it is one of the most widely used large-scale general-purpose time sharing system that includes the following capabilities: command system, language processors, data management, multiprocessing, public storage, configuration control facilities, conversational and nonconversational task execution, and no operational constraints on jobs. Comfort [Com65], Gibson [Gib66], and Lett and Koenigsford [Let68] present introductions to TSS/360. Other time sharing systems, such as MULTICS [Cor65] are at least as well known as TSS but are not used in as many installations.

One of the major reasons TSS is presented is that it includes several advanced concepts that are significant regardless of the system in which they are included. This set of advanced concepts contains:

1. an advanced command system,
2. virtual memory,
3. page-oriented data management,
4. dynamic loading, and
5. a three-level operating concept.

Whenever possible, topics are presented as general concepts. In fact, the topics can be studied independently of the system in which they are embedded.

Controlled Access

The design philosophy behind TSS is that users have access to the system by means of telecommunication facilities (least lines, ordinary telephone lines, and hard wire connections) and that access must be controlled and the integrity of programs and data must be protected. Protection is maintained through the command. system, through the catalog structure and data set naming conventions, and by an established procedure for controlling access to the system.

When the TSS system is generated, a system manager and a system operator are "JOINed" to the system. When a person is JOINed to the system, it means that he may use the system, and his user ID, password, charge numbers, and user attributes are in a table maintained as an indexed sequential data set. (The name

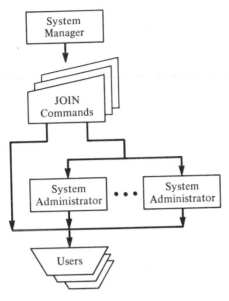

Fig. 9.1 Managing access to the system.

of this data set is TSS*****.SYSUSE; the prefix TSS***** denotes the data set is owned by the system.) Initially only the system manager and the system operator have an entry in SYSUSE. A system administrator can also be established; he is JOINed by the system manager. Both the system manager and the system administrators (there can be several) can JOIN users to the system. ("JOIN" is a function of the command system that is invoked with the command JOIN and permits the above information to be entered for users of a terminal; the nature of the command system is presented later.) When it is desired to remove a user's record from SYSUSE, either the system manager or the system administrator can issue a QUIT command. The concept of managing access to the system is suggested by Fig. 9.1. More specifically, each user has an entry in SYSUSE and his user ID and password must be entered correctly when he desires to use the system; otherwise, he is denied access. His user attributes (called his "profile") govern how he uses the system.

System Utilization

The system can be used in a conversational mode or in a nonconversational mode. When using the system in the conversational mode, a terminal device is used so that user can interact with the system on a dynamic basis. Nonconversational use of the system is initiated via a terminal or via the card reader as a batch job to be run in the multiprogramming mode.

In the conversational mode, the user connects his terminal by a dial-up procedure or by simply turning the terminal "on" in a hard wired configuration. The user presses ATTENTION to initiate a "sign on" procedure and his keyboard is unlocked so that he can send information to the system—frequently referred to as "entering information into the system." The system operates as follows:

1. The user's keyboard is unlocked so that he can enter information. (The computer has issued a "read" to the terminal.)

2. The user types the information on the terminal device; as each character is typed, it is sent to the computer. The user presses RETURN to end the message and a special character is sent to the computer. The keyboard is now "locked."†

3. The necessary processing is performed by the system the next time the user's task is given control of the CPU. (Conversational work is time sliced by the system's supervisor program.)

4. If a system function was requested, it is performed and the results (if any) are typed at the user's terminal. The keyboard is unlocked so that the user can enter his next command.

5. If a processing program is executed, then it can request input from the terminal or from a data set; similarly, it can send output to the user's terminal or write it to a data set. (The program may require a dialogue between the user and the computer.) When the execution of the processing program is complete, the keyboard is unlocked so that the user can enter his next command.

When the user requests that a system function be performed for him or that a processing program be executed, it is initiated the next time his task is given the CPU and is continued during subsequent time slices until that function or program is complete. The conversational mode is characterized in another way: The system input device (SYSIN) and the system output device (SYSOUT) for a task are the user's terminal. When the user completes his work, he "signs off" with the LOGOFF command. The period between sign on and sign off is termed a *terminal session.* The actual clock time between sign on and sign off is referred to as *connect time.* The actual *CPU time* used is usually considerably less than connect time.

In the *nonconversational mode,* the user cannot interact with the system and is not connected to it with a terminal device. A nonconversational task may be time sliced or multiprogrammed depending upon the scheduling algorithm used. Nonconversational tasks are initiated in two ways:

1. by entering a batch job into the system by the card reader; and

---

†Techniques for keyboard management differ. Some systems keep the keyboard unlocked at all times and information sent to the computer is put into buffers. These buffers are "read" the next time the associated task is given control of the CPU.

2. by initiating a nonconversational task with a command entered in the conversational mode.

In the latter case, the user can enter a command that initiates a system defined function, such as printing a data set on the line printer or writing a data set on a magnetic tape, or he can request that the system execute a data set that contains the input stream for a batch job. In either case, the nonconversational task operates independently of the task that initiates it.

The user can also enter data into the system via the card reader or via magnetic tape. These data are stored in the system as a data set for subsequent use by a conversational or nonconversational task.

The Task Concept

The basic unit of work to the system and to the user is a *task*. To the system, a task is represented by a control block that is linked to the control blocks for other tasks and is anchored in a table called the "System Table." A task can be active, ready, waiting, etc., and the control block is marked as such. A task is either conversational or nonconversational. When a user signs on at a terminal, a conversational task is created for him. When a batch job is selected for processing, for example, a nonconversational task is created for him.† The structure of a conversational task and a nonconversational task is the same. The primary difference between the two kinds of tasks is with regard to SYSIN and SYSOUT and how the CPU is allocated to them—i.e., how they are scheduled for execution.

To the user, a task is a work session that involves one or more of the following:

1. the successive execution of one or more processing programs and system functions in the conversational mode;
2. a batch job that may involve the execution of one or more processing programs and system functions;
3. the specification of a system command (such as PRINT) for which a nonconversational task is created.

In short, a task is a terminal session or a batch job. If a task creates a second task, the second task is nonconversational and is processed independently. Subtasking is not permitted nor is it possible for one conversational task to create another conversational task. Later, Task Management routines that operate in support of a task are introduced. These routines should be distinguished from OS task management. In OS, task management refers to the manner in which the supervisor allocates the CPU to tasks. In TSS, Task Management refers to

---

†A batch job can be entered into the system at any time by the operator. The job is stored on direct-access storage until selected for execution by a "batch monitor." A batch job can also be initiated by a user at a terminal.

routines that support a given task. Thus, Supervisor routines are *not* called task management in TSS.

Storage Classification

Three categories of storage are defined in TSS: main storage, auxiliary storage, and external storage. Unfortunately, naming conventions differ from other systems. *Main storage* is the main storage of the computer. It is allocated in units of 4096 bytes, called pages, by the Supervisor program. When a program is being executed by the CPU, pages containing machine code and data that are being actively referenced (i.e., that are needed for that program to operate) must be in main storage.

When several programs (i.e., tasks) are concurrently being executed in a time sharing environment,[†] the programs and data for all users that are active (i.e., currently signed on) cannot be held in main storage at the same time. Direct-access storage used to hold main storage pages temporarily during system operation is termed *auxiliary storage*. When the system operates, pages containing programs and data are constantly being moved back and forth between main storage and auxiliary storage as different tasks are given control of the CPU. *External storage* is used to hold data sets and libraries. It is used during program execution for normal IO processing, for permanent storage of data files, and for storing libraries of programs. External storage is divided into three classes: public storage, private storage, and system storage.

In a time sharing environment, the number of concurrent users is expected to be much greater than the number of separate IO volumes available. Thus, the concept of on-line *public storage* is defined. When the TSS system is started up (i.e., IPLed), a number of public devices are defined. In general, most direct-access devices in the system are designated as public devices. When a user's task is created, that task automatically has access to all of the public volumes on the public devices via the data management system and the system catalog. Public storage is allocated by system routines, and access to it for input and output operations is provided by data management routines. Public storage is *on-line* in the sense that public volumes are always mounted. When a user creates a data set, he gives it a data set name and assigns it data set attributes. Subsequently, that data set is referenced by name, and the system is given responsibility for locating the data set and providing access to it. The system also protects the data set from being accessed by other users, unless the owner of the data set allows it to be shared. Data sets on public storage are always cataloged. Unless specified otherwise, a user is always assigned public storage when he creates a new data set.

[†]In a time sharing environment, concurrent execution means the following: (1) When the system configuration contains one CPU, then the tasks are time sliced; and (2) in an n-plex system, the tasks are time sliced but n tasks can be in a state of execution at the same time since n CPUs are operating in parallel.

Private storage refers to the use of private volumes on devices allocated to private use. The user requests a private volume when he defines a data set and the system then requests that the operator mount the specified volume if it is not already mounted. Private volumes may contain cataloged or uncataloged data sets; if a cataloged data set is stored on a private volume, then the serial number of the volume is kept in the catalog in addition to the "private" attribute. When the user requests a cataloged data set on a private volume by data set name alone, the operator is requested automatically to mount the appropriate storage volume.

TSS uses two control volumes (termed *system storage*) that are always mounted: the Initial Program Load (IPL) Control Volume and the Auxiliary Control Volume.† The *IPL Control Volume* contains system routines and the *Auxiliary Control Volume* (called the AUX Control Volume) contains the catalog, program libraries, and user tables. Control volumes are presented later.

System Concepts

A time sharing system is characterized in a variety of ways:

1. by the way the user uses the system to get his work done,
2. by the way that main storage is managed,
3. by the way that the CPU is allocated to tasks, and
4. by the way that IO is performed.

In a multiprogrammed operating system, a job consists of a set of job steps and a job step specifies the execution of a processing program. Other specifications, such as the DD statement, augment the execution of the processing program as specified with the EXEC statement. In a general-purpose time sharing system, each time a user enters a command, some function is performed and the results of that function exist for the duration of the terminal session—unless those results are nullified or superseded. Thus, if a user loads a program, that program stays loaded until it is explicitly unloaded or the user signs off the system. Similarly, if a user defines a data set (with a DDEF statement that is similar to a DD statement), that data set is defined for the duration of the terminal session—unless, of course, that definition is canceled with a "release" command. This operational philosophy is consistent with the way that time sharing systems are used. A terminal session is not completely preplanned and the requests that the user makes of the system are, at least in part, determined by the results that the user obtains in the conversational mode on a dynamic basis.

At first glance, the notion of loading a program that stays loaded for the duration of a terminal session implies either small programs or large storage. However, the concept of virtual memory is used that gives the user the operational

---

†Actually, the IPL Control Volume is used during "startup" only. Once the system is "up," this volume can be demounted.

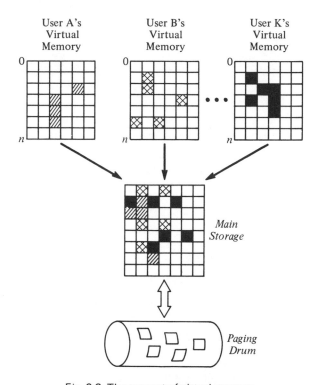

Fig. 9.2 The concept of virtual memory.

advantage of having a large single-level storage. *Virtual memory* is a technique that gives the user an address space as large as the addressing capability of the computer.† The actual size of main storage available on a 360/67 using TSS is 512K to 2,048K bytes. Each user's virtual memory is mapped into a combination of main storage and an auxiliary storage volume—such as a magnetic drum or magnetic disk. Main storage as well as virtual memory and the auxiliary storage volume are managed on a page basis. When the user references a page in his virtual memory, the hardware checks to see if it is in main storage. If it is, then execution continues. If it is not in main storage, then an interruption is generated and the Supervisor brings the needed page into main storage so that it can be used. In a nutshell, this is the concept of virtual memory; it utilizes both hardware features and software support. The notion of virtual memory is depicted conceptually in Fig. 9.2. When using virtual memory, a page is easily

†On the System/360 Model 67, 24-bit addressing gives the user a virtual memory of 16 million bytes (i.e., $2^{24}-1$); 32-bit addressing gives a virtual memory of 4 billion bytes (i.e., $2^{32}-1$). The mode of addressing is set by a bit in the program status word.

shared by including the same main storage page in two or more users' virtual memory. Virtual memory is managed through the use of page tables—a set of page tables is created for each task by the Supervisor when that task is initiated. The software and hardware details for using virtual memory are presented later.

The process of moving pages between main storage and auxiliary storage (and also external storage) is termed *paging*. Paging operates as a high-priority IO operation so that needed pages are brought into main storage as quickly as possible. The process of moving pages from main storage to auxiliary storage is also important since main storage space is frequently required for pages that are "currently" needed by an operating program. When a task needs a page and that page must be brought into main storage, the CPU does not wait but goes on to another task. The task needing the page is put into "page wait." When the needed page is finally brought into main storage, then the waiting task is made "active" so that it can complete its time slice the next time it is given control of the CPU.

The paging process is also used for input and output. Data sets on direct-access volumes are organized by the system into 4096-byte pages and use the high-priority paging process for input and output. Only the needed pages of a data set are in main storage at one time. Data sets of this sort are termed *virtual data sets;* three types of virtual organization are defined: "virtual sequential," "virtual indexed sequential," and "virtual partitioned." Virtual organization is essentially the same as having a fixed block size of 4096 bytes. The processing of virtual data sets involves advanced concepts in operating systems technology that are presented in Chapters 10 and 11.

Conventional data sets (such as in OS/360) are termed physical data sets—in contrast to virtual data sets. The capability of handling data sets of this type is necessary for compatibility with other systems. TSS contains facilities for both physical *and* virtual data sets. Physical data sets are not discussed further here since they were introduced in Parts One and Two of this book.

9.2 PROGRAMMING SYSTEMS

To the user, the "appearance" of a general-purpose time sharing system is determined by the programming systems available for using the computer. Programming systems involve seven general capabilities: (1) the command system used to address the system; (2) language processing; (3) libraries; (4) loading; (5) program checkout facilities; and (6) data management facilities.

Command System

The command system is the principal means by which the user directs the system. Many command system facilities are also available to the user through system-defined assembler language macro instructions.

The format of a command is:

Operation   *Operand*

command-name   zero or more operands separated by commas

such as

DDEF DDNAME=MFILE,DSORG=VS,DSNAME=BOOK.ONE

or
RUN LSQUARE

Commands are grouped into six categories:

1. *Task management* commands, such as LOGON (to identify a user to the system), EXECUTE (execute a previously defined nonconversational task), and ABEND (eliminate current task and start a new one).
2. *Data management* commands, which are further classified as data set management, text editing, data editing, and bulk output. Examples are: *data set management,* such as DDEF (define a data set), DELETE (delete data set entry from a user's catalog), and SHARE (allow one user to share a data set belonging to another user); *text editing,* such as EDIT (invoke the text editor) and CONTEXT (perform context editing); *data editing,* such as DATA (build virtual data set) and MODIFY (modify a record in a virtual data set); and *bulk output,* such as PRINT (print a data set on the line printer) and WT (write a data set on magnetic tape).
3. *Program management* commands, such as FTN (to invoke the FORTRAN compiler), LOAD (place an object module in virtual memory), and RUN (initiate execution of a loaded object module or load an object module not previously loaded and initiate execution of it).
4. *Command creation* commands, such as PROCDEF (defines a command procedure) and BUILTIN (defines an object module to be invoked by a command name).
5. *User profile management* commands, such as DEFAULT (establish default values or conditions) and SYNONYM (rename a command, operand, or expression).
6. *Message handling* commands, such as EXPLAIN (obtain an explanation of a message).

The same commands are used in either the conversational or nonconversational modes of operation.   Some commands are useful only in the conversational mode but are assigned reasonable interpretations when used in the nonconversational mode.

The command language discussed here falls into the same general category as the job control language presented in Part Two. Each statement is not initiated with special characters (such as the //s) for one or more of the following reasons:

1. When commands are entered from the terminal, special characters are bothersome and are more characters to type.
2. The input job stream is not processed beforehand by a component such as a reader/interpreter in OS.   Special characters provide information to the reader/interpreter as to what cards are JCL statements and what cards are programs or data.   In a time sharing system, the system responds immediately to a command (i.e., it is not processed beforehand in some way) by performing a function or calling in a program.   If that program needs data it issues its own "read" to the SYSIN device.
3. The system provides a specific means of entering data into the system so that the problem of distinguishing statements from data is not as significant.

With the command language, one operational characteristic is important.   The command system is an executable component of the system that allows dynamic user interaction.   In other words, the command system actually operates in the computer during the execution of a job to process commands that are entered. Once a program finishes execution or the execution of a system function is completed, program control passes to the command system.   The command system then reads SYSIN and processes the next command.   After each "step" in the task (obviously not after each time slice), control always returns to the command system.   In OS, to cite a counterexample, the JCL statements are completely processed before a job begins execution.

Language Processors, Object Modules, and Libraries

Language processors are designed to operate in the conversational mode.   The user invokes a language processor (such as the FORTRAN compiler) with a program management command, such as

FTN

or

RUN FTN

The FORTRAN compiler (in this case) is loaded into the user's virtual memory, if it is not there already, and it proceeds to do a FORTRAN compilation in one of two modes: (1) The source module is prestored; and (2) the source module is to be entered via the terminal or, in the case of a batch job, via the input stream. The user specifies the mode of compilation as an input parameter.

If the source module is to be entered from the terminal, the compiler prompts the user for source lines, stores them in public storage, and provides syntactical error checking as the lines are entered.   The source program is placed in public storage as a source data set in case modifications or recompilation is required. Language processing is suggested in Fig. 9.3.   Some language processors do not provide terminal input and diagnostics and require that the source module be

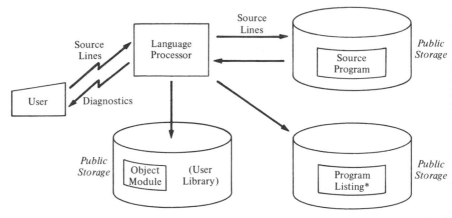

*The program listing data set is usually printed and then erased in most instances.

Fig. 9.3 Language processing in a time sharing environment.

prestored. However, since a language processor operates as a processing program to the system, it can always be executed in the conversational or nonconversational mode.

The object module is composed of three sections:

1. a *program module dictionary* (PMD) that contains control information;
2. a *text* portion (TXT) that contains the object code; and
3. an optional *internal symbol dictionary* (ISD) that can be used during program checkout.

An object module is always produced in 4096-byte page format.

Object modules are stored automatically in a library implemented as a partitioned data set using virtual organization (called a virtual partitioned data set). When each user is JOINed to the system by either the system manager or system administrator, he is automatically given a user library organized as a virtual partitioned data set referred to as his USERLIB. A user's object modules are automatically stored by the language processor in that user's user library. Whenever a user requests that a program be executed, it is fetched from his user library. The only exception exists when a user defines a JOBLIB. If a JOBLIB is defined, the language processor automatically puts an object module into the most recently defined JOBLIB; similarly, when loading a program, the system searches the JOBLIBs from the one most recently defined backwards to the USERLIB. A job library is defined as follows:

DDEF data-definition-name,DSORG=VP,DSNAME=data-set-name,
      OPTION=JOBLIB

and is a virtual partitioned data set.

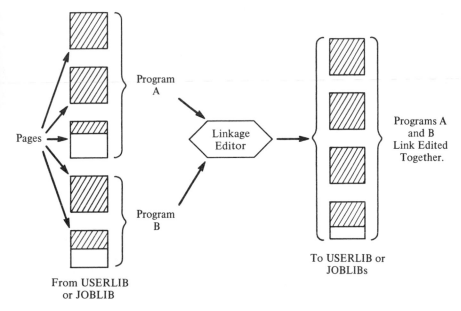

Fig. 9.4 Overview of linkage editor processing.

As described in the next section, object modules need not be link edited before execution since they can be loaded dynamically. However, object modules can be combined by the linkage editor to conserve the number of main storage pages needed for execution and possibly to save execution time. An overview of linkage editor processing is given as Fig. 9.4. As in OS, the linkage editor can be used to edit object modules, and so on. However, in OS, linkage editing is necessary as an explicit job step or a part of the loading process in the event that a loader is used. In TSS, programs are loaded on a dynamic basis for several reasons:

1. A terminal session is frequently unplanned.
2. The use of virtual memory eliminates the need to structure a program to fit into available storage.
3. Because virtual memory and paging are used, there is no need to have all pages of a program in main storage (in fact, only needed pages are moved into main storage).

For these reasons, programs are loaded dynamically in TSS.

Dynamic Loading

Normally, a routine that performs a loading function performs three operations: (1) allocation of storage, (2) loading of program text, and (3) relocation. In

TSS, the allocation is performed when a program is explicitly loaded (e.g., a LOAD command is entered). However, no program text is moved until a specific page of that program is needed on a "demand" basis. When a program is dynamically loaded, virtual memory is allocated to that program and the subprograms needed by it. This involves creating page table entries (discussed later) for the needed pages and updating the task's "task dictionary table" (TDY). Later, when a page of the program is needed on a "demand" basis, the text for that page is brought into main storage (loading) and relocation of address constants is performed. Once a page is processed by the dynamic loader, it need not be processed again. Thus, if a page of a program is never used, that page is never moved to main storage and the address constants included in that page are never relocated.

Program Checkout

The time sharing operational environment permits a user to checkout and debug his program using facilities of the time sharing system. In general, the user can insert debugging statements in his program and have results typed at his terminal on a dynamic basis. This mode of operation requires that a program be actually designed for checkout or modified accordingly.

The *program checkout subsystem* (PCS)† permits a program to be checked out without making modifications to it. PCS is used as follows:

1. The user loads his program into virtual memory but does not request that it be executed.
2. The user enters debugging statements such as: ‡

   AT symbolic-location DISPLAY variable

   or

   AT symbolic-location IF condition SET variable=expression

3. The program checkout system places an SVC instruction at the specified "symbolic location." The corresponding interruption is designed to pass control to routines to perform the requested action.
4. The user RUNs his program and PCS statements are executed as required.
5. Modifications are made to the source program using the text editor features of the command system.
6. The source program is recompiled or reassembled using the "prestored" option.

---

†In early versions of TSS/360, PCS stood for "program checkout subsystem." In a later version, the function of the program control system was extended to include checkout facilities. As a result, the meaning of the acronym PCS was changed to "program control system."

‡Optionally, a user can request an internal symbol dictionary along with his object module. This dictionary is used during debugging to locate symbolic variables.

PCS statements can be entered or removed at will. When a program is completely checked out, the PCS statements are removed and the source program need not be reprocessed by a language processor. PCS commands include AT, IF, DISPLAY, DUMP, RUN, SET, and STOP.

Data Management

The data management facilities of TSS parallel those of OS presented in Part Two. The use of public storage actually simplifies data management from the user's point of view since many options are handled by default or by access methods defined over virtual data sets (i.e., those organized on a page basis).

In general, the following conventions, facilities, and requirements apply to data management:

1. Data sets are located through a catalog by data set name.
2. Data sets are accessed via "access method" routines.
3. Data sets must be OPENed and CLOSEed.
4. Automatic buffering and deblocking is performed, as required.
5. Data sets may be copied or modified by using facilities of the command system.
6. IO devices and external storage allocation are managed by the system.
7. Normal IO programming conventions are used.

Subsequent chapters present more detailed aspects of data management. However, time sharing presents other problems. The volume table of contents (VTOC) was used in OS (and initially in TSS) to locate data sets on a given volume. When the number of opens and closes is relatively low, the concept poses no operational problems. In OS, for example, the number of jobs is limited to 15 so that only a few data sets are in the process of being used at one time. However, when the number of users is large, the number of data sets being opened and closed is very large and the number of disk seeks to the VTOC is correspondingly great. In particular, the real time necessary to open and close a data set becomes noticeably long. Therefore, the VTOC is eliminated for TSS volumes, and data set "descriptor" information is kept in the catalog. This concept cuts down on IO traffic through the data channels and improves performance.

9.3 VIRTUAL MEMORY AND PAGING

The concept of virtual memory is introduced earlier in this chapter. More specifically, it is a combination of hardware and software facilities that gives the user the operational advantage of having a large address space; each user's address space is mapped into a combination of real main storage and auxiliary direct-access storage.

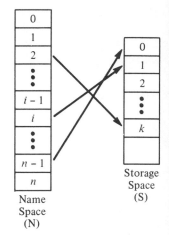

Fig. 9.5 Mapping between a name space and a storage space.

Introduction to Virtual Memory

The design philosophy behind virtual memory and paging is that a main storage address serves two purposes: (1) It represents that name of a data item; and (2) it represents the location of the data item. By considering the two items separately, the name can be used in a table lookup operation to determine the location of the data item. The process of mapping between a name space and a storage space is depicted in Fig. 9.5. The process is essentially the same as applying a function (f N$\rightarrow$S) to each argument in the name space to arrive at a location in the storage space. When used as a storage management technique, some data items are not in main storage, so the function is undefined for some arguments. Virtual memory is usually *segmented*, which means that storage is regarded as a collection of "blocks" or "segments." Within a segment, information is stored linearly. Segments are named symbolically or linearly. Segments that are named linearly have a segment number so that segments can be arranged consecutively in much the same way that information within a segment is arranged linearly. Denning [Den70] surveys the concept of virtual memory and presents the notions given above in a more general context.

One method of implementing virtual memory is to organize a linearly segmented name space and the address space into page-size units, such that addresses within a page need not be translated. Page locations are translated using a table lookup procedure. Figure 9.6 depicts the use of a single-level page table. A single-level page table has distinct disadvantages (see Dennis [Dns65] and Arden, Galler, O'Brien, and Westervelt [Ard66]); the most important is that the page table becomes excessively long and must be in main storage when the task to which it corresponds is in the state of execution. This disadvantage led to the development of what is known as two-level page tables. With two-level page tables, each user's virtual memory is divided into segments such that a page table exists for each segment and only the page tables required for execution of

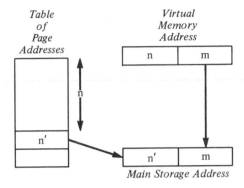

Fig. 9.6 Address translation using a single-level page table.

a task need be located in main storage. In addition, segments can be defined to serve special purposes; for example, pages are shared among tasks by utilizing a shared segment. The use of two-level page tables is depicted in Fig. 9.7.

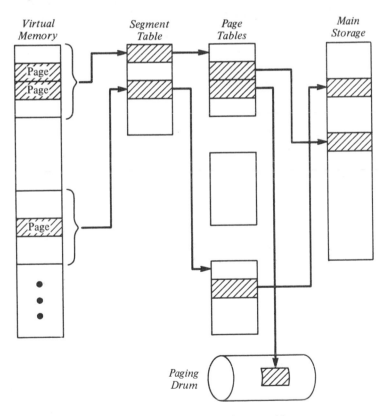

Fig. 9.7 The use of two-level pages tables.

Succeeding sections describe dynamic address translation and paging, which are a means of implementing virtual memory. Some advantages of virtual memory can now be listed:†

1. Adjacent virtual memory pages need not occupy adjacent main storage areas.
2. Not all of a user's program need be in storage simultaneously and can be retrieved when needed (called demand paging).
3. The user is permitted a large address space for programs and data.
4. The operating system can manage storage dynamically.

Additional background information on virtual memory is available from Flores [Flo67] and Oppenheimer and Weizer [Opp68]. Randell and Kuehner [Ran68] survey the area of dynamic storage allocation and describe linear and segmented name spaces.

Dynamic Address Translation

Virtual memory operates with a hardware feature known as *dynamic address translation*. Each effective address (see Chapter 3) formed by the CPU is translated to a real main storage address prior to each storage reference when operating in the "relocate" mode. (The computer used for a description of dynamic address translation in the System/360 Model 67; TSS/360 is designed to be the primary operating system for this computer.)

The Model 67 includes several hardware additions to a normal System/360 computer; those related to dynamic address translation are:

1. An extended PSW (program status word) that permits a "normal" mode and a "relocate" mode. When operating in the normal mode, the computer operates as any System/360 computer. When in the relocate mode, dynamic address translation is performed.
2. A set of "control registers" used during dynamic address translation. In particular, one control register (called the *segment table register*) points to the segment table.
3. A DAT box‡ (DAT is an acronym for Dynamic Address Translation). The DAT box physically performs the address translation and generates a program interruption if the referenced page is not in main storage or the virtual memory page has not been allocated (i.e., a page table entry does not exist for it.)
4. A small high-speed associative memory. The dynamic translation of addresses requires two storage references to access the segment and page tables. The main storage locations of the last eight pages referenced are

---

†See Johnson and Martinson [Joh69].
‡The DAT box is also referred to as the *Blaauw Box* after G. A. Blaauw who designed it.

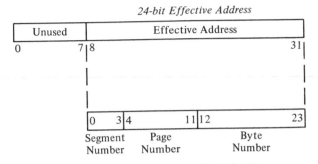

Fig. 9.8 Twenty-four-bit effective address and the virtual memory logical address.

stored in this associative memory. When an address is to be translated, the segment-page fields of the virtual memory address are compared in parallel with the virtual memory addresses in the associative memory. If a match is found, the corresponding main storage address is taken directly from the associative memory and no storage accesses are required for the segment and page tables. (The associative memory is discussed later.)

When operating in a virtual memory environment, the CPU computes an effective address for storage references in the usual fashion. This fact is important and means that a program contains virtual memory addresses and not main storage addresses. If the CPU is operating in the "normal" mode, then the effective address becomes the physical main storage address. When operating in the relocate mode, dynamic address translation takes place as described in the following paragraphs.

The CPU computes a 32-bit effective address; however, only the low-order 24 bits of it are used.† The 24-bit effective address and the corresponding virtual memory logical address are depicted in Fig. 9.8. The logical virtual memory address (hereafter referred to as simply the "virtual memory" address) is divided into three parts: segment number, page number, and byte number. Thus, there are 4096 bytes per page and 256 pages per segment. Ordinarily, pages within a segment are allocated consecutively. However, segments are used for different purposes (e.g., a shared segment) so the ith segment need not be completely allocated before a page allocation is made to the $(i+1)$st segment, or any other segment as a matter of fact. Each task requires the following for execution:

1. a table register value that gives the segment table origin;

---

†The 360 Model 67 also incorporates a 32-bit relocate mode which gives a virtual memory size of 4 billion bytes. It is not presented here; the reader is directed to references [TSSe] and Gibson [Gib66].

2. a segment table that gives the origin of the page tables; and
3. a page table for each segment.

Each page table entry gives the phsyical main storage address of the corresponding page. These tables are created by the Supervisor for each task; the tables are updated as the system operates and pages are moved between main storage and auxiliary storage.

The page table entry requires the following information:

1. main storage address (A);
2. a flag (F) denoting whether the main storage address is valid or invalid; and
3. an external page address (E) giving the device address and relative page number within the device.

A conceptual page table entry is given as Fig. 9.9. If the main storage address is invalid, then the external page address tells where the page can be found so that it can be brought into main storage by the Supervisor on a demand basis. In actual practice, the three entries are disjoint in the sense that the main storage address and the flag are found in a page table entry (per se) and the external page address is found in an external page table entry.

When a task is given control of the CPU, its segment table is brought into main storage,† and the table register is set to point to the origin of the segment table. The page tables are brought in on a demand basis. Assume for this discussion that the page tables are also resident in main storage. The 32-bit table register is depicted in Fig. 9.10 and is used to locate a segment table entry in Fig. 9.11. The segment table entry, depicted in Fig. 9.12, points to a page table origin. During dynamic address translation, the page number (bits 4–11 of the virtual memory address) are added to bits 23–30 of the segment table entry to give the physical address of the page table entry (see Fig. 9.13), that is, if the virtual

Main Storage Address (A)	Flags (F)	External Page Address (E)

Fig. 9.9 *Conceptual* page table entry.

Segment Table Length	Segment Table Origin	000000
0 7	8 25	26 31

Fig. 9.10 Table register for dynamic address translation (points to the segment table).

†An auxiliary segment table is also present in main storage; it is presented under "paging."

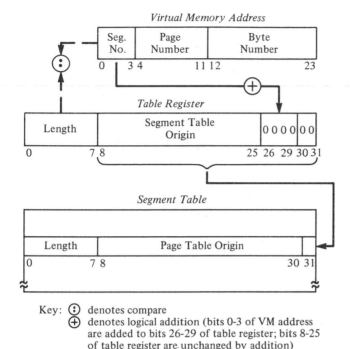

Key: ⊙ denotes compare
      ⊕ denotes logical addition (bits 0-3 of VM address
         are added to bits 26-29 of table register; bits 8-25
         of table register are unchanged by addition)

Fig. 9.11 Locating a segment table entry.

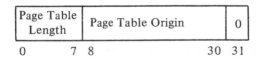

Fig. 9.12 Segment table entry.

nemory page number does not exceed the length of the page table specified as
bits 0-7 of the segment table entry. If the virtual memory page number exceeds
he length of the page table, then an appropriate program interruption occurs
ince that virtual memory page has not been allocated. At this stage, a page
able entry has been located; if the page is in main storage, then the entry should
nclude the main storage address of that page. The page table entry is depicted
n Fig. 9.14. Bits 0-11 of the page table entry give the high-order 12 bits of the
nain storage address that corresponds to the virtual memory address. (The low-
rder 12 bits of the main storage address are the same as the low-order 12 bits of
ne virtual memory address since there is no relocation within a page.) The
alidity of the address contained in the page table entry is governed by bit 12—
alled the *availability bit*. If bit 12 is zero, then the required page is in main stor-

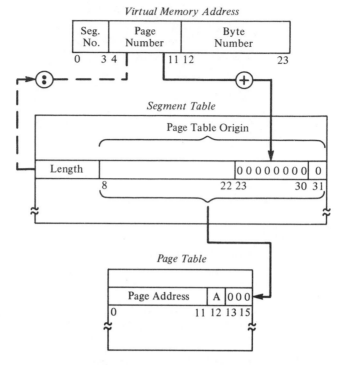

Virtual Memory Address

Key: ⊙ denotes compare
     ⊕ denotes logical addition (bits 4-11 of VM address
        are added to bits 23-30 of the segment table
        entry; bits 8-22 are unchanged)

Fig. 9.13 Locating a page table entry.

Main storage address	A	000
0 11	12	13 15

A denotes available bit:
    0 denotes main storage address is valid
    1 denotes main storage address is invalid
      (page is not in main storage)

Fig. 9.14 Page table entry.

age and the address is valid. If bit 12 is one, then the page is not in main storage
and the address is invalid. If an availability bit of one is encountered by the
hardware during dynamic address translation, an interruption is initiated so that
the Supervisor can bring the required page into main storage.

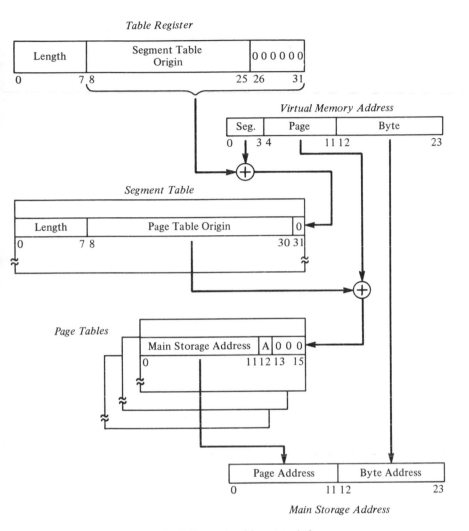

Fig. 9.15 Dynamic address translation.

The complete process of dynamic address translation is depicted in Fig. 9.15. Although the translation is performed by the hardware (the tables are built by software), each translation requires two storage references to reference the segment table and the page table. In the relocate mode, each storage reference would require three storage accesses instead of the customary one, resulting in a performance degradation. Therefore, in the Model 67, dynamic address translation is augmented with a small associative memory (see Fig. 9.16). The associative memory is located in CPU local storage and includes 8 registers, each 31 bits

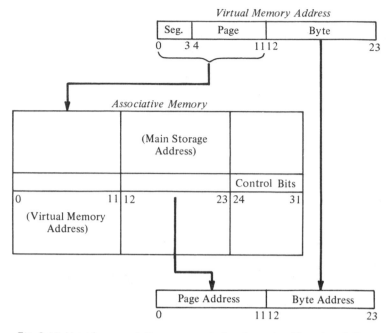

Fig. 9.16 Use of an associative memory during dynamic address translation.

wide.† When a virtual memory address is to be translated, the segment and page numbers (bits 0–11 of the VM address) are compared with bits 0–11 of each associative register in parallel. If an equal match is found, bits 12–23 become the page address directly and the storage accesses for the segment and page tables need not be made. (In the Model 67, the use of the associative memory adds 150 nanoseconds to each storage access, whereas use of the segment and page tables requires at least two microseconds.) Of the remaining six bits, in each associative register, two additional bits are defined: a "used" bit and a "valid" bit. The *valid bit* denotes whether the entry refers to a page that is in storage. If the valid bit is zero, the corresponding entry is not used during associative address compare. The valid bit for an entry is set to one when that entry is used during relocation. When the table register is loaded, the valid bit in each associative register is set to zero, which invalidates all entries. The table register is normally reset when a new user is given control of the CPU and the register is changed to point to the new user's segment table. The *used bit* is set to one when an associative register entry is used during dynamic address translation. The used bits are also reset to zero when the table register is loaded. When all the used bits are set to one, they are automatically reset to zero by the hardware and process is repeated. During dynamic address translation, the associative

†In the 32-bit mode, each register is 39 bits wide.

compare and the search through segment and page tables are initiated together. If an equal compare is made in the associative registers, relocation is performed from the associative registers and the table search is terminated. If no equal comparison is made, the main storage page address from the page table entry is used during relocation and that page address is put into the associative memory with the valid bit and the used bit set to one. The virtual memory and main storage page addresses displace the lowest-numbered associative register with its

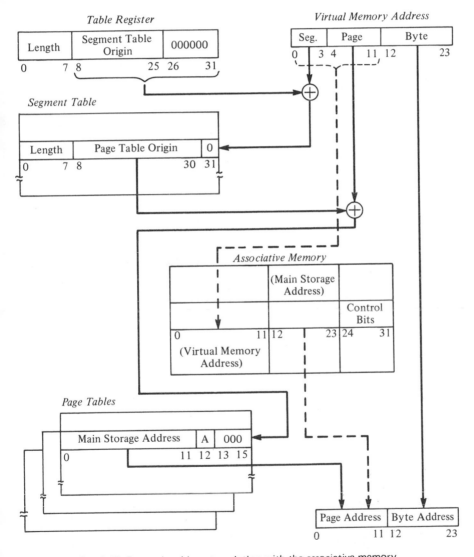

Fig. 9.17 Dynamic address translation with the associative memory.

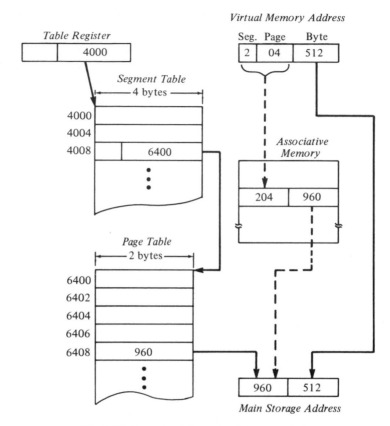

Fig. 9.18 Example of dynamic address translation.

used bit set to zero. This algorithm replaces the "least used" entries; as a result, the "last used" or "most frequently used" page addresses reside in the associative memory. The associative memory is hardware controlled and is not addressable by an operating program. A complete picture of dynamic address translation is given as Fig. 9.17, and an example of the process is given as Fig. 9.18. The ultimate objective of this chapter is to describe the paging process; however, one additional topic is required—storage protection.

Storage Protection

The storage protection feature is modified on the Model 67 to include fetch, reference, and change bits. Recall that the storage protection facility normally involves a 4-bit storage protection key that is associated with each 2048-byte block (i.e., a half page) of main storage. There are also protection key fields in the program status word (PSW) and the channel address word (CAW). If the

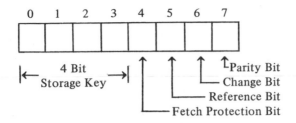

Fig. 9.19 Storage protection extension.

protection key does not match the storage key, then the CPU or the channel, respectively, cannot store information in the corresponding 2048-byte block. The only exception exists when the protection key is zero, which permits access to all of main storage. Storage protection is extended with fetch, reference, and change bits as depicted in Fig. 9.19. When the fetch bit is set to one, then that 2048-byte block is also fetch (read) protected as well as write (store) protected. The *reference bit* is set to one whenever the block is referenced. During paging, the paging processor inspects the two reference bits (one for each 2048-byte half page) for pages that are shared among tasks. If a shared page has not been referenced in a given period of time, it is "paged out" to auxiliary storage. The *change bit* is set to one when a page is changed. During the "page out" operation, the paging processor inspects the change bit. If it is zero and a copy of that page resides on auxiliary storage, then there is no reason to write the page on auxiliary storage and the block of main storage can be reassigned immediately. If, on the other hand, one of the 2048-byte blocks of a page has been changed, then the page must be written to auxiliary storage before that block of main storage can be reassigned.

Paging

Although dynamic address translation gives the means of implementing virtual memory, software support is also necessary for creating and maintaining segment and page tables, moving pages in and out of main storage, and handling program interruptions that result from paging exceptions. *Paging* is the process of moving pages between main storage and auxiliary storage on a dynamic basis under the control of the Supervisor program.

When a task is initiated as a unit of work to the system (i.e., the task is created), a control block called the *task status index* (TSI) is built for that task. The TSI for a task resides in main storage for the duration of a terminal session. Associated with each TSI is another variable-length control block the *external task status index* (XTSI) that partially resides in main storage when the task is active. The XTSI contains the segment and page tables for a task. The segment table is built when the task is initiated as are page tables for an *initial virtual*

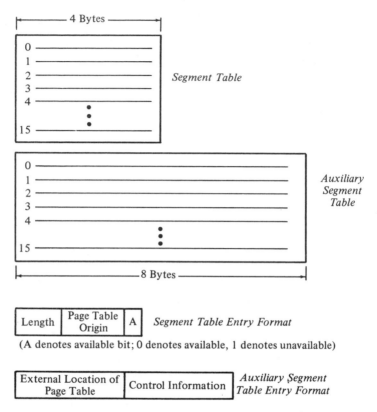

Fig. 9.20 Segment table and auxiliary segment table.

memory (IVM) that is automatically given to each user. As an example, IVM includes the routines of the command system. Other page tables are built dynamically as virtual memory is allocated to a task.

The form of the segment table is given in Fig. 9.20. Also depicted is the auxiliary segment table. The segment table points to page table origins. If a page table is not in main storage, it is marked as such† and the auxiliary segment table points to its location on auxiliary storage. If a page table is not in main storage during dynamic address translation, an interruption is generated and the paging process brings it in from auxiliary storage and the segment table is modified to point to the page table's new location. Later, when the task is "paged out," the page table is placed on auxiliary storage and its location is placed in

---

†Bit 31 of a segment table entry serves this purpose. If bit 31 is zero, the page table is in main storage and the "page table origin" field of that entry points to it. If bit 31 is one, then the corresponding auxiliary segment table entry gives the location on auxiliary storage of the page table.

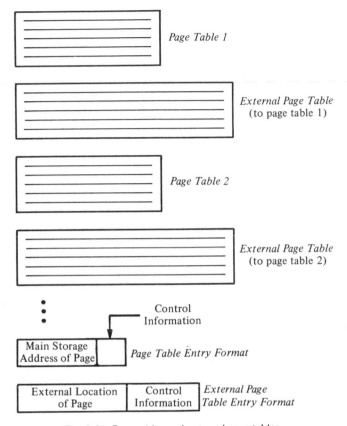

Fig. 9.21 Page tables and external page tables.

the respective auxiliary segment table entry. The page is again marked as un-available in the segment table.

The form of the page table is given in Fig. 9.21. When a page table is in main storage, so is its corresponding external page table. If the dynamic address translation hardware encounters a page marked as unavailable, the resultant pro-gram interruption causes the required page to be "paged in" by the paging processor. The location on auxiliary storage of the required page is determined from the external page table. When a page is "paged out," its page table entry and external page table entry are modified accordingly.

As mentioned previously, a task's segment table, auxiliary segment table, page tables, and external page tables are located in the task's extended task status index (XTSI). Before a task is dispatched for execution, the segment table por-tion of its XTSI is brought into main storage. Other pages are brought on a "demand" basis. In other words, only the "needed" pages are "paged in." At any point in time, the relationship of several tasks' virtual memories and main storage can be viewed conceptually as in Fig. 9.2. The phenomenon of "page buildup" occurs until a task has enough pages in main storage to sustain continued execution. When a task is waiting for a page to continue execution (or possibly to begin execution, as the case may be), it is put into a "page wait" state. When the needed page comes in, the Supervisor again puts that task into the "ready" state for subsequent dispatching. It should be remembered here that when a task is waiting for a page, another task is using the CPU. A task accumulates CPU time in this manner until its time slice is used up. That task is put into the "time slice end" state and its pages are marked to be paged out. The process of moving out the pages of a task is governed by the following conventions:

1. If a page has been changed, then it is marked to be paged out; if it previously occupied space on auxiliary storage, then that space is released for reuse.
2. If a page has not been changed and a copy exists on auxiliary storage, then the main storage occupied by that space is released for reuse.

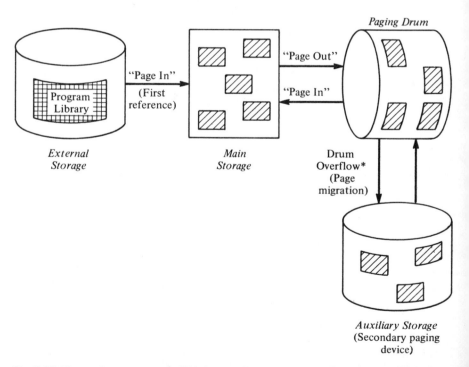

Fig. 9.22 The paging process. (∗ This is a conceptual representation; "page migration" is performed by the Resident Supervisor and pages are read from drum into main storage and are then written out to disk.)

This is a characteristic of demand paging, and each time a task is given the CPU, it must build up enough pages to execute. (Denning [Den68, Den70] discusses the problems associated with building up a working set of pages.) In some cases, "page reclaiming" is possible. *Page reclaiming* refers to the practice of reclaiming a page that has been marked to be paged out; it occurs when a task is given control of the CPU before the pages could be "paged out."

The paging process is depicted in Fig. 9.22. As the system operates, pages are constantly being moved between main storage and a direct-access storage device. The paging device (frequently drum storage) is formatted to handle pages in an efficient manner. The drum has a limited capacity, so infrequently used pages are migrated from the drum to disk. (In at least one case, the paging drum is replaced with large-capacity storage with notable success; see Lauer [Lau67] and Fikes, Lauer, and Vareha [Fik68]).

It should be emphasized at this point that "virtual memory and paging" is a storage management technique. As such, it is only one aspect of a total time sharing system. Other factors that greatly influence the operation of a time sharing system are the scheduling algorithm, storage allocation techniques, data management, the supervisor, and multiprocessing capability. As with the use of virtual memory, these other factors are oriented toward a system that provides rapid "response."

9.4 SYSTEM CONTROL STRUCTURES

Storage Organization and Control

In a conventional multiprogramming operating system, main storage is divided into two areas each representing one level of control. The structure of a two-level operating system is depicted in Fig. 9.23. Level one facilities operate in support of level two programs, even when several user tasks reside in the user area.

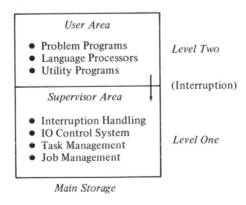

Fig. 9.23 Conventional two-level operating system.

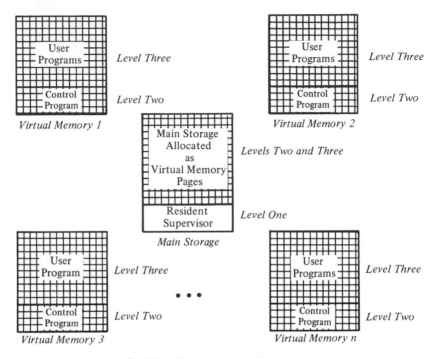

Fig. 9.24 Three-level operating system.

In a virtual memory based system, two storage areas must be managed—main storage and virtual memory. A three-level operating system is used to control the two types of storage. Figure 9.24 depicts a three-level operating system. The "resident supervisor" controls the allocation of "real" resources and is resident in main storage at all times. Each user's virtual memory is divided into two areas: a privileged control program that provides the conventional support services (this is level two) and the user's program area (which is level three). The Resident Supervisor and the virtual memory control programs differ in important ways. The Resident Supervisor has the following characteristics:

1. There is one Resident Supervisor per system (regardless of the number of CPUs).
2. It operates in the supervisor state.
3. It runs in the nonrelocated mode (i.e., the normal 360 mode).
4. It is not time sliced.
5. It is resident in main storage at all times.

The level two virtual memory control programs have the following characteristics:

1. There is one assigned to each user.

2. They operate in the problem state.
3. They run in the "relocate" (i.e., virtual memory) mode.
4. They are time sliced.
5. They can be "paged in" and "out" of main storage.

The major difference between level one and level two is that level one programs operate in the supervisor state and are core resident. The major difference between level two and level three is that level two programs operate with a PSW protection key of zero (as does level one) whereas level three programs have a nonzero PSW protection key.†

Thus, storage protection keys protect the control programs against being accessed by level three programs. Distinct level three tasks are protected against each other through dynamic address translation and the page tables. (Obviously, when one or more pages are shared, the respective page table entries point to the same block of main storage.)

The assignment of storage keys to main storage blocks operate in conjunction with the above conventions and are given as Table 9.1.

TABLE 9.1 STORAGE PROTECTION KEYS

Storage type		Key
Task Virtual Storage	User read/write	1
	User read only	2
	Privileged	2
Pages being written out		3
IORCB buffer[a]		4
Resident supervisor code		5

[a]An input/output request block (IORCB) is used for input/output operations on physical data sets.

Resident Supervisor

The system operates under the control of a supervisor program that is resident in main storage; it is called the Resident Supervisor. The Resident Supervisor is mainly an interruption handler that sorts the five interruption types of the System/360 into more specific categories and stacks them for subsequent processing. The Resident Supervisor is "interrupt-driven," and interruptions are processed on a priority basis. With regard to the operation of the system and its objectives, some interruptions (such as an IO paging interruption) are simply more important than others.

In a time sharing system, where response time is significant, an interruption is usually associated with a condition or event that must be resolved before a task

†More specifically, the PSW protection key of level three programs is set to one.

can continue execution. Moreover, the "round robin" type of scheduling† implies that at any point in time, any ready task has a reasonably good chance of "getting" the CPU. Thus, all interruptions are processed, within the priority structure of the system, before the CPU is dispatched to another task.

In general, the Resident Supervisor operates with interruptions enabled as do programs that operate in virtual memory. When an interruption occurs, other interruptions are temporarily disabled until a control block can be formed for the interruption that occurred and that control block can be placed on an appropriate queue. If the system was operating in the supervisor state when the interruption occurred, then the Resident Supervisor resumes its processing from the point of interruption so that work can be performed in an orderly manner. If the system was operating in the problem state when the interruption occurred, then the status of that task is "saved in" its TSI and control remains in the Resident Supervisor until all of its work is complete.

The operational flow of control between user tasks and the Resident Supervisor is suggested in Fig. 9.25 (see Lett and Konigsford [Let68]). A more detailed version of this figure is given later; however, the major components of the Resident Supervisor are depicted.

Before considering the components of the Resident Supervisor, the functions that it performs on a system-wide basis are given to indicate why the Supervisor is organized in the precise manner that it is. Resident Supervisor functions can be grouped as follows:

1. interruption handling,
2. task control,
3. timer control and task dispatching,
4. main storage allocation,
5. auxiliary storage allocation,
6. reading and writing pages (paging),
7. nonpaging IO,
8. task accounting, and
9. error retry and recovery.

The components of the Resident Supervisor are grouped into six categories as shown in Fig. 9.26; they are described as follows:

1. *Interrupt stacker.* This component is the only entry to the Resident Supervisor. The interrupt stacker classifies interruptions, builds appropriate GQEs (see next section), and places the GQEs on appropriate queues.
2. *Queue scanner.* This component provides a sequencing mechanism by which interruptions are processed. The queue scanner uses a scan table (see

†The term "round robin" is used figuratively since a round-robin scheduling algorithm is not used.

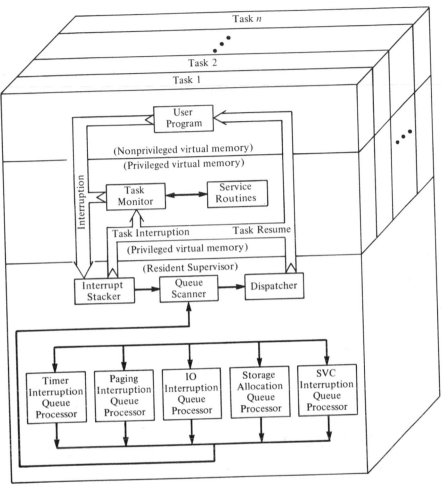

Fig. 9.25 Simplified flow of control between user tasks and the Resident Supervisor.

next section) to which the various queues are anchored and passes control to the queue processors.

3. *Queue processors.* Each queue processor is designed to process a GQE on its queue and return to the queue scanner. Some exceptions exist (such as the paging drum queue processor) where the queue processor processes all GQEs on its queue before returning to the queue scanner.

4. *Dispatcher.* The dispatcher selects a task to be given CPU control and places that task in execution.

5. *Supervisor service routines.* These routines provide general services re-

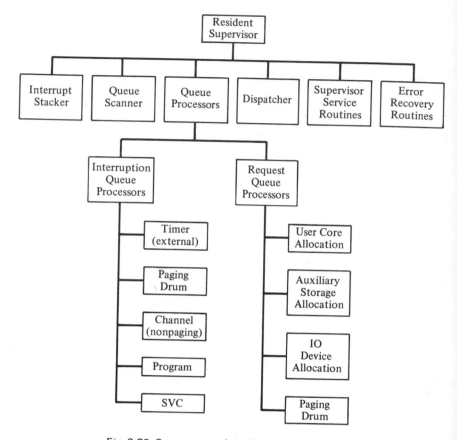

Fig. 9.26 Components of the Resident Supervisor.

quired by other routines. Examples are queue control, IO service, and task service.

6. *Error recovery routines.* These routines operate in response to machine error conditions and provide recording, recovery, and reconfiguration services.

The queue processors are the most extensive component since they perform most of the work done by the Resident Supervisor, including a great many system facilities that are available through macro instructions and corresponding SVC interruptions. The various queue processors are discussed in more detail in Chapter 11.

The design of the Resident Supervisor is relatively "clean" as evidenced by the preceding paragraphs. Control blocks and tables are used extensively in TSS; as such, they represent an additional level of system control.

System Control Blocks and Tables

As in most operating systems, a variety of system control blocks and tables are defined and used. The discussion here is limited to the most significant of these control blocks and tables as far as system control is concerned.

Six control blocks and tables are described: (1) the generalized queue entry (GQE), (2) the task status index (TSI), (3) the extended task status index (XTSI), (4) the page control block (PCB), (5) the scan table, and (6) the system table.

The generalized queue entry (GQE) contains a description of work to be done by the Resident Supervisor or a device controlled by the Resident Supervisor. In most cases, a GQE is built by the interrupt stacker to record information associated with an interruption. However, in some cases, a GQE is built by one queue processor to have work performed by another queue processor. A GQE contains the following information:

1. pointer to the TSI,
2. pointers to preceding and succeeding GQEs on the same queue,
3. pointer to the page control block if the GQE is associated with a paging request,
4. pointer to an IO request block or a message control block, if the GQE is associated with nonpaging IO,
5. flags (page in or page out),
6. instruction length code,
7. GQE movement information,
8. sense data (from an IO operation),
9. channel status word,
10. channel logout data,
11. interruption code, and
12. symbolic device code.

In TSS, the GQE is fixed at a length of 64 bytes.

A *task status index* (TSI) is associated with each task in the system. The TSIs reside on a TSI queue that is anchored in the system table. A task's TSI is resident in main storage between LOGON and LOGOFF. The TSI contains the following information:

1. user identification,
2. task identification,
3. task priority,
4. SYSIN and SYSOUT device addresses,
5. pointer to XTSI,
6. pointer to task interruption queue (of task interruptions as compared to system interruptions),

  7. pointer to task symbolic device list,
  8. task status flags,
  9. task interruption mask,
  10. lock byte for multiprocessing, and
  11. task interruption pending flags.

In TSS, the TSI is fixed at a length of 128 bytes.

The *extended task status index* (XTSI) is an extension to the TSI that does not have to be permanently resident in main storage between LOGON and LOGOFF. The XTSI contains a fixed-length portion and a variable-length portion. The fixed portion contains save areas for the program status word, control registers, general-purpose registers, and floating-point registers plus the following: TSI pointer, time slice information, and timer information. The variable-length portion contains the segment table, auxiliary segment table, page tables, and external page tables. The XTSI is paged in and out of main storage but is not part of a user's virtual memory.

A *page control block* (PCB) controls the movement of a virtual memory or XTSI page between main storage and auxiliary or external storage. The PCB is pointed to by the GQE for a paging request. The PCB contains the following information:

  1. main storage address of page,
  2. virtual memory address of page,
  3. auxiliary or external address of the page, and
  4. flags that specify the status of the paging operation.

A single PCB can be used to control three paging operations and is linked to a succeeding PCB. In TSS, the PCB is fixed at a length of 64 bytes.

The *scan table* is used by the queue scanner and serves as an anchor for all GQE queues. The scan table (depicted in Fig. 9.27) contains an entry for each interrupt type, for each device, and for each resource allocated. Each scan table entry contains the following:

  1. pointer to first GQE on the queue,
  2. pointer to last GQE on the queue,
  3. location of the queue processor,
  4. queue processor lock byte, and
  5. flags, including a queue empty flag and queue processor suppress flags.

Each scan table entry is 16 bytes in length.

The *system table* is a fixed area in the Resident Supervisor that contains system parameters as well as pointers to the active TSI chain, inactive TSI chains, and the resident shared page index (RSPI) that controls all shared page operations for the system.

Collectively, the Resident Supervisor routines, the interruption structure, the

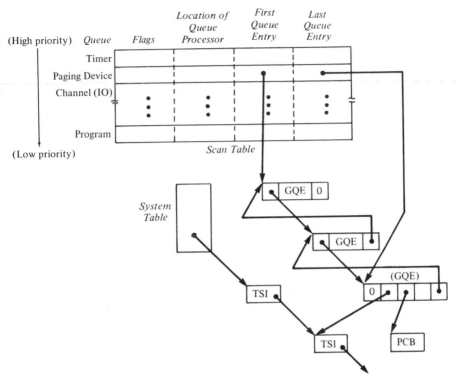

Fig. 9.27 Conceptual view of the scan table.

control blocks, and the tables control the execution of the system. The Resident Supervisor routines are processors that operate on queues and tables creating new ones. At any point in time, the state of the system can be determined from the contents of the various queues and tables. The manner in which the system operates is described in Chapter 11.

9.5 TASK CONTROL STRUCTURES

To the Resident Supervisor, each task appears as a virtual computer system. A task is allocated main storage, virtual storage, space on public volumes, access to private devices, and CPU time. In response to interruptions, the Resident Supervisor handles service requests and satisfies conditions that arise and then passes CPU control to an active task, as determined by a scheduling algorithm. Special conditions that must be resolved at the system level (i.e., level one) are handled by the Resident Supervisor directly. Conditions that can be handled at the task level are passed back to the task to be processed by a level two monitor program —called the Task Monitor. The purpose of this section is to present the manner in which tasks are controlled by the Resident Supervisor and the Task Monitor.

Task Initiation

A task is created in one of two ways: (1) A user signs on at the terminal; or (2) a routine of the system creates a task. (Actually, a system routine creates a task in both cases; however, procedures for establishing a conversational task are sufficiently different to warrant special attention.)

When the user dials the telephone number of the computer system, receives a high-pitched tone, and denotes that he wants to enter the DATA mode, he establishes a connection with the transmission control unit of the computer.† As yet, he has not created a task. The user presses ATTENTION and an IO interruption is initiated by the channel. The interruption is "fielded" by the interrupt stacker and a GQE for it is built; the GQE is queued on the channel interrupt queue. Subsequently, the channel interrupt processor is called upon to process this GQE. The channel interrupt processor determines the symbolic device address associated with the interruption. If there is no IO operation pending on the device, then it is determined that the IO interruption is unsolicited (i.e., it is "asynchronous"). A "device group table" is checked to see if a task is associated with the device. If there is no task associated with the device, then a "Task Initiation" routine is called. This routine creates a TSI and an initial XTSI and transfers the GQE from the channel interrupt queue to the TSI. An asynchronous IO flag is set in the TSI. The new TSI is linked to the TSI chain and an exit is made to the Queue Scanner routine of the Resident Supervisor. Subsequently, this "task" is scheduled for execution. A "task interrupt control" routine is called by the Dispatcher to determine if any task interruptions are pending. (In this case, there is.) Therefore, the "task interrupt control" routine specifies that the task should be started at a task interruption processing routine of the Task Monitor (see "Initial Virtual Memory"). Control is returned to the Dispatcher, which gives CPU control to the task. The Task Monitor is entered and it recognizes that the interruption pertains to an initial attention. The Task Monitor calls a Virtual Memory Task Initialization routine that performs preliminary processing for a task, establishing the following data sets: SYSIN, SYSOUT, the catalog, system library (SYSLIB), macro library, system accounting table, and system messenger file, and invokes a LOGON routine that validates the user's identity. After logon is complete, the user's library—USERLIB—is opened and control is passed to the command system. The user can now enter commands.

Nonconversational tasks are created by two "system tasks" that operate at level two; they are the "batch monitor" task and the "bulk IO" task. The "batch monitor" controls the execution of nonconversational processing programs (i.e., tasks) and maintains a batch work queue (BWQ). When the user enters a command to create a nonconversational task, such as EXECUTE or

---

†When the user's terminal device is directly attached to the computer system, he simply turns the device on and the required connection is established.

PRINT, that command effectively places an entry in the batch work queue. The batch work queue is processed by the Batch Monitor by creating tasks for processing programs and by passing input and output requests to the Bulk IO task. The creation of a task from within the system is initiated with a "create TSI" macro instruction; in general, the process of creating a nonconversational task is essentially the same as for creating a conversational task. Obviously, differences, such as the allocation of SYSIN and SYSOUT, are handled appropriately.

The bulk IO task performs another important function for the system: it reads cards and creates data sets. The Bulk IO task is created when the system is started (called "startup," which is analogous to the IPL sequence in OS) or with an operator command. If the Bulk IO task exists, it is activated when the operator starts the card reader. If a batch job is read in, the Bulk IO task creates a data set out of it and makes an appropriate entry in the batch work queue. If data cards are read in, the Bulk IO task creates a data set out of them and catalogs the data set name for subsequent use by a conversational or a nonconversational task.

Initial Virtual Memory

In a batch-oriented operating system, such as OS, job control information (i.e., control cards or JCL) is frequently processed before the job is initiated for execution. In the time sharing system, however, job control information is processed dynamically as it is entered by the user. Therefore, each task must initially include a set of programs that allow it to "get off the ground." These programs are called *initial virtual memory* (IVM) and are automatically "given" to a task when its TSI and XTSI are created. IVM contains three important programs:

1. the *task monitor* that provides control services for programs executing in the task's virtual memory;
2. the *command system* that reads and interprets user commands and performs the requested actions; and
3. the *dynamic loader* that "loads" object modules into virtual memory, as required.

The programs that comprise IVM occupy a public segment and are shared among users. Thus, only one copy of IVM programs exists in the system; moreover, these programs are link loaded together so that they occupy a minimum number of virtual memory pages. IVM programs occupy the same virtual memory addresses in each user's virtual memory.

The Command System and the Dynamic Loader are presented in Chapter 10; the Task Monitor is covered next.

Task Monitor

The Task Monitor performs the same functions for an individual task that the Resident Supervisor performs for the entire system. Clearly, the processing of some types of interruptions are a task's responsibility and should be performed in that task's privileged virtual memory. A GQE for an interruption of this type is queued on the task's TSI. The Task Interrupt Control (TIC) routine recognizes the case and specifies an entry to the Task Monitor to process the interruption—which is now called a "virtual interruption" or a "programmed interruption." Some programmed interruptions can be masked off and this facility is handled by the Task Monitor. In general, the reason that programmed interruptions are necessary is that the task for which an interruption is intended may not be the next one dispatched.

In order to devise a virtual interruption scheme analogous to the real interruption mechanism, a virtual PSW (VPSW) and an interrupt storage area (ISA) are defined. A VPSW is the virtual counterpart of the real PSW and reflects virtual memory addresses rather than real storage addresses. The ISA is page 0 of segment 0 in each user's virtual memory. Control and sense data, interrupt conditions, and old and new VPSWs are stored there for use by a task and the Task Monitor. (The ISA is analogous to "lower core" in some computers.†)

When the Task Monitor receives an interruption, it creates a queue linkage entry (QLE) analogous to the GQE of the Resident Supervisor. The QLE is placed on an appropriate queue and the Task Monitor calls upon a "Scanner/Dispatcher" to invoke virtual memory queue processors for the various QLEs.

Some virtual interruptions serve only to pass program control from a nonprivileged program to a privileged routine; since this operation requires a change of the task's PSW protection key, the services of the Resident Supervisor are needed.‡ Other interruptions result from an actual program interruption, a request to have an IO processing operation completed in virtual memory, etc.

Task Status

At any point in time, a task can be in one of several states. The state that a task is in determines whether or not it can use the CPU and where its pages are. Only tasks for which a TSI exists are considered; in other words, the status of a task before LOGON and after LOGOFF is not of concern.

In general, a task can be active or inactive. An *active task* is active in the sense that it is undergoing a time slice, has just finished a time slice, is waiting for page, or is waiting for input/output operation. An *inactive task* is waiting for a response from the terminal; this response is typically measured in seconds, minutes, or hours (in the case the user has gone out for lunch without logging off). Tasks are also put on the inactive queue for what is referred to as an IO delay, such as waiting for a private volume to be mounted. Active tasks can be either

---

†In System/360, the ISA is the virtual memory counterpart to the prefix storage area (PSA) of the CPU.

‡The instruction to load a new PSW is a privileged operation that must be executed when the CPU is in the supervisor state.

"dispatchable" or "eligible." A task that is classed as *dispatchable* is in one of the following states:

1. in execution,
2. waiting for execution,
3. waiting for a page, or
4. waiting for (nonterminal) IO.

These tasks are accumulating pages in main storage and are also accumulating CPU time, that is, when they are in execution. Tasks on the dispatchable list are effectively being multiprogrammed. The situation requires a note of explanation. As mentioned, the system uses demand paging. What this means is that a task executes for a few microseconds and another page is needed. An interruption occurs through dynamic address translation and the Supervisor brings the page in. The process continues until the task has accumulated a "working set" of pages; the phenomenon is called "page buildup." At any point in time, there are usually several tasks going through page buildup. Thus, the CPU is given to one of the dispatchable tasks that is ready for execution. Scheduling is presented in Chapter 11.

When a task has accumulated its time slice—usually in "bits and pieces" of CPU time—it is taken off the dispatchable list and put on an "eligible" list. An *eligible task* has completed a time slice and is waiting for a new one. When a task completes a time slice, the main storage assigned to its pages (often called

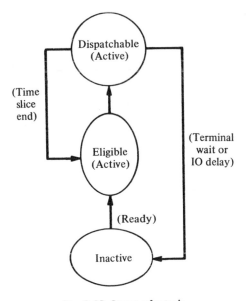

Fig. 9.28 States of a task.

core blocks) are released for use by other tasks. Tasks move from the eligible list to the dispatchable list on a modified round robin basis as the dispatcher looks for work. Obviously, the manner in which the lists are managed is a scheduling problem and is discussed under that subject. The *states* of a task are depicted in Fig. 9.28.

It is important to recognize that an operating system of this type is usually supported by a very fast computer and that a task moves between the different states at a high rate of speed. Task status is also affected by the amount of main storage that is available. A task is moved from the eligible list to the dispatchable list as soon as space is available for its pages. Thus, if the number of users is low relative to the size of main storage, then a task moves quickly from the eligible list to the dispatchable list and it experiences good response time (and the user is happy). If the number of users is high relative to the size of main storage, then some delay takes place between the time a task enters and leaves the eligible list, and the response time is not as good (and the user is not as happy). The situation is influenced, obviously, by the characteristics of the tasks and by the scheduling algorithm used.

9.6 COMMENTS ON THE CHARACTERISTICS OF A GENERAL-PURPOSE TIME SHARING SYSTEM

Although a general-purpose time sharing system and a multiprogrammed operating system process user programs in much the same manner, their respective design philosophies are markedly different. (Obviously, programs are compiled or assembled, loaded, and executed in both kinds of systems.) The fact that a user can "converse" with a time sharing system seems to be the major design factor for the following reasons:

1. Response time is of prime importance.
2. The CPU is scheduled differently to provide good response time.
3. Jobs are not usually preplanned such that job control statements must be processed dynamically.
4. The fact that rapid multiplexing among tasks exists requires that the Resident Supervisor process interruptions on a system-wide basis rather than on a task-oriented basis.
5. Rapid multiplexing between tasks requires a Task Monitor that operates in virtual memory to control task execution.

The next chapter, "System Operating Environment," emphasizes the appearance of the system to a user task operating in virtual memory. In spite of the "user orientation" of the chapter, it is impossible to subordinate the dynamic characteristics of a general-purpose time sharing system, and this is the difficulty in designing an effective open time sharing system. There are many components in an operating system of this type: the paging process, the scheduling algorithm and dispatcher, main storage allocation, external storage allocation, input and output processes, program loading, task control, device allocation, and the structure of the supervisor—to name only a few. The components do not necessarily compete for the resources of the system, but they do use these resources, and therefore cause conflicts to some degree. Most of these components have been studied and are well understood. However, principles for developing effective operating systems from these components are not as well developed. Currently, most operating systems are designed and developed with the aid of simulation models.

10

SYSTEM
OPERATING
ENVIRONMENT

10.1 VIRTUAL MEMORY SYSTEMS

The objective behind a three-level operating system is to provide task control in an open time sharing environment. Privileged system routines that operate in each user's virtual memory supply the required level of control. When a task is created, it is given an initial virtual memory (IVM) that includes three major components: the Task Monitor, the Command System, and the Dynamic Loader. Also included in IVM are certain data management access routines and a variety of service programs. The contents of IVM can be established during system generation; in fact, some installations have included the FORTRAN compiler in IVM. IVM is common to all users' virtual memory; in fact, these routines are shared by users of the system. The process of sharing is depicted conceptually in Fig. 10.1

Privileged routines that execute in virtual memory are a logical extension to the Resident Supervisor. They operate with a PSW protection key of zero, so that they can access tables and a user's virtual memory, and have a stroage key that is different from that of a user task and its PSW.

The user communicates with components that operate in virtual memory with the command system and through assembler language macro instructions. In general, the user does not interface directly with the Task Monitor or the Dynamic Loader; however, these components operate in support of a task. The Command System uses a command language—analogous, in a sense, to the job control language introduced previously. Data Management structures are

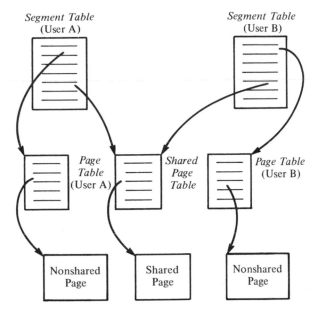

Fig. 10.1 Conceptualization of shared pages.

also included in TSS and they are similar to those of OS or of any operating system. A system catalog is used, along with access methods and various techniques for data set organization. A "virtual access method" (referred to as VAM) is provided for use with public storage. VAM groups data records into page-sized (4096 bytes) blocks so that they can be transferred between public storage and main storage by the paging routines.

10.2 DATA MANAGEMENT STRUCTURES

Although a time-sharing system is heavily dependent upon data management facilities, these facilities (like a time sharing system itself) are "user-oriented" rather than "system-oriented," in order to provide the level of service demanded in a time sharing environment. Therefore, data management structures include data set names, the catalog, virtual access methods, physical access methods, record formats, data set sharing, IO operations, and data management commands.

In general, the subject matter presented here is a logical extension to the concepts presented in Chapters 6, 7, and 8.

Data Set Naming Conventions

A data set name is a series of one or more simple names separated by periods; e.g.,

BIGFILE

or

AB.KT3.FIN1

A data set name that is not simple is termed a *qualified name* and relates to the hierarchical structure of the system catalog. In TSS, qualified data set names are used to provide data set security.

Because of the multiaccess characteristics of a time sharing system, several users ordinarily have access to the information stored in the system. The system protects a user's data sets against inadvertent access by other users and against planned infiltration by persons seeking information.

Each user is assigned a "user ID" when he is joined to the system. He must provide the user ID to gain access to the system, among other things, and that user ID is used to structure his entries in the system catalog. Each time a user specifies a data set name, his user ID is prefixed to that name as an additional level of qualification. Thus if the user's ID is BRODGERS and his data set is named MFILE, then the system uses the qualified data set name BROD-GERS.MFILE. The process of prefixing the user's ID to the data set name is performed automatically by the command system so that one user cannot access another user's data set—unless explicitly permitted to share that data set by the other user.

Catalog Structure

The first hierarchical level in the catalog is a *master index* that includes an entry for each user joined to the system. The master index effectively structures the catalog into a set of user catalogs.

The primary entry in the catalog is termed an *S block* and is used for two purposes: as an index entry and as a data set descriptor. When used as an *index entry*, an S block points to other S blocks at the same level. When used as a *data set descriptor*, an S block points to the data set control block (DSCB) and the list of authorized sharers of that data set. Consider the qualified names in Fig. 10.2; a conceptual view of a corresponding catalog structure is given as Fig. 10.3. A subentry to any given master index entry is regarded as a *user catalog*, since corresponding S blocks belong to the respective user. The lowest-level entries in any user catalog are data set descriptors that point to the sharer list for a data set and to the data set. For VAM direct-access volumes, the descriptor points to the data set which also contains its own DSCB. For OS type direct-access volumes, the descriptor points to the VTOC of that volume.[†] For

---

[†]VAM data sets on direct-access volumes do not use a VTOC; the catalog entry points directly to the data set. This design technique is feasible since all VAM data sets are cataloged. In OS, as a counterexample, all data sets are not cataloged and a VTOC is necessary to locate a data set on a direct-access volume. TSS could use a VTOC (in fact, early versions of TSS did use a VTOC); however, many data sets are "opened" and "closed" in a time sharing environment and the seek time to the VTOC becomes excessive.

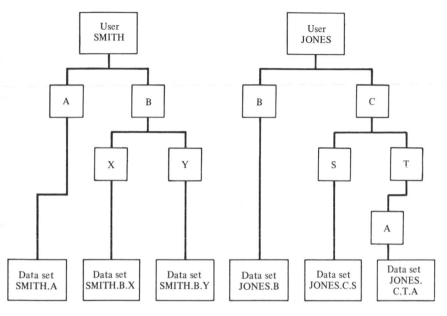

Fig. 10.2 An example of qualified data set names (see Fig. 10.3).

magnetic tape volumes, the descriptor gives the volume identification so that it can be mounted by the operator.

The catalog structure can be viewed in a slightly different fashion, as depicted in Fig. 10.4; this figure depicts how the data set JONES.C.S of Fig. 10.2 is located.

The data set control block (DSCB) illustrated in Figs. 10.3 and 10.4 performs essentially the same function as the DSCB described in Chapters 6, 7, and 8. The form of the DSCB varies depending upon the data set it describes.

In TSS, most data sets are cataloged. More specifically, virtual access method (VAM) data sets are cataloged when they are defined. Data sets entered into the system and placed on public storage by bulk IO facilities are also cataloged automatically by the system. Physical data sets (as in OS) are cataloged only when explicitly requested by the user.

Virtual Access Methods

Virtual access method (VAM) data sets are stored as page-size (4096 bytes) blocks so that they can be accessed by the system paging programs. VAM data sets are organized in three ways: (1) virtual sequential (VSAM), (2) virtual indexed sequential (VISAM), and (3) virtual partitioned (VPAM). The *virtual sequential access method* (VSAM) is designed for data sets that are written and read sequentially. The access method uses an "external page map" that is stored

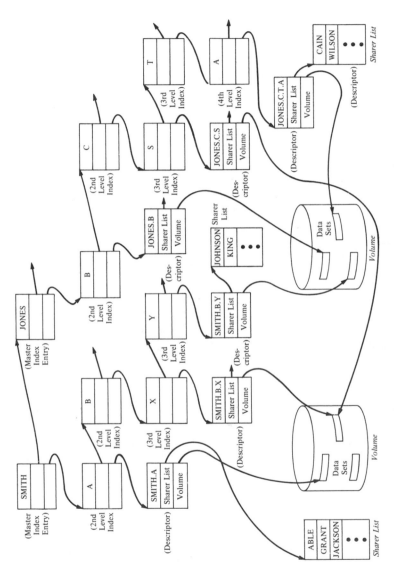

Fig. 10.3 Conceptual view of the catalog (see Fig. 10.2).

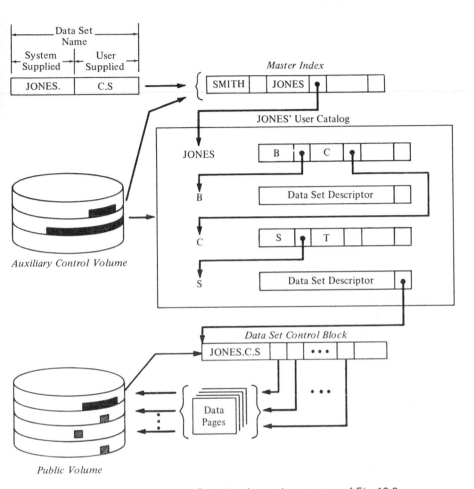

Fig. 10.4 Another means of viewing the catalog structure of Fig. 10.3.

along with the data set. When a VSAM data set is opened, the "external page map" is brought into main storage to form a Relative External Storage Correspondence Table (RESTBL). The RESTBL is used by the access routines, located in a task's virtual memory, to transfer VSAM pages between main storage and public storage. A VSAM data set is suggested by Fig. 10.5.

The *virtual indexed sequential access method* (VISAM) is the virtual storage counterpart of the indexed sequential access method considered previously. VISAM data sets include three kinds of pages: (1) directory pages, (2) data pages, and (3) overflow pages. The *directory page* serves as the master index to the data set and contains one entry for each page of the data set. That entry includes the lowest key on the page and the relative location of the page in public storage. Each *data page* includes the keys and the data records contained in that

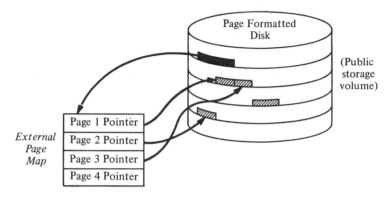

Fig. 10.5 Conceptual view of virtual sequential data set organization.

page. The keys entries are maintained in collating sequence so that a binary search can be made as required. Because of additions, deletions, and insertions, data records are not necessarily maintained in any specific order. When an insertion is made to the data set that would cause a page overflow, an *overflow page* is used. An overflow page is located by a key entry in a data page. A VISAM data set is depicted in Fig. 10.6.

The *virtual partitioned access method* (VPAM) is analogous to the OS partitioned data set organization. VPAM data sets permit virtual sequential members and virtual indexed sequential members; they are frequently used for program libraries stored as either object modules or source modules. A VPAM data set includes directory pages and member pages. The *directory page* gives the page location of each member of VPAM data set. *Member pages* take the form of either VSAM or VISAM pages, discussed previously. The form of a VPAM data set is suggested by Fig. 10.7.

Virtual data sets are a convenience from both the user's point of view and the system's point of view. Space on public storage volumes (i.e., direct-access volumes) is allocated in page-size extents. Thus, external storage management is simplified and a data set (or even parts of it) need not occupy contiguous tracks. The reader should refer to Figs. 10.5, 10.6, and 10.7 here and note that pages of a VAM data set are always located through an "external page map" or a "directory page." As a result, the user need not specify primary and secondary allocations and a data set can grow in size, as required. In short, VAM data sets provide many of the advantages normally associated with the use of linked lists. Lett [Let69] presents an overview of the data management structures in TSS.

Physical Access Methods

Physical access methods, in contradistinction to virtual access methods, are needed for compatibility with other systems and for utilizing nonstandard IO devices with the system. TSS includes three physical access methods: BSAM,

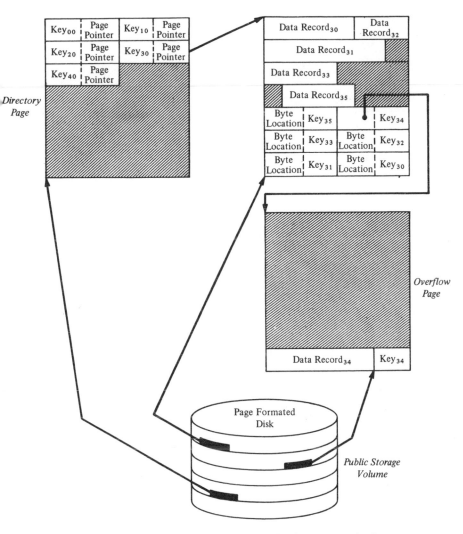

Fig. 10.6 Example of virtual indexed sequential data set organization.

QSAM, and IOREQ.   BSAM and QSAM have been introduced previously.
IOREQ (which stands for IO Request) permits a user to write his own
channel program.

Physical access methods use an interesting technique to insure that buffer
pages are in main storage, to compensate for virtual memory addresses, and to
guard against a time slice end condition occurring at the wrong time.   The
access method builds an input/output control block (IORCB) that is passed to
the Resident Supervisor with the SVC instruction used to initiate IO processing.
The IORCB contains the following:

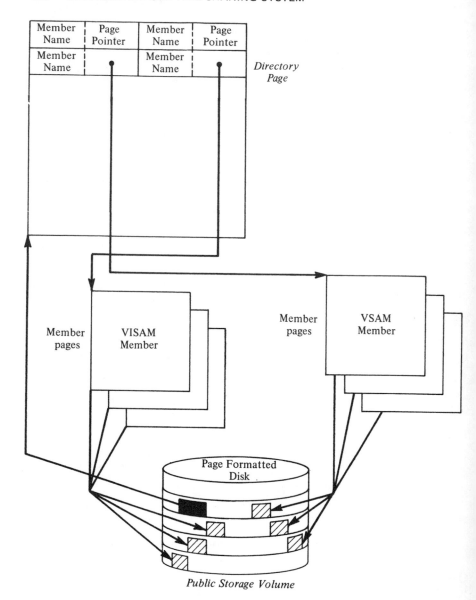

Fig. 10.7 Example of virtual partitioned data set organization.

1. the SVC instruction,
2. symbolic device address,
3. a data buffer or a list of page addresses (for cases where the block exceeds a page in length), and
4. a channel program.

SVC	Symbolic Device
	Address and
	Control information
Data Buffer	
or	
List of Pages	
Channel Program	

Fig. 10.8 Input/output request control block (IORCB).

The IORCB is depicted in Fig. 10.8. Prior to initiating the IO operation, the Resident Supervisor must make adjustments for the fact that the IO system uses physical storage addresses and the access method uses virtual memory addresses.

When "physical access method" input and output is performed by the Supervisor, the physical storage address of the IORCB is determined and the contents of the IORCB are moved to a supervisor work area. Virtual memory addresses in the page list and the channel program are adjusted to correspond to physical storage addresses. The following discussion describes why the SVC instruction is in the IORCB and demonstrates one type of design problem that arises in the development of operating systems. Control is transferred from the access method, which executes in virtual memory, to the Resident Supervisor with an SVC instruction generated by the expansion of an IOCAL (IO call) macro instruction. (IOCAL also passes the address of the IORCB to the Resident Supervisor.) However, a time slice end could occur at an unfortunate time, that is, after the IORCB has been built and just before IOCAL SVC has been executed. At the beginning of the next time slice, the IOCAL SVC would be executed but the IORCB page would very likely be paged out. To circumvent this problem, the IOCAL SVC is placed in the IORCB and it is executed remotely (with an EXECUTE instruction). This technique serves two purposes: (1) The IORCB is in main storage at the time the SVC is executed; and (2) the address of the IORCB is passed to the Resident Supervisor, implicitly, as the address of the SVC instruction.

The above technique is characteristic of the kinds of techniques that must be employed in the design and implementation phases of operating system development.

Record Formats

Record formats in page-oriented data management systems are a logical extension to the concepts presented earlier. Fixed-length, variable-length, and undefined-length records are defined for VSAM and VISAM data sets. (This obviously includes VPAM data sets that can have VSAM and VISAM members.) Fig. 10.9 depicts VSAM record formats. For fixed-length and variable-length records, the system automatically keeps track of overlap across page boundaries.

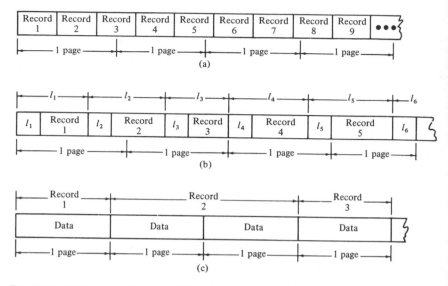

Fig. 10.9 VSAM record formats. (a) Fixed-length records. (b) Variable-length records. (c) Undefined-length records.

An undefined-length record must consist of an integral number of pages and always begins on a page boundary.

Fig. 10.10 depicts VISAM record formats. The system automatically provides directory pages. Records cannot exceed page boundaries; however, the user can specify the percentage of data pages that are to be initially filled (see Fig. 10.6). If many record insertions are anticipated, IO processing time can be decreased by minimizing the number of overflow pages that will eventually be needed. VISAM records can have initial or embedded keys and can assume fixed-length and variable-length record formats.

A special form of the VISAM data set is the "line data set." A *line data set* includes variable-length records and has a line number as a key (see Fig. 10.11). The line data set is designed for use with language processors and other programs where the line number is generated by the program requesting the data.

Record formats for physical data sets are fundamentally the same as presented in Chapters 6, 7, and 8 and are not presented further.

Data Set Description

The *data control block* (DCB)—see Chapter 7—is used as the primary means of communication between a task, the access method, and the IO routines. A DCB is required for each data set used by a program; the skeleton of the DCB is created by the DCB macro instruction in assembler language, by a compiler, or by a program dynamically during its execution. The DCB that is eventually used

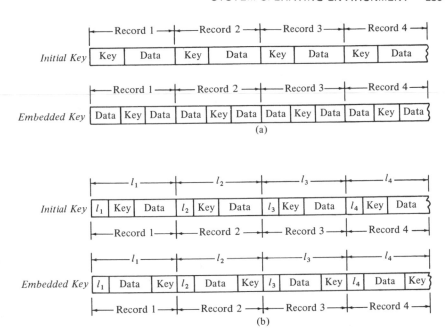

Fig. 10.10 VISAM record formats (VISAM records cannot exceed page boundaries). (a) Fixed-length records. (b) Variable-length records.

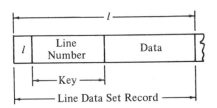

Fig. 10.11 Record of a line data set.

during IO processing describes a data set and is completed when the data set is opened. It receives its information from the skeleton DCB, the define data command (DDEF), or the data set control block (DSCB) of the data set. The DCB resides in a user's program and can be modified during program execution. A field in the DCB contains the rare combination of characters *%*%. This field is inspected periodically as a means of measuring the integrity of the DCB.

The fields in the DCB vary depending upon the data set described. In general, virtual data sets require less descriptive information than physical data sets. A data set is described by the following parameters contained in the DCB:

Data definition name (DDNAME)
Data set organization (DSORG)
Record format (RECFM)

Logical record length (LRECL)
End of data exit address (EODAD)
Error exit address (SYNAD)
Key length (KEYLEN)
Relative key position (RKP)
Space to be left on VISAM pages (PAD)
Macro instruction and facilities (MACRF)
Device type (DEVD)
Optional control program services (OPTCD)
Block size (BLKSIZE)
System error recovery indicator (IMSK)
Problem program exit list (EXLST)
Number of READ or WRITE macro executions before CHECK (NCP)
Number of buffers (BUFNO)
Buffer alignment (BFALN)
Buffer length (BUFL)
Error options for uncorrectable IO errors (EROPT)

Table 10.1 lists the access methods to which the different parameters apply.

TABLE 10.1   ACCESS METHODS TO WHICH DCB PARAMETERS APPLY

Parameter	VSAM	VISAM	VPAM	BSAM	QSAM	IOREQ
DDNAME	X	X	X	X	X	X
DSORG	X	X	X	X	X	X
RECFM	X	X	X	X	X	
LRECL	X	X	X	X	X	
EODAD	X	X	X	X	X	
SYNAD		X	X[a]	X	X	X
KEYLEN		X	X[a]	X		
RKP		X	X			
PAD		X	X[a]			
MACRF				X	X	
DEVD				X	X	
OPTCD				X	X	
BLKSIZE				X	X	
IMSK				X	X	
EXLST				X	X	
NCP				X		X
BUFNO				X		
BFALN				X		
BUFL				X		
EROPT					X	

[a]Denotes that parameter applies to VISAM members only.

As in OS, the DCB also points to the access method routine for a given set of IO operations. This address is supplied when the data set is opened. (In TSS, the access method routine resides in a task's virtual memory and is shared among different tasks.)

Data Set Definition

"Data set definition" is the process of associating a data set with an IO procedure. In addition to specifying data set characteristics, data definition is also used to complete the DCB and to establish job libraries. A data set definition is established with the DDEF command or with a DDEF macro instruction. Once a DDEF is made, it is valid for the duration of the task (i.e., the terminal session) unless nullified with a RELEASE command. Thus, a data file created in one program can be conveniently used in a subsequent program.

The key parameter in a data set definition is the "ddname" field that establishes a link between the problem program and the data set. The ddname field also serves another important function: It can be used to specify data sets that have special meaning to the time sharing system.

In the conversational mode, a DDEF command is processed immediately.[†] Special precaution is taken in the nonconversational mode since a request for a private device can tie up the resources of the system. In the nonconversational mode, private device requirements must be established with the SECURE command. A nonconversational task remains queued until its private device requirements can be met.

A data set definition provides the following information to the system:

Data definition name (DDNAME)
Data set name (DSNAME)
Data set organization
Data control block (DCB) information
Unit and volume requirements
Storage requirements
Retention options
Access level
Data set status
Data set options (concatenation of data sets, job library)

A DDEF command takes the following simplified form for VAM data sets on public storage:

DDEF   DDNAME=data definition name [,DSORG={VS|VI|VP}] ,
      DSNAME=data set name

[†]It follows that the processing for the DDEF macro instruction is also performed when that macro is executed, which is to be expected.

where VS denotes VSAM, VI denotes VISAM, and VP denotes VPAM data sets. The extended DDEF command format includes an extensive set of parameters that use the following keywords (in addition to the three given): DCB, UNIT, SPACE, VOLUME, LABEL, DISP, OPTION, and RET (retention period). Moreover, the DCB parameter includes subparameters relevant to the DCB.

The form of the DDEF macro instruction is:

Name	Operation	Operand
[symbol]	DDEF	{operand-list│operand-addr}

For example,

DDEF MFILE,VS,DSNAME=OLD.MAST

If the "operand-addr" operand is used, then the address of the operand list, stored as a string of characters in main storage, is given.

The reader has probably predicted how the system operates in response to a DDEF command. The command system interprets the DDEF command and executes a DDEF macro instruction. Most TSS commands have counterparts as macro instructions—including the RELEASE command mentioned in this section.

In response to the DDEF command, the system builds a Job File Control Block (JFCB) that contains the following information:

1. DDNAME,
2. DSNAME,
3. DCB parameters, and
4. data set control information.

In building a JFCB, the command system may have to utilize device management routines, external storage allocation routines, and catalog service routines. After the JFCB is built, it is linked to a chain of JFCBs called the Task Definition Table (TDT). The TDT is anchored in an area of a task's virtual memory called the "interrupt storage area." A TDT is constructed for each task and exists only for the duration of that task. When a DDEF is made, the TDT is searched for a JFCB with the same DSNAME. If a JFCB with the same DSNAME is found, then the new DDNAME is substituted for the old DDNAME. Thus, only one JFCB can exist for a data set. A redefinition of a data set would occur when it is used as output from one program (i.e., the "old DDNAME") and input to another program (i.e., the "new DDNAME").

Open and Close Processing

The JFCB is used during OPEN processing to complete the DCB and construct the DSCB for new data sets. The form of the OPEN macro instruction is the same as given in Chapter 7, that is,

Location	*Operation*	*Operand*
[symbol]	OPEN	(DCB address, . . .)

and the functions performed in response to the execution of the macro are essentially the same. For physical data sets, a Data Extent Block (DEB) is built as a privileged extension to the DCB. For virtual data sets, a Relative External Storage Correspondence Table (RESTBL) is built to establish a correspondence between data set pages and external volume and page numbers. Both control blocks are discussed in more detail in Chapter 11.

In TSS, a request for volume mounting is usually made when the DDEF is issued and not when the OPEN macro is executed. This method can be used since data definitions are processed dynamically during a terminal session. (In OS, on the other hand, data definitions are processed by the interpreter prior to job step execution.)

As in OS, the CLOSE macro instruction disconnects a data set from a user's program. The DCB is restored to its original form and DSCB, label, and volume disposition processing are performed.

Data Set Access

The *access methods* used for IO processing are included as part of the user's initial virtual memory and are comprised of nonprivileged and privileged components. The user communicates with the nonprivileged component (of the access method routine) that uses an ENTER macro instruction, which generates an SVC instruction, to enter the privileged component of the access method. All access methods use the Resident Supervisor for actual IO operations. The available access methods are summarized in Table 10.2. The access methods are used with assembler language macro instructions or by equivalent machine code generated by a compiler. In general, logical records are retrieved using either the move mode or the locate mode, and special macro instructions are available for use with VISAM and VPAM for performing IO processing characteristic to those access methods. Explicit IO buffering is not used with virtual access

TABLE 10.2   ACCESS METHODS

Device	*Data Set Organization*	*Access Method*
Direct access	Virtual sequential	VSAM
	Virtual indexed sequential	VISAM
	Virtual partitioned	VPAM
	Basic sequential	BSAM
	Queued sequential	QSAM
Magnetic tape	Basic sequential	BSAM
	Queued sequential	QSAM

methods since it is inherent in the page-sized blocks and the manner in which the system does IO. With physical access methods, traditional IO buffering facilities are available (see Chapter 7).

An obvious difference between a conversational task and a nonconversational task is that the system input unit (SYSIN) for a conversational task is the user's terminal while the SYSIN for a nonconversational task is the task's input stream on direct-access storage. Similarly, the conversational user's system output unit (SYSOUT) is the user's terminal while the SYSOUT for a nonconversational task is a task output stream on direct-access storage. Many programs are developed to run in either mode. When developing a program that reads SYSIN, the user uses a gate read (GATRD) macro instruction. This macro reads SYSIN regardless of the mode of execution of a user's task. Similarly, the user uses a gate write (GATWR) macro instruction to write to the SYSOUT data set. As with GATRD, GATWR places a record on the task's SYSOUT—regardless of the mode of execution. In either case, the IO routine uses privileged task information to determine if a task is conversational or nonconversational. (Recall that the SYSIN and SYSOUT device addresses for a task are contained in its TSI; all tasks have a SYSIN and a SYSOUT.)

A frequent sequence of IO operations in a time sharing environment is to write a record to SYSOUT followed by a read of a record from SYSIN. Two macro instructions support this need:

GTWAR—write a record to SYSOUT and read a record from SYSIN.
GTWSR—write a record to SYSOUT and read a record from terminal SYSIN.

In the latter case, the task is terminated if the task is nonconversational.

One of the significant characteristics of the time sharing environment is that it lends itself to the sharing of programs and data sets on a dynamic basis. Program sharing has been introduced earlier and is covered in detail in Section 10.4. Data set sharing is discussed here. Because of the catalog structure and the technique of automatically prefixing a user's ID as a level of qualification to each data set name,[†] one user cannot access another user's data sets unless authorized to do so. Data sets are shared through the catalog. A data set is normally "unshared"; it becomes "shared" when its owner enters a PERMIT command allowing it to be shared and denoting the users who can share it. When issuing a PERMIT for another user to share his data set, the user can specify the level of access:

1. *Read-only access.* The sharer may only read the data set but may not change it.
2. *Read-write access.* The sharer may read or write the data set but may not erase it; i.e., the sharer may not "delete" it from the system.

[†]Obviously, special conventions must be used with OS data sets on direct-access volumes, which are located through the VTOC.

3. *Unlimited access.* The sharer can treat the data set as his own. He may read, write, or erase it.

The list of sharers is part of the owner's catalog entry for a data set as depicted in Fig. 10.3. The sharer may share another user's data set only when he (the sharer) enters a SHARE command for the data set. The command system verifies that the sharer is permitted to share the data set and builds a catalog entry for the sharer. As an example, assume SMITH owns data set LITTLE. RIVER and agrees to share it with user JONES with read-only access; user JONES wishes to refer to the data set by the name BIG.CREEK. User SMITH issues the following PERMIT command:

PERMIT DSNAME=LITTLE.RIVER,USERID=JONES,ACCESS=RO

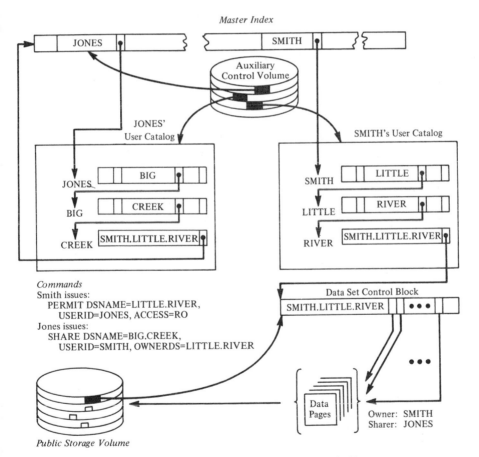

Fig. 10.12 Data set sharing through the catalog facility.

and subsequently, user JONES issues the following SHARE command:

SHARE DSNAME=BIG.CREEK,USERID=SMITH,OWNERDS=LITTLE.RIVER

The catalog entries resulting·from the preceding PERMIT and SHARE commands are reflected in Fig. 10.12, which depicts both users' catalog entries.

When providing a data set sharing facility, the system must define an "interlock" facility to prevent several users from simultaneously attempting to update the same record. With virtual access methods, the interlock conventions would necessarily be dependent upon whether a VSAM, VISAM, or VPAM data set is being shared. Defining a set of useful interlock conventions is left as an exercise for the reader.

Other Data Management Facilities

Obviously, a wide range of IO functions have not been covered, including other access methods and the use of bulk IO facilities. Access methods not covered are:

  TAM—terminal access method,
  MSAM—multiple sequential access method, and
  DRAM—drum access method.

All are designed for use by privileged or system programs. The *multiple sequential access method* (MSAM) is designed for use with unit record devices and uses command chaining in a channel program to perform functions such as printing an entire page on the line printer with a single IO instruction. The reader is directed to references [TSSb] and [TSSd] for information on these access methods.

Bulk IO refers to the process of transferring data sets to system output devices (at the user's request) or of prestoring data in the system (at the operator's request). Bulk IO is covered later in this chapter.

10.3 COMMAND SYSTEM

Introduction

The command system allows the user to communicate with the system dynamically or on a preplanned basis, depending upon whether the system is being used in a conversational mode or a nonconversational mode, respectively. It should be remembered here that all commands, regardless of the mode of operation, are executed as they are read by the command system that executes from each user's virtual memory as a shared privileged program. In fact, the command system is part of each user's initial virtual memory.

Each user is given a "skeleton profile" when he is joined to the system. The profile is stored in the user's USERLIB as a VPAM member. In short, the profile governs how the system responds to the user and specifies the following: default values for command operands, character set, message brevity, prompting required, etc. The user can change his profile through commands available for that purpose (more specifically the commands are DEFAULT, SYNONYM, and PROFILE) and the changes are reflected in the profile stored in his USERLIB. When the user "logs on" for a new terminal session, his updated profile is retrieved from his user library for use by the command system. The basic philosophy is that as the user gains expertise in using the system, his operational needs change and he establishes his own conventions for using the system.

The purpose of this section is to provide information on how the TSS system is used and on the facilities available for using it. Although this material is also useful in its own right, it primarily supplies background information for Chapter 11, which describes the structure of the system and how it operates. Compared with OS job control language, the TSS command system includes a large number of commands that perform a variety of functions. The commands are conveniently grouped into six categories:

1. task management,
2. data management,
3. program management,
4. command creation,
5. user profile management, and
6. message handling.

The commands in each category are discussed collectively; however, the operands to a specific command often provide insight into how the command is used and into what it does. Therefore, at least a minimal operand structure is given for each command, whenever possible. In general, specific operands are not discussed. The metasymbols used for describing the commands are given as Table 10.3. The structure and use of the command system also involves operational conventions—such as those required for any complex system. As a result, the topics covered initially cover task initiation, typing conventions, task termination, etc. For additional information on the command system, the user is directed to a paper by McKeehan [Mck69] and the *Command System User's Guide* [TSSc].

Task Initiation and Operational Conventions

When the user establishes a "connection" to the system and presses ATTEN-TION, he indicates that he wishes to "log on" to the system in the conversational mode. He is prompted by the system to identify himself so that he may use the system. The procedure is somewhat as follows:

> *User:* [Dial up, then ATTENTION]
> *System:* B001 LOGON TASKID=0008 10/01/72 15:30
> *User:* jones,act34,,,jack
> *System:* __

TABLE 10.3   METASYMBOLS USED WITH COMMAND FORMATS

Symbol(s)	Name	Function
{}	Braces	Used to delimit syntactical units or alternatives; e.g., {operand=[value]}
[ ]	Brackets	Used to delimit optional syntactical units; e.g., [(member name)] or [NAME=entry point name] or [charge number]
|	Vertical stroke	Represents "exclusive or" and separates alternative syntactical elements; e.g., {ACCEPT| SKIP|END}. Selection of an alternative element is also specified by vertical stacking; e.g., $$\begin{Bmatrix} ACCEPT \\ SKIP \\ END \end{Bmatrix}$$
. . .	Ellipsis	Denotes that the preceding syntactical unit may be repeated one or more times; e.g., (data set name [,...]) or {term = [value]} [,...]

The system types in capital letters; the user normally enters information in lower case letters. (This is a simple convention but helps to distinguish between the two when looking at a terminal printout. Usually, the upper and lower cases are "folded" into the same internal codes; however, this is a function of the user's profile.) The user enters a user identification, password, account number, and other control information. If the user is accepted by the system, he is prompted with an underscore indicating that he may enter commands. The underscore concept works as follows:

1. The command system is ready for the user to enter a command.
2. The command system types an underscore and back spaces. The keyboard is unlocked. The carriage is not moved up.
3. The user enters information on the same line and presses RETURN.

That is, for example:

System/User: ̲run myprog   [RETURN]

Whenever the user can enter a command, he is prompted with the underscore. Normally, an underscore is typed by the command system when the execution of the previous command is complete or the user presses ATTENTION to interrupt the system and gain access to the command system. (It should be pointed out that when a user "converses" with a processing program, he establishes his own conventions for prompting the person at the terminal—if required.)

The procedures given above are conventions established by the designers of TSS for using the system. Any time sharing system has similar conventions. Other conventions are required:

1. When the user wishes to change a character of a line, he simply backspaces to the point of error and retypes the remainder of the line. (A good practice is to move the carriage up a line so the user can see his change.) That is, for example:

    _rum myprog   [BACKSPACE to "m," move up carriage]
       n myprog   [RETURN]

2. When the user wishes to continue a line (when entering commands), he types a hyphen, then RETURN, and continues on the next line.

The procedure for correcting character errors is significant from both the system's and the user's points of view. From the system's point of view, the BACKSPACE characters are transmitted to the system and it must sort out the exact composition of the line entered. From the user's point of view, a composite symbol formed by backspacing and overstriking is not possible. This limitation has led the designers of several other systems to define a "delete" character in addition to the backspace character. The *delete character* is used for deleting characters (i.e., correcting errors) so that the backspace character is free for use in constructing composite symbols. The left arrow (←) is frequently used as a delete character such that the previous example might look as follows:

    _rum myprog ← ← ← ← ← ← ← ← n myprog   [RETURN]

The delete character is not defined in TSS.

When initiating a nonconversational task, the user must explicitly use the LOGON command as follows:

    LOGON   JONES,ACT34,,,JACK

since the input is coming from a prestored data set. Other than the LOGON command, TSS commands are used the same in the nonconversational mode as in the conversational mode. A nonconversational task can be "logged on" in one of two ways: (1) as a batch job read into the system by the operator; and (2) with the EXECUTE command (entered in the conversational mode) that establishes a task (in the nonconversational mode) for an input job stream composed of commands, programs, and data prestored as a data set on public storage. Both of these cases require the LOGON command, as shown. A nonconversational task can also be established with the BACK command that switches a task from the conversational mode to the nonconversational mode and with a bulk IO command entered as a user command or an operator command. The cases involving the BACK command and bulk IO do not require a LOGON command. Nonconversational tasks are discussed later.

Commands are always read by the command system from the task's SYSIN device.[†] System messages, prompting, responses, and system output are always sent to a task's SYSOUT device. (The symbolic SYSIN and SYSOUT device addresses are stored in the task's TSI.)

Task Termination and Abnormal Conditions

A user terminates his terminal session (and his task as well) when he enters a LOGOFF command. At that time, the command system asks the user the desired disposition of uncataloged data sets on private volumes. These data sets subsequently may be cataloged, erased, or ignored. In the last case, a default disposition is selected by the system depending upon the type of device and on the type of data set.

An abnormal task termination (ABEND) occurs when errors prevent a task from continuing. The following general functions are performed by the system:

1. Task IO is terminated.
2. System interlocks caused by the tasks are released.
3. An ABEND message is written to the task's SYSOUT device.

If warranted by the severity of the error conditions, the following functions may also be performed:

4. Data sets are closed.
5. Uncataloged data sets are erased.
6. Shared modules are unlinked.
7. A LOGOFF is issued for the "old" task.
8. A "new" task is logged on for the user.

The system then attempts to resume execution of the "new" task.

An abnormal termination can also be initiated by the user with the ABEND command. The user normally enters an ABEND command when his virtual memory is sufficiently "messed up" that continuation of the task would be undesirable. Use of the ABEND command performs the functions given above and provides the user with a new task so that he may "start over."

A conversational task is also terminated with the BACK command. The user initiates a conversational task and builds a data set on public storage containing commands, programs, and data to complete the work to be performed. He then enters the BACK command, with the data set name of the prestored input stream

---

[†]The only exceptions to this rule are defined procedures and the CALL DATA DEFINITION command.

as an operand. The conversational task is switched by the system from the conversational mode to the nonconversational mode. In other words, the conversational task is effectively terminated and a nonconversational task is created. With the BACK command, the prestored input stream need not contain the LOGON command.

A bulk IO task is automatically terminated when the data transfer operation is complete. In addition, the user or the system operator can use the CANCEL command to terminate a nonconversational task during its execution or before it is selected for execution. Whenever a nonconversational task is entered into the "batch work queue," a batch sequence number (BSN) is assigned and is displayed to the user or the operator. This BSN is used to identify that task and is used as an operand to the CANCEL command.

Task Management Commands

Task management commands allow the user to control the manner in which the system operates on his task. Task management command formats are summarized in Table 10.4.

The LOGON command is used to initiate a task and to identify a user to the system. This command is not used in the conversational mode since it is implicit in the "dial up" procedure. After the initiation of a task is complete, the system attempts to invoke a user-defined command procedure named ZLOGON. If this procedure does not exist, then the system does nothing and continues with task execution. If the user defines a procedure named ZLOGON and stores it in his procedure library, then it is invoked automatically by the com-

TABLE 10.4   TASK MANAGEMENT COMMAND FORMATS

Operation	*Operand*
ABEND	
BACK	DSNAME=data set name
CANCEL	BSN=batch sequence number
EXECUTE	DSNAME=data set name
LOGOFF	
[LOGON][a]	user identification, [password], [addressing], [charge number], [control section packing], [maximum auxiliary storage], [pristine]
SECURE	$\left\{ \begin{array}{l} (TA=number\ of\ devices\ [,type\ of\ device])\ ) \\ (DA=number\ of\ devices\ [,type\ of\ device])\ ) \end{array} \right\} [,\dots]$
TIME	[MINS=minutes]
USAGE	
ZLOGON	

[a]The pristine parameter to the LOGON command indicates whether the user wants access to previously defined defaults, synonyms, procdefs, and his USERLIB.

mand system. The user can use the ZLOGON procedure to prompt the user for additional identification, to perform initialization, or to enter a special processing mode. The TIME command establishes a time limit for the execution of a task; it is ordinarily used with nonconversational tasks. The EXECUTE command is used to initiate a nonconversational task; the input job stream for this task is previously stored as a data set on public storage. The SECURE command is used in the nonconversational mode to reserve private devices for private volumes. In the nonconversational mode, private devices needed for task execution must be reserved before the task is initiated so that batch jobs do not completely tie up the operation of the system. The SECURE command is not used with conversational tasks, and private devices are requested dynamically as part of the processing of the DDEF command. The BACK command converts a conversational task to a nonconversational task for completion of its processing. The CANCEL command causes a nonconversational task to be terminated prior to or during its execution. The ABEND command terminates the current task and establishes a new task with a "fresh" initial virtual memory. The USAGE command provides usage statistics, on the current task, to the user, and the LOGOFF command is used to terminate the task from which it is entered.

The philosophy of having several commands to perform task management functions is illustrative of the time sharing mode of operation—especially in the conversational mode. The user need not completely preplan his entire job and he can enter control information at his convenience.

Data Management Commands

Data management commands, which allow the user to manage and process his data sets, fall into four categories: data set management, text editing, data editing, and bulk output.

Data set management commands are used to identify, store, retrieve, catalog, define, and erase data sets. Data set management command formats are summarized in Table 10.5. The DDEF command is used to define a data set and provide its attributes to the system. The CDD command (for call data definition) retrieves DDEF commands that have been prestored as a VAM data set. The RELEASE command nullifies a data definition made with a previously executed DDEF command. The CATALOG command is used to create or alter a catalog entry for a data set. The RET command is used to modify a catalog entry for a virtual access method (VAM) data set and EVV is used to create catalog entries for VAM data sets on a private volume. EVV is used when an entire volume of data sets is moved from one system to another. The DELETE command removes an entry from the user's catalog. This command applies to data sets on private volumes and shared data sets owned by another user. The ERASE command frees direct-access storage assigned to a data set and deletes its catalog entry. The PERMIT command provides authorization or withdraws authorization for

TABLE 10.5   DATA SET MANAGEMENT COMMAND FORMATS

Operation	Operand
CATALOG[a]	DSNAME=data set name [,STATE={N|U}] [,ACC={R|U}] [,NEWNAME=data set name]
CDD	DSNAME=data set name $\left[,\begin{cases}\text{data definition name} \\ \text{(data definition name } [,\ldots]\text{)}\end{cases}\right]$
CDS	DSNAME1=input data set name [(member name [,...])], DSNAME2=copy data set name [(member name)] [,ERASE={Y|N}] [,BASE=first line number, INCR-increment] [,REPLACE={R|I}]
CLOSE	[DSNAME=data set name] [,TYPE=T] [,DDNAME=data definition name]
DDEF[a]	DDNAME=data definition name [,DSORG={VI|VS|VP}], DSNAME=data set name
DDNAME?	JOBLIB={Y|N}
DELETE	[DSNAME=data set name]
DSS?	$\left[\text{NAMES}=\begin{cases}\text{data set name} \\ \text{(data set name } [,\ldots]\text{)}\end{cases}\right]$
ERASE	[DSNAME=data set name]
EVV	DEVICE=device type, VOLUME=(volume serial number [,...]) [,USERID=user identification]
JOBLIBS	DDNAME=data definition name
PC?	$\left[\text{NAMES}=\begin{cases}\text{data set name} \\ \text{(data set name } [,\ldots]\text{)}\end{cases}\right]$
PERMIT	DSNAME={data set name|*ALL} [,USERID={(user identification[,...])|*ALL}] [,ACCESS={R|RO|RW|U}]
POD?	DSNAME=data set name[,DATA=Y] [,ALIAS=Y] [,MODULE={ALL|module name}]
RELEASE	DDNAME=data definition name[,DSNAME=data set name] [,{SCRATCH|HOLD}]
RET	DSNAME=data set name,RET=retention code
SHARE	DSNAME=data set name,USERID=owner's user identification [,OWNERDS={owner's data set name|*ALL}]
TV	DSNAME1=tape data set name[,DSNAME2=VAM data set name]
VT	DSNAME1=VAM data set name [,DSNAME2=tape data set name]
VV	DSNAME1=current data set name [,DSNAME2=new data set name]

[a]Other forms of this command exist.

another user (or users) to access a data set (or data sets) owned by the user. The SHARE command creates a catalog entry for a data set owned by another user; permission to share the data set must be previously made with the PERMIT command. Four commands terminate with a question mark (?) and request data set management information from the system:

DSS?–Provide status of cataloged data sets ("data set status").
PC?–Provide abbreviated status of cataloged data sets ("present catalog").
POD?–Provide information on member of VPAM data set ("partitioned organization directory").
DDNAMES?–Display JFCBs for current task.

The JOBLIBS command allows the user to move a defined JOBLIB to the top of the chain of JOBLIB JFCBs so that it is searched first. The CLOSE command is used to close data sets that are not closed at the program level when the normal path of processing is interrupted. Four commands allow data sets to be copied:

VT–Copy VAM data set from public storage to tape.
TV–Copy VAM data set from tape to public storage.
VV–Copy a VAM data set in direct-access storage.
CDS–Create a new copy of a data set permitting a certain amount of data set modification.

Text editing commands are used with the text editor to perform specific functions. In general, the text can be any form of information, such as a program or a report, organized as a VISAM data set.[†] Most open time sharing systems provide a text editor of some sort since text editing lends itself to the conversational mode of operation. Text editing is an area of specialization within operating systems technology and reflects, to some extent, the viewpoint of the designer of the text editor. Therefore, the text editing commands, in TSS, are not given in detail but are only listed to give the reader an idea of the text editing facilities that are nominally available in an open time sharing system:

EDIT–Invoke the text editor and specify the data set to be edited.
END–Terminate processing of the text editor.
REGION–Specify a region of a data set.
DISABLE–Cause all modifications to a data set to be remembered so that the data set may be restored to its original form.
ENABLE–Cause only the most recent change to a data set to be remembered.
STET–Delete change made by previous command.
POST–Cause all modifications to a data set to be retained (i.e., finalized).

[†]The text editor accepts two kinds of VISAM data sets: the line data set, mentioned previously, and a region data set, which is a line data set stratified into regions that are assigned names.

CONTEXT—Specify a context (sequence of characters or line) in which a change should be made.

CORRECT—Replace or insert characters in one or more lines (region) of a data set.

REVISE—Change or delete specified lines (changes follow the REVISE command).

UPDATE—Add or insert lines in the region previously established (additions or insertions follow the UPDATE command).

EXCERPT—Insert lines from a data set (the current data set or another data set) into the current data set.

EXCISE—Delete lines from current data set.

INSERT—Insert lines in the current data set (insertions follow the INSERT command).

NUMBER—Cause lines to be numbered.

LIST—Display lines on user's SYSOUT device.

LOCATE—Locate a character string in the current region.

Data editing commands are used to create, modify, and display VAM data sets. Table 10.6 summarizes the format of the data editing commands. The DATA command can be used as part of an input job stream (conversational or non-conversational) to build a VSAM or a VISAM line data set. The MODIFY is used to insert, delete, or replace lines from a VISAM data set or a VISAM member of a VPAM data set. In the TSS system, the advantage of the MODIFY command over the text editor is that the MODIFY command allows the key to be located anywhere in the record of the VISAM data set or VISAM member of a VPAM data set. Without exploring the subject in depth, this appears to be a useful design philosophy: Provide a flexible editor (the text editor) for a limited

TABLE 10.6 DATA EDITING COMMAND FORMATS

Operation	Operand
DATA	DSNAME=data set name $$\left[,\text{RTYPE} = \begin{Bmatrix} \text{I} \\ \text{LINE} \\ \text{FTN} \\ \text{CARD} \\ \text{S} \end{Bmatrix} \left[\text{BASE=first line number,INCR=increment} \right] \right\}$$
LINE?	DSNAME=data set name $$\left[\begin{Bmatrix} \text{line number} \\ \text{(first line number, last line number)} \end{Bmatrix} [,\ldots] \right]$$
MODIFY	SETNAME=data set name [,CONF=R] [,LRECL=record length, KEYLEN=keylength, RKP=relative key position, RECFM={V|F}] [,FTN={Y|N}]

TABLE 10.7   BULK OUTPUT COMMAND FORMATS

Operation	Operand
PRINT	DSNAME=data set name [,STARTNO=starting position] [,ENDNO=ending position] $\left[,PRTSP = \left\{ \begin{matrix} EDIT \\ \left\{ \begin{matrix} 1 \\ 2 \\ 3 \end{matrix} \right\} \end{matrix} \right\} \ [,HEADER=H] \ [,LINES=lines\ per\ page]\ [,PAGE=P] \right]$ [,ERASE={Y|N}] [,ERROROPT={ACCEPT|SKIP|END}] [,FORM=paper form] [,STATION=station number]
PUNCH	DSNAME=data set name [,STARTNO=starting position] [,ENDNO=ending position] [,STACK={1|2|3|EDIT}] [,ERASE={Y|N}] [,FORM=card form]
WT	DSNAME=data set name, DSNAME2=tape data set name [,VOLUME=tape volume number] [,FACTOR=blocking factor] [,STARTNO=starting position] [,ENDNO=ending position] $\left[,PRTSP = \left\{ \begin{matrix} EDIT \\ \left\{ \begin{matrix} 1 \\ 2 \\ 3 \end{matrix} \right\} \end{matrix} \right\} \ [,HEADER=H] \ [,LINES=lines\ per\ page]\ [Page=P] \right]$ [,ERASE={Y|N}]

form of data set (i.e., the line data set) and provide a limited facility (the MODIFY command) with a general form of data set (i.e., the generalized VISAM record). The LINE? command obtains a VISAM record (or set of records) and displays them on the task's SYSOUT device.

Bulk output commands create nonconversational tasks that transfer data sets from public storage to system output devices (such as the printer, punch, and tape). The bulk IO task created runs asychronously to the task that creates it and is analogous to the SPOOLing operation mentioned previously. Table 10.7 gives command formats for the bulk output commands. The PRINT command causes a data set to be printed on the system's line printer (i.e., not the user's SYSOUT device—whatever it is). Similarly, the PUNCH command causes a data set to be punched and the WT command causes a data set to be written on magnetic tape in a format for subsequent printing.

Program Management Commands

Program management commands are used to initiate language processing and to control the processing of programs. *Language processing* involves invoking a specific language processor and supplying parameters for the type of processing to be done. For compilation or assembly in the conversational mode, the source program is entered line by line from the terminal or it is prestored. From the terminal, statements are analyzed by the compiler as they are received and diagnostic information is returned to the terminal as it is generated. Thus, the user can make modifications immediately. When the source program is prestored, diagnostic information is sent to terminal so that the user can use the MODIFY command or the text editor to change the prestored source program prior to having it reprocessed. In the batch mode, the source program may be contained in the input job stream or be prestored. Diagnostic information is sent to the task's SYSOUT device. The program listing ordinarily provided with language processing is placed in public storage as a VAM data set. The user may inspect the listing with the LINE? command or have it printed with the PRINT bulk output command. The commands for invoking the assembler, FORTRAN compiler, linkage editor, and PL/I compiler are ASM, FTN, LNK, and PLI, respectively. Operands are specific to the language processor involved and are not covered.

Program control commands provide the capability for the user to have his programs loaded and executed and then to interact with them directly while they are being executed. This topic has been introduced earlier (Chapter 9) under the general topic of program checkout. Program control command formats are summarized in Table 10.8.

The LOAD command causes an object module to be loaded in a user's virtual memory by the dynamic loader; execution of that object module is not initiated. The UNLOAD command removes an object module from a user's virtual memory. The CALL command passes control to the specified entry point. If the object module is not already loaded, then the dynamic loader is called to have the module loaded before execution is attempted. If no entry point is specified, then the last module referenced is called. The RUN command is used

TABLE 10.8 PROGRAM CONTROL COMMAND FORMATS

Operation	Operand
AT	Instruction location [, . . .]
BRANCH	INSTLOC=instruction location
CALL	[NAME=entry point name [,module parameters]]
DISPLAY	data field name [, . . .]
DUMP	data field name [, . . .]
GO	
IF	condition
LOAD	[NAME=entry point name]
QUALIFY	MNAME=[link edited module name.] object module name
REMOVE	statement number [, . . .]
RUN	[LOC=entry point name]
SET	{data location=value} [, . . .]
STOP	
UNLOAD	[NAME=entry point name]

in one of two ways: (1) to initiate the execution of a program from the point at which it was interrupted with the ATTENTION key; or (2) to continue the execution of a program after it was interrupted by a sequence of PCS statements of the form: AT . . . STOP. The GO command is used to resume execution of an interrupted program and is equivalent to the RUN command without an operand. The BRANCH command is used during program checkout to dynamically change the flow of the program or to continue execution of a program, after an interruption, at a different location. The REPEAT command is used to have the last nonprompting message, issued by the system, repeated.

The remaining program control system (PCS) commands are designed specifically for use during program checkout. (The BRANCH and GO commands, given above, are also primarily PCS program checkout commands.) Ordinarily, the user will load his program and place ATs, followed by commands that aid in program checkout, in the loaded program. When the appropriate control point is reached in the user's program, the PCS commands following the AT are executed conditionally or unconditionally, as the case may be. The following PCS commands are used:

AT—Establish a control point in a program.

IF—Specify that the following statements are conditional.

SET—Alter the contents of machine registers, program variables, and virtual memory locations.

DISPLAY—Display the contents of machine registers, program variables, and virtual memory locations on the user's SYSOUT device.

DUMP—Dump registers, variables, and memory locations on a data set defined as PCSOUT (in the "ddname" field).

QUALIFY—Specify an implicit level of qualification to internal variables.

STOP—Halt execution of a program and return control to the command system; this is the same as a dynamic interruption and the interrupted program can be restarted.

REMOVE—Remove ATs and PCS statements following the ATs.

Obviously, program management facilities are terminal-oriented in the sense that a user can sit at his terminal and completely manage the execution and debugging of his program. Thus, the normal delays, customarily associated with batch processing, are eliminated. PCS commands can also be used in the batch mode but are limited by the fact that the entire run must be preplanned.

Command Creation Commands

Commands can be created, in TSS, in one of two ways:

1. as a series of commands defined with the PROCDEF command; and
2. as an object program established as a command with the BUILTIN command.

Procedures are headed with the PROCDEF command and are stored in the user's library on public storage. A typical procedure takes the form:

```
          PROCDEF UPDATE
100  PARAM DS1,DS2
200  DDEF  INPUT,VS,DSNAME=DS1
300  DDEF  OUTPUT,VS,DSNAME=DS2,DISP=NEW
400  DISPLAY 'UPDATE PROG IN EXECUTION'
500  RUN UPDAT30
600    END
```

and would be invoked with a command of the form:

```
          update  bigfox,catrun
```

As a result, the command system would execute the following commands as though the user had entered them directly:

```
DDEF  INPUT,VS,DSNAME=BIGFOX
DDEF  OUTPUT,VS,DSNAME=CATRUN,DISP=NEW
DISPLAY 'UPDATE PROG IN EXECUTION'
RUN  UPDAT30
```

The concept of a command procedure is important here, and not the details of how one is constructed. The user can develop simplified procedures for using a complicated system or he can use a command procedure to avoid entering a similar sequence of commands repeatedly. Command procedures also add to the versatility of a time sharing system and permit the commands of one system to emulate the commands of another system—an important feature is compatibility and conversion.

The BUILTIN command provides a facility whereby an object module written in assembler language can be invoked via the command system—in effect, adding a command to the system. Operands adhere to command rules instead of object-module call rules such that the user is extending the capability of the system. Table 10.9 gives "command creation" command formats. The reader is directed to references [TSSa] and [TSSc] for further details on command creation.

TABLE 10.9 COMMAND CREATION COMMAND FORMATS

Operation	Operand
BUILTIN	NAME=command name [,EXTNAME=macro name]
PROCDEF	NAME=procedure name

TABLE 10.10   USER PROFILE MANAGEMENT COMMAND FORMATS

Operation	Operand
DEFAULT	{operand=[value]} [,...]
PROFILE[a]	[CSW={N|Y}]
SYNONYM	{term-[value]} [,...]

[a]CSW refers to whether command symbols should be stored as part of the profile.

User Profile Management Commands

The user can tailor the command system to his needs with the "user profile management commands." As mentioned previously, each user has a profile, stored as member (SYSPRX), of his USERLIB. When the user logs on to the system, this profile is read into virtual memory and governs how the command system responds to the user. (A prototype profile is stored as member (SYSPRX) of the system library (SYSLIB). If a user logs on and he has no profile in his USERLIB—which will occur when he logs on for the first time after being joined or when he erases the profile from his USERLIB—then the prototype profile is fetched from SYSLIB and copied into his USERLIB and into virtual memory.) Each user's profile contains defaults and synonyms.

The DEFAULT and SYNONYM commands allow the user to change defaults and synonyms, respectively, for the current task. The PROFILE command replaces the profile stored in USERLIB with the task profile of the current task. The formats of user profile management commands are given as Table 10.10.

Message Handling Commands

Two commands involve the messages that are sent to the user. Messages are stored as member (SYSMLF) of the system library (SYSLIB) or as member (SYSMLF) of a user's USERLIB. Each message has an identification code. When it is desired to send a message to a user's SYSOUT device, the PRMPT assembler language macro instruction is issued. The operand to PRMPT specifies a message identification. The user's USERLIB and then SYSLIB are searched for the message identification and the associated message is written to SYSOUT. By editing the message file in his USERLIB, the user can change the messages that are sent to him. The method by which messages are stored in the system message file (SYSMLF) also permits an explanation to be stored there. The EXPLAIN command allows the user to request explanations of a message, a part of a message, or a word in a message. The PRMPT command allows the user to reference the message file, to have a message displayed, and to have inserts, similar to arguments, placed in a message. The formats of message handling commands are given in Table 10.11.

TABLE 10.11   MESSAGE HANDLING COMMAND FORMATS

Operation	Operand
EXPLAIN	$\left\{\begin{matrix} \text{MSGID} \\ \text{ORIGIN} \\ \left\{\begin{matrix} \text{word} \\ \text{TEXT} \\ \text{RESPONSE} \\ \text{MSGE} \\ \text{MSGS} \end{matrix}\right\} \text{[,message identification]} \end{matrix}\right\}$
PRMPT	MSGID=message identification [,INSERTn=inserted character [,...]]

Comments on the Command System

The large number of commands presented in this section imply a great deal. Although one could debate whether *all* of the commands are necessary, it should be evident that at least a fairly large number are required and that fact is a sharp contradiction to the basic three statements (i.e., JOB, EXEC, and DD) used in the OS job control language. The key point is that an interactive open time sharing system provides a great deal of flexibility that is reflected in the complexity of the underlying system.

10.4   PROGRAM SHARING

One of the fundamental concepts in time sharing is that of sharing: program sharing and data set sharing. Data set sharing through the system catalog was introduced earlier and the concept is obviously extended to allow several users to access the same data set concurrently. Program sharing has also been introduced but the mechanism by which that is accomplished was not covered.

Control Sections

A control section is a block of machine coding (i.e., instructions and/or data) whose virtual memory locations can be relocated at load time without affecting the logic of the program. A control section begins on a page boundary and may extend to several pages as required. A control section occupies consecutive byte locations in virtual memory. In real storage, however, the pages of a control section, more than likely, do not occupy adjacent pages; moreover, not all pages of a control section are necessarily in real storage at the same time.

In ordinary programming, a control section contains both machine instructions and data. Compilers usually generate a single control section for a source module; in assembler language, the programmer can define several "named" control sections and have them assembled as a single source module. Ordinary control sections are given the attribute "read/write" since they modify themselves during execution—if only to store the value of a variable. Control sections are frequently referred to as CSECTs.

Prototype Sections

If a program is to be shared among users, then it must not modify itself during execution. This is accomplished by placing variables and storage areas in a block of storage called a prototype section (PSECT) such that the machine instructions left in the CSECT are not self-modifying and are given the attribute "read only." Thus, when a user shares a shared program, it shares the readonly CSECT and possesses a read/write PSECT of its own.

Attributes of Programs

Programs possess attributes, as do ordinary variables, and those attributes are included along with the other control information in the object module. The attributes that apply to program sharing are public/private and readonly/read-write. A shared program is one with one or more public readonly CSECTs and at least one private PSECT for storing variables and data.

Loading

Program sharing is implemented through the dynamic loader. When loading a shared program into a user's virtual memory, the dynamic loader recognizes that

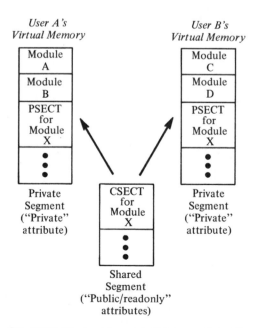

Fig. 10.13 Sharing of module X by users A and B.

the readonly CSECTs are to be shared and makes entries in the user's page tables to point to the physical copy of the program. The dynamic loader dynamically builds a PSECT for the user, as described in the object module, and places it in the user's private virtual storage. The CSECT is coded to obtain the location of the PSECT dynamically so that it can be shared by any task that requests its services. Program sharing is suggested by Fig. 10.13.

10.5 BATCH PROCESSING, BULK IO, AND SYSTEM OPERATIONS

Batch Processing

Most time sharing systems allow "background" jobs to be processed when the resources of the computer system are not being fully utilized in providing time sharing service. One of the tasks that is initiated when the system is "started up" is a high-priority system task termed the "batch monitor." The *batch monitor* controls the execution of nonconversational tasks. When a conversational user logs on to the system, a task is established immediately and it is permitted to "time share" the resources of the computing system. When a nonconversational task enters the system, it is assigned a batch sequence number (BSN) and is put into a *batch work queue* for subsequent processing. Jobs are also entered into the batch work queue as a result of the EXECUTE command or by one of the bulk IO commands. Jobs are selected for execution from the batch work queue by the batch monitor in response to a request for work by the system scheduler and are multiprogrammed in the usual fashion. Deck setup for batch jobs is suggested by Fig. 10.14. The same commands and operational procedures are used in the nonconversational mode as in the conversational mode.

Bulk IO

Bulk IO is performed by a *bulk IO task* established when the system is "started up" or with an operator command. The bulk IO task controls bulk IO processing in response to user and operator commands and when cards are entered from the card reader. (Bulk IO processed in support of a task operates independently of the task.)

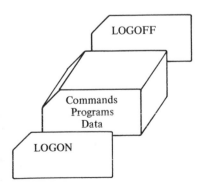

Fig. 10.14 Batch job deck setup.

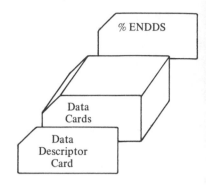

Fig. 10.15 Deck setup for entering data
cards via the card reader.

TABLE 10.12   FORMAT OF THE DATA
DESCRIPTOR CARD

Operands
DATASET, user identification, data set name, [format]
[starting number] , [ending number] , $\left\{\begin{array}{l} \text{LINE} \\ \text{FTN} \\ \text{COMP} \\ \text{CARD} \end{array}\right\}$, [error]

An attention indicator generated when the operator readies the card reader causes the bulk IO task to read cards from the card reader and build a VAM data set. If the input cards are a batch job, the bulk IO task signals the batch monitor to place an entry for that job in the batch work queue. If a data set is being entered in card form, the data set is cataloged as specified in a "data descriptor card." The form of a data set entered via the card reader is suggested by Fig. 10.15. The format of the *data descriptor card* is given in Table 10.12.

System Operations

The system operator controls the operation of the system by performing the following functions:

1. start up and shut down,
2. configuration control,
3. task communications and system control,
4. task control, and
5. bulk IO initiation.

The operator starts the TSS system by performing an IPL sequence and by specifying the system configuration. When it is time to shut the system down, the operator broadcasts to all conversational users that the system is to be shut down and subsequently terminates system activity with a SHUTDOWN command. The operator is able to send a message to all users with the BCST command.

The operator manages the configuration of the computer system by issuing HOLD and DROP commands. The HOLD command prevents a device from being assigned for system use. The DROP command cancels the effect of a previously entered HOLD command. A HOLD command is frequently issued for a device when that device must be made unavailable for system use because of required maintenance.

When the TSS system operates, the system sends messages to the operator to have functions, such as to mount a tape, performed and to enter information for the system's use. The operator replies to system messages with the REPLY command. In addition, the operator can send a message to all users with the BCST command or to a specific user with the MSG command. The operator can have the operator's log[†] printed with the PRINT command.

The operator can effect task operation with two commands: CANCEL and FORCE. The CANCEL command terminates a nonconversational task before it has been executed or during its execution. The FORCE command terminates a conversational task and is used when the task is in suspended state or it is adversely affecting the performance of other tasks.

The operator is responsible for entering cards through the card reader and for having the contents of a magnetic tape read into the system with the RT (read tape) command. The ASNBD command is used to manage IO devices for bulk IO operations. The operator also performs volume mounting, as mentioned earlier, in response to system messages.

The format of operator commands is given in Table 10.13. The role of the system operator in a general-purpose time sharing system is briefly discussed here because it is sufficiently different than in typical batch multiprocessing systems to warrant its study. In an open time sharing system, the operator is less concerned with the mechanics of operating the system and more concerned with how the system is operating as a whole. In general, he has no control over which tasks are run, whereas in a batch multiprocessing system, he can control the work the system performs by starting appropriate readers, initiators, and writers.

10.6 SYSTEM MANAGEMENT

In most operating environments, the system is controlled, at least in part, by the person entering jobs into the system and by the system operator. In an open time sharing system, however, direct physical control is impossible and the system is designed to manage itself. Obviously, this is impossible in the "general

---

†The operator's log is a data set of operator console traffic.

TABLE 10.13   FORMAT OF OPERATOR COMMANDS

Operation	Operand
ASNBD	{A|D} (symbolic device address) [,...]
BCST	TEXT=text of message
CANCEL	BSN=batch sequence number
DROP	symbolic device address [,...]
FORCE	USERID=user identification
HOLD	symbolic device address [,...]
MSG	USERID=user identification, TEXT=text of message
PRINT	DSNAME=SYSLOG(integer) [,STARTNO=first byte position] [,ENDNO=last byte position] [,PRTSP={1|2|3}] [,HEADER=H] [,LINES=lines per page] [,PAGE=P] [,ERROROPT={ACCEPT|SKIP|END}] [,FORM=page form]
REPLY	MSGNO=message number [,TEXT=text of message]
RT	{VOLUME=volume serial number,TATYPE=tape type CTLG={CTLG|YES}} [USERID=user identification] ,DSNAME1=input data set name [,DSNAME2=new data set name] [,LINE=LINE] [,ERROROPT={ACCEPT|SKIP|END}]
SHUTDOWN	

sense" and that is why the system manager and system administrator are defined (see Chapter 9).

The system manager and the system administrator are responsible for who uses the system. This responsibility is discharged through the JOIN facility and through privilege classes, priorities, and authorization codes. When a user is joined to the system, he is assigned a privilege class and an authorization code that collectively determine the system facilities he can use and the functions he can perform.

Privilege Classes and Authorization Codes

The system manager and the system operator are prejoined to the system. All other users are joined by the system manager or a system administrator that has been joined by the system manager. A user's privilege class is contained in his entry in SYSUSE (the data set containing a list of all users and their attributes) and that information is transferred to his TSI when he logs on. The appropriate field in a user's TSI is inspected by system routines that are sensitive to the user's privilege code. The privilege codes defined in TSS are given in Table 10.14.

Users with a privilege class of D are distinguished by an *authorization code* that is also included in a user's SYSUSE entry and his active TSI. The following authorization codes are defined:

TABLE 10.14   PRIVILEGE CLASSES

Type of User	Privilege Class	Joined by
System manager	F	Prejoined at system generation
System operator	A	Prejoined at system generation
System administrator	B	System manager
System monitor[a]	E	System manager
Privileged system programmer	D	System manager
System programmer	D	System manager or system administrator
User	D	System manager or system administrator

[a]The *system monitor* is a person concerned with system evaluation, analysis, and performance. He uses a system component called the *Time Sharing Support System* that provides both static and dynamic facilities for performance measurement and functional analysis.

U—normal user that is not permitted to utilize system programs directly;

P—system programmer that can use certain macro instructions, privileged SVC codes, and system programs; and

O—privileged system program that can use all macro instructions, SVC codes, and system programs.

As far as authorization codes P and O are concerned, many functions are performed by the system programmer that the normal user has no need to perform. One of these functions is the reassembly of system routines that utilize system macros not available to the normal user. In general, the user with the appropriate authorization code can access this macro library. Most operating systems have macros of this sort that aid in system development but are not of general use to the normal user.

System Management Functions

Functions defined for the system manager determine the system management commands that he can use:

1. Join other users (JOIN).
2. Withdraw permission to use the system (QUIT).
3. Terminate any nonconversational task (CANCEL).
4. Determine the contents and status of any data set in the system (PC?, DSS?, LINE?).
5. Extract accounting information from the system (USAGE).

TABLE 10.15   FORMAT OF SYSTEM MANAGEMENT COMMANDS

Operations	Operand
CANCEL	BSN=batch sequence number
DSS?	[USERID=user identification] $\left[,\text{NAMES}=\begin{Bmatrix}\text{data set name}\\(\text{data set name }[,\dots])\end{Bmatrix}\right]$
JOIN	USERID=user identification [PASSWORD=identifier], CHARGE=charge number [,PRIORITY=priority] [,PRIV=(privilege [,...])][,AUTH=authority] [RATION=key][,BATCH={Y|N}]
LINE?[a]	DSNAME=data set name $\left[,\begin{Bmatrix}\text{line number}\\(\text{first line number, last line number})\end{Bmatrix}[,\dots]\right]$
LOGOFF	
[LOGON]	user identification, [charge number], [confirmation],[message option],[password]
PC?	[USERID=user identification] $\left[\text{NAMES}=\begin{Bmatrix}\text{data set name}\\(\text{data set name }[,\dots])\end{Bmatrix}\right]$
QUIT	USERID=user identification
USAGE	[USERID=user identification]

[a]The data set name used is a fully qualified name including the owner's userid.

Similarly, the system administrator can perform the same functions—but only for users that he has joined. The format of system management commands is given in Table 10.15. When a system manager or a system administrator desires to access the system, he logs on as any other user and a conversational task is created for him. When he has finished his work, he logs off in the usual manner. Thus, there is a certain amount of consistency in how the system is used, which is desirable in any general-purpose time sharing system.

11 | SYSTEM STRUCTURE AND OPERATION

11.1 INTRODUCTION

The objective of this chapter is to provide additional insight into the structure and operation of the TSS system. The subject matter has been introduced earlier in a more general context. Most of the topics can be studied independently; collectively, they represent the "state of the art" in operating systems technology. Only topics deemed to be of "most general" use are covered, including:

1. the resident supervisor,
2. scheduling,
3. storage allocation,
4. paging,
5. the dynamic loader,
6. data management, and
7. multiprocessing.

The reader is directed to references [Com65], [Gib66], [Let68], and [TSSi] for information on topics that are not covered.

Overall System Flow

The structure of TSS and its overall system flow are given in Fig. 11.1. The reader should recognize the three levels of the system:

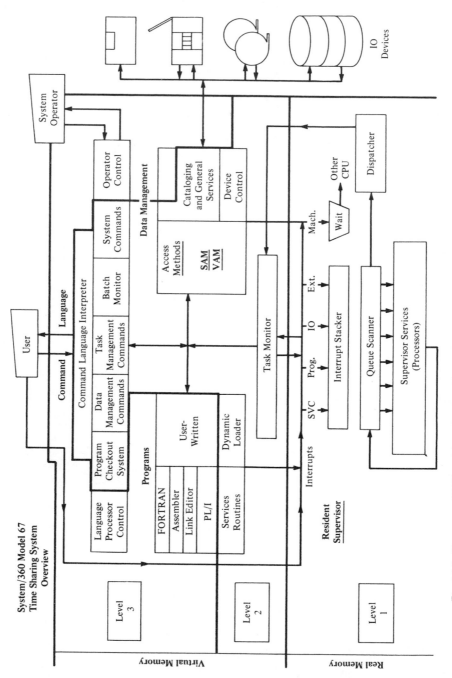

Fig. 11.1 Structure of TSS and overall system flow. (*Courtesy International Business Machines Corporation.*)

1. Level one—The *resident supervisor* that is permanently resident in main storage and operates in the supervisor state.
2. Level two—*Privileged system routines* that reside in a user's virtual memory and operate in the problem state with privileged protection keys.
3. Level three—*User programs* and *language processors* that reside in virtual memory and operate in the problem state with user protection keys.

The only entry to the Resident Supervisor is via an interruption that is handled by the interrupt stacker routine. Control is passed between Resident Supervisor routines with the branch instruction or by placing a generalized queue entry (GQE) on an appropriate queue for subsequent processing. Most Resident Supervisor routines exit to the Queue Scanner that controls the execution of Queue Processors on a priority basis. Except for minor exceptions, Resident Supervisor routines execute with interruptions enabled (in contrast to OS) and do not issue SVC interruptions. In general, program interruptions from the Resident Supervisor are not expected, since it is tested and supposed to be "bug" free, and are classed as system failures. Machine check interruptions are processed by error recovery routines. External and IO interruptions can come in when the Resident Supervisor has control of the CPU and are processed by the interrupt stacker.

Program control is passed to user tasks by loading a new PSW (i.e., a new status word) with an address field that points to an appropriate main storage location that corresponds to a user location in virtual memory. When CPU control is dispatched to a user task in this fashion, the "problem state" bit in the new PSW is set to place the computer system in the problem state. Similarly, the new PSW associated with an interruption (see Chapter 3) does not have the "problem state" bit set so that the computer system enters the supervisor state when an interruption is accepted.

Startup

The system is "started up" in one of two ways: (1) as the result of an IPL sequence by the operator; and (2) in response to a call from a reconfiguration routine of the Resident Supervisor. The latter case results from a system restart following a system error. The result is the same in either case: A STARTUP program is invoked that readies the system for utilization. The STARTUP program is composed of two components: STARTUP prelude and STARTUP proper. The execution of STARTUP prelude precedes that of STARTUP proper; the following functions are performed by STARTUP prelude:

1. The physical addresses of the IPL control volume and the operator's console are determined.
2. A list of defective main storage pages is generated so that the resident supervisor can prevent them from being allocated.

3. The configuration control block (CCB) is read in from the SYSCCB data set and located in main storage. The CCB is a collection of tables that describes the hardware configuration and installation parameters.

In a multiple CPU environment, STARTUP prelude determines the active CPU and performs a configuration analysis. After performing a variety of other control functions, STARTUP prelude reads in and passes control to the "STARTUP proper" program.

The primary function of STARTUP proper is to link load the Resident Supervisor and Initial Virtual Memory (IVM). The routines of the Resident Supervisor are contained in the data set RESSUP and the routines of Initial Virtual Memory are contained in the data set SYSIVM. Both data sets are contained on the IPL control volume. The Resident Supervisor is left in main storage and IVM is placed on an auxiliary paging device. The link loading is significant. A load list that contains names of routines exists for both the Resident Supervisor and IVM. During STARTUP, the operator is asked whether he wants to establish a library hierarchy of installation-supplied routines. If not, routines are link loaded, according to the load list, from the RESSUP and SYSIVM data sets, respectively, on the IPL control volume. If installation-supplied libraries are specified, then these libraries are searched first for routines on the load list. The STARTUP proper program also creates a skeletal XTSI for the location of IVM pages on auxiliary storage, constructs shared page tables for public CSECTS (see Chapter 10), writes the IVM CSECTS on the auxiliary paging device, constructs a storage map for the dynamic loader, initializes the Core Block Table (used for main storage allocation), sets the storage protection keys, initializes the system Table, establishes the Main Operator Task, and creates a GQE representing an operator attention and places it on the Main Operator Task's TSI. (In a multiple CPU system, other CPUs are also started.) Finally, the STARTUP proper program exits to the Resident Supervisor.†

Main Operator Task

The main operator task is interrupt driven, as is the Resident Supervisor and many other components of the system. The "attention" GQE created during startup causes the CPU to be dispatched to the Main Operator Task, which is the only task in the system at this time. After the operator is logged on, a Main Operator Housekeeping Routine (MOHR) is called that performs initialization and opens appropriate data sets. MOHR also sets a flag that allows other tasks to be created. This flag prevents conversational users from "dialing in" and logging on before system initialization is complete. Lastly, MOHR issues an SVC instruction to the Resident Supervisor to create and initialize the Batch Monitor Task. MOHR is invoked during startup only.

†Obviously, other functions are performed during startup. At this level of presentation, however, some operations must be subordinated to a more detailed discussion.

The two main processing routines of the Main Operator Task are: the Operator External Interrupt Processor; and the Main Operator Control Program. Both routines are primarily concerned with operator communications and are entered only in response to interrupt conditions.

The Operator External Interrupt Processor (OXIP) is the link between the command system and the main operator task. OXIP formats messages or replies and places entries in a "message queue." The Main Operator Control Program (MOCP) maintains the message queue and communicates with the operator. It is entered during a time slice of the Main Operator Task,† when no commands are being processed, to perform console IO operations. If no console operations are required, MOCP places the Main Operator Task in the wait status.

Messages are maintained in four lists for processing by MOCP:

1. The *major list*—contains high-priority messages to be sent to the operator.
2. The *normal list*—contains normal messages to be sent to the operator.
3. The *reply list*—contains replies entered by the operator. Replies are correlated with messages by number and a flag is set in the original message when the reply is received.
4. The *wait list*—contains messages that have been sent to the operator and for which the reply has not been received. If a reply is not received in a specified time, the message is reissued.

Batch Monitor

The *Batch Monitor Task* is created and initiated by the Main Operator Housekeeping Routine. The Batch Monitor maintains the batch work queue (BWQ), which is implemented as a VISAM data set. If the BWQ does not exist (e.g., when the system is started up), then the Batch Monitor creates the BWQ data set. In general, the BWQ is maintained between "shutdown" and "startup" such that when the system is restarted, the Batch Monitor must inspect the BWQ to determine the status of batch jobs that have not been processed.

The Batch Monitor Task is time sliced. During normal processing, it creates nonconversational tasks, initiates bulk IO requests, and assigns batch sequence numbers. The Batch Monitor operates in response to request flags set by command language processing routines. During its time slices, the Batch Monitor inspects these flags for pending requests and initiates either batch tasks or bulk IO tasks as resources permit.

In general, the Batch Monitor and the Main Operator Task operate at a high-priority level so that they receive frequent time slices. Only one Batch Monitor and one Main Operator Task exist in the system. Information is passed between Command System routines and the Batch Monitor and Main Operator Task via control blocks, queues, and tables.

---

†The Main Operator Task is time sliced as any user task.

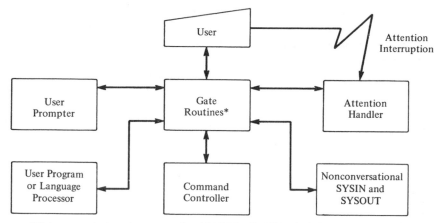

*Gate macro instruction processing (GATRD, GATWR, GTWSR—See Chapter 9).

Fig. 11.2 Operational flow of the command system.

Command System

Whereas the Batch Monitor and Main Operator Tasks represent single tasks in the system, the "Command System" routines reside in each user's virtual memory and are shared. That is, each user uses the Command System as though it were his own. The TSS Command System is designed to process a large number of single commands—each represented by an appropriate processing routine. Conceptually, the processing of commands is a relatively simple function. Much of the complexity is a result of default, synonym, and definitional facilities.

The operational flow of the Command System is given in Fig. 11.2. As far as command processing is concerned, the key component is the "command controller," which utilizes the other components as required. The structure of command processing is depicted in Fig. 11.3.

Task control is passed from the Task Monitor to the *Command Analyzer and Executor* (CA&E) as the result of an attention interruption, task initialization, or the completion of the execution of a command or a processing program. The Command Analyzer and Executor receives its input via the *Source List Handler*, which retrieves input commands from a defined procedure or prompts the user for his next command, and uses a *Verb Scanner* routine and the *Combined Dictionary Handler* to isolate a particular command and pass control to the appropriate processing routines. (The dictionary handler utilizes the user's profile SYSPRX—to identify the command entered.) The command processing routines use the *Scan Routine* to isolate and validate parameters. The *Gate Routines*, which process the GATRD, GATWR, GTWAR, and GTWSR macro instructions, and *Virtual Memory Task Initiatlization* have been mentioned previously.

The function and use of the Command System are not directly related to how

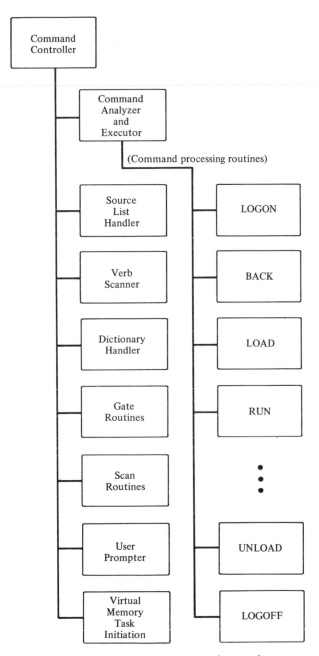

Fig. 11.3 The structure of command processing.

and when a task receives control of the CPU; task control is a Resident Supervisor function. A task's control point can be in the Command System, the Task Monitor, the Dynamic Loader, a language processor, an access method routine, a user program, etc.—however, this control point must be in virtual memory. When a task requests a Resident Supervisor function, then that task is put into a "delay" status and it is not dispatched for execution until the request is satisfied. Otherwise, program control passes between the virtual memory programs, mentioned above. All tasks are time sliced or multiprogrammed (or both). Thus, for example, a task can be executing in the Command System when its time slice is over (i.e., a timer "goes off"); the next time that task is given the CPU, execution resumes from where it was interrupted in the Command System. Here is where multiprogramming and time slicing are used together. When the Command System prompts the user for a command, the task is put into a "terminal wait" state and CPU control is dispatched to another task. This is multiprogramming. When the timer "goes off" on an executing task, time slicing takes place. In general, a task accumulates bits of CPU time until the duration of its time slice is exceeded. It is then returned to the end of the queue (figuratively speaking) while other tasks are given time slices.

Control Volumes

TSS system storage is introduced in Chapter 9. The *IPL Control Volume* includes the IPL control record and the STARTUP prelude program, as well as the following VPAM libraries:

TSS*****.SYSCCB   TSS*****.SYSIVM
TSS*****.STARTUP   TSS*****.SYSBLD
TSS*****.RESSUP   TSS*****.APGENX

The prefix TSS***** is the "user ID" of the system and prevents these data sets from being accessed by a normal user. SYSCCB contains the configuration control block that is built during system generation. STARTUP contains the "startup proper" program, and RESSUP and SYSIVM contain the Resident Supervisor and Initial Virtual Memory modules, respectively. SYSBLD and APGENX are used during system generation.

The *Auxiliary Control Volume* contains the following system data sets:

TSS*****.SYSCAT—the System Catalog
TSS*****.SYSLIB—the System Library
TSS*****.SYSMAC—the System Macro Library (normal users)
TSS*****.MACNDX—index to SYSMAC by macro name
TSS*****.ASMMAC—the System Assembler Macro Library (privileged users)
TSS*****.ASMNDX—index to ASMMAC by macro name
TSS*****.USERLIB—privileged system programmer's library
TSS*****.SYSUSE—table of system users

TSS*****.SYSMLF–System Message Table
SYSOPERO.SYSLOG–operator's log

It would seem that the contents of the Auxiliary Control Volume could easily exceed the capacity of a single direct-access volume. This is where the privileged system programmer (with a user ID of TSS*****) would log on and transfer one or more of the above data sets to another public volume. In fact, he could use the VV command (VAM to VAM) given in Chapter 10.

As the system is used, new generations and versions of the system data sets given here are normally required. For that reason, a low-order qualification of the form:

$$GxxxxVyy$$

is suffixed to all system data sets. Thus, the fully qualified name of the RESSUP data set is:

$$TSS*****.RESSUP.GxxxxVyy$$

This facility, termed a *generation data group*, is available for all data sets through the DDEF processing routine of the Command System. It allows "generations" of a data set to be identified. The reader should consult references [Let69] and [TSSc] for additional information on this subject.

11.2 RESIDENT SUPERVISOR

The purpose of this section is to present additional detail on the Resident Supervisor, introduced in Section 9.4. The reader should refer to Figs. 9.25 and 9.26, which depict the "overall system flow" and the "components of the Resident Supervisor," respectively. The structure of the Resident Supervisor and operational flow between components is depicted in Fig. 11.4. Most components, included in Fig. 11.4, are introduced in an earlier chapter.

Interrupt Stacker

As mentioned in Chapter 9, all interruptions go through the interrupt stacker that classifies and analyzes interruptions on the basis of type, origin, and severity. These interruptions can be grouped into three logical categories:

1. emergency interruptions that must be processed immediately, such as a machine check interruption;
2. interruptions that require nontrivial processing by the Resident Supervisor; and
3. SVC and program interruptions that do not require Resident Supervisor processing but request a change in task status (e.g., from the nonprivileged to the privileged state) or present a condition (such as fixed-point underflow) that can be resolved in virtual memory.[†]

[†] In a case such as this, task control is effectively passed to the Task Monitor that contains facilities for resolving task-oriented interruptions.

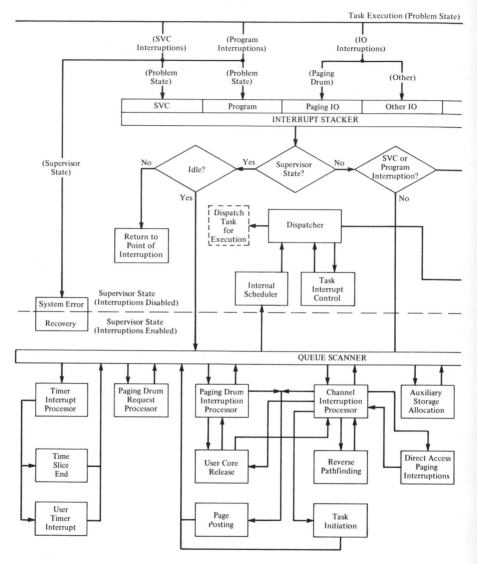

Fig. 11.4 Structure and organization of the Resident Supervisor.

Emergency conditions cause "error recovery" procedures to be invoked directly. After task-oriented interruptions are recognized, program control is passed directly to appropriate processing routines (see Fig. 11.4). The major concern here is with "supervisor-oriented" interruptions.

The interrupt stacker is entered when a new PSW is swapped for an old PSW.

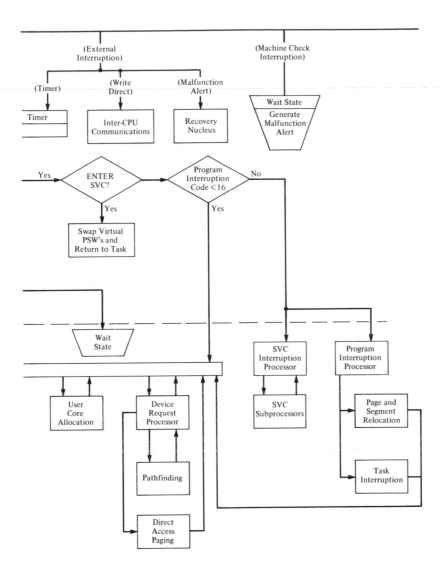

Fig. 11.4 Continued.

The new PSW has bits set to disable further interruptions while a record is made of the interruption that just occurred. Upon entry, the interrupt stacker saves critical information on the interrupted program (location counter, condition codes, status fields, necessary registers). This is called a *short save*. A *generalized queue entry* (GQE) is built for the interruption and it is placed on an appropriate queue. If the system was in the supervisor state prior to the interruption, program control is returned to the interrupted routine by restoring the CPU to the exact state it was in prior to the interruption. Otherwise, the system was in the problem state and the complete status of the task is saved in its TSI.† This is called a *long save*. Interruptions are then enabled and the interrupt stacker exits to the Queue Scanner.

Queue Scanner

The *Queue Scanner* uses the scan table to schedule the order in which work is performed by the Resident Supervisor. As mentioned in Chapter 9, each interruption type, each device, and each resource is represented in the scan table. More specifically, the Resident Supervisor includes several Queue Processors, each programmed to process a specific request or to handle a given condition. The Scan Table contains an entry for each queue processor. A Scan Table entry essentially consists of an anchor for the queue of GQEs that reflect the work that is stacked up for a particular queue processor. The only exceptions are the Device Queue Processor and the Paging Drum Processor. A queue exists for *each* paging drum in the system and for *each* device in the system; each of these queues is also anchored in the Scan Table and ordered by priority. The Paging Drum Processor handles all GQEs for the paging drums and the Device Queue Processor handles all GQEs for the other IO devices.

The various Scan Table entries permit the queues to be placed in priority order. The Queue Scanner selects the highest-priority queue that has work to do (i.e., the highest-priority queue containing at least one GQE). Control is passed to the corresponding queue processor to do the work reflected in the first GQE on its queue. After the queue processor finishes processing that GQE, it returns to the Queue Scanner. Why? Because it is desirable to process GQEs in priority order (e.g., to keep the paging drum going) and a high-priority interruption might come in while a lower-priority GQE is being processed.

There are times when a queue processor cannot be used by one CPU because it is being used by another CPU that has set the "lock byte." When this situation occurs, the Queue Scanner bypasses that queue processor and finds another "unit of work" that needs to be performed.

When the Queue Scanner determines that there is no more work for the Resident Supervisor to do, either because all the GQEs have been processed or the queue processors for which there is work are busy, the Queue Scanner passes control to the Dispatcher to allocate the CPU to a task.

Dispatcher

The primary function of the Dispatcher is to allocate the CPU to a task. The precise manner in which a task is selected is covered in the section on schedul-

† Actually, task control information is saved in its Extended TSI (i.e., its XTSI).

ing. In general, however, a TSI, representing a task, is selected from a dispatchable TSI list anchored in the System Table. (A task is dispatchable only if it has pages in main storage.) The Dispatcher calls a routine, termed Task Interrupt Control (TIC), to determine if task interruptions are pending. If so, task control is altered so that the task will be entered at a routine designed to process the task interruption. TIC returns to the Dispatcher. The Dispatcher then places the task in execution by:

1. setting the TSI status flag to "in execution";
2. recording the task identification in the Resident Supervisor;
3. setting the internal timer to the task's time slice value;
4. loading task control information (registers, etc.) from the XTSI; and
5. loading a PSW that will cause execution of the task to be started at a specific address in main storage.

Once the execution of a task commences, it continues to execute until an interruption occurs. That interruption can be initiated by an SVC instruction or a "program fault" in the executing program or an independent event, such as an IO completion, machine check condition, or the expiration of the timer.

If no task is ready for execution, the Dispatcher puts the CPU into the wait state (see Chapter 3) with interruptions enabled. The CPU subsequently leaves the wait state when an interruption is received by that CPU.

CPU scheduling is presented in Section 11.6.

Queue Processors

Queue processors are grouped into three categories: (1) interruption queue processors, (2) request queue processors, and (3) error control processors. One queue processor can call upon the services of another queue processor by placing a GQE on its queue. This technique, together with service routines, minimizes the amount of machine code that comprises the Resident Supervisor.

Interruption queue processors correspond to the types of interruptions presented earlier and frequently use "request queue processors" to complete their processing. Five interruption queue processors are used:

1. timer interruption queue processor,
2. paging drum interruption queue processor,
3. channel interruption queue processor,
4. program interruption queue processor, and
5. SVC interruption queue processor.

Request queue processors are used by interruption queue processors and certain Resident Supervisor routines. The following request queue processors are used:

1. user core allocation (allocates main storage),
2. auxiliary storage allocation (allocates public storage),

3. device queue processor (initiates IO processing), and
4. paging drum queue processor (initiates "page in" and "page out" requests).

Error control processors are entered as the result of hardware or software error conditions. These processors, covered later, provide error recording, error recovery, and system reconfiguration facilities. The SVC interruption processor is of major concern since it provides a great many facilities to user programs (tasks) executing in either the privileged or nonprivileged state. The SVC interruption processor identifies a particular SVC request by a number n, where $0 \leqslant n \leqslant 256$, that is the operand to the SVC instruction and is stored in the old SVC PSW when the SVC interruption occurs. The SVC interruption processor passes control to an SVC subprocessor, designed to process that type of request. For example, the "create TSI subprocessor" operates in response to the CRTSI macro instruction. Similarly, the "terminal IO wait subprocessor" operates in response to the TWAIT macro instruction. Most Resident Supervisor services that operate in response to a request from virtual memory are implemented as SVC subprocessors.

Other SVC interruptions, initiated in the nonprivileged problem state, request services available from privileged programs that execute in virtual memory. (The SVCs corresponding to the CATALOG and DDEF macro instructions fall into this category.) In cases such as this, a virtual memory entry is made to the Task Monitor, which subsequently invokes the required virtual memory routine.

The Resident Supervisor does not issue SVC calls to itself but passes control via the branch instruction or by placing GQEs on Scan Table queues. Thus, SVC calls are not nested. The only supervisor state SVC that is defined is in response to a software error (SYSERR) that is detected by the software. This SVC causes error recovery routines to be entered as described below.

Supervisor Service Routines

As in any operating system, service routines are developed for use by queue processors and other Resident Supervisor routines. Some examples are: queue control, page handling, and inter-CPU communication. Routines of this type are implemented as closed subroutines that are called by system macro instructions. These macros are distinct from normal user macros and are available only to a user with an authorization code of P or O (see Chapter 10). These macros are stored in the ASMMAC library and are normally used during system development and maintenance. When an attempt is made to OPEN this data set by the assembler program, the privilege class of the associated task is inspected. If it is "nonprivileged" then the execution of that task is abnormally terminated.

Error Recovery and Control Procedures

Although system errors in an operating system environment are always serious, the potential danger is perhaps greater with an open time sharing system than with a typical batch processing system. The obvious reasons for this are inherent in the large number of on-line concurrent users and the use of public storage for storing programs and data. Toward this end, error recovery, retry, and recording, along with reconfiguration facilities, are of prime importance.

The manner in which errors are processed is dependent upon the origin and severity of the error condition. Errors are grouped into the following categories: (1) hardware errors (CPU, main storage, channel control units), (2) paging IO errors, (3) task IO errors, and (4) system software errors. (These categories do not include task programming errors.) *Hardware errors* are classified as internal (CPU, main storage) or external (channel controller). *Paging IO errors* are caused by equipment malfunction in the channel, control unit, or device and are processed by Resident Supervisor routines. *Task IO errors* originate in the same way but are usually processed by system routines that execute out of virtual memory. *System software errors* are classified as major (affecting the system as a whole) or minor (localized to a task). Error processing is initiated in the same manner for all types of errors: (1) The error environment is recorded for subsequent analysis; (2) the error condition is analyzed; (3) retry is attempted; and (4) execution is resumed or error recovery is performed. An overview of error processing is given in Fig. 11.5. Hardware errors and paging IO errors are presented here. The reader is directed to reference [TSSi] for details of task IO errors and system software errors.

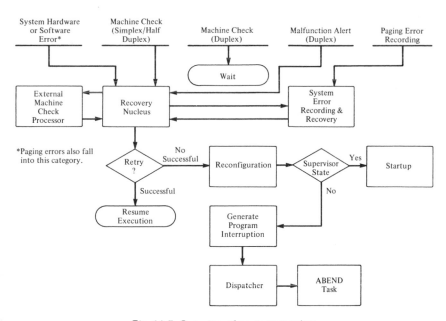

Fig. 11.5 Overview of error processing.

Although hardware error processing is necessarily machine-dependent, the principles involved are general enough to apply to other systems, as well. Other than the error itself, the two most important considerations are:

1. whether the computer system is single CPU or a duplex system; and
2. whether the computer was operating in the supervisor state or the problem state when the error occurred.

When the circuitry of the computer detects a hardware error, a machine check interruption is generated. This interruption, for obvious reasons, cannot be masked off. The CPU receiving the interruption (i.e., the one that has the hardware error) logs out hardware status information into "fixed logout areas" in main storage. In a duplex system, the malfunctioning CPU sends a malfunction alert to the other CPU as an external interruption and then enters the wait state. The "good" CPU will check out the "bad" CPU. When the good CPU receives the malfunction alert, it enters a Recovery Nucleus routine that is part of the Resident Supervisor. In a single CPU system, the "failing" CPU enters the Recovery Nucleus directly.

The function of the *Recovery Nucleus* is to assess the extent of the damage, do error recording, and take appropriate action. For *external machine checks*, an appropriate processor is called to analyze the error and perform retry operations if possible. This processor invokes the error recording module of the System Environment Recording and Retry (SERR) routines to record the occurrence of the error. For solid errors, the channel controller is made unavailable and the system is restarted (i.e., it goes through startup again). Otherwise, execution of the system is resumed. For *internal machine checks*, SERR is called to check out the system (CPU data paths, instructions, and main storage) and provide a damage report. For instruction errors, the Recovery Nucleus attempts an instruction retry, if it is possible. If retry is impossible or the instruction fails again, the Recovery Nucleus enters a Reconfiguration routine that determines if the operation of the system can continue. Internal machine check processing is summarized in Table 11.1. In general, the system is restarted or put into the wait state if the error occurs when the computer is executing in the supervisor state since the probability that the error condition affects several users is high. On the other hand, continued operation of the system is attempted when the error occurs when the computer is executing in the problem state. The task in execution when the error occurred is abnormally terminated. Also, reconfiguration of the system is performed dynamically if a half duplex or duplex system is involved. If a main storage error affects less than four user pages, those pages are marked unavailable in the "Core Block Table" (see the section on storage allocation). Otherwise, global damage is assumed and the entire storage module† is reconfigured out if possible.

†A storage module for the 360/67 computer contains 256K bytes.

TABLE 11.1 DECISION TABLE DESCRIBING THE RESULTS OF INTERNAL MACHINE CHECK PROCESSING[a]

Condition Stub	Condition Entry
Instruction error	Y Y Y Y N N N Y Y Y Y N N N N Y Y Y Y N N N
Restart possible (failing CPU)	Y Y N N - - - Y Y N N - - - Y Y N N - - -
Main storage error	N N N N Y Y Y N N N N Y Y Y N N N N Y Y Y
Less than 4 user pages faulty	- - - - - Y N - - - - Y N - - - - Y N
Supervisor state	Y N Y N Y N N Y N Y N Y N N Y N Y N Y N N
Simplex system	Y Y Y Y Y Y Y N N N N N N N N N N N N N N
Half duplex system	N N N N N N N Y Y Y Y Y Y Y N N N N N N
Duplex system	N N N N N N N N N N N N N N Y Y Y Y Y Y

Action Stub	Action Entry
Wait state (failing CPU)	X X X X X X
Operator intervention	X X X X X X
Automatic system reconfiguration	X X X X X X
Automatic restart (i.e., startup)	X X X X X X X
ABEND task	X X X X X X X X X
Mark faulty pages unavailable	X X X
Resume system operation	X X X X X X X

Key: Y—Yes   X—Take designated action
N—No   - —Irrelevant condition

[a]This table is included for pedagogical purposes and may not represent the precise action taken in all cases for all generations of the TSS/360 system.

The processing of paging errors is another area where the eventual disposition of the condition is dependent upon the state of the system when the error occurs. A paging IO error can occur at either of two times during a paging operation: (1) during the process of starting the operation; and (2) during the data transfer portion of the IO operation. If the operation cannot be started, an alternate path to the device is tried in an attempt to complete the operation. For data transfer errors, the operation is retried along the same path and then along an alternate path if the retry attempt fails. A routine called "Standard Area Retry" is called if it cannot be determined if the error is caused by a failing device, a defective volume, or a bad page (on a volume). An overview of paging IO error processing is given in Fig. 11.6. The analysis of the error condition is continued until a cause is determined so that the system can continue operation or signal a system hardware error. A device is diagnosed as unavailable if it is defective or if no path exists to it. A major hardware error is signaled if the primary paging device becomes unavailable. If a paging device other than the primary paging device becomes unavailable, operation of the system is continued. A "page location" on a paging device can become defective when the corresponding track is defective, while the device remains intact. On a page-out op-

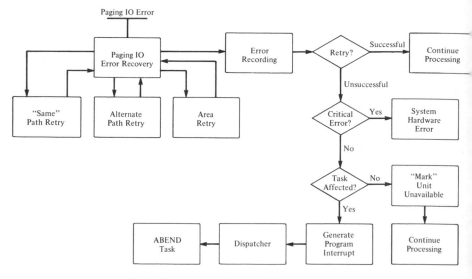

Fig. 11.6 Overview of paging IO error processing.

tion, the page location (on the paging device) is marked as unavailable and the operation is retried. On a page-in operation, the task is either abnormally terminated or allowed to continue depending upon the nature and severity of the condition. The results of paging IO error processing are given in Table 11.2. Detailed analysis of this table, as well as Table 11.1, is left as an exercise for the reader.

Comments on the Resident Supervisor

Although all of the components of the Resident Supervisor are important from the standpoint of overall system operation, some are considered to be more germaine to the study of operating systems. Topics that are grouped into this category are: storage allocation, paging, scheduling, dynamic loading, input and output facilities, and multiprocessing. These subjects comprise the remainder of the chapter. Sayers [Say71] presents a comprehensive survey of the field of operating systems and includes an introduction to most software components normally found in an operating system.

11.3 STORAGE ALLOCATION

Storage allocation in TSS involves main storage, virtual storage, auxiliary storage, and external storage. Allocation is handled by Resident Supervisor queue processors in response to task SVC instructions or requests by other Resident Supervisor routines.

TABLE 11.2 DECISION TABLE DESCRIBING THE RESULTS OF PAGING IO ERROR PROCESSING[a]

Condition

Condition	Condition Entry
Defective path[b]	Y Y Y Y Y Y Y Y Y
Alternate path available	Y N N N N N N N N
Defective device	Y Y Y Y Y Y Y Y Y Y Y
primary paging unit	Y
auxiliary paging unit	Y Y Y Y Y Y Y Y Y Y Y Y Y Y Y Y Y Y
Defective page (on device)	Y Y Y Y Y Y Y Y Y Y
Relocation	
task page	Y Y Y Y Y Y Y Y Y
shared page	Y Y Y Y Y Y
Paging operation	
page in	Y Y Y Y Y Y Y Y Y Y Y Y Y Y Y Y Y Y Y Y Y Y
page out	Y Y Y Y Y Y Y Y Y Y Y Y
VAM request	Y Y Y Y Y Y Y Y
TWAIT request	Y Y Y Y
IOCAL operation	Y Y Y Y Y Y Y Y
System operation[c]	Y Y Y Y Y Y Y Y

Action

Action	Action Entry
Mark device unavailable	X X X X X X X X X X X X X X X X X X X
Mark path unavailable	X X X X X X X X X X X X
Signal system hardware error	X X X X
Mark page unavailable	X X
Allocate new page and retry	X X X X X X X X X X X X X X
ABEND task	X X X X X X X X X X
Request operator FORCE task	X X
Continue task operation	X X X[d] X X X X X[d] X X X X[d] X X
Continue system operation	X X X X X X X X X X
Mark page unavailable (on device)	X X X X

Key: Y–Yes   N–No   X–Take designated action

[a]This table is included for pedagogical purposes and may not represent the precise action taken in all cases for all generations of the TSS/360 system.
[b]Channel controller, channel, or control unit.   [c]Dispatcher or page posting.   [d]The task may continue without reading the page.

Main Storage

Main storage is allocated in 4096-byte blocks termed *pages*. During startup, a Core Block Table (CBT) is built for the pages that comprise main storage. Each page has an entry in the CBT and is assigned to one of three categories: (1) assigned for user allocation; (2) assigned to the Resident Supervisor; and (3) defective or partitioned pages. A page that falls into the last category, either statically during startup or dynamically as part of error recovery procedures, it not allocated for use. Resident Supervisor allocation is contiguous in lower storage; the five pages following the Resident Supervisor "machine code" are also assigned for use in building control blocks. All other pages are made available for task use.

The user portion of main storage is managed by the User Core Allocation Queue Processor in response to requests during page-in operations and when virtual memory pages allocated by the GETMAIN macro instruction are referenced. User pages are "in use" or "not in use." *In-use pages* are assigned to the tasks in the system and are located through their respective page tables. A page is not placed in the "not in use" category until all IO and paging operations that use it are completed; moreover, XTSI pages are not released until all activity for that task is quiesced and the XTSI itself is paged out. The CBT entries for not-in-use pages are placed into one of three lists: (1) *available list*—not being used; (2) *pending list*—pages assigned to tasks in time slice end, terminal wait, or in IO wait; and (3) *preferred pending list*—user pages for tasks in time slice end, terminal wait, or in IO wait that must be in main storage for the task to begin execution. For a given task, preferred pending list pages consist of XTSI pages and the task's PSW page—i.e., the page in which the task was executing when it was interrupted. Two types of requests can be made for user storage: (1) to reclaim a page (before it is paged out) previously assigned to that task; and (2) for initial assignment of a page to a task. The process is depicted in Fig. 11.7. When a request is made to reclaim a page, the CBT is searched for that page. If it can be reclaimed, a "read in" from the paging device is saved. Otherwise, an assignment is attempted from the available, pending, and preferred pending lists, in that order. Similarly, when a request is made for a "new" page, the available, pending, and preferred pending lists are searched. The User Core Allocation Queue Processor maintains a page count. If the count drops below a "high core" threshhold, a "low core indicator" is turned on. The *low core indicator* denotes that additional pages should not be assigned until task pages are released. (When a task reaches time slice end, its pages are placed on the pending and preferred pending lists and the page count is increased.) If a storage request is made and either the low core indicator is set or no storage is available, then an attempt is made to release shared pages. If this attempt fails, then the task that is least likely to be dispatched is placed in a time slice end status, thus making pages available for assignment.

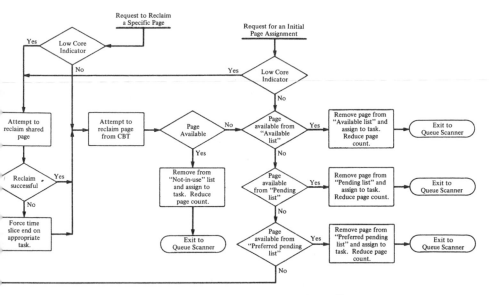

Fig. 11.7 Operation of the User Core Allocation Queue Processor.

The pages assigned to the Resident Supervisor during startup are chained together on a *Reserve List* and are used by the Supervisor Core Allocation and Supervisor Core Release subroutines. The unit of suballocation within the Resident Supervisor is a 64-byte block, most frequently used to build GQEs. Reserve pages used for suballocation are removed from the Reserve List and chained together and divided into blocks. The first block of each page contains an "available" block count and a bit map that denotes the blocks that are available. The Supervisor Core Allocation/Release subroutines also maintain six "quick cells" that point to the blocks most recently returned and reduce the amount of fragmentation during suballocation. A request for supervisor storage can fall into one of three categories:

1. request for one 64-byte block,
2. request for several contiguous 64-byte blocks, and
3. request for a full page.

The last request is satisfied from the Reserve List. The Reserve List is replenished by "borrowing pages" from the user area, as required.

Virtual Memory

A request for virtual memory allocation is made in response to a user's GETMAIN macro instruction or a request for virtual memory space by the dynamic loader. In addition, system service routines that operate in behalf of a task sometimes require virtual memory for tables. Virtual memory allocation is performed by a system routine that operates in a task's virtual memory. Actual manipulation of page and segment tables is performed by Resident Supervisor SVC processing routines.

Three macro instructions are defined for virtual memory allocation/release. These macros expand as SVCs that effectively transfer program control to a privileged virtual memory program, called "Virtual Memory Allocation (VMA)." The macros are:

GETMAIN–Allocate private virtual memory.
FREEMAIN–Free private virtual memory.
EXPAND–Expand an existing area of virtual memory.

Resident Supervisor SVC subprocessors perform appropriate processing in response to the following privileged macro instructions:

ADDPG–Add pages to a task's virtual memory by creating necessary page table entries.
ADSPG–Add shared pages to a task's virtual memory by creating necessary shared page table entries.
CNSEG–Connect a segment table entry to a shared page table.
DELPG–Remove pages from a task's virtual memory by deleting page table entries.
DSSEG–Disconnect a segment table entry from a shared page table.
MOVXP–Move page table entries from one table to another.

More specifically, a user issues a macro instruction in the first class that invokes Virtual Memory Allocation (VMA). VMA performs the required function by invoking Resident Supervisor SVC processing routines with a macro instruction in the second class. For example, the GETMAIN routine is called to allocate storage to a user program or in response to a system service routine. GETMAIN executes an ADDPG macro instruction to perform the actual allocation (i.e., modify the task's page tables). Similarly, the FREEMAIN routine releases virtual memory by issuing a DELPG macro instruction.

Auxiliary Storage

Auxiliary storage is used during dynamic address translation paging to hold IVM and user pages that are not being used at a given point in time. Auxiliary storage volumes are formatted to process page-sized blocks. TSS uses a drum as the primary paging device, with disk storage as secondary paging devices. (In some cases, an extra drum is used for paging and in others—see [Fik68] and [Lan67] — large-capacity storage is used as a pseudo-paging device.) Obviously, space on the primary paging device is at a premium; the system protects itself against a single user "clogging up" the drum. The *Auxiliary Storage Allocation Queue*

Processor maintains a count of the pages remaining on the drum. If the count falls below a system limit, task pages are migrated to the secondary paging device. The Auxiliary Storage Allocation Queue Processor also uses a "fair share" value that reflects a nominal number of pages on the primary paging device that should be allocated to a single task. When the remaining pages fall below the limit mentioned previously, a task is selected for page migration. Page migration entails moving a task's pages, in excess of the fair share, from the primary to the secondary paging device(s). The task selected for page migration is on the inactive list; it is the task on that list with the highest number of pages in excess of its fair share.

Ordinarily, requests for auxiliary storage are assigned by the Auxiliary Storage Allocation Queue Processor from the primary paging device. The secondary paging device is used when the available space on the primary paging device has reached the minimal level. The following procedure is applied during time slice end processing: If a task has not exceeded its fair share of space on the primary paging device, then its pages are written to the primary paging device. If the task has exceeded its fair share of space on the primary paging device, however, then its pages are written to a secondary paging device.

An *auxiliary storage allocation table* (ASAT) is built during startup for use by the Auxiliary Storage Allocation Queue Processor. The ASAT contains a bit directory of available pages for each paging device in the system. The directories for each type of paging device are chained together in the ASAT table to facilitate storage allocation.

During operation of the system, each task's auxiliary storage requirements (from the user profile) are compared with the currently available auxiliary storage on both primary and secondary devices. If insufficient auxiliary storage is available, the task is denied access to the system. When the total amount of available auxiliary storage is at a minimal level during system operation, the amount of auxiliary storage assigned to a task is compared dynamically against a system limit. If a task exceeds its limit, a warning message is issued so that the conversational user can UNLOAD programs, thereby reducing his auxiliary storage requirements. Nonconversational tasks are abnormally terminated.

Several comments are in order. When there are few users on the system, most paging is done to the primary device, and page reclaiming is frequently possible. Thus, response time is good. When the number of users is higher, the secondary paging device must be used, and page reclaiming is not as prevalent. Thus, response time is not as good as in the first case. Limitations on page requirements take effect only when the amount of available auxiliary storage is low.

External Storage Allocation

External storage allocation involves the allocation of space on direct-access volumes used for external storage. Allocation facilities fall into two classes:

sequential access method (SAM) allocation and virtual access method (VAM) allocation. SAM allocation is performed through the VTOC for a given volume and can be used with private storage in TSS in a manner analagous to the way it is used in OS. VAM allocation can be used with either public or private storage in TSS. VAM allocation is discussed here.

VAM volumes are divided into 4096-byte blocks referred to as pages. Each volume includes a Page Assignment Table (PAT) that is located through the volume label and specifies the status of each page on the volume. The status of a page on a VAM volume can be one of the following:

1. assigned as a data set page,
2. unassigned,
3. assigned as a DSCB page, or
4. defective and unavailable for assignment.

Public volumes are located through a Public Volume Table (PVT) maintained by the External Storage Allocation Processor. The PVT contains the volume identification of all volumes designated as public storage.

A page in public storage is located with an external page address that consists of a relative volume number and a relative page number on that volume. The relative volume number is an index to the PVT table and the relative page number is an index into the "assigned page" part of the PAT table. A list of private VAM volumes is also maintained by the system so that all VAM data sets can be processed in the same manner.

11.4 PAGING

The reasons for paging and the manner in which it is used are introduced in Chapter 9. The purpose of this section is to describe briefly how paging is performed using the facilities of the Resident Supervisor. *Paging* is the process of moving 4096-byte blocks of information between main storage and auxiliary storage and between main storage and external storage.

Initiation of Paging

The paging process is initiated by an event that occurs when the system is operating. The event can be a hardware interruption or a request by a Resident Supervisor routine to initiate a paging operation. In addition to the initiation of a paging operation, the paging process also involves the handling of IO interruptions associated with the completion of a paging operation and the "posting" of the completion of that event.

Page in refers to the operation of bringing a page into main storage from either an auxiliary storage device or an external storage device. It can be initiated in one of the following ways:

1. A *page relocation exception interruption* is triggered when a task references a page that is not in main storage. (See "Dynamic Address Translation" in Chapter 9.)
2. The *Dispatcher* requests the first XTSI page of a task scheduled for execution.
3. The *Task Interrupt Control routine* requests the ISA (Interrupt Storage Area) page of a task to establish a virtual PSW (VPSW).
4. The *Page Posting routine* brings in the remaining XTSI pages.
5. The *Page Out Service routine* moves a VAM page from auxiliary storage to external storage. The page is paged in from auxiliary storage and paged out to external storage.
6. The *IO Call (IOCAL) SVC Processor* brings in IO buffer pages from auxiliary storage.

Page out refers to the operation of moving a page from main storage to either auxiliary storage or external storage. It can be initiated in one of the following ways:

1. The *Timer Interrupt Queue Processor* during time slice end (TSE) moves a changed page to auxiliary storage.
2. The *Page Out Service* routine moves a VAM page from main storage to external storage.

The page in and page out processes use queue processors and routines that are introduced later. These components process GQEs as mentioned previously. When a paging operation is involved, a Page Control Block (PCB) is built and is chained to the GQE. Each PCB can contain up to three page control block entries, referred to as PCBEs. A PCBE is needed for each 4096-byte block of information that is paged in or out. A page control block is depicted in Fig. 11.8.

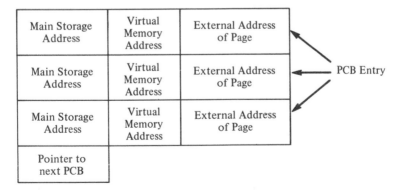

Fig. 11.8 Page control block (PCB).

Ordinarily, a request to move a page to auxiliary storage, for example, involves more than one operation. First, a GQE for the operation and a PCB for the pages to be moved are built. The PCB is linked to the GQE and the GQE is placed on the Auxiliary Storage Allocation queue for subsequent processing. After auxiliary storage is allocated for the page, the Auxiliary Storage Allocation Queue Processor moves the GQE to the Page Drum Queue or to the Page Direct Access Queue to have the page written out. Later, when the operation is complete, the GQE and the PCB are released.

Paging Processors and Service Routines

Paging is performed by queue processors called by the Queue Scanner. The queue processors use paging service routines, as required. These queue processors and service routines are:

1. *Program Interrupt Queue Processor.* Handles a page relocation exception; a PCB for the needed page is constructed and attached to a GQE. The GQE is enqueued on the User Core Allocation queue.
2. *Timer Interrupt Queue Processor.* Initiates time slice end (TSE) procedures for a task and handles "terminal wait" (TWAIT) migration of pages from the primary to the secondary paging devices. In case of TSE, changed pages of a task and its XTSI are written to auxiliary storage and the main storage occupied by these pages is released.
3. *User Core Allocation Queue Processor.* Allocates a page of main storage for each PCB entry. This processor uses the Core Block Table and does page reclaiming as described in Section 11.3.
4. *User Core Release Routine.* Releases a main storage page by setting its Core Block Table Entry to "not in use" and by placing an entry on one of the three queues: unassigned, pending, and preferred pending.
5. *Auxiliary Storage Allocation Queue Processor.* Allocates an auxiliary storage page to each entry in the PCB attached to the GQE. Uses the bit directory mentioned in Section 11.3.
6. *Auxiliary Storage Release Routine.* Releases pages on auxiliary storage that are no longer required.
7. *Page Drum Queue Processor.* Builds a channel program to handle all paging operations specified by the PCBs of all GQEs queued. This processor either initiates IO or appends the channel program to a running channel program.
8. *Page Drum Interrupt Queue Processor.* Processes interrupts resulting from paging operations on the primary paging device (i.e., the drum). Posting procedures are performed for completed operations.
9. *Page Direct Access Queue Routine.* Handles direct-access paging operations (secondary paging device) specified by the PCB of one GQE. Called by the IO Device Queue Processor.

10. *Page Direct Access Interruption Subroutine.* Handles the interruptions resulting from direct-access paging operations (secondary paging device) initiated by the Page Direct Access Queue Routine. Called by the Channel Interruption Processor.

11. *Page Out Service Routine.* Handles a VAM page out SVC interruption. VAM pages may reside in main storage or on auxiliary storage. VAM pages in main storage are transferred to external storage. VAM pages on auxiliary storage are read into main storage and then transferred to external storage.

12. *Page Posting Routine.* Posts in a task's TSI, XTSI, or Shared Page Table (SPT) the status of a user's pages after a paging operation has been completed.

13. *Delete TSI Routine.* Releases all main storage and auxiliary used by a task; is called during LOGOFF.

These processors and routines are invoked, as required, during paging operations. Some interesting aspects of drum paging are covered next followed by a "walk-through" of drum paging. A study of disk paging parallels that of drum paging and is left as a research and analysis project for the reader.

Drum Paging IO

The performance characteristics of a virtual memory based system is heavily dependent upon the paging process. Toward that end, two techniques are used to transfer pages between main storage and the drum as quickly as possible; slot sorting and command chaining. *Slot sorting* is the process of allocating auxiliary storage and arranging the transfer of pages such that the maximum number of pages are transferred per drum revolution. More specifically, the drum contains 200 tracks; nine pages can be stored in two tracks. (Therefore, the drum holds 900 pages. The exact capacity of the drum is not important but it is something to work with.) Thus, there are 100 track positions, each containing 9 page positions. The corresponding page position in each of the 100 track positions is termed a slot. (See Fig. 11.9.) If the channel program is arranged appropriately, 9 pages can be transferred between the drum and main storage in two drum revolutions—one page in each slot regardless of the track position because read/write heads can be switched electronically. Slot sorting maximizes the efficiency of the paging process by providing activity for each slot as the drum rotates. The paging operation has been studied both theoretically and experimentally by Denning [Den72], in which he presents an analysis of the efficiency of a paging drum.

Command chaining is used in the channel program to keep the drum continually running—i.e., constantly transferring information to and from main storage. In order to inform the Paging Drum Interruption Processor that a given paging operation has been completed, a "program controlled interruption" is generated

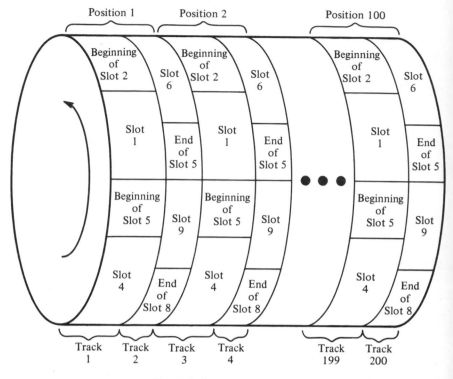

Fig. 11.9 Paging drum format.

as part of the channel program. In other words, the drum keeps running while the Resident Supervisor is informed of the fact that the previous page transfer operation has been completed. Channel commands are added to the end of the executing channel program so that IO need not be reinitiated for each paging operation.† (It has been said that with a heavily loaded system using this technique, a "start IO" command could be issued to the drum in the morning and the drum could run all day without requiring another "start IO.")

Figure 11.10 depicts the manner in which paging drum IO is managed. The Scan Table points to GQEs and PCBs that represent the work to be done. The System Table contains a Drum Interface Control Block (DICB) that effectively points to a Drum Interface Block (DIB) that is constructed for each page drum GQE. The DIB includes control information and the channel programs for PCBs on that GQE. The control blocks depicted in Fig. 11.10 are used by the Page Drum Queue Processor and the Page Drum Interruption Processor to perform the paging operations as described in the next section.

---

†This is accomplished with a transfer-in-channel channel command.

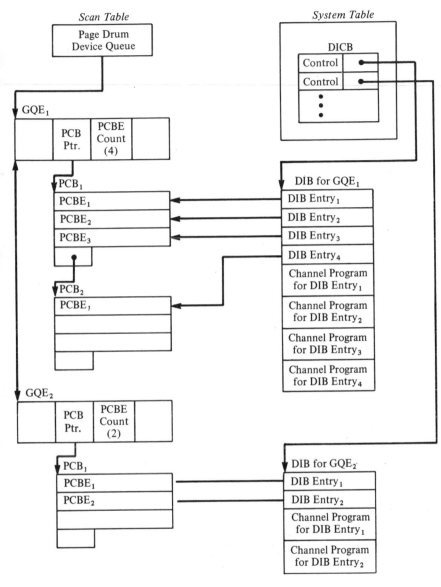

Fig. 11.10 Control blocks (simplified) used to manage paging drum IO.

Drum Paging Operations

This section gives a "walkthrough" of a drum page in operation and a drum page out operation. The various queue processors and service routines perform a wide variety of functions such that it is impractical to present the material as a

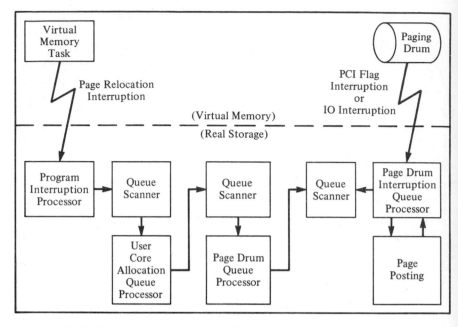

Fig. 11.11 Conceptual view of paging in from the primary paging device (drum).

flow diagram similar to those used in earlier chapters. Therefore, the various functions are listed in the order that they are performed.

A conceptual view of the page in process is depicted in Fig. 11.11. The process is initiated by a program interruption resulting from a virtual memory task that references a page that is not in main storage. The interruption is fielded by the Interrupt Stacker that recognizes the type of interruption and the condition and passes control directly to the Program Interruption Processor after building a GQE for the interruption.

Program Interruption Processor:
1. Checks the page table entry to verify that the page is still not available and determines the external address of the page.
2. Creates a PCB containing the virtual memory and external address of the page.
3. Links the PCB to the GQE and turns on "read" flags in both control blocks.
4. Marks the task status in its TSI to "page wait."
5. Enqueues the GQE on the User Core Allocation queue.
6. Exits to the Queue Scanner.

Subsequently, control is passed to the User Core Allocation Queue Processor to process the GQE.

User Core Allocation Queue Processor:
1. Allocates a block of main storage (i.e., a page) using the Core Block Table and its associated lists and inserts the main storage address of the block in the PCB.
2. Enqueues the GQE on the appropriate device queue, depending upon where the page is located. (It is the drum in this example.)
3. Exits to the Queue Scanner.

Subsequently, control is passed by the Queue Scanner to the Page Drum Queue Processor that processes *all* GQEs on its queue. (The Page Drum Queue Processor description also applies to page out operations.)

Page Drum Queue Processor:
1. Creates a Drum Interface Block (DIB) for each GQE; the DIBs are chained together.
2. Makes an entry in the DIB for each PCB entry on the GQE.
3. Connects the DIB chain to the currently executing DIB chain or to the System Table (DICB) if no drum channel program is in execution.
4. Performs slot sorting.
5. Creates a channel program for each page.
6. Issues a start IO to the drum or inserts a transfer-in-channel command into the last channel program in the DIB chain.
7. Exits to the Queue Scanner.

The page is in the process of being read in. When the operation is complete, an IO interruption is received. The Interrupt Stacker receives the interruption, builds a GQE, and passes control to the Queue Scanner. The Page Drum Interruption Processor is entered to process all GQEs on its queue. (Note that the Page Drum Interruption Processor handles interruptions for both incoming and outgoing pages.)

Page Drum Interruption Processor:
1. Examines channel conditions to determine the reason for the interruption. If an error condition is indicated, appropriate error routines are called.
2. Unchains DIBs for completed paging operations.
3. Performs specific posting operations (see #7 and #8).
4. Calls Supervisor Core Release to release storage occupied by DIB, PCB, and GQE control blocks.
5. Exits to Page Drum Queue Processor if it has work to do.
6. Otherwise, exits to the Queue Scanner.
7. For a read operation (page in):
   a. Each DIB entry points to a PCB entry to be posted.
   b. Turns on page IO complete flag in the PCB entry.

    c. Calls Page Posting to update associated page table.
    d. Searches for the next DIB in the chain.
  8. For a write operation (page out):
    a. Again, each DIB entry points to a PCB to be posted.
    b. Calls User Core Release to release the main storage block pointed to by the PCB.
    c. Calls Page Posting to update associated page table.
    d. Turns on page IO complete flag in the PCB.

As the Page Drum Interruption Processor, the Page Posting Routine is called for a page in or a page out operation.

Page Posting Routine:
  1. For incoming virtual memory pages:
    a. Inserts the main storage address from the PCB entry in the appropriate page table entry and marks page available (i.e., turns off unavailable bit).
    b. Sets storage keys of page from a field in the external page table entry.
    c. If page is marked as unprocessed by the Dynamic Loader, creates a task interrupt for the Dynamic Loader that executes in virtual memory.
    d. Returns to caller.
  2. For outgoing virtual memory pages:
    a. Inserts the external location of the page (found in the PCB entry) into the appropriate external page table entry.
    b. Decrements the page IO count; if zero, marks the task's TSI to "time slice end (TSE)." The TSI is located through the GQE.
    c. Returns to caller.

The paging process also brings in XTSI pages that contain a task's segment and page tables. These pages are processed in a slightly different manner; the reader is directed to reference [TSSi] for additional information on this subject.

A conceptual view of the page out process is depicted in Fig. 11.12. The process is initiated by a timer interruption (or by a simulated timer interruption† when a Resident Supervisor routine builds a GQE and places it on the timer queue). The timer interruption is fielded by the Interrupt Stacker that builds a GQE for it and places it on an appropriate queue. The interrupt Stacker exits to the Queue Scanner. Subsequently, the Timer Interruption Processor is called to process the first GQE on its queue.

Timer Interruption Processor:
  1. Creates a PCB entry containing virtual memory addresses, main storage addresses, and external addresses for each "available" page in the task's page tables. Next:

†If the Resident Supervisor desires to place a task in "time slice end" for one of several reasons (excessive paging, main storage required, etc.), it uses this method.

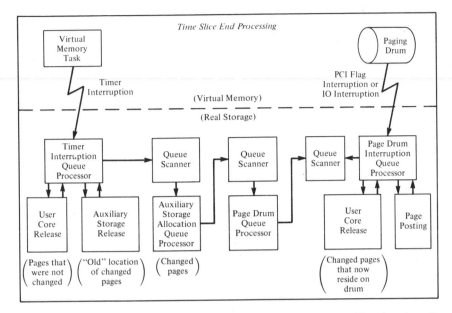

Fig. 11.12 Conceptual view of paging out to the primary paging device (drum) at time slice end.

a. Marks the pages unavailable.
b. Calls the Auxiliary Storage Release Routine to release auxiliary storage assigned to changed pages.
c. Turns on the "unavailable" bit in the PCB of unchanged pages.
d. Turns on "write" bit in the PCB of changed pages.
e. Calls the User Core Release Routine to release main storage for all unchanged pages.
f. Turns on the "drum preference" bit for PSW and XTSI pages.†
g. Links the PCBs for changed pages together and chains them to the GQE.
h. Enqueues the GQE on the Auxiliary Storage Allocation queue.
i. Exits to the Queue Scanner.

The Auxiliary Storage Allocation Queue Processor is invoked by the Queue Scanner to process the GQE.

Auxiliary Storage Allocation Queue Processor:
1. Assigns auxiliary storage locations to PCB entries as described in Section 11.3.
2. Turns on the suppress flag in the Scan Table to lock out this processor if auxiliary storage is exhausted.

†Recall that the PSW page is the page in which the task was executing when the interruption occurred.

3. Enqueues the GQE on the Page Drum queue.

4. Exits to the Queue Scanner.

The remainder page out process is then processed by the Page Drum Queue Processor as described previously.

11.5 DYNAMIC LOADING

The Dynamic Loader executes in a task's virtual memory and is entered via a virtual task interruption to perform relocation or through the LOAD macro instruction to perform allocation. The reasons for utilizing a dynamic loading process are given in Section 9.2.

Basic Concepts

The dynamic loader is used to locate a program in a library and make that program available for subsequent execution. An object module is comprised of four entities:

1. A *heading* containing the module name, length, entry point, and other control information.
2. A *control section dictionary* for each section of the module. It includes:
    a. A definition table of external entry point definitions (DEFs).
    b. A reference table of external entry points referenced (REFs).
    c. A relocatable dictionary that points to address constants that have to be relocated.
    d. A virtual memory page table for the control section.
3. The *machine code* (TXT) of the object module.
4. An *Internal Symbol Dictionary* (ISD) of internal symbol names and relative locations.

The Dynamic Loader does a link loading of a module and all subprograms called by that module. It maintains a *Task Dictionary Table* (TDY) in virtual memory that includes the REFs and DEFs of all modules. When an object module is requested either in response to a LOAD or to satisfy a REF, program libraries are searched in the following order:

1. user JOBLIBS (in reverse order of creation),
2. the user's USERLIB, and
3. the system library (SYSLIB).

The Task Dictionary Table is built for task during task initiation and includes entries that correspond to Initial Virtual Memory (IVM) program. As the user LOADs and UNLOADs programs, the contents of the Task Dictionary Table change. However, since the user is operating in virtual memory, he need not be concerned with the number of programs that are concurrently loaded.

The Allocation Phase

The allocation phase of the Dynamic Loader is entered in response to a LOAD or a CALL command. The Task Dictionary Table is inspected to determine if the requested module is already loaded in the task's virtual memory. If the module is loaded, the Dynamic Loader returns to the user through the Task Monitor. Otherwise, the Dynamic Loader searches the library hierarchy to locate the requested module and performs the following functions:

1. allocates virtual memory (i.e., calls Virtual Memory Allocation) for the requested module by making segment and page table entries;
2. marks all page table entries created as "unavailable" and "unprocessed" by the relocation phase of the Dynamic Loader;
3. processes DEFs and REFs and dynamically loads subroutines as required; and
4. exits to the Task Monitor to pass control to the user.

At this point, all page table entries have the following characteristics:

1. No main storage address exists.
2. Each page is marked as "unavailable" and "unprocessed."
3. The external location of the page refers to its location in external storage (i.e., in the library in which it is stored).

No text is moved and no relocation is performed.

The Relocation Phase

The relocation phase of the Dynamic Loader is entered when an "unprocessed" flag is recognized during page posting (see Section 11.4). At this point, a page containing program text is in main storage, but address constants are not adjusted to correspond to the location of the page. A task interruption is created to invoke the Dynamic Loader the next time the task is given control of the CPU. The Dynamic Loader relocates the address constants on that page and returns control, via an SVC, to the Resident Supervisor to complete the processing of that page. The address constants contained in a page that has been relocated are not adjusted again, and that page is paged out to auxiliary storage, whenever appropriate. Thus, a page is brought in from external storage and the address constants on that page are relocated only when that page is referenced on a demand basis.

The loading process is complex because of the different classes of programs that can be loaded (privileged/nonprivileged, shared/nonshared) and because modules can also be UNLOADed—a process that requires extensive bookkeeping operations. For that reason, the Dynamic Loader is not discussed further except for the following case.

It was mentioned previously that when programs are shared, each task has a private "data part," and the "program part" is shared with other tasks. The data part is generally known as a PSECT (prototype section which, by the way, can also contain executable machine code). PSECT control information is also contained in the object module and virtual memory for it is requested by the Dynamic Loader for a task when a shared program is loaded. The task's page tables are connected with a shared page table for the "program part" of shared programs.

11.6 SCHEDULING

Task scheduling in a time sharing environment is a complex process and involves different philosophies on how scheduling should be performed. TSS uses a table-driven scheduler that allows an installation to readily change scheduling parameters to meet its operational needs. It is described here. Early versions of TSS used a modified round robin type of scheduling, which is also covered after a brief introduction.

Basic Scheduling Methods

A particular algorithm for scheduling reflects the characteristics of a given system: how main storage is managed, the hardware configuration, and the attributes of the user environment. Doherty [Doh70] and Hellerman [Hel69] discuss various aspects of scheduling in a time sharing environment.

The most basic method is known as *round robin scheduling.* Using this method, all tasks are serviced on a first-come-first-served basis using a single queue. Whenever a task reaches the end of a time slice or it can no longer use the CPU for some reason, it is placed on the end of the list and the next task on the queue is given a slice of CPU time. Tasks are either resident in main storage or are "swapped in and out" as needed from an auxiliary device. A variation to round robin uses a *function work slice.* With this approach, the time slice technique is augmented such that a task is allowed to keep the CPU until a certain amount of work is performed—such as the completion of a compilation or until a certain number of statements are interpreted and executed. Round robin methods have the distinct disadvantage that "compute-bound" tasks and "terminal response" tasks are treated equally; thus, the method is satisfactory when tasks are permanently resident in main storage for the duration of execution but is not satisfactory otherwise. As mentioned previously, terminal response is significant and the scheduling algorithm should reflect that realization.

With an *exponential scheduling* strategy, several scheduling queues are maintained, each with a given priority. As a task enters the system, it is assigned to a queue on the basis of its storage requirements—with lower storage requirements being assigned a higher priority since they facilitate storage management. The scheduling queues are serviced on a priority basis; no queue is serviced unless higher-priority queues have already been completed. Terminal response tasks (i.e., those that do not complete their time slice because of terminal IO) are kept in the highest-priority queue—thus assuring good terminal response. If a task is computing at the end of its time slice, it is placed in the next lower-priority queue. However, lower-priority queues are given longer time slices, of the order 2t,4t,8t,..., so that once in execution, a compute-bound task stays in execution longer. Exponential scheduling has "human factors" appeal in that a terminal-oriented user, who is assigned frequent time slices, is very aware of the behavior of his task whereas the behavior of a compute-bound task is generally transparent to the user.

Modified Round Robin Scheduling with Variable Time Slices

Prior to the use of a schedule table, TSS used a modified round robin scheduling algorithm. The algorithm is designed to work with a paging system and attempts to reduce the total amount of paging that is performed by the system.

Active and inactive queues of tasks are maintained as described in Section 9.5. The Scheduler allocates the CPU to tasks on the active queue. As depicted in Fig. 11.13, the Scheduler maintains two pointers, called the "commutator" and the "wall." The commutator and the wall cyclically pass through the TSI queue as the system operates. The tasks above the commutator are ready for their next time slice. The tasks below the wall are ready for their current time slice. The tasks between the commutator and the wall are undergoing a time slice and are multiprogrammed. These tasks have assigned pages in main storage.

The Scheduler scans the active queue between the commutator and the wall (referred to as "in the wall"); it gives the CPU to the first task it encounters that is in the "ready" state. If no task in the wall is ready, the wall pointer is moved down to include an additional task. When a task that is included in the wall finishes its time slice, it is marked accordingly. When the task pointed to by the commutator reaches time slice end, the commutator is moved down the active queue. It stops when a "ready" or "page wait" task is encountered. If a task in time slice end status is encountered when the commutator is moved down, it is passed over and marked "ready" for its next time slice. When an inactive task becomes active, it is placed in the active queue just below the wall pointer.

One of the difficulties with demand paging and this scheduling algorithm is that "page buildup" occurs such that when a task can best use the CPU, it reaches time slice end and its pages are paged out.† A modification to the above algorithm during time slice and processing operates as follows:

1. If the paging time during the time slice exceeds the CPU time (the time slice value), the task is set to "ready" and does not give up its pages.

---

†This technique presents a potential problem, referred to as *thrashing*, wherein the system spends an inordinate amount of resources in moving pages into and out of storage. This problem has been studied by Denning [Den68b].

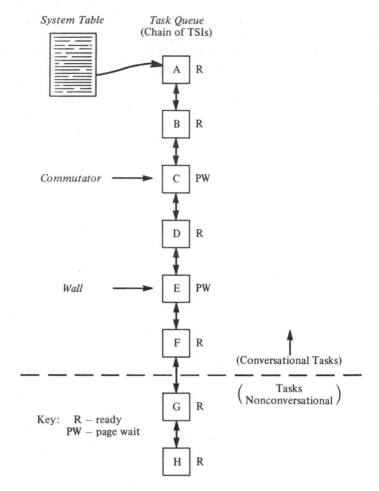

Fig. 11.13 Active queue for modified round robin scheduling.

2. The task stays in the wall and continues to accumulate pages and use CPU time.
3. Additional time slices are given to the task, as outlined in step (1).
4. The system compensates for giving n additional time slices to the task by setting the task to time slice end the next n times it is included in the wall.

Thus, on the average, a task receives one time slice for every k time slices given by the Scheduler if there are k users in the system.

Table-Driven Scheduling

A table-driven scheduler uses the dispatchable, eligible, and inactive lists, given in Section 9.5, along with a schedule table that attempts to adjust the scheduling algorithm to the dynamic characteristics of a task.

The schedule table contains parameters such as time slice duration, time between time slices, number of pages allowed, priority, next level in the table (when the current time slice is ended), the level to be entered when TWAIT is ended, etc. Table 11.3 depicts a sample schedule table. When a task enters the system, it is assigned a level (i.e., a row in the schedule table). When that task is given the CPU, it is time sliced according to the entries in that row. The row also specifies the task's level for its next time slice based on the operational characteristics of the task.

Tasks on the dispatchable list are going through a time slice and accumulate pages. When time slice end is reached, the pages are released and the task is classified as being compute-bound or paging-bound. This classification is based on the schedule table level assigned to the task and the number of page "reads" performed for that task during the time slice. The task is placed on the eligible list. Later, when the task is moved to the dispatchable list, its placement is determined by whether it is paging-bound or compute-bound. Paging-bound tasks are ordered ahead of compute-bound tasks.

The eligible list includes tasks that are waiting for a "new" time slice. The list is ordered by priority and by "scheduled start time." *Scheduled start time* (SST) is a value stored in a task's TSI. It is computed when a task enters the eligible list as a function of actual clock time and the interval between time slices for a given level of the schedule table. When the Dispatcher is looking for work and desires to move a task from the eligible list to the dispatchable list, it chooses the highest-priority task on the eligible list. Within the same priority level, the task is selected that is most behind schedule using its scheduled start

TABLE 11.3 SAMPLE SCHEDULE TABLE

Level	Priority	Time Slice Duration	Interval at Which a Time Slice Should be Given	Next Level	TWAIT Level
0	0	50ms	0ms	1	0
1	1	100ms	3000ms	1	0
2	1	100ms	3000ms	3	2
3	2	200ms	5000ms	4	2
4	2	200ms	7000ms	5	2
5	3	500ms	10000ms	5	4

time. The reader is again directed to Doherty [Doh70] for additional insight into how a schedule table can be used to improve the responsiveness of a system.

Although an effective open time sharing system is a complex system of interconnecting components, the scheduling algorithm appears to be the key to "good" terminal response. The subject has been studied extensively by several researchers, and a variety of analytical models have been developed for system analysis and for simulation purposes. The bibliography includes several references on the subject.

11.7 INPUT AND OUTPUT CONSIDERATIONS

The purpose of this section is to extend the data management concepts presented in Chapters 9 and 10. Miscellaneous topics are presented that are not covered elsewhere. The material is analogous to the corresponding section in Chapter 8; however, TSS and OS are structurally different and that difference is reflected in the manner in which the subjects are presented. The actual flow of IO operations in OS is covered in Chapter 8. In TSS, on the other hand, much of the VAM input and output is performed by paging routines, so this section is more concerned with structural and physical properties of VAM operations. Physical input and output are not covered since they are introduced in Chapter 9 and are similar to those in OS.

Device Allocation

One of the primary objectives of an open time sharing system is to make the user's program and the control program independent of a particular IO configuration. Moreover, the system also should be insensitive to dynamic changes in the configuration. Another consideration is that a single device may have more than one hardware address since a given control unit can be connected to more than one channel, etc. As a result, each device in TSS is assigned a symbolic address that is used by the access methods. The Resident Supervisor (see Fig. 11.4) uses a "pathfinding" subroutine to translate a symbolic device address into a physical device address that reflects a channel controller, a channel attached to the channel controller, a control unit attached to the channel, and a device attached to the control unit. The IO address format of the host computer† is depicted in Fig. 11.14.

2 bits	3 bits	4 bits	4 bits
Channel Controller	Channel	Control Unit	Device

Fig. 11.14 IO address format.

†That is, the 360 Model 67.

Devices are reserved for system use or are available for allocation to users. System devices are used for control volumes and are specified during system generation. Devices that are currently available to users are established during startup. These devices include terminal devices and data recording devices. More specifically, communication lines are allocated, rather than terminal devices, since TSS is primarily a dial-up system. Recording devices can be either public or private. Public and private device assignments are also established during system generation and are used to mount public and private volumes, respectively. The above conventions also apply to the use of magnetic tape units and unit record devices.

The system maintains two tables in shared virtual memory that govern device allocation: the Symbolic Device Allocation Table (SDAT) and the Available Device Table (ADT). Each device has an entry in the SDAT table; the entries are sorted by symbolic device address. Each SDAT entry includes the following types of information: device status, device use (system, public, private, etc.), concurrent IO requests allowed, number of concurrent users of the device,† gross space available for allocation, and the address of the volume's VTOC. The SDAT table is formed during system generation. During Startup, each entry is marked as: (1) partitioned out of the system, (2) nonexistent, (3) unavailable (i.e., malfunctioning), and (4) available.

The Available Device Table includes an entry for each device that is not assigned as a system device, auxiliary storage device, or a public device. Each ADT entry points to its corresponding SDAT entry.

The method by which private devices are assigned is easily determined. The Private Device Management routine searches the ADT to locate a particular device type. The ADT points to the SDAT that gives device status, etc. The operation of the HOLD and DROP commands is equally straightforward. The HOLD command processor simply sets the device status in its SDAT entry to "partitioned off." Similarly, the DROP command sets the device status to "available."

Pathfinding

The purpose of the Pathfinding subroutine is to find a physical path to a device specified by a symbolic device address. The Pathfinding subroutine uses Pathfinding Tables built during system generation; these tables are modified during startup to reflect the existing system configuration. Thus, IO components that are partitioned, nonexistent, or malfunctioning are flagged. One of the major objectives of pathfinding is to reduce the number of times that a device is busy when needed because a component in the path is busy. Toward that end, the Pathfinding Tables maintain the status of each component, that is, if it is busy

---

†This would apply primarily to direct-access devices.

or it is not busy. When a component is assigned to a data path, it is marked as "busy." When the operation is complete, the component is marked as "not busy." The Pathfinding Tables are:

1. a symbolic-to-actual-address conversation table that gives a physical address for each symbolic address;
2. a device group table for each control unit or switch that lists paths to that component;
3. a channel table that includes an entry for each channel;
4. a control-unit-assigned-to-channel table that lists the control units assigned to a given channel; and
5. a control unit table that contains an entry for each control unit in the system.

The Pathfinding Subroutine determines a path to a given device by selecting a path and verifying that it is free. If it is determined that a component in a path is busy by inspecting its respective table, an alternate component is selected and the process is repeated. A device is busy only if all paths to it are busy.

The Pathfinding Subroutine is a routine of the Resident Supervisor; it performs the following functions:

1. determines an available path to a device and reserves the components along that path;
2. releases the components of a path when an IO operation is complete;
3. modifies Pathfinding Table entries for partitioned or malfunctioning components; and
4. determines the symbolic address that is associated with a given physical address.

The Pathfinding Subroutine is used by the Device Queue Processor and the Channel Interrupt Processor of the Resident Supervisor.

VAM Input and Output Processing

VAM input and output processing is performed in a similar manner to the way in which physical input and output is performed. Each data set used by a task requires a data definition (DDEF), a DCB, and a JFCB. The DCB is included as part of the virtual memory task and it is completed when the data set is opened. The JFCB is created during data definition and the JFCB created is chained to other JFCBs for the task in a list called the Task Definition Table (TDT). The Task Definition Table is used during LOGOFF to manage the disposition of uncataloged data sets and is used during the library search procedure for a requested object module. The Task Definition Table is also used during DDEF processing to determine if a data set is currently defined.

The process of opening a data set is depicted conceptually in Fig. 11.15. The

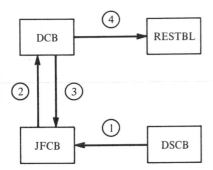

Fig. 11.15 Conceptual view of data flow during open processing for a VAM data set.

last control block built during open processing is the Relative External Storage Correspondence Table (RESTBL). The RESTBL is the logical counterpart of the Data Extent Block (DEB)† used with physical data sets and contains the "external page map" of a VAM data set. VAM orders the pages of a data set by relative page number from the beginning of the data set, and the external page map contains the relative volume number (in the public/private volume table) and the relative external storage page number (on that volume) for each page in the data set. The format of the RESTBL entry for each data set page is given in Fig. 11.16. The RESTBL entries are ordered by data set relative page number.

A VAM input operation proceeds as follows (see Fig. 11.17):

1. The RESTBL is built in a task's virtual memory during open processing.
2. The task requests that a record is read into virtual memory by using a VAM access method.
3. A page-sized buffer is obtained by the access method in virtual memory.
4. The external address of the data set page (containing the record) is obtained from the RESTBL and placed in the External Page Table (XPT) entry of the buffer page. The data set page has not moved, as yet, but its physical location in external storage is in the task's XPT. The buffer page is marked as not being in main storage.
5. When the record is addressed in the virtual storage buffer, a relocation interruption occurs and the data set page is brought into main storage from external storage by the paging routines.

Flags	Relative Volume Number	Relative Page Number

Fig. 11.16 Format of a RESTBL entry for one VAM data set page.

---

†The DEB is regarded as a "protected" extension to the DCB.

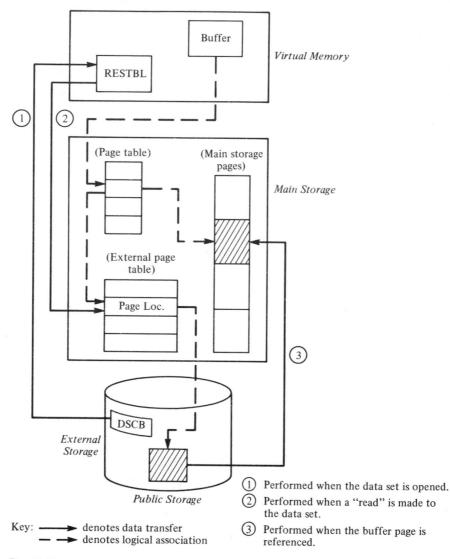

Fig. 11.17 Data flow and the relationship of control blocks during a VAM input operation.

The end result, obviously, is that only the needed pages of a data set are brought into main storage, and the input and output operations are performed efficiently by the paging routines. The development of a VAM output procedure (similar to the input procedure just given) is left as an exercise for the reader.

The objective has been to introduce the concept of a virtual access method and how it operates. The complete process is indeed more sophisticated and includes much of the detail associated with physical input and output. Virtual access methods perform blocking, deblocking, and most of the other IO operations that are ordinarily available with a physical access method. In short, the primary difference between the two techniques involves data set organization and the manner in which actual input and output operations are performed.

11.8 MULTIPROCESSING

The term *multiprocessing* refers to multiple CPUs operating concurrently. The term *multiprocessing system* refers to a system configuration that contains more than one main CPU. Usually, the CPUs share a common main storage. TSS is designed around a duplex system that shares main storage, channels, and devices. The storage units utilize a distributed crossbar switching technique referred to as "multiple tails" such that each CPU, as well as the channel controllers, can reference the same storage unit at the same time. The implication is that each CPU can share the Resident Supervisor and virtual memory routines.

The CPUs operate asynchronously and use the queues built by the Resident Supervisor to control the work that is performed. Whenever a critical table, routine, or list is referenced, a *lock byte* is tested. If the lock byte is set, the CPU cannot use that resource and either waits or goes on to process another unit of work. If the lock byte is not set, the resource is used and the lock byte is set. In this manner, the system is protected against both CPUs attempting to update the same table at the same time.

As an example, assume that CPU enters the Queue Scanner, sets the lock byte, and determines that it has no supervisor work that can be performed at this time. Control would then pass to the Dispatcher to allocate CPU_1 to a task. The Dispatcher's lock byte is set, and CPU_1 is given to a task that is marked "in execution." Suppose that in the meantime, CPU_2 finishes whatever it was doing and also can find no supervisor work to do. CPU_2 waits on the Dispatcher's lock byte until CPU_1 is finished and then enters the Dispatcher. In allocating a task to CPU_2, the Dispatcher passes over the task being executed by CPU_1 because it is on the dispatchable list but is "in execution." The Dispatcher allocates CPU_2 to another task. Assuming that no interruptions are received by either CPU in the meantime, both CPUs are executing in the problem state. When an interruption is received by one (or both) of the CPUs, the active task is suspended and that CPU enters the Resident Supervisor. A given task, for example, can have its successive time slices executed by either CPU in a quasi-random fashion.

Machine check, program, external, and SVC interruptions are received by the CPU with which they are associated. An IO interruption is received by the CPU that initiated the respective IO operation. During normal processing, it may be necessary for a given CPU to address any channel in the system. This facility is permitted through the channel controller mentioned in Chapter 3.

Thus, the system's work queues can be processed by either of the CPUs. Conceivably, both CPUs could be executing in the same Resident Supervisor routine, provided that the setting of a lock byte is not required. On the other hand, only one CPU could be executing in a given task since the manner in which the task queues are handled would prevent that from occurring.

During startup, one CPU serves as the master and loads system routines and builds system tables as mentioned previously. When startup is complete, the master CPU sends an external interruption to the other CPU to "start it." Execution of both CPUs then proceeds in parallel.

When a machine check occurs in one CPU, it sends an external interruption to the other CPU (called a malfunction alert) and enters the wait state. The "good" CPU then uses the Recovery Nucleus routines to "check out" the failing CPU.

Multiprocessing is used for several reasons:

1. to increase reliability and availability;
2. to provice "load leveling" in a time sharing environment; and
3. to increase throughput.

Multiprocessing also represents a savings in storage requirements over two independent computer systems running simultaneously since the Resident Supervisor and reentrant virtual memory routines can be shared among the CPUs.

QUESTIONS FOR PART THREE

Chapter 9

1. Why is it necessary to control access to a time sharing system?
2. Explain why a nonconversational mode of operation is required in most operating environments.
3. Contrast the difference between JCL processing in OS and command processing in TSS.
4. Distinguish between roll out/roll in and paging.
5. Explain why the use of data set names and the catalog are necessary with public storage.
6. What is a "segmented name space"?
7. Why is the segment table used?
8. Describe how the associative registers operate.
9. What function does the Auxiliary Segment Table serve? The External Page Table?
10. When is the reference bit used? The change bit?
11. What does the XTSI contain?
12. What steps are involved when a user page is "paged out"?
13. Why is page reclaiming used?
14. What function does a *queue processor* serve?
15. Why is the *scan table* used?
16. Describe the purpose of having an initial virtual memory.
17. Describe, in your own words, the process of page buildup.
18. How could page buildup be avoided?
19. Distinguish between the "dispatchable" list and the "eligible" list.

Chapter 10

20. How is the hierarchical structure of the catalog used in TSS?
21. Why is a VISAM overflow page used?
22. What is the "sharer list"?
23. Why are physical access methods required?
24. In what way are VAM record formats less complicated than OS record formats?
25. Why are "gate read" and "gate write" used?
26. Distinguish between SHARE and PERMIT. (Would you rename these commands? How would you do it?)
27. What function does a user's profile serve?
28. Distinguish between the "backspace" character and the "delete" character. What is the significance of the delete character?
29. How could you use ZLOGON to provide another level of security to your programs and data?
30. Give a good example of when the BACK command could be used.
31. How would you move a collection of data sets from one TSS system to another?

32. Contrast PROCDEFs with assembler language macros.
33. When would a message be changed in the system message file? Comment on the use of TSS in a multinational environment.
34. Distinguish between a CSECT and a PSECT.
35. Distinguish between CANCEL and FORCE and between HOLD and DROP.
36. How could a user enter a large ámount of data into the system?
37. When is a batch sequence number (BSN) used?

Chapter 11

38. Draw a state diagram of Resident Supervisor interruption processing.
39. Comment on the process of link loading the Resident Supervisor and Initial Virtual Memory during STARTUP. How frequently is this done?
40. Describe how the structure of the command system is designed to utilize a user profile.
41. TSS does not allow multitasking. Can you imagine why? Are there any operational "dangers" in allowing this facility in a general-purpose time sharing environment?
42. Distinguish between a "short save" and a "long save."
43. List the differences between interruption queue processors and request queue processors.
44. How would the Queue Scanner and Dispatcher have to be modified so that TSS would be useful in a real-time environment?
45. List the conditions and components that must be analyzed by the Recovery Nucleus.
46. Contrast the use of the Core Block Table in TSS with the FBQE chain in OS. What are the similarities?
47. What is *page migration* and how does it work? Why is it used?
48. Compare demand paging with the concept of a "working set" of pages (See Denning [Den68a].) How could the working set concept be implemented in TSS?
49. When would dynamic loading be an inefficient (and perhaps irritating to the user) method for loading object modules? From a paging viewpoint, how does it reduce the paging load? Design a loader for TSS that would operate in the conventional manner but in a virtual memory environment.
50. Develop a flow diagram of the dynamic loading process.
51. The process of pathfinding is a particularly good example of a case where a design trade-off is made between efficiency and reliability. Elaborate on this concept.
52. Describe what is meant by the following statement: "VAM input and output procedures effectively allow a data set to be mapped into virtual memory."

REFERENCES
AND BIBLIOGRAPHY*

Aho, A., P. J. Denning, and J. D. Ullman, "Principles of optimal page replacement," *Journal of the ACM*, Vol. 18, No. 1, January 1971.

■Ale72 Alexander, M. T., "Organization and features of the Michigan Terminal System," *Proceedings of the 1972 Spring Joint Computer Conference*, AFIPS Vol. 40, 1972.

■Ard66 Arden, B. W., B. A. Galler, T. C. O'Brien, and F. H. Westervelt, "Program and addressing structure in a time-sharing environment," *Journal of the ACM*, Vol. 13, No. 1, 1966.

■Aro69 Aron, J., et al., "Information systems in perspective," *Computing Surveys*, Vol. 1, No. 4, 1969.

Balzer, R. M., "EXDAMS—Extendable Debugging and Monitoring System," *Proceedings of the 1969 Spring Joint Computer Conference*, AFIPS Vol. 34, 1969.

Bard, Y., "Performance criteria and measurement for a time-sharing system," *IBM Systems Journal*, Vol. 10, No. 3, 1971.

Barron, D. W., *Assemblers and Loaders*, New York, American Elsevier Publishing Co., 1969.

Barron, D. W., *Computer Operating Systems*, London, Chapman and Hall, Ltd., 1971.

*Specific references are keyed to the text as shown. General references and the bibliography are included to support the subject matter presented and to provide material for term papers and research. An attempt has been made to include at least one reference to each topic covered in the book.

Batson, A., S. Ju, and D. C. Wood, "Measurements of segment size," *Communications of the ACM*, Vol. 13, No. 3, March 1970.

Belady, L. A., "A study of replacement algorithms for virtual storage computers," *IBM Systems Journal*, Vol. 5, No. 2, 1966.

Belady, L. A., and C. J. Kuehner, "Dynamic space-sharing in computer systems," *Communications of the ACM*, Vol. 12, No. 5, May 1969.

Belady, L. A., R. A. Nelson, and G. S. Shedler, "An anomaly in space-time characteristics of certain programs running in a paging machine," *Communications of the ACM*, Vol. 12, No. 6, June 1969.

Bell, C. G., and A. Newell, *Computer Structures: Readings and Examples*, New York, McGraw-Hill Book Co., 1971.

■Ber71   Berztiss, A. T., *Data Structures: Theory and Practice*, New York, Academic Press, 1971.

Bernstein, A. J., and J. C. Sharp, "A policy-driven scheduler for a time-sharing system," *Communications of the ACM*, Vol. 4, No. 2, 1971.

Betourne, C., J. Boulenger, J. Ferrie, and C. Kaiser, "Process management and resource sharing in the multiaccess system ESOPE," *Communications of the ACM*, Vol. 13, No. 12, December 1970.

Bobrow, D. G., J. D. Burchfield, D. L. Murphy, and R. S. Tomlinson, "TENEX, A Paged Time Sharing System for the PDP-10," *Communications of the ACM*, Vol. 15, No. 3, March 1972.

■ Boh71   Bohl, M., *Information Processing*, Chicago, Science Research Associates, 1971.

Brawn, B. S., and F. G. Gustavson, "Program behavior in a paging environment," *Proceedings of the 1968 Fall Joint Computer Conference*, AFIPS Vol. 33, 1968.

■Bro70   Brown, G. D., *System/360 Job Control Language*, New York, John Wiley & Sons, Inc., 1970.

■Cad70   Cadow, H. W., *OS/360 Job Control Language*, Englewood Cliffs, N.J., Prentice-Hall, Inc., 1970.

Calingaert, P., "System performance evaluation: survey and appraisal," *Communications of the ACM*, Vol. 10, No. 1, January 1967.

Cantrell, H. N., and A. L. Ellison, "Multiprogramming system performance measurement and analysis," *Proceedings of the Spring Joint Computer Conference*, AFIPS Vol. 32, 1968.

■ Cen67   Cenfetelli, A. R., "Data management concepts for DOS/360 and TOS/360," *IBM Systems Journal*, Vol. 6, No. 1, 1967.

■Cha68   Chapin, N., "A deeper look at data," *Proceedings of the ACM National Conference*, 1968.

■ Cha71   Chapin, N., *Computers: A Systems Approach*, New York, Van Nostrand Reinhold Co., 1971.

Christensen, C., and A. D. Hause, "A multiprogramming, virtual memory system for a small computer," *Proceedings of the 1970 Spring Joint Computer Conference*, AFIPS Vol. 36, 1970.

■ Cla66   Clark, W. A., "The functional structure of OS/360: Part III. Data Management," *IBM Systems Journal*, Vol. 5, No. 1, 1966.

■Cod70   Codd, E. F., "A relational model of data for large shared data banks," *Communications of the ACM*, Vol. 13, No. 6, June 1970.

■Cod71   Codd, E. F., "Further normalization of the data base relational model," *IBM Research Report*, RJ 909, August 31, 1971.

Coffman, E. G., Jr., "Analysis of two time-sharing algorithms designated for limited swapping," *Journal of the ACM*, Vol. 15, No. 7, July 1968.

Coffman, E. G., Jr., M. J. Elphick, and A. Shoshani, "System deadlocks," *Computing Surveys*, Vol. 3, No. 2, June 1971.

Coffman, E. G., Jr., and L. Kleinrock, "Computer scheduling methods and their counter measures," *Proceedings of the 1968 Spring Joint Computer Conference*, AFIPS Vol. 32, 1968.

Coffman, E. G., Jr., and T. A. Ryan, Jr., "A study of storage partitioning using a mathematical model of locality," *Communications of the ACM*, Vol. 15, No. 3, March 1972.

Coffman, E. G., Jr., and L. C. Varian, "Further experimental data on the behavior of programs in a paging environment," *Communications of the ACM*, Vol. 11, No. 7, July 1968.

Cohen, L. J., *Operating System Analysis and Design*, Washington, D.C., Spartan Books, 1970.

Colin, A., *Introduction to Operating Systems*, New York, American Elsevier Publishing Co., 1971.

Collmeyer, A. J., "Data base management in a multi-access environment," *Computer*, Vol. 4, No. 6, November/December 1971.

■Com65   Comfort, W. T., "A computing system design for user service," *Proceedings of the 1965 Fall Joint Computer Conference*, AFIPS Vol. 27, 1965.

Considine, J. P., and A. H. Weiss, "Establishment and maintenance of a storage hierarchy for an on-line data base under TSS/360," *Proceedings of the 1969 Fall Joint Computer Conference*, AFIPS Vol. 35, 1969.

Corbato, F. J., C. T. Clinger, and J. H. Saltzer, "Multics—the first seven years," *Proceedings of the 1972 Spring Joint Computer Conference*, AFIPS Vol. 40, 1972.

■Cor62   Corbato, F. J., M. Merwin-Daggett, and R. C. Daley, "An experimental time-sharing system," *AFIPS Conference Proceedings*, Vol. 21, 1962.

■Cor63   Corbato, F. J., et al., *The Compatible Time-Sharing System*, Cambridge, Mass., The M.I.T. Press, 1963.

■Cor65   Corbato, F. J., and V. A. Vyssotsky, "Introduction and overview of the MULTICS system," *Proceedings of the 1965 Fall Joint Computer Conference*, AFIPS Vol. 27, 1965.

Courtois, P. J., F. Heymans, and D. L. Parnas, "Concurrent control with 'Readers' and 'Writers,'" *Communications of the ACM*, Vol. 14, No. 10, October 1971.

Cuttle, G., and P. B. Robinson (eds.), *Executive Programs and Operating Systems*, New York, American Elsevier Publishing Co., 1970.

■Dal68   Daley, R. C., and J. B. Dennis, "Virtual memory, process, and sharing in MULTICS," *Communications of the ACM*, Vol. 11, No. 5, May 1968.

Daley, R. C., and P. G. Neumann, "A general-purpose file system for secondary storage," *Proceedings of the 1965 Fall Joint Computer Conference*, AFIPS Vol. 27, 1965.

Daniels, E. L., and L. Harris, "Remote job entry," *Datamation*, April 1969.

■Dav69 Davis, G. B., *Computer Data Processing*, New York, McGraw-Hill Book Co., 1969.

■Dav71 Davis, G. B., *Introduction to Electronic Computers* (2nd Ed.), New York, McGraw-Hill Book Co., 1971.

De Meis, W. M., and N. Weizer, "Measurement and analysis of a demand paging time-sharing system," *Proceedings of the ACM 24th National Conference*, 1969.

Deniston, W. R., "SIPE: a TSS/360 software measurement technique," *Proceedings of the ACM 24th National Conference*, 1969.

Denning, P. J., "Effects of scheduling on file memory operations," *Proceedings of the 1967 Spring Joint Computer Conference*, AFIPS Vol. 30, 1967.

Denning, P. J., "Equipment configuration in balanced computer systems," *IEEE Transactions on Computers* C-18, November 1967.

■Den68*a* Denning, P. J., "The working set model for program behavior," *Communications of the ACM*, Vol. 11, No. 5, May 1968.

■Den68*b* Denning, P. J., "Thrashing: its causes and prevention," *Proceedings of the 1968 Fall Joint Computer Conference*, AFIPS Vol. 33, 1968.

■Den70 Denning, P. J., "Virtual memory," *Computing Surveys*, Vol. 2, No. 3, 1970.

Denning, P. J., "Third generation computer systems," *Computing Surveys*, Vol. 3, No. 4, December 1971.

Denning, P. J. (Chairman), "An undergraduate course on operating systems principles," *Computer*, Vol. 5, No. 1, January/February 1972.

■Den72 Denning, P. J., "A note on paging drum efficiency," *Computing Surveys*, Vol. 4, No. 1, March 1972.

Denning, P. J., and S. C. Schwartz, "Properties of the working-set model," *Communications of the ACM*, Vol. 15, No. 3, March 1972.

■Dns65 Dennis, J. B., "Segmentation and the design of multiprogrammed computer systems," *Journal of the ACM*, Vol. 12, No. 4, 1965.

Dennis, J. B., "A position paper on computing and communications," *Communications of the ACM*, Vol. 11, No. 5, May 1968.

■Dod69 Dodd, G. G., "Elements of data management systems," *Computing Surveys*, Vol. 1, No. 4, 1969.

■Doh70 Doherty, W., "Scheduling TSS/360 for responsiveness," *Proceedings of the 1970 Fall Joint Computer Conference*, AFIPS Vol. 37, 1970.

Donovan, J. J., *Systems Programming*, New York, McGraw-Hill Book Co., 1972.

Dykstra, E. W., "Solution of a problem in concurrent programming control," *Communications of the ACM*, Vol. 8, No. 9, September 1965.

Dykstra, E. W., "The structure of the THE-multiprogramming system," *Communications of the ACM*, Vol. 11, No. 5, May 1968.

Elspas, B., M. W. Green, and K. N. Levitt, "Software reliability," *Computer*, Vol. 4, No. 1, January/February 1971.

Estrin, G., and L. Kleinrock, "Measures, models and measurements for time-shared computer utilities," *Proceedings of the ACM National Conference*, 1967.

Fano, R. M., and E. E. David, "On the social implications of accessible computing," *Proceedings of the 1965 Fall Joint Computer Conference*, AFIPS Vol. 27, 1965.

Fenichel, R. R., and A. J. Grossman, "An analytic model of multiprogrammed computing," *Proceedings of the 1969 Spring Joint Computer Conference*, AFIPS Vol. 34, 1969.

Fik68 Fikes, R. E., H. C. Lauer, and A. L. Vareha, "Steps toward a general-purpose time-sharing system using large capacity core storage and TSS/360," *Proceedings of the ACM National Conference*, 1968.

Fine, G. H., C. W. Jackson, and P. V. McIssac, "Dynamic program behavior under paging," *Proceedings of the ACM National Conference*, 1968.

Fischler, M. A., and A. Reiter, "Variable topology random access memory organization," *Proceedings of the 1969 Spring Joint Computer Conference*, AFIPS Vol. 34, 1969.

Flores, I., *Computer Software*, Englewood Cliffs, N.J., Prentice-Hall, Inc., 1965.

Flores, I., *Computer Programming*, Englewood Cliffs, N.J., Prentice-Hall, Inc., 1966.

Flo67 Flores, I., "Virtual memory and paging," Part I. *Datamation* (August, 1967), Part II. *Datamation* (September, 1967).

Flo69 Flores, I., *Computer Organization*, Englewood Cliffs, N.J., Prentice-Hall, Inc., 1969.

Flo70 Flores, I., *Data Structure and Management*, Englewood Cliffs, N.J., Prentice-Hall, Inc., 1970.

Flo71 Flores, I., *Job Control Language and File Definition*, Englewood Cliffs, N.J., Prentice-Hall, Inc., 1971.

Flynn, M. J., and A. Podvin, "Shared resource multiprocessing," *Computer*, Vol. 5, No. 2, March/April 1972.

Fos70 Foster, C. C., *Computer Architecture*, New York, Van Nostrand Reinhold Co., 1970.

Foster, J. M., *List Processing*, New York, American Elsevier Publishing Co., 1967.

Fraser, A. G., "On the meaning of names in programming systems," *Communications of the ACM*, Vol. 14, No. 6, 1971.

Freeman, D. N., "A storage hierarchy system for batch processing," *Proceedings of the 1968 Spring Joint Computer Conference*, AFIPS Vol. 32, 1968.

Freeman, D. N., and R. R. Pearson, "Efficiency vs responsiveness in a multiple-services computer facility," *Proceedings of the ACM National Conference*, 1968.

Friedman, T. D., "The authorization problem in shared files," *IBM Systems Journal*, Vol. 9, No. 4, 1970.

Fuchel, K., and S. Heller, "Considerations in the design of a multiple computer system with extended core storage," *Communications of the ACM*, Vol. 11, No. 5, May 1968.

Gaines, R. S., "An operating system based on the concept of a supervisory computer," *Communications of the ACM*, Vol. 15, No. 3, March 1972.

Gecsei, J., D. R. Slutz, and I. L. Traiger, "Evaluation techniques for storage hierarchies," *IBM Systems Journal*, Vol. 9, No. 2, 1970.

■Gib66   Gibson, C. T., "Time sharing in the IBM System/360 Model 67," *Proceedings of the 1966 Spring Joint Computer Conference*, AFIPS Vol. 28, 1966.

Glaser,-E. L., J. F. Couleur, and G. A. Oliver, "System design of a computer for time-sharing applications," *Proceedings of the 1965 Fall Joint Computer Conference*, AFIPS Vol. 27, 1965.

Gold, M. M., "Time-sharing and batch processing: an experimental comparison of their values in a problem-solving situation," *Communications of the ACM*, Vol. 12, No. 5, May 1969.

Graham, G. S., and P. J. Denning, "Protection—principles and practice," *Proceedings of the 1972 Spring Joint Computer Conference*, AFIPS Vol. 40, 1972.

Graham, R. M., "Protection in an information processing utility," *Communications of the ACM*, Vol. 11, No. 5, May 1968.

Haberman, A. N., "Prevention of system deadlocks," *Communications of the ACM*, Vol. 12, No. 7, July 1969.

Haberman, A. N., "Synchronization of communicating processes," *Communications of the ACM*, Vol. 15, No. 3, March 1972.

Hansen, P. B., "The nucleus of a multi-programming system," *Communications of the ACM*, Vol. 13, No. 4, April 1970.

Hatfield, D. J., and J. Gerald, "Program restructuring for virtual memory," *IBM Systems Journal*, Vol. 10, No. 3, 1971.

■Hei61   Heising, W. P., and R. A. Larner, "A semi-automatic storage allocation system at loading time," *Communications of the ACM*, Vol. 4, No. 10, October 1961.

Hellerman, H., *Digital Computer System Principles*, New York, McGraw-Hill Book Co., 1967.

■Hel69   Hellerman, H., "Some principles of time-sharing scheduler strategies," *IBM Systems Jounral*, Vol. 8, No. 2, 1969.

Higman, B., *A Comparative Study of Programming Languages*, New York, American Elsevier Publishing Co., 1967.

Holt, A. W., "Program organization and record keeping for dynamic storage allocation," *Communications of the ACM*, Vol. 4, No. 10, October 1961.

Holt, R. C., "Comments on prevention of system deadlocks," *Communications of the ACM*, Vol. 14, No. 1, January 1971.

Hopgood, F. R. A., *Compiling Techniques*, New York, American Elsevier Publishing Co., 1969.

Iliffe, J. K., *Basic Machine Principles*, New York, American Elsevier Publishing Co., 1968.

Iliffe, J. K., and J. G. Jodeit, "A dynamic storage allocation scheme," *Computer Journal*, Vol. 5, October 1962.

Irons, E. T., "A rapid turnaround multi-programming system," *Communications of the ACM*, Vol. 8, No. 3, March 1965.

Jamison, F. L. (Chairman), *Comparative Operating Systems: A Symposium*, Princeton, N.J., Auerbach Publishers Inc., 1969.

Jodeit, J. G., "Storage organization in programming systems," *Communications of the ACM*, Vol. 11, No. 11, November 1968.

Joh69 Johnson, O. W., and J. R. Martinson, "Virtual memory in Time Sharing System/360," *TSS/360 Compendium*, IBM Corporation, Data Processing Division, 1969.

Johnstone, J. L., "RTOS—extending OS/360 for real time spaceflight control," *Proceedings of the 1969 Spring Joint Computer Conference*, AFIPS Vol. 34, 1969.

Kat70 Katzan, H., *Advanced Programming: Programming and Operating Systems*, New York, Van Nostrand Reinhold Co., 1970.

Katzan, H., "Operating systems architecture," *Proceedings of the 1970 Spring Joint Computer Conference*, AFIPS Vol. 36, 1970.

Kat71 Katzan, H., *Computer Organization and the System/370*, New York, Van Nostrand Reinhold Co., 1971.

Katzan, H., "Storage hierarchy systems," *Proceedings of the 1971 Spring Joint Computer Conference*, AFIPS Vol. 38, 1971.

Kay, R. H., "The management and organization of large scale software development projects," *Proceedings of the 1969 Spring Joint Computer Conference*, AFIPS Vol. 34, 1969.

Kilburn, T., D. B. G. Edwards, M. J. Lanigan, and F. H. Sumner, "One-level storage system," *IEEE Transactions*, Vol. EC11, No. 2, April 1962.

Kimbleton, S., "Performance evaluation—a structured approach," *Proceedings of the 1972 Spring Joint Computer Conference*, AFIPS Vol. 40, 1972.

Kin64 Kinslow, H. A., "The time sharing monitor system," *AFIPS Conference Proceedings*, Vol. 25, 1964.

Kleinrock, L., "A continuum of time sharing scheduling algorithms," *Proceedings of the 1970 Joint Computer Conference*, AFIPS Vol. 36, 1970.

Knu68 Knuth, D. E., *The Art of Computer Programming*, Vol. 1, *Fundamental Algorithms*, Reading, Mass., Addison-Wesley Publishing Co., 1968.

Lampson, B. W., "A scheduling philosophy for multiprocessing systems," *Communications of the ACM*, Vol. 11, No. 5, May 1968.

Lam69 Lampson, B. W., "Dynamic protection structures," *Proceedings of the 1969 Fall Joint Computer Conference*, AFIPS Vol. 35, 1969.

Lan69 Lanzano, B. C., "Loader standardization for overlay programs," *Communications of the ACM*, Vol. 12, No. 10, October 1969.

Lasser, D. J., "Productivity of multiprogrammed computers—progress in developing an analytic prediction method," *Communications of the ACM*, Vol. 12, No. 12, December 1969.

Lau67 Lauer, H. C., "Bulk core in a 360/67 time-sharing system," *Proceedings of the 1967 Fall Joint Computer Conference*, AFIPS Vol. 31, 1967.

Let69 Lett, A. S., "The approach to data management in Time Sharing System/

360," *TSS/360 Compendium*, IBM Corporation, Data Processing Division, 1969.

■Let68 Lett, A. S., and W. L. Konigsford, "TSS/360: a time-shared operating system," *Proceedings of the 1968 Fall Joint Computer Conference*, AFIPS Vol. 33, 1968.

Liskov, B. H., "The design of the Venus Operating System," *Communications of the ACM*, Vol. 15, No. 3, March 1972.

■Mcc63 McCarthy, J., F. J. Corbato, and M. M. Daggett, "The linking segment subprogram language and linking loader," *Communications of the ACM*, Vol. 6, No. 7, July 1963.

■Mck69 McKeehan, J. B., "An analysis of the TSS/360 Command System II," *TSS/360 Compendium*, IBM Corporation, Data Processing Division, 1969.

McKinney, J. M., "A survey of analytical time-sharing models," *Computing Surveys*, Vol. 1, No. 2, June 1969.

Madnick, S. E., "Multi-processor software lockout," *Proceedings of the ACM National Conference*, 1968.

Madnick, S. E., and J. W. Alsop, II, "A modular approach to file system design," *Proceedings of the 1969 Spring Joint Computer Conference*, AFIPS Vol. 34, 1969.

■Mea62 Mealy, G. H., "Operating Systems" (date 1962), in S. Rosen (ed.), *Programming Systems and Languages*, New York, McGraw-Hill Book Co., 1967.

■Mea66 Mealy, G. H., "The functional structure of OS/360: Part I. Introductory survey," *IBM Systems Journal*, Vol. 5, No. 1, 1966.

■Mea67 Mealy, G. H., "Another look at data," *Proceedings of the 1967 Fall Joint Computer Conference*, AFIPS Vol. 31, 1967.

Meeker, J. W., N. R. Crandall, F. A. Dayton, and G. Rose, "OS-3: the Oregon State open shop operating system," *Proceedings of the 1969 Spring Joint Computer Conference*, AFIPS Vol. 34, 1969.

Meyer, R. A., and L. H. Seawright, "A virtual machine time-sharing system," *IBM Systems Journal*, Vol. 9, No. 3, 1970.

Morris, R., "Scatter storage techniques," *Communications of the ACM*, Vol. 11, No. 1, January 1968.

Mullery, A. P., and G. C. Driscoll, "A processor allocation method for time sharing," *Communications of the ACM*, Vol. 13, No. 1, January 1970.

Murphy, J. E., "Resource allocation with interlock detection in a multi-task system," *Proceedings of the 1968 Fall Joint Computer Conference*, AFIPS Vol. 33, 1968.

Nemeth, A. G., and P. D. Rovner, "User program measurement in a time-shared environment," *Communications of the ACM*, Vol. 14, No. 10, October 1971.

Nielsen, N. R., "The simulation of time-sharing systems," *Communications of the ACM*, Vol. 10, No. 7, July 1967.

Nielsen, N. R., "An analysis of some time-sharing techniques," *Communications of the ACM*, Vol. 14, No. 2, February 1971.

O'Connell, M. L., "A file organization method using multiple keys," *Proceedings of the 1971 Spring Joint Computer Conference*, AFIPS Vol. 38, 1971.

O'Neill, R. W., "Experience using a time-shared multiprogramming system with dynamic address translation hardware," *Proceedings of the 1967 Spring Joint Computer Conference*, AFIPS Vol. 30, 1967.

Opler, A., "Dynamic flow of programs and data through hierarchical storage," *Proceedings of IFIP Congress*, 1965.

Opp68   Oppenheimer, G., and N. Weizer, "Resource management for a medium scale time-sharing operating system," *Communications of the ACM*, Vol. 11, No. 5, May 1968.

OS   IBM System/360 Operating System publications:
   a. Advanced Checkpoint/Restart Planning Guide, Form GC28-6708
   b. Concepts and Facilities, Form GC28-6535
   c. Data Management Services, Form GC28-3746
   d. Input/Output Supervisor Program Logic Manual, Form GY28-6616
   e. Input/Output Support (OPEN/CLOSE/EOV), Form GY28-6609
   f. Introduction, Form GC28-6534
   g. Introduction to Control Program Logic, Form Y28-6605
   h. Job Control Language, Form GC28-6539
   i. Job Control Language Reference, Form GC28-6704
   j. Linkage Editor and Loader, Form 28-6538
   k. MVT Guide, Form GC28-6720
   l. MVT Job Management Program Logic Manual, Form GY28-6660
   m. MVT Supervisor, Form GY28-6659
   n. Supervisor and Data Management Macro Instructions, Form GC28-6647
   o. Supervisor Services, Form GC28-6646
   p. System Programmer's Guide, Form GC28-6550
IBM Corporation, White Plains, New York.
See also: Brown [Bro70], Cadow [Cad70], Cenfetelli [Cen67], Clark [Cla66], Flores [Flo70 and Flo71], Mealy [Mea66], Sayers [Say71], and Witt [Wit66].

O'Sullivan, T. C., "Exploiting the time-sharing environment," *Proceedings of the ACM National Conference*, 1967.

Pan68   Pankhurst, R. J., "Program overlay techniques," *Communications of the ACM*, Vol. 11, No. 2, February 1968.

Parkhill, C. V., *The Challenge of the Computer Utility*, Reading, Mass., Addison-Wesley Publishing Co., 1966.

Patton, P. C., "Trends in data organization and access methods," *Computer*, Vol. 3, No. 6, November/December 1970.

Pinkerton, T. B., "Performance monitoring in a time-sharing system," *Communications of the ACM*, Vol. 12, No. 11, November 1969.

Ran68   Randell, B., and C. J. Kuehner, "Dynamic storage allocation systems," *Communications of the ACM*, Vol. 11, No. 5, May 1968.

Richards, M., "BCPL: a tool for compiler writing and system programming," *Proceedings of the 1969 Spring Joint Computer Conference*, AFIPS Vol. 34, 1969.

Rse64   Rosen, S., "Programming systems and languages–a historical survey," *AFIPS Conference Proceedings*, Vol. 25, 1964.

Rse67   Rosen, S. (ed.), *Programming Systems and Languages*, New York, McGraw-Hill Book Co., 1967.

Rsi69 Rosin, R. F., "Supervisory and monitor systems," *Computing Surveys*, Vol. 1, No. 1, March 1969.

Ryder, K. D., "A heuristic approach to task dispatching," *IBM Systems Journal*, Vol. 9, No. 3, 1970.

Sackman, H., "Time-sharing versus batch processing: the experimental evidence," *Proceedings of the 1968 Spring Joint Computer Conference*, AFIPS Vol. 32, 1968.

Say71 Sayers, A. P. (ed.), *Operating Systems Survey*, Princeton, N.J., Auerbach Publishers Inc., 1971.

Say69 Sayre, D., "Is automatic folding of programs efficient enough to displace manual?" *Communications of the ACM*, Vol. 12, No. 12, December 1969.

Schatzoff, M., R. Tsao, and R. Wiig, "An experimental comparison of time sharing and batch processing," *Communications of the ACM*, Vol. 10, No. 5, May 1967.

Scherr, A. L., "Time sharing measurement," *Datamation*, April 1966.

Scherr, A. L., *An Analysis of Time-Shared Computer Systems*, Cambridge, Mass., The M.I.T. Press, 1967.

Schroeder, M. D., and J. H. Saltzer, "A hardware architecture for implementing protection rings," *Communications of the ACM*, Vol. 15, No. 3, March 1972.

Schwartz, J., E. G. Coffman, and C. Weissman, "A general purpose time sharing system," *AFIPS Conference Proceedings*, Vol. 25, 1964.

Schwemm, R. E., "Experience gained in the development and use of TSS/360," *Proceedings of the 1972 Spring Joint Computer Conference*, AFIPS Vol. 40, 1972.

Selwyn, L. L., "Computer resource accounting in a time sharing environemnt," *Proceedings of the 1970 Spring Joint Computer Conference*, AFIPS Vol. 36, 1970.

Shedler, G. S., and S. C. Yang, "Simulation of a model of paging system performance," *IBM Systems Journal*, Vol. 10, No. 2, 1971.

Shemer, J. E., "Some mathematical considerations of time-sharing scheduling algorithms," *Journal of the ACM*, Vol. 14, No. 4, April 1967.

Smith, L. B., "A comparison of batch processing and instant turnaround," *Communications of the ACM*, Vol. 10, No. 8, August 1967.

Stimler, S., "Some criteria for time-sharing system performance," *Communications of the ACM*, Vol. 12, No. 1, January 1969.

Teorey, T. J., and T. B. Pinkerton, "A comparative analysis of disk scheduling policies," *Communications of the ACM*, Vol. 15, No. 3, March 1972.

Tho71 Thomas, A., Jr., *System/360 Programming*, San Francisco, Rinehart Press, 1971.

Tonik, A. B., "Development of executive routines, both hardware and software," *Proceedings of the 1967 Fall Joint Computer Conference*, AFIPS Vol. 31, 1967.

Trapnell, F. M., "A systematic approach to the development of system programs," *Proceedings of the 1969 Spring Joint Computer Conference*, AFIPS Vol. 34, 1969.

■TSS   IBM System/360 Time Sharing System publications:
  a. Assembler Programmer's Guide, Form C28-2032
  b. Assembler User Macro Instructions, Form C28-2004
  c. Command System User's Guide, Form GC28-2001
  d. Concepts and Facilities, Form GC28-2003
  e. IBM System/360 Model 67 Functional Characteristics, Form GA27-2719
  f. Manager's and Administrator's Guide, Form C28-2024
  g. Operator's Guide, Form C28-2033
  h. Preliminary Technical Summary, Form C20-1647
  i. System Logic Summary, Program Logic Manual, Form Y28-2009
  j. System Programmer's Guide, Form C28-2008
  IBM Corporation, White Plains, New York.
  See also: Comfort [Com65]; Fikes, Lauer, and Vareha [Fik68]; Gibson [Gib66]; Johnson and Martinson [Joh69]; Lauer [Lau67]; Lett and Konigsford [Let68]; Lett [Let69]; and McKeehan [Mck69].

Van Horn, E. C., "Three criteria for designing computer systems to facilitate debugging," *Communications of the ACM*, Vol. 11, No. 5, May 1968.

■Vys65   Vyssotsky, V. A., "Structure of the MULTICS supervisor," *Proceedings of the 1965 Fall Joint Computer Conference*, AFIPS Vol. 27, 1965.

Wallace, V. L., and D. L. Mason, "Degree of multiprogramming in page-on-demand systems," *Communications of the ACM*, Vol. 12, No. 6, June 1969.

Wegner, P., "Communication between independently translated blocks," *Communications of the ACM*, Vol. 5, No. 7, July 1962.

Wegner, P. (ed.), *Introduction to System Programming*, New York, Academic Press, 1964.

Wegner, P., "Machine organization for multiprogramming," *Proceedings of the ACM National Conference*, 1967.

Weizer, N., and G. Oppenheimer, "Virtual memory management in a paging environment," *Proceedings of the 1969 Spring Joint Computer Conference*, AFIPS Vol. 34, 1969.

Wilkes, M. V., "Slave memories and dynamic storage allocation," IEEE Transactions, Volume EC-14, April 1965.

Wilkes, M. V., *Time-Sharing Computer Systems*, New York, American Elsevier Publishing Company, 1968.

Wilkes, M. V., "A model for core space allocation in a time-sharing system," *Proceedings of the 1969 Spring Joint Computer Conference*, AFIPS Vol. 34, 1969.

Wirth, N., "On multiprogramming, machine coding, and computer organization," *Communications of the ACM*, Vol. 12, No. 9, September 1969.

■Wit66   Witt, B. I., "The function structure of OS/360: Part II. Job and task management," *IBM Systems Journal*, Vol. 5, No. 1, 1966.

Witt, B. I., "M65MP: an experiment in OS/360 multiprocessing," *Proceedings of the ACM National Conference*, 1968.

Wood, T. C., "A generalized supervisor for a time-shared operating system," *Proceedings of the 1967 Fall Joint Computer Conference*, AFIPS Vol. 31, 1967.

Additional entries

Abell, V. A., Rosen, S., and R. E. Wagner, "Scheduling in a general purpose operating system," *Proceedings of the 1970 Fall Joint Computer Conference*, AFIPS Vol. 37, 1970.

Badger, G. F., Johnson, E. A., and R. W. Philips, "The Pitt time-sharing system for the IBM System/360: Two years experience," *Proceedings of the 1968 Fall Joint Computer Conference*, AFIPS Vol. 33, 1968.

Bernstein, W. A., and J. T. Owens, "Debugging in a time-sharing environment," *Proceedings of the 1968 Fall Joint Computer Conference*, AFIPS Vol. 33, 1968.

Brawn, B. S., and F. G. Gustavson, "Program behavior in a paging environment," *Proceedings of the 1968 Fall Joint Computer Conference*, AFIPS Vol. 33, 1968.

Day, P., and H. Krejci, "An operating system for a central real-time data processing computer," *Proceedings of the 1968 Fall Joint Computer Conference*, AFIPS Vol. 33, 1968.

Dean, A. L., Jr., "Development of the LOGICON 2+2 system," *Proceedings of the 1970 Fall Joint Computer Conference*, AFIPS Vol. 37, 1970.

Dickinson, R. V., and W. K. Orr, "System Ten—A new approach to multiprogramming," *Proceedings of the 1970 Fall Joint Computer Conference*, AFIPS Vol. 37, 1970.

Freibergs, I. F., "The dynamic behavior of programs," *Proceedings of the 1968 Fall Joint Computer Conference*, AFIPS Vol. 33, 1968.

Kuehner, C. J., and B. Randell, "Demand paging in perspective," *Proceedings of the 1968 Fall Joint Computer Conference*, AFIPS Vol. 33, 1968.

Ossanna, J. F., and J. H. Saltzer, "Technical and human engineering problems in connecting terminals to a time-sharing system," *Proceedings of the 1970 Fall Joint Computer Conference*, AFIPS Vol. 37, 1970.

Scherr, A. L., and D. C. Larkin, "Time-sharing for OS," *Proceedings of the 1970 Fall Joint Computer Conference*, AFIPS Vol. 37, 1970.

Sedgewick, R., Stone, R., and J. W. McDonald, "SPY—a program to monitor OS/360," *Proceedings of the 1970 Fall Joint Computer Conference*, AFIPS Vol. 37, 1970.

INDEX